Learning
WordPerfect® 5.0

Learning
WordPerfect® 5.0

Annette J. Thomason

Utah Valley Community College

Houghton Mifflin Company ■ **Boston**

Dallas   Geneva, Illinois

Palo Alto   Princeton, New Jersey

ISBN: 0-395-47799-9

ABCDEFGHIJ-SM-9543210-89

Contents

2 Faster Cursor-Movement and Deleting Methods, More Editing Commands, and Working with the Print Menu   37

3 Margins, Spacing, Tabs, and Other Format Settings   75

4 More Format Tips Including Centering, Bolding, and Underlining   107

16 Working with Fonts, Special Printing Techniques, and Desktop Publishing 417

17 Helps for Manuscripts 443

About This Book

This text manual is designed as an easy-to-understand and simple-to-use introductory tutorial for the WordPerfect® 5.0 word processing program. It is written for a variety of users from those who have had very little previous experience with either computers or word processing to those who need an easy way to learn a new program or upgrade to a new version. Instructions are provided in an uncomplicated step-by-step fashion beginning with basic commands and progressing to intermediate and advanced commands in later chapters. The presentation of the material lends itself to either a classroom or self-instructional environment.

Practice exercises and illustrations are included throughout, and frequent summaries and self-check activities are provided to help review and reinforce important concepts and procedures. To help reduce the time required for keyboarding, a Student Exercise Disk containing the material students are instructed to type in each chapter is provided in each copy of the text. These materials can be retrieved and used to complete the practice assignments if desired.

The book covers all the major features of WordPerfect® 5.0 including among others, entering, editing, printing, saving and retrieving documents; formatting with margin changes, tabs, and spacing; bolding, centering, and underlining; doing searches; using block functions; macros; and merging. It also includes instruction on the speller and thesaurus, sorting and selecting, tabulation, columns, and math, as well as indexes, outlines, tables of contents, windows, footnotes, and many other features. All the features of version 5.0 including graphics and desktop publishing, document handling, document compare, automatic referencing, setup, and styles are presented.

You will find this book most helpful and your time most effectively used if you will read through each lesson **before** beginning to work at the computer. Be sure to follow the instructions carefully and **proofread** your work thoroughly. Helpful TIPS are provided throughout and there are many suggestions on ways you can use WordPerfect® 5.0 to increase your skill and productivity for both personal and professional endeavors.

Use this book as a workbook. You may want to highlight sections or make notes in the margins. And be sure to jot down the answers to the Self-Check Quizzes at the end of each lesson for reference. Feel free to turn back to any section you may not fully recall or to work through an exercise more than once if you like. You're in full control.

Now turn to Chapter 1 and let's get started. This is going to be interesting and fun.

Acknowledgments

With much gratitude I acknowledge the helpful assistance, support, and encouragement of the many teachers, students, colleagues, and family who have contributed greatly to the completion of this text.

And to my Mom, who gave me opportunities she didn't have and was a supporter of women even before it was popular, I offer special thanks for encouragement and faith without which much of this would never have come to pass.

Annette Thomason

Orem, Utah

1

Getting Acquainted and Once Over Lightly

Welcome to word processing with **WordPerfect 5.0.** You're about to begin one of the most rewarding and valuable adventures of your career. After completing this chapter, you will be able to:

- use special keys on the keyboard to communicate with WordPerfect.
- enter text with WordPerfect.
- edit and change text.
- save a document on the disk.
- select various print options
- print a document.
- retrieve files from the disk.
- exit to the operating system.
- use many word-processing terms correctly.

Overview of Word Processing

Word processing means creating and manipulating written text. For years people have been using typewriters, pens and pencils, or scissors and tape to create and manipulate text. When you do word processing, however, you do those functions on a computer.

The main difference between a computer and a typewriter is that the computer can store your work in a way that is both permanent and easily changeable. With a typewriter, you have to retype a whole page if you make a mistake or change your mind about phrasing or the placement of a paragraph. On a computer, using a word-processing program like WordPerfect, you can make whatever changes you want without having to retype unaffected parts of the text.

Once you have learned to use your computer for correspondence and other typing projects, you'll wonder how you ever got along without it. Let's get started by taking a look at the keyboard.

Looking at the Keyboard

The computer keyboard resembles an ordinary typewriter keyboard plus a number of extra keys.

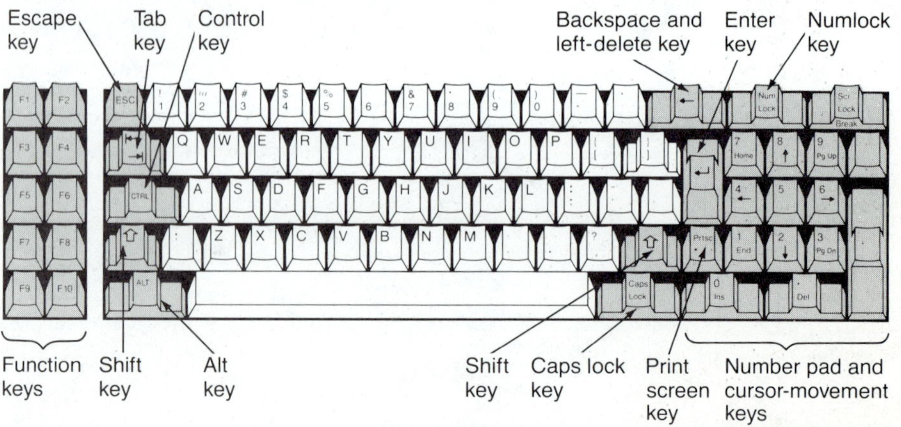

Locate the function keys marked **F1** through **F10**.

Find the **Esc**, **Ctrl**, **Alt**, and **PrtSc** keys.

The key with opposing arrows is the **Tab** key and the keys with fat upward pointing arrows are the Shift keys. Notice that there is a **Shift** key on each side of the keyboard.

Find the ten-key number pad. Four of the keys (the 4, 8, 6, and 2 keys) may have arrows on them. Pressing one of these keys when there is text on the screen will cause the **cursor** (the blinking dash that marks your location on the screen) to move in the direction of the arrow. If your computer has a separate set of keys for cursor movement, they will move the cursor the same way.

The long key with the bent arrow (↵) is the **Enter or Return** key, which corresponds to the carriage return on a typewriter. The large key at the upper right with the left-pointing arrow (←) is the **Backspace** and left-delete key.

The **Caps Lock** key will make alphabetic characters on the keyboard type in all capital letters, and the **Num Lock** key will override the cursor arrows on the 10-key pad and make those keys type numbers instead of moving the cursor. Tapping the Caps Lock and Num Lock keys will turn these features On and Off.

There are also several other keys with special markings, which you will learn about later.

Near the function keys you should have a plastic template with commands listed on it. To execute commands printed in **blue**, you will hold down the Alt key and tap the appropriate function key (like typing a capital letter, but using Alt rather than the Shift key). Those printed in **red** require the Ctrl key and the appropriate function key. Commands printed in **green** are executed by holding down the Shift key and tapping the function key. For commands printed in **black**, use only the function key itself.

Computer Equipment

For simplicity's sake, the instructions in this text assume that you are working on a standard equipment configuration composed of an IBM or compatible computer with two disk drives, a minimum of 512K of memory, a monochrome monitor and access to a dot matrix printer that is capable of printing graphics.

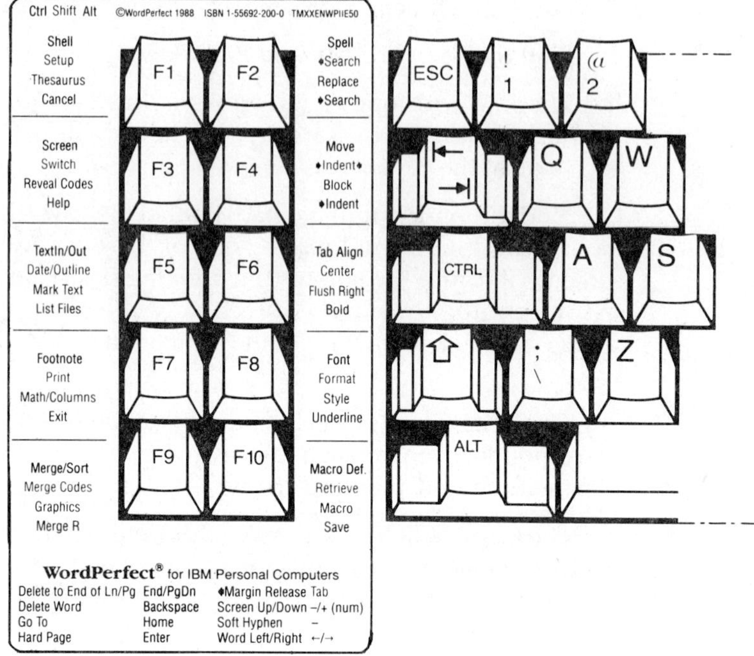

This assumption does not imply that your system must meet only those requirements, however, just that it has at least that capability. You could also, for instance, have access to a laser printer, be working from a hard disk, be on a network, have a color monitor or be working on a computer with only one disk drive. If your system configuration includes any of these or other options, simply make appropriate adjustments when starting the program, selecting printers, and specifying drive or directory locations for such operations as saving or retrieving files.

If you have only one drive, you will need to change disks occasionally to use the one available drive for multiple operations. Because of the size of the WordPerfect 5.0 program itself, it is recommended that you have at least two drives. Many experts advise that you use a hard disk and at least 640k of internal memory when working with WordPerfect 5.0.

In the event that your setup varies from the standard two-drive configuration assumed, refer to your WordPerfect manual, instructor, or lab assistant for any special instructions you may need to start the WordPerfect program and to deal with the differences in your particular situation. Among other things you may need to know, the name of the directory the WordPerfect program is stored in on your hard disk, what code words to use to log onto the network, and how to specify the path for auxiliary directories or files.

Inserting Disks and Starting the Computer

■ To begin, put a DOS disk in Drive A, which is on the left if the disk drives are side-by-side, and on top if the drives on your machine are stacked. Remember that the disk should be inserted with the label up/label last. (If you have never worked with disks before, be sure to read the guidelines for proper handling and care of disks in the appendix.) Then close the drive latch by carefully snapping it down.

■ Now put your student exercise disk or a blank formatted data disk in Drive B, which is on the right side if the disk drives are side-by-side and on the bottom if they are stacked, and close the latch.

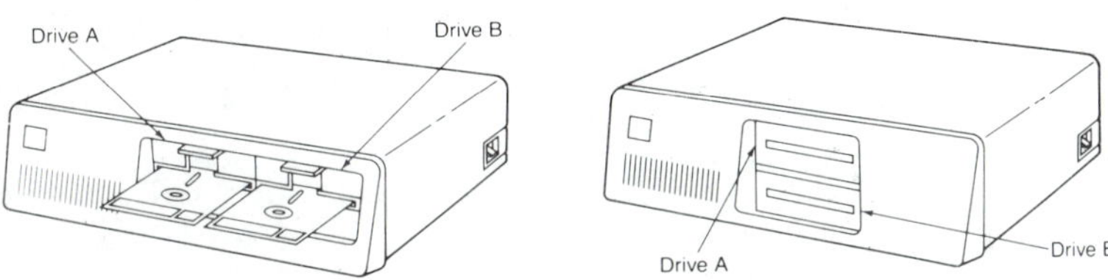

REMEMBER: Disks should always be inserted ___________________________

____

NOTE: If part of the DOS has been copied to your WordPerfect disk, you will not need to use the DOS disk in this manner. You can bypass the DOS disk and insert the disk marked WordPerfect 1 into the A drive and start the computer (boot) from there to set the date and time. In either event, you will need to have the CONFIG.SYS file on your WordPerfect 1 disk; and you should follow the instructions given below for date and time. If DOS will not fit onto the disk marked WordPerfect1, you may need to delete the help files to make room for it.

TIP: Instructions you are to do are preceded by a solid box—■—throughout this text. Also note that keys you should press and text you should type are displayed in bold print.

◼ Reach around to the side or back of your machine and raise the big switch to the On position. At first nothing will happen. The machine is performing a short self-diagnostic test. In a few seconds the red light on Drive A will go on, and you will be asked if you want to enter the current date. You can either enter today's date, using the month-day-year format (MM-DD-YY) shown, or simply press the Enter key to use the date given. Whichever you choose, that date will be used to date stamp your files when they are stored.

TIP: If you are using a network or have special features on your computer, you may not see the date and time messages; they will be entered automatically for you. If this is the case, simply move on to the next section.

Since the format is MM-DD-YY, if today's date were August 10, 1988, you would enter 8-10-1988 or 8-10-88.

◼ Type in **today's date** and press **Enter**. (Do not type the name of the day of the week, such as Tue.)

The next prompt will be:

```
C:\>TIME
Current time is 10:34:56.65
Enter new time:
```

The time shown on your computer will vary depending on the setup of your machine. The format is hour: minutes: seconds.thousandths of seconds, or HH:MM:SS.TSTS. It is not necessary to supply seconds or thousandths of seconds if you wish to omit them. You must, however, pay close attention to the punctuation between each part of the time specification. Note that a period separates the seconds from the thousandths of seconds.

If the time were 10:45 a.m., you would enter 10:45:00 or 10:45. If it were 2:30 p.m., however, you would enter 14:30. WordPerfect operates on a 24-hour clock, because it has no way to tell a.m. from p.m. Whatever time you enter will be used to set the internal clock in the computer, and it will then keep track of the time for you.

◼ Type in the **current time** and then press **Enter**.

The date and time you supply will be used by WordPerfect to date and time stamp your files when they are saved. Later, if you wish to find a file created on a certain date or at a certain time, you can locate it by looking in the directory. This feature can be very helpful if you have many files that are similar. It can also help keep your files organized.

To Review

Change the following times from the 24-hour clock to regular time followed by a.m. or p.m.

23:10 _______________

16:40 _______________

02:00 _______________

04:35 _______________

Insert the correct punctuation in the following dates:

10   8   87   4   1   88   1   23   88

TIP: You will see an A> prompt after you enter the date and time. (If you are working with a hard disk, the prompt will display a C> or C:\.)

CONFIG.SYS File

Before moving ahead, you should check to be sure there is a CONFIG. SYS file on your DOS disk (or in the C:\ root directory on a hard drive) that includes statements like the following:

Files = 20

Buffers = 20

TIP: If this statement is not inserted into the CONFIG.SYS file, you will get an error message when you try to start WordPerfect indicating that there are insufficient file handles. Adding the statements shown above will tell DOS to open more files than it normally does so that you can run WordPerfect correctly.

To determine whether the CONFIG.SYS file exists, make sure A> is showing on the screen and either your WordPerfect 1 disk with DOS on it or the DOS disk itself is in the A drive. If you are using a hard drive, be sure that you are working in the Root Directory which is C:\.) Then, in either event, type the following:

◾ **DIR/W**

◾ Then press **Enter**. A listing of files will appear. If CONFIG. SYS is among them, type **TYPE CONFIG.SYS** and press **Enter**.

■ The contents of the CONFIG.SYS file will appear. Look for the statements "Files = 20, Buffers = 20" (or more) If they are there, move ahead.

■ If the CONFIG.SYS file is not on your DOS disk (or root directory) or the file exists but the statements are not included, refer to your instructor, lab manager, or the appendix of your WordPerfect reference manual on how to add the file and/or the statements. Then reboot your computer and move ahead.

■ Type **B:** (B colon) and press the **Enter** key. The prompt will change to B>. If necessary, remove the DOS disk and put it back into the paper jacket. Then insert the disk labelled WordPerfect 1 into the A drive. (If you are working with a hard drive, you may want to specify the directory to store your work files in at this point.)

■ Then type **A:WP** (A colon WP) and press **Enter** again, as shown below. (You would type something like C:\WP50\WP for a hard drive. To specify the location of the program correctly, you will need to know the name of the directory the program is stored in. It will likely be WP50 as indicated above, but ask your instructor or lab manager to verify.)

TIP: | It does not matter whether you use upper-case or lower-case characters. WordPerfect will load and you will be ready to begin.

```
A>B:                    <Press Enter>
B>A:WP                  <Press Enter>
```

or

```
C>:\(Location where you want to store your work files)
C>:\(The directory where the WordPerfect 5.0 program is stored)\WP
```

Since it requires two disks to load WordPerfect 5.0 into the memory of your machine, you will soon see the following message if you are using a dual disk machine.

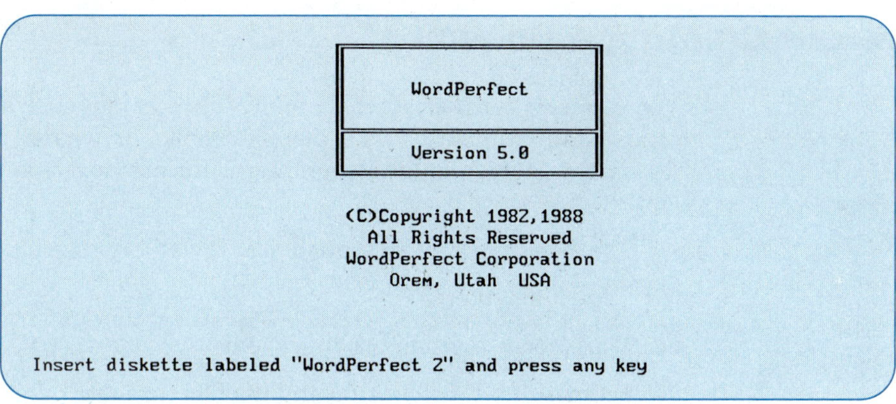

NOTE: If you are using a hard drive, both disks will be automatically loaded into the memory of your machine and there will be no need to change disks.

TIP: Occasionally the message **Are other copies of WordPerfect running? (Y/N)** will appear across the bottom of your screen as WordPerfect is loading. If this should happen, press N (for No), and WordPerfect will continue to load.

Now get comfortable in your chair. Use the knobs on the side or bottom of your screen to adjust the brightness and contrast. If you like, prop this manual between the top of the keyboard and the monitor. Then follow along. This is going to be fun.

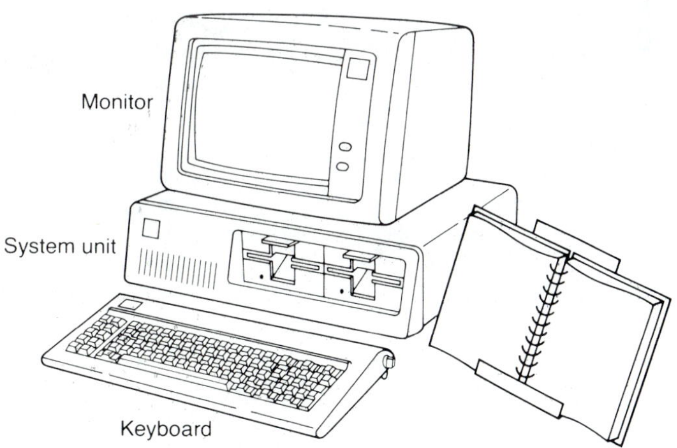

Creating a Document

You can use WordPerfect to do many kinds of jobs such as writing a letter, a report, an outline, a book, a memo, a table, or whatever. These are called documents, which is the generic term for any text you create with Word-Perfect.

The steps to create an attractive and well-organized document are:

1. Type it in (enter).

2. Make corrections and changes (edit).

3. Set margins, tabs, spacing and the like (format).

4. Store it on a disk (save).

5. Produce a copy on paper (print).

6. Recall it for further corrections or changes (retrieve).

If you need to make further changes in your document after it is initially typed, you can retrieve it and repeat any or all of these steps to produce the final document without having to retype the entire text.

The first step in word processing is to enter some text. So let's get started.

The Status Line and Entering Text

The status line at the bottom right-hand side of your screen will look like the following:

                                                            Doc 1 Pg 1 Ln 1"   Pos 1"

This is WordPerfect's way of telling you where the cursor (the small blinking dash) is on the page. Right now it is on the first document, page 1, 1 inch from the top of the paper (Ln) and 1 inch from the left edge of the page (Pos).

TIP: If the information in the status line on your machine appears as Doc 1 Pg 1 Ln 1 Pos 10, that means the same thing. WordPerfect can display the status line information in a variety of ways and the defaults on your machine may have been changed. Do not be concerned. Both methods will arrive at the same end. You will learn how to change the format for the status line in a later chapter.

A standard sheet of paper is 8 1/2 inches wide by 11 inches long. Vertically, there are 6 lines per inch, for a total of 66 lines. Horizontally, pica type—which you are using—accommodates 10 characters per inch, for a total of 85 spaces or characters across the page. Pica type is often called 10-pitch. The center point on the page is 42. If you were using elite type, or 12-pitch, which is smaller, you would have 12 characters per inch for a total of 102 possible characters across. The center point would be 51.

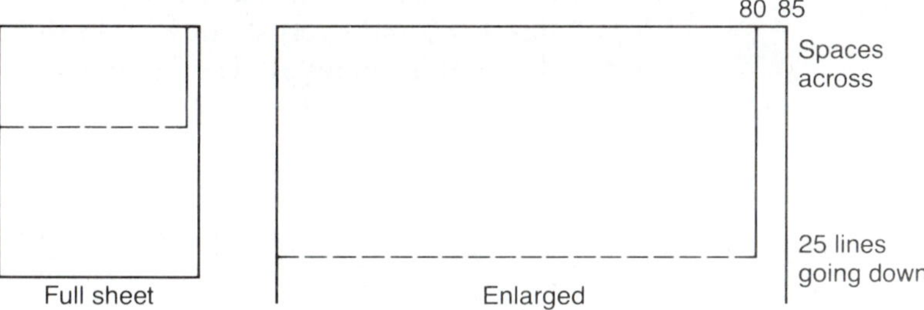

Most computer screens display only 80 columns across (horizontal spaces) and 25 lines down (vertical) at any one time. The way in which what you see on the screen corresponds to a standard sheet of paper is shown in the figure above on this page.

As WordPerfect uses up the 24 available screen lines (25 less one for the status line), it scrolls down to the next line. When this happens, the top lines disappear off the top of the screen because there is not enough room for them. Do not be concerned. They are being saved in the computer's memory and can easily be retrieved and returned to the screen later.

◼ Now type the following text on your machine. You do not need to press the Enter key at the end of a line to move the cursor to the beginning of the next line. WordPerfect will do this for you automatically, using the word wrap feature. Also, don't worry about correcting errors on this first draft. You'll have an opportunity to go back and do that later.

TIP: Remember to insert two blank spaces (tap the Space Bar twice) after a period or other punctuation at the end of a sentence. Indent (press the Tab key) at the beginning of each paragraph, and leave a blank line between paragraphs. To insert a blank line, press the Enter key twice. This will end the previous paragraph and move the cursor down the screen two lines.

Charlie is the name of my miniature Doberman pinscher who is just eight months old. Dobermans come of German stock and are well known as watchdogs and seeing-eye dogs for the blind. Charlie is a proud specimen of the breed. His chest and forelegs are powerful, and he has slim, tapering hindquarters. Some Dobermans are copper-colored, but Charlie is black and tan. He has a short, smooth coat and generally looks like a terrier.

Charlie is practically full-grown, even though he is less than a year old. He stands about eleven inches high and weighs less than six pounds. He has an independent nature, an iron will, and is very venturesome. When we are outside he is kept on a leash because he has a strong desire to chase anything that moves including flies, birds, kites, cats, and even shadows. On the other hand, he is the kind of dog that becomes attached to just one person; and he gives all his devotion and obedience to me.

Charlie had a pretty rough start in life. When he was just a few months old, he was taken away from his mother and given to me. That changed his young life completely. He became familiar with new surroundings and new people and learned almost overnight to get along without his playmates. Hardest of all was learning to give his devotion and allegiance to a new owner, but he made that adjustment quickly.

Saving Documents (Interim Save)

Before going any further, you should save what you have typed by transferring a copy of it from the temporary memory of your machine to permanent storage on a disk or hard drive. That way it will not be lost if the power should fail, you bump the cord, or some other accident erases the temporary memory of your machine.

There are two ways to save.

1. The Interim Save (F10) will put a copy on the disk and will leave the text in the computer's memory and on the screen so you can continue working on it. You will learn this method first.

2. The Exit (Save) Clear Screen (F7) will also put a copy of the document on the disk, but it will then erase your document from both the screen and the temporary memory of the machine so you can begin another document or quit for the day. You will use this method later when you finish this document.

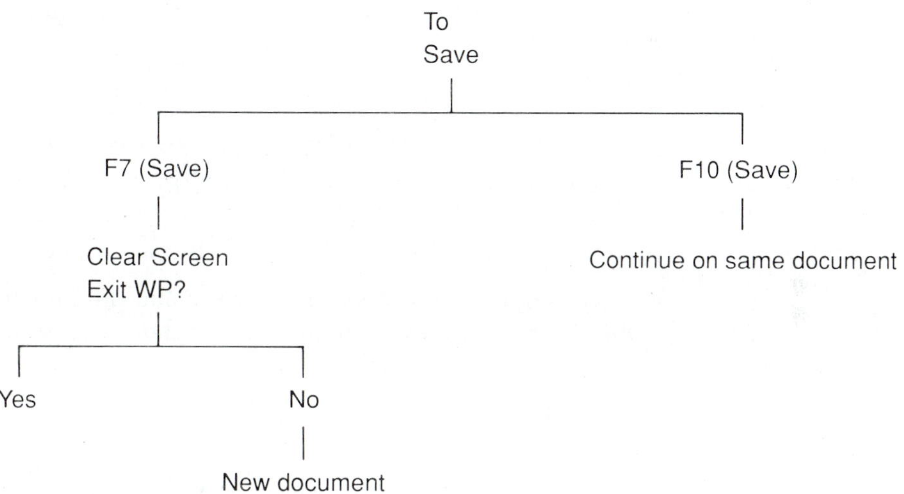

The method you choose will depend on what you plan to do after you have saved. This time, because you plan to continue working with your document, and therefore will not want it erased from the screen and temporary memory of your machine, you will want to use the interim-save function. Look at the F10 key. Notice that the word **Save** is printed in black on the template beside it.

▣ Commands printed in black do not require a second key to execute, so simply press the **Save (F10)** key. When you do, the following prompt should appear in the lower left-hand corner of your screen:

WordPerfect is asking you for the name under which you wish to save your document. Here are some tips to keep in mind when naming documents:

1. The name cannot be longer than eight characters, or contain any spaces. You may also add a period (.) and a three letter extension to your document names if you wish.

2. Use symbols such as * and : and / with caution. WordPerfect uses a number of symbols for special commands, and using the same symbol in a filename could cause your file to be saved improperly. It is better to avoid using symbols at all.

3. The name should provide a clue to what your document contains, in case you forget the filename and have only the list of document titles in which to find it.

◩ Name this document Charlie.1 Type **Charlie.1** beside the cursor at the prompt.

◩ Press the **Enter** key to let WordPerfect know you are ready to move ahead.

TIP: The computer will not respond correctly to the use of the letter "O" for the number 0, or to the use of the letter "l" for the number 1. You must use the appropriate number keys for the computer to respond correctly.

A red light on the disk drive will come on, and the message **Saving B:Charlie.1** will appear in the lower left-hand corner of the screen. When the light goes off, your document has been saved on the disk but has not been erased from the screen or the memory of your machine. You now have two copies of Charlie—one on the screen and one on the disk. Now you can continue working with the text on the screen. You will note that the drive and filename now appear in the lower left-hand corner of your screen:

```
B:\CHARLIE.1                                    Doc 1 Pg 1 Ln 2.4" Pos 3.5"
```

TIP: The "Ln" and "Pos" positions shown on your computer may vary slightly from that shown in the text. Do not be concerned. Such differences can be caused by variations among printers, font selections, or other features of your particular equipment setup and should not affect the ultimate outcome of your projects.

To Review

What are the rules for naming your document? _______________________

____

What key should you press to save your document when you wish to con-

tinue working on it? _______________________

____

Cursor Movement

Using the arrow keys on your keyboard, (↑, ↓, →, and ←) move the cursor
around the text until you feel comfortable with the way these keys work.

TIP: If the cursor does not move and numbers appear instead, turn Num Lock off
by tapping the Num Lock key.

You can either move one space at a time by tapping the key once for each
character, or you can zip in the direction of the arrow by holding the key down
until you want the cursor to stop. Notice that the cursor will not go beyond
the outer limits of the text. Also notice what happens in the status line as you
move the cursor around: the numbers for **Pos** and **Ln** will change to show
where the cursor is on the screen.

TIP: You may notice that the symbol for the left-arrow key is short ←, and the
symbol for the Backspace key is longer ←——.

To Review

Draw the key that will move the cursor in the direction indicated.

Up a line: _______________________

To the left: _______________________

Down a line: _______________________

To the right: _______________________

Defaults

As you look at your text, you will notice that WordPerfect has established some settings for margins, spacing, and other aspects of format.

```
     Charlie is the name of my miniature Doberman pinscher who
is just eight months old. Dobermans come of German stock and
are well known as watchdogs and seeing-eye dogs for the
blind. Charlie is a proud specimen of the breed. His chest
and forelegs are powerful, and he has slim, tapering
hindquarters. Some Dobermans are copper-colored, but Charlie
is black and tan. He has a short, smooth coat and generally
looks like a terrier.

     Charlie is practically full-grown, even though he is less
than a year old. He stands about eleven inches high and
weighs less than six pounds. He has an independent nature, an
iron will, and is very venturesome. When we are outside he is
kept on a leash because he has a strong desire to chase
anything that moves--flies, birds, kites, cats, and even
shadows. On the other hand, he is the kind of dog that
becomes attached to just one person; and he gives all his
devotion and obedience to me.

     Charlie had a pretty rough start in life. When he was
just a few months old, he was taken away from his mother and
given to me. That changed his young life completely. He
became familiar with new surroundings and new people and
learned almost overnight to get along without his playmates.
A:\CHARLIE.WP                                  Doc 1 Pg 1 Ln 1" Pos 1"
```

These initial settings which are built into WordPerfect and automatically come up when it is started are called defaults. You can change any of the defaults any time you wish. But it is important to be aware of the setting that WordPerfect starts with, so you will know what to expect:

1. The text is single-spaced.

2. The margins are set 1 inch in from both left and right sides of the page.

3. The type size is pica, or 10-pitch, which means that there are 10 characters to the inch. (Therefore the center point of the page is on space 42, or in other words 4.2 inches from the left edge of the page.)

4. Word wrap is On. This means that you don't need to press Return or Enter at the end of each line.

5. The tabs are preset every 1/2 inch.

6. Justification is On. Though it is not apparent on the screen, when your document is printed it will have a justified (even) right-hand margin.

Some less obvious defaults are:

7. Line settings for six lines to the inch going down the page.

8. A one-inch automatic top and bottom margin, which the printer will add.

9. A maximum of 54 lines of text per page.

10. Insert is On.

Measuring In Inches

The fact that margins, tabs, and other settings are indicated in inches may seem a little confusing, especially if you are used to specifying their positions at a particular place such as 10 and 74 margins and 5 space tabs. However, with the variety of different sized fonts and other options available in WordPerfect 5.0, identifying and maintaining any particular position on the page becomes more difficult. You may already have experienced some of this problem in converting from pica to elite size type or vice versa.

As you recall, pica has 10 spaces to the inch but elite has 12. Therefore, to obtain one-inch side margins using pica type, you would set the margins at 10 and 74. However, to obtain the same one-inch margin using an elite type size, they would need to be set at 12 and 90. If you tried to use pica margins with elite type, or vice versa, the printout would not have even margins and would be lopsided on the page. The same kind of problem occurs when 5 space tabs are used. Tabs every 5 spaces result in a stop every 1/2 inch with a pica type but not with elite type, which requires tabs every 6 spaces to achieve the same 1/2 inch distance. In addition, center point for pica is 42 and for elite it is 51. The figure shown below illustrates these differences.

1 inch = 10 spaces pica, 12 spaces elite

10	42	74 Pica
12	51	90 Elite
1" left margin	Center	1" right margin

As you can imagine, this problem is greatly compounded when many type sizes and fonts are available. And even though it is fairly easy to memorize the settings and compensate for the differences between two sizes that vary only in width such as pica and elite do, most users of word processing would not want to memorize all the differences for the great variety of fonts they now have access to that are not only wider or narrower but also taller or shorter than the standard.

Therefore, to overcome the need to learn the specifics of each font, as well as the requirement to change the settings each time the font is changed, WordPerfect now has a built-in conversion table that makes margin, tab, and other changes automatically when a different font is specified.

As a result, when you indicate a one-inch margin, WordPerfect identifies the font being used and inserts the correct setting to provide that margin regardless of the font size. If you change the font, WordPerfect automatically changes the margin setting to maintain the one-inch distance. It's as simple as that. Therefore, even though converting from spaces to inches may seem a little confusing at first, the effort to reorient your thinking will result in much greater capability and less trouble when you are using various fonts and other graphic functions in your work.

Finally, because of the adjustments WordPerfect makes to maintain the settings you specify, things sometimes don't come out exactly even horizontally or vertically on the space or line. Therefore, you may often see indicators such as **Ln 5.33"** and **Pos 2.16i**. This simply means that the cursor is 5-1/3 inches down the page and slightly beyond two inches horizontally from the left edge. Do not be concerned. These figures are the result of differences caused by the type style or font currently in use and the fact that some things don't divide evenly. Be assured that WordPerfect will take them into account and, when printed, your document will appear as you specify.

TIP: In addition to displaying inches in two ways (" and i), WordPerfect is able to display units of measure in centimeters and points. It can also display measurements similar to those used by WordPerfect 4.2, although these will often appear with decimals.

To Review

Indicate the defaults for each of the following:

Spacing: _____________   Left/right margins: ___________

Center: _____________   Pitch: _______________________

Tabs: _______________   Lines/inch: __________________

Top margin: __________   Lines/page: __________________

Word wrap: ___________   Justification & insert: __________

Editing Text and Correcting Errors

The following commands will help you to correct any typing errors you may
have made. Read through this list carefully, and locate the keys on your
keyboard before you begin to make corrections.

Backspace
> (Top row on the right) Backspaces and deletes the character to the
> immediate left of the cursor.

Del
> Deletes the character above the cursor (and will delete to the right of
> the cursor if held down).

Space Bar
> Inserts a space to the immediate left of the cursor.

Ctrl + Backspace
> Holding down these two keys together deletes the entire word above
> the cursor.

Ins   (Default)
> Typing a character with Insert On inserts the character to the imme-
> diate left of the cursor and moves the rest of the text one space to the
> right. No characters are deleted.

Typeover

Typing a character with Insert Off (the word **Typeover** will appear in the
lower left-hand corner of the screen) inserts the character above the cursor, in
place of whatever was previously in that position. Thus the old character is
erased.

Notice that the **Ins** key is a toggle switch. Press it a couple of times and
watch the word Typeover flash On and Off at the bottom left of the screen. You
can shift from one condition to the other with a press of the key. Certain
commands, which you will learn more about later, work differently depending on whether Ins is On or Off.

■ Look over what you have typed. When you find the first error, use the arrow
keys to move the cursor until it is blinking just under or just to the right of the
incorrect letter. Then use the appropriate editing key to fix the error. Continue
until you feel comfortable with these editing commands and have corrected
all the errors in the text.

NOTE: If you made no errors while entering the text, type a sentence or two containing deliberate errors so that you can practice using these editing commands.

Saving Documents (Exit/Clear Screen)

When you have corrected all your errors, you are ready to update the copy you made on the disk when you saved it before. This is necessary because the changes you have just made are stored only in the temporary memory of the computer. The copy on the disk has not been affected at all and still has all the errors in it. To update the copy on the disk, you may use either of the two methods you learned earlier, depending on what you plan to do after you have saved.

You already know how to save with the Save (F10) key (Interim Save), let's try the Exit/Clear Screen (F7) method.

◻ Find the F7 key; notice that the word **Exit** is printed in black on the template beside it. WordPerfect will not allow you to exit from the program without considering saving, so a save function is built into the exit procedure.

◻ Because Exit is printed in black, simply press the **F7** key. The prompt shown below will appear:

```
Save document? (Y/N) Yes
```

TIP: If you have made no changes in your document since it was saved last, you will see the prompt **Text was not modified** on the right-hand side of the status line. This reminder will tell you when it is not necessary to resave a document.

WordPerfect is asking whether you wish to save the document. You may respond Y(es) or N(o). Because WordPerfect assumes that you will want to save, the default is shown as Yes. If your answer is No, type an N. Pressing any other key, including a Y, will mean Yes (the default) to WordPerfect.

TIP: This is how WordPerfect handles your responses to questions it asks as you go along. You must press a specific key if your response is different from the default. Pressing any other key will enter the default.

◼ Type **Y** (or press any key but N). The following words will appear:

```
Document to be saved: B:\CHARLIE.1  (or C:\(directory name)\Charlie.1)
```

You will notice that WordPerfect has remembered what you named the document before and has entered it for you (Charlie.1). If you wish to use the same name again, simply press the Enter key. You do not need to retype the name. If you wanted to use another name, however, you could just type it in. The old name would disappear and WordPerfect would use the new name instead.

This is just an update of the same file, let's use the same name again.

◼ Press **Enter** to tell WordPerfect to use the same name.

Oops! WordPerfect knows that it can store only one file under any given name. If it puts the new version on the disk under the old name, the old file will be destroyed similar to when you record over something on a cassette tape. So it asks you whether you want to replace the file you already have on your disk with the revised one on your screen.

```
Replace B:\CHARLIE.1? (Y/N) No
```

This safety feature is built in to prevent you from accidentally destroying files you may want to keep.

Because the old file on the disk is the one with all the errors, you will want to replace it with the updated and corrected version. (If you wanted to keep the old version, you would have to give this new version a different name.) Because your response is different from the default, which is N (for No), you will need to type a Y (for Yes) to tell WordPerfect to replace the old file (thus destroying it) with the new version.

◼ Type **Y**. The red disk-drive light should come on, indicating that the updated version is being saved. (You will see the message **Saving B: CHARLIE.1** in the lower left-hand corner of the screen.) When WordPerfect is finished saving your document, the following message will appear on the screen:

```
Exit WP? (Y/N) No                              (Cancel to return to document)
```

Clear Screen (and Memory)

With this message, WordPerfect is giving you the choice to stop using Word-Perfect for the day, to work on a new document, or to return to the document on your screen.

If you say Y(es) at this point, the WordPerfect program will be erased from the memory of your machine and control will be returned to the operating system. You can tell when this has happened because an A>, B>, or C> will appear on your screen. You should choose this option when you are finished for the session and are ready to turn your machine off.

If you say N(o), WordPerfect will erase the document on the screen and the temporary memory of your machine and will return to the word-processing program ready to start on another document or project. You should choose this option when you wish to clear the screen and memory and continue to use WordPerfect.

If you do not want to clear the screen and memory, you may press Cancel (F1) to return to your document. This is similar to what happens when you use the Interim Save (F10) command.

☐ Because you are not yet ready to quit for the day, but do want the screen/memory cleared, press **N** to tell WordPerfect not to exit. The screen and memory will clear, and you'll be ready to start on another document.

Congratulations! You have now entered, edited, and saved your first document. You also have a clear screen to start a new document.

Retrieving and Printing a Document

But just a minute. . . . you also need a paper copy (also called hard copy) of the material you have just typed. Because you have exited and cleared the memory and the screen, you can retrieve your document from the disk in order to print it.

TIP: It is not necessary to save a document before printing it. And you do not need to Exit before printing.

■ Before you do this, make sure the screen is clear (no text in the memory or on the screen). Then find the key that says Retrieve. It is printed in green on the template next to the Save (F10) key.

■ Since commands printed in green require the use of both the Shift key and the function key, hold down either **Shift** key and then press (lightly tap) the **Retrieve** (F10) key. The following will appear:

```
Document to be retrieved:
```

■ Type the document name (in this case **CHARLIE.1** or **C:\(directory name\Charlie.1**) and press the **Enter** key.

The document will immediately appear back on your screen. If you wanted, you could add to, delete, or make more changes in the document now. Since you want to print it without changes, let's send the document to the printer.

■ Looking at the function keys, you will notice that the word **Print** appears in green near the F7 key. With your document showing on the screen, hold down a **Shift** key and tap the **F7** to prepare WordPerfect to print. The menu shown on page 24 will appear:

WordPerfect is asking for information about how and what you want to print, the printer you want to use, and what you want the printed copy to look like.

TIP: Notice that the numbers and letters that run down the side as well as one of the letters in each of the descriptions are bolded. You may press either the number/letter at the left or the bolded letter in the description to select any option. You may type either an upper–case or lower–case letter.

If you select Full Document (**1**), WordPerfect will print everything in your document from what is stored in its internal memory.

If you select **P**age (**2**), WordPerfect will print only the page the cursor is on (the page that is showing on your screen), again from its internal memory.

If you select **D**ocument on Disk (**3**), WordPerfect will print either specified pages or the entire document from the file you stored on your disk

```
Print

        1 - Full Document
        2 - Page
        3 - Document on Disk
        4 - Control Printer
        5 - Type Through
        6 - View Document
        7 - Initialize Printer

Options

        S - Select Printer
        B - Binding                     0"
        N - Number of Copies            1
        G - Graphics Quality            Medium
        T - Text Quality                High




    Selection: 0
```

TIP:

The distinction between what is stored in the computer's internal (temporary) memory and what is stored on the disk is important. Even though it is always a good idea to do so, documents or pages printed from internal (temporary) memory do not need to be saved to disk first. In addition, if you have retrieved a document and made changes but not resaved it (and thus updated the contents of the file on the disk), what appears on the printed page will depend on whether the computer goes to its memory or to the disk to get the material.

If you select **C**ontrol Printer (**4**), WordPerfect will allow you to give the printer some special commands including those to cancel print jobs, change the printing order, and/or start and stop the printer. You can also see the listing of jobs waiting to be printed if you wish. You will work with these commands more later.

If you select **T**ype Through (**5**), your text will go directly to the printer as you enter it, like a typewriter. Not all printers support this feature, and you will also learn more about how to use it in a later chapter.

◼ If you would like to see the options that choices 4, and 5 offer, type those numbers (or the bold letter) and take a look. Do not change any of the settings. Press the Space Bar or Exit (**F7**) to return to the print menu.

TIP: You have already used Cancel (F1) to exit from a menu you do not want. When this command is used, WordPerfect "forgets" any changes that may have been made as it returns to its original position. However, if you want to save the changes as you leave the menu, use Exit (F7). In addition, because WordPerfect often steps through a series of menus, you may need to press Cancel (F1) or Exit (F7) several times to step back through the menus one by one. Finally, you can also save and leave many of the menus by pressing the Space Bar.

If you select **View** (**6**), you can view on the screen how the document will look when it is printed. You will work with this feature in Chapter 2.

If you select **Initialize** (**7**), any soft fonts (loaded from a disk) currently in the printer's memory will be erased and the printer will be returned to initial or beginning settings.

Additional options will allow you to identify the printer you are using, set a binding width (additional space on the left margin to allow for binding), specify the number of copies you want printed, and determine the quality of print (draft, medium, or high) for both graphics and text.

Printer Definitions

There are many variations and ways to customize your printer setup which you will learn about in a later chapter. For the time being, however, we will work with only the basics and save the rest until then.

NOTE: If the printer you are using has already been specified or if you elect to use the default standard printer, you may skip this section and move on to the next. However, if the printer has not previously been identified for your computer or the default printer will not work, you will need to select a printer now. Then once it is done, it is not necessary to change the setting any more unless you change printers.

▪ From the Print menu, press **S** for Select Printer to bring up the menu shown on page 26.

The asterisk beside Standard Printer tells you that it is the current selection. If there are other printers listed, you could move the cursor (highlighted area) up or down with the arrow keys to another choice and press 1 to select it. This would move the asterisk to that printer, and WordPerfect would know that was the printer definition it should use.

Other choices along the bottom line of the menu allow you to specify additional printers, edit or change specifications for a particular printer, copy the setup, delete a printer from the list, or obtain help in the form of information about a particular printer.

```
Print: Select Printer

*Standard Printer




1 Select; 2 Additional Printers 3 Edit; 4 Copy; 5 Delete; 6 Help: 1
```

■ Select **Additional Printers** (**2**) to see a listing of additional printers that you can select from. If you are using a dual disk computer, the following message will appear:

```
Select Printer:  Additional Printers

Printer files not found

    Use the Other Disk option to specify a directory for the
    printer files. Continue to use this option until you find the
    disk with the printer you want.



1 Select; 2 Other Disk; 3 Help; 4 List Printer Files; N Name Search: 1
```

TIP: If you are using a hard drive, it is not necessary to change disks to find the one containing the correct files for your printer. These files will likely all have been copied onto the hard disk and will list when **Additional Printers** (**2**) is selected.

Other choices on this menu allow you to review help screens with information about the selected printer, list all the files for printers that have been selected, and search for a printer by name.

▣ Select **O**ther Disk (**2**) to display the following message:

```
Directory for printer files:
```

▣ WordPerfect is asking where it should look for the printer files. Type **B:**

▣ Remove your data disk in drive B and replace it with the Printer 1 disk. Then press **Enter**. Immediately a listing of printer files found on the Printer 1 disk will appear similar to the following:

```
Select Printer:   Additional Printers

Brother HL-8
Dataproducts LZR-1230
HP LaserJet
HP LaserJet 2000
HP LaserJet Series II
HP LaserJet+, 500+
LaserImage 1000
NEC Silentwriter LC-860+
Okidata LaserLine 6
Okidata Laserstar 6


1 Select; 2 Other Disk; 3 Help; 4 List Printer Files; N Name Search: 1
```

NOTE: There are four printer disks, each with a portion of the available printer definitions. The printer files on a hard disk will have a different arrangement since they are all grouped together into one place. If you are using a hard disk, you can simply search the alphabetized list of printer files to find the one that matches your printer and move ahead.

TIP: You may wonder why it is necessary to be so specific and why each printer is different; and the reason is that most printers have their own unique codes to enable them to recognize and print things like underlines, bolded text, and other special features. These printer definitions "define" the way such text is to be handled to each printer so that it will be printed correctly.

▣ Look on the outside of your printer case to find the brand name of the printer you are using. Then find the matching name in the list of printers on the screen. If it is not there, remove the Printer 1 disk and insert the Printer 2 disk.

◼ Then press **Other Disk (2)** and **Enter** to see the listing of printers on the Printer 2 disk. Continue with the Printer 3 disk and the Printer 4 disk if necessary.

◼ When you find the correct printer, highlight it, and choose **Select (1)** and **Enter**. WordPerfect will transfer a copy of the printer definition file for the printer you have selected to the WordPerfect 2 disk in the A drive. While it is doing this, you will see a message indicating the fonts are being updated and some helps and hints on the printer you have selected.

TIP: If you do not find your printer on any of the disks, an additional 50 or so printer files are available from WordPerfect (1-800-321-4566). The README files on the printer disks provide further information.

◼ When the fonts are finished, press **Exit (F7)** to move to the Printer Edit menu shown below.

◼ Remove the Printer disk from Drive B and return your data disk to the drive.

TIP: As you may have noticed, you can also reach this menu by choosing **Edit (3)** on the previous menu.

```
Select Printer: Edit

        Filename                        <Printfile.PRS>

    1 - Name                            <Printer name>

    2 - Port                            LPT1:

    3 - Sheet Feeder                    None

    4 - Forms

    5 - Cartridges and Fonts

    6 - Initial Font

    7 - Path for Downloadable
          Fonts and Printer
          Command Files




    Selection: 0
```

There are several items on this menu that involve fonts and other things that you will work with later, but for now, the Port is what you want to look at. WordPerfect will use the port you specify to send output to the printer. Your computer may have either a parallel or serial port, or both. Parallel ports are typically identified with the prefix LPT (meaning "line printer") and serial ports are typically identified with COM prefixes.

▣ Choose **Port (2)** to bring up the following menu across the bottom of the screen under the Edit menu:

```
Port: 1 LPT 1; 2 LPT 2; 3 LPT 3; 4 COM 1; 5 COM 2; 6 COM 3; 7 COM 4; 8 Other: 0
```

As you can guess, it is possible to have up to three parallel ports and four serial ports, as well as certain other types, in use at once. You are being asked to specify which port this particular printer occupies.

TIP: The following instructions are for a typical dot matrix configuration. You may need to adjust them to fit your own situation if it is different.

▣ Since it is more common to use a parallel port for a dot matrix printer, press **1** to specify the first LPT port. Then press **Exit (F7)** to move to the Printer Selection menu.

TIP: If you are using a serial port and select COM, you will be asked to specify a baud rate, parity, number of stop bits, and character length. Check the Help option on the menu or ask your instructor or lab assistant for information on what data to supply at this point.

▣ At the Printer Select menu, highlight the name of the printer you want and **Select (1)** it. An asterisk (*) will appear beside the active printer. Then press **Exit (F7)** to leave the menu and return to the Print menu.

Printing

Now that the printer has been selected, let's give WordPerfect the command to print. Your document is only one page long, so options 1 (Full Document) and 2 (Page) would produce the same result. The difference between these selections is apparent only when your document is several pages long.

Before printing with either option, you should check to be sure the printer is ready. Make certain it is turned on, the paper is aligned and in position to print, and the printer is on-line and ready to accept material from your machine.

▣ Now, because you want the entire document printed, select Full Document **(1)**. If you use the 1, remember to press the number 1, not the letter l.

Printing should begin within a few seconds. When it is finished, carefully tear the printed copy of your document off the printer at the perforated page separation, and trim off the edges if necessary.

TIP: You may notice an occasional line that is not justified on the right-hand side. This is caused by the printer's inability to "squeeze" the line together enough. Ignore it for the time being. You will learn how to overcome this problem later when you work with the hot-zone command.

Exiting from WordPerfect

When you have finished for the day or are ready to end your session with WordPerfect, you should **always** exit from the program.

To do this, you must first decide whether you want to save whatever you have been working on. If you don't save your document in its current form, everything you have entered into the computer's temporary memory since you last saved will be lost when WordPerfect is restarted or your computer is turned off.

The fact that the temporary memory is cleared following the Exit procedure is important to remember when you are deciding which Save function to use. Even though the prompts and the steps are very similar for both, the end result is not, because you **do not** lose what is on the screen and in the temporary memory with the Save (F10) method, and you **do** when using Exit (F7).

For practice, let's save again. Find Exit on the template near the F7 key. Notice that it is printed in black and therefore does not need a second key to function appropriately.

■ Press the **Exit (F7)** key. The following prompt will appear in the lower left-hand corner of your screen:

```
Save document? (Y/N) Yes
```

For the time being, let's assume that you want to save your document.

■ Press **Enter** or type **Y**. This will bring up the following prompt:

> Document to be saved:

■ Let's change the name. Type in **CharlieA.1** and press the **Enter** key.

The red light will come on, and WordPerfect will save your document under the new name. You now have two copies of your text, one under Charlie.1 and one under CharlieA.1.

When it is finished, another message will appear:

> Exit WP? (Y/N) No   (Cancel to return to document)

■ This time you do want to exit, so you should press the **Y** key.

The red light on the disk drive will come on once again, and you will see the B> or C> (depending on which drive is active and whether you are using a floppy disk or a hard drive).

You have now exited to the operating system. When the red disk-drive light has gone off, you are ready to take the disks out (if necessary) and turn the machine off. (Remember that to avoid possible damage to your disk, you should **never** insert or remove a disk when the red disk light is on.)

You should follow the Exit procedure outlined above anytime you are finished with a wordprocessing session and are ready to leave WordPerfect and/or turn the machine off.

Isn't this fun!

Summary

TO	PRESS
Interim save	Save (F10)
Save/exit document	Exit(F7); Save doc.? Y; Exit WP?N
Retrieve	Retrieve (Shift-F10)
Print	Print (Shift-F7); then 1 or 2
Exit from WP	Exit (F7); Save doc.? Y or N; Exit WP? Y
Clear screen	Exit (F7); Save doc.? Y or N;Exit WP? N

Activities

You should have completed the following:

Charlie.1	*Original Document*
CharlieA.1	*Edited Document*

Chapter Review

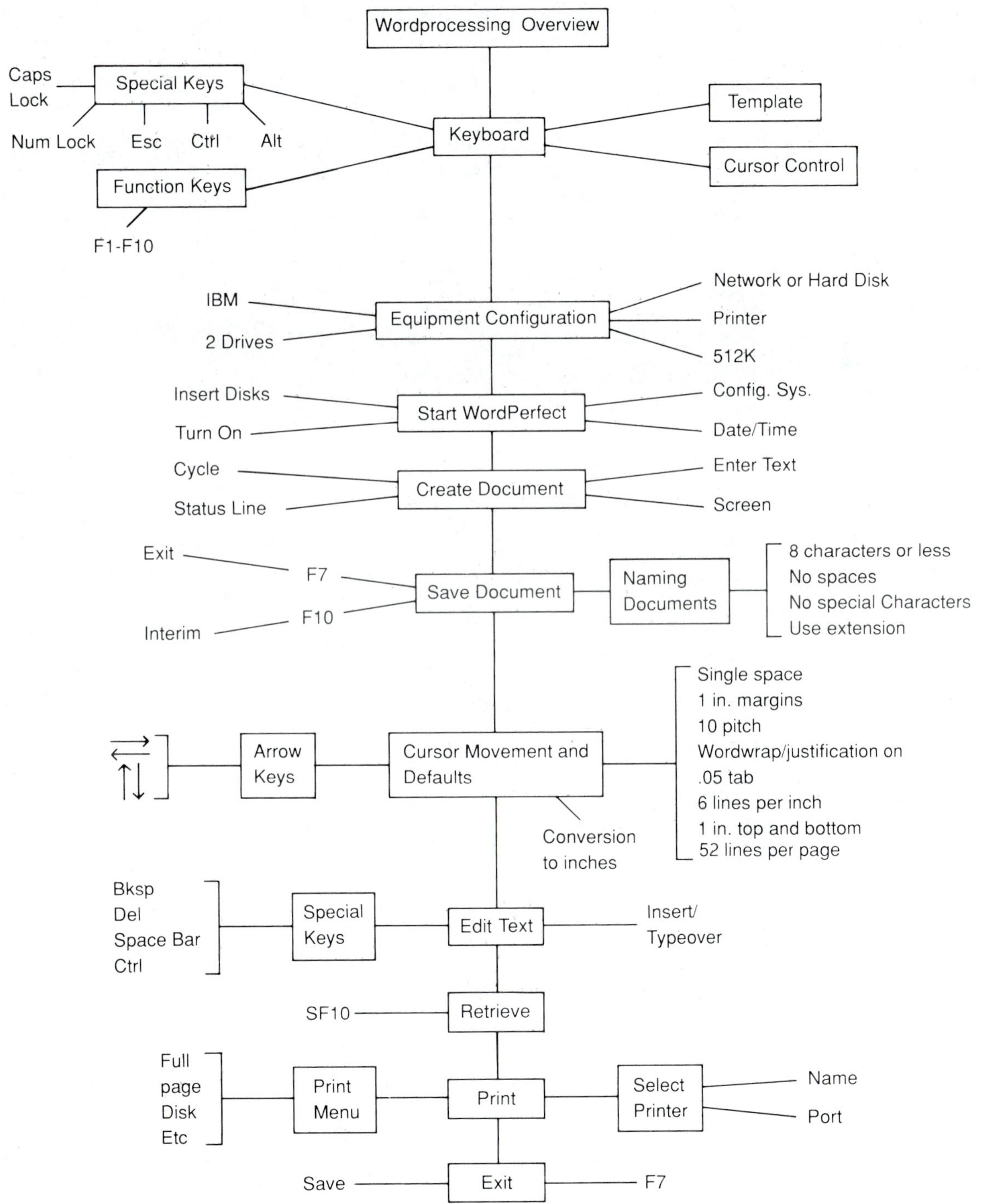

Self-Check Quiz 1

1. What function will each of the following keys perform?

   a. ←   b. ↵

   c. |⇄| d. ←

2. Using the template as a guide, what keys should you press to activate commands printed in each of the following colors?

   Red ________________________________

   Blue ________________________________

   Black ________________________________

   Green ________________________________

3. What are the steps in the document creation cycle?

4. What does the following status line tell you?

   B: Charlie.1   Doc 1 Pg 3 Ln 2" Pos 1.9"

   ____

5. In what position should you hold a disk when you insert it into the machine? ____

6. What is the difference between saving with Interim Save (F10) and Save (F7)? ____

7. Indicate what will happen when each of the following keys is used.

   a. Del ____

   b. Ins (Typeover) ____

   c. Tab ____

   d. Enter ____

   e. Backspace ____

   f. Up arrow ____

   g. Num Lock ____

   h. Caps Lock ____

8. Describe the difference in the way the delete function works with Del and with Backspace Delete.

9. If you wish to save your document, what commands should you use?

10. What is the advantage of using inches for margins and tabs?

11. What does it mean when the red disk-drive light comes on?

12. What key strokes should you use to retrieve a document?

13. What key strokes should you use to print a document?

14. Why must you define the printer before printing?

15. What kind of port would each of the following require:

    COM1
    LPT1

16. Can you interchange the l and 1 keys and the O and 0 keys? Why or why not?

17. What are the defaults for each of the following:
    a. Left/right margins _______________________
    b. Tabs _______________________
    c. Inches per page _______________________
    d. Spacing _______________________
    e. Paragraph indentation _______________________
    f. Word wrap _______________________

18. List three things you should remember when naming documents.

19. What should appear on the screen before you turn off the machine?

Extra Practice

For extra practice on the material covered in Chapter 1, do the following:

a. Using WordPerfect 5.0, enter several pages of text from a book from another class, the daily newspaper, or a magazine.

b. Use Save (F10) to save your document as Pract1a. Then proofread carefully and correct any errors you find.

c. For practice, resave your document using Exit (F7) and exit from Word-Perfect.

d. Re-enter WordPerfect and retrieve your document to the screen.

e. Print your document.

f. Use WordPerfect to enter an assignment, such as a report or paper for one of your classes. Proofread it carefully and correct any errors you find. When you are finished, save it as Pract1b and print it. Hand in the paper to your instructor.

g. Using WordPerfect, write a letter to a friend. Edit your work, save it to the disk, and print it.

2

Faster Cursor-Movement, and Deleting Methods, More Editing Commands, and Working with the Print Menu

Moving the cursor one space at a time and deleting text one character at a time can be slow and time-consuming. This chapter will show you some faster ways to do those functions. You will also review some commonly used proofreader marks. Then you will learn to print a document from the disk, print multiple copies, use printer control commands, and view your document in WYSIWYG (What You See Is What You Get) fashion. You will also learn some tips for troubleshooting the printer and how to use the type-through feature.

After completing this chapter, you will be able to:

- use a number of special commands, such as PgUp/Down and Screen Up/Down, GoTo, End, and Esc to move the cursor around your text.

- delete words, lines, and parts of a page all at once.

- use undelete and restore to retrieve deleted text.

- cancel unwanted commands.

- recognize and use commonly accepted proofreaders' marks

- print documents from the disk

- use the Type-through feature to address envelopes and other items.

- use the View command to see a document as it will appear when printed.

- use the printer control commands to check the status of your print jobs and stop and restart the printer

- print multiple copies of a page or document

- solve common printing problems and troubleshoot the printer.

Getting Started

- To begin, insert your disks and turn on your computer. Enter the current date and time.

- As soon as WordPerfect is loaded into the memory and you see the status line at the bottom of the screen, quickly type the sentence **Now is the time for all good men to come to the aid of their country** ten times as shown below. Use word wrap and do not be concerned if your lines do not end exactly at the

---

Now is the time for all good men to come to the aid of their country. Now is the time for all good men to come to the aid of their country. Now is the time for all good men to come to the aid of their country. Now is the time for all good men to come to the aid of their country. Now is the time for all good men to come to the aid of their country. Now is the time for all good men to come to the aid of their country. Now is the time for all good men to come to the aid of their country. Now is the time for all good men to come to the aid of their country. Now is the time for all good men to come to the aid of their country. Now is the time for all good men to come to the aid of their country.

---

same place as the example. Do not take time at this point to correct your errors; you'll have a chance to do that later. If you wish, you can retrieve the file **Nowis.2** from the Student Exercise disk using Retrieve (Shift-F10).

◙ Before going any further, save your material with the name **Nowis.2** and clear the memory and your screen using **Exit** (**F7**). Replace the file if asked.

◙ Then retrieve **Nowis.2** with **Retrieve** (**Shift-F10**).

TIP: It is important for the temporary memory to be clear before retrieving a document. If there is already a document in the memory, the one you retrieve will be added to it and you will end up with a file composed of both documents mixed together.

Quick Cursor Movements

Now that you've typed a document, you can practice moving the cursor around in it using the Home key and the Arrow keys. Try each of the following to see what happens:

TIP: Some commands are entered by pressing keys consecutively, and others are entered by holding down one key while you press another.

Keys that should be pressed consecutively are shown separated by commas (Home, Home, Up Arrow).

Those that should be pressed together are shown with a hyphen between them (Ctrl-F10)

TIP: When both the function name and the function-key number are given, one or the other will be in parentheses like the following: F7 (Exit) or Exit (F7).

Home, Up Arrow	Moves cursor to the top of the screen.
Home, Right Arrow	Moves cursor to the right end of the line.
Home, Left Arrow	Moves cursor to the left end of the line.
Home, Down Arrow	Moves cursor to the bottom of the screen.
Ctrl-Right Arrow	Moves cursor one word to the right.
Ctrl-Left Arrow	Moves cursor one word to the left.

TIP: Any group of characters followed by a space is defined as a word by Word-Perfect. All of the following would be treated as words:

move, A61/23, $235.

Home, Home, Up Arrow	Moves cursor to beginning of document.
Home, Home, Down Arrow	Moves cursor to end of document.

Isn't that slick!

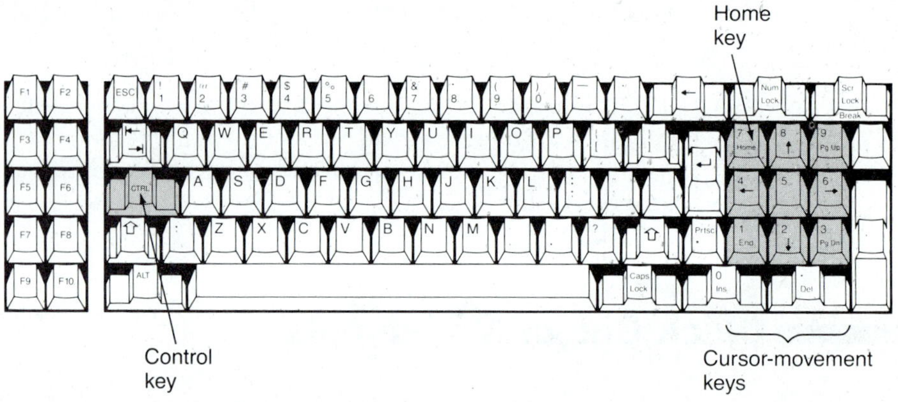

Faster Ways to Delete

There are also faster ways to delete words, lines and blocks of text with WordPerfect.

Backspace

▣ First, position the cursor in the middle of a line and hold down the **Backspace** ← key.

Whoops! As you can see, this command will continue to delete to the left, one character at a time, as long as you hold the key down. (Shades of Pac-Man.)

▣ Now press the **Ins** key, so that Typeover shows in the lower left-hand corner of your screen, and then press the **Backspace** key again to delete.

Things work differently with Ins Off. WordPerfect is now inserting spaces in place of the characters it deletes. When you have tried this command with Ins both On and Off, turn Ins On so that Typeover does not show on your screen. Then go on.

Del

In contrast to the Backspace command, the Del command causes the cursor to stay put. The letter above the cursor is deleted and the text to the right of the cursor moves toward it.

▣ Now hold down the **Del** key and see what happens. Again the delete is continuous. This time, though, the characters above and to the right of the cursor are deleted. (It looks almost like they fall into a hole.)

Ctrl-Backspace

An entire word can be deleted by positioning the cursor under the word you want to take out, holding down the Ctrl key and pressing the Backspace key.

▣ Try it on a few words.

Ctrl-End

You can erase to the end of the line by positioning the cursor at the beginning of the text you want to delete, holding down the Ctrl key and pressing End (or, on some computers, EOL for **end of line**).

▣ Delete a couple of lines. Notice that material is deleted above the cursor and to the right. Watch carefully because when the cursor is moved the words after the deletion will fill the empty spot.

Ctrl-PgDn

You can delete part of a page by using the Ctrl and PgDn (or, on some computers, EOP for **end of page**) keys together.

▣ Move the cursor to a point three lines from the bottom of your text. Hold down **Ctrl** and press **PgDn** to delete those lines.

▣ WordPerfect will ask you to confirm that you really want to delete to the end of the page. Answer **Y**(es). If you answered N(o), the delete command would be ignored. This is WordPerfect's way of helping you avoid errors that could not be recovered. Delete an additional two lines if you wish.

Home, Backspace

Pressing Home and then Backspace will delete to the left from the cursor to the next blank space. If the cursor were in the middle of a word, part of the word would be deleted; if the cursor were at the end of a word, the whole word would be erased. The cursor must be on the blank space after the word, otherwise it leaves the last letter.

Home, Del

Pressing Home and then Del will delete to the right from the cursor to the next blank space. Again, you can delete either part of a word or the whole word with this command, depending on where the cursor is placed.

Insert Off

Pressing the Space Bar when Insert is Off (Typeover is displayed at the bottom of your screen) will delete characters as spaces are added. When Insert is On and the Space Bar is pressed, text is pushed to the right without being deleted as spaces are inserted.

▣ To see how this works, move the cursor to the middle of a line. Then press **Ins** to display Typeover at the bottom left of your screen.

▣ Press the **Space Bar** a few times to see what happens. Notice that characters are deleted as the cursor moves across the screen.

▣ Now press **Ins** to return to Insert On status. Again press the **Space Bar** and watch what happens. The text will be pushed to the right as spaces are inserted.

Exit (No Save)

Finally, you can delete an entire file from the temporary memory simply by not saving it when you Exit. When you are asked if you want to save the file, answer N(o) and it will be erased from the temporary memory without saving on the disk.

Summary

In summary, use the following commands to Delete:

a.	Backspace	Continuous delete to the left of the cursor.
b.	Del	Continuous delete to the right of the cursor.
c.	Ctrl-Backspace	Deletes a word at a time.
d.	Ctrl-End (EOL)	Deletes from the position of the cursor to the right-hand end of the line.
e.	Ctrl-PgDn (EOP)	Deletes from the position of the cursor to the end of the page.
f.	Home, Backspace	Deletes to the next blank space on the left.
g.	Home, Del	Deletes to the next blank space on the right.
h.	Exit/No Save	Deletes unsaved file.

Undelete

If you delete something and then regret your action and want to retrieve the text, WordPerfect has the answer.

To make it possible to restore deleted material, WordPerfect remembers the last three deletions you made and stores them in temporary files. To retrieve one of these files, simply position the cursor where you want the text restored and press Cancel (F1). The text of the last deletion will appear highlighted at the cursor, and the following menu will appear across the bottom of the screen:

```
Undelete: 1 Restore; 2 Previous Deletion: 0
```

If you want to restore this text at the cursor, all you need to do is select **Restore (1)**. The deleted material will be inserted wherever the cursor is.

If you want to see one of the other two deletions, select **P**revious deletion **(2)** and another deletion will appear.

Now that you've learned how to move the cursor quickly, and some new tricks for deleting (and restoring), go back and clean up this project to get it ready to print.

◻ Correct any errors and retype where necessary to restore the original text of Now is the time . . . typed ten times, corrected, and ready to save. Use the fast cursor-movement and delete commands wherever possible.

◻ When you are finished, resave your document using the **Save (F10)** key. Name it **Nowis.2**. Confirm replacement with **Y**(es).

Cancel

Occasionally you will begin a command and then change your mind. How do you back out without changing your document? WordPerfect has the answer.

◻ To see how it works, press **Retrieve (Shift-F10)**. A message asking which document you wish to retrieve will appear at the lower left-hand corner of your screen.

```
Document to be retrieved:
```

Whoops! You don't want to retrieve any text. You're ready to print. To get out of this predicament, notice that the word **Cancel** appears in black next to the F1 key. This command will allow you to cancel or stop the command.

◻ Press **Cancel (F1)** (since it's printed in black, no other key is needed). The message in the lower left-hand corner will disappear. WordPerfect has cancelled your previous command, and you can now proceed with another action.

The Cancel command can be used to cancel any menu or status line prompt if you change your mind or find you have entered a wrong command.

TIP: When you use the Cancel (F1) command this way, WordPerfect "forgets" any changes you may have made and simply returns to the settings it had before you pressed Cancel. If you wish to save any changes, you must use Exit (F7) to leave the command.

Proofreaders' Marks

Now let's do a longer document so you can work with some commands to move through the text in longer jumps. While we're at it, let's review some of the commonly accepted proofreaders' marks so you can use them to edit as you go along. Study the following until you know them well and can use them from memory:

Meaning	Proofreaders' marks
Insert	seventen
Close up	seven teen
Delete	seventeenn
Delete and close up	seventeeen
Transpose	seventene
Spell out	(17) Sp
Period	⊙
Move to the right	
Move to the left	
Ignore correction	stet--means "let it stand"
New paragraph	¶
Single space	ss
Double space	ds
Triple space	ts
Capitalize	seventeen
Lower-case	Seventeen
Add a space	seventeenyears
Underline	seventeen underline
Bold	seventeen
Comma	

SAVE OFTEN! Be sure to save your documents every page or so. Experts recommend saving every ten minutes. This is a good habit to develop so that you will not risk losing a great deal of material if something should happen to your computer. It is also a good idea to save anytime you are interrupted or must leave your computer for a short time.

Use the Save function on the Save (F10) key for interim saves on the following document, and name it TV.2. Say Y(es) when you are asked if you want to replace the file on the disk. That way you can just continue with your work after each save, and WordPerfect will help you keep the copy on the disk updated. Use the Exit (F7) key to save when you are completely finished and wish to shift to another project.

TIP: It is possible to instruct WordPerfect to back up your document automatically every few minutes and you will learn how to do that in a later chapter. For the time being, however, get in the habit of doing the backups yourself on a regular, fairly frequent basis.

☐ Type the text below, following the instructions given. You may if you wish, retrieve TV.2 from the Student Exercise disk and continue on. Note that you must correct all errors indicated by the proofreaders' marks.

    a. Use default settings for margins, tabs and spacing.

    b. Edit as you go along by responding to the proofreaders' symbols. When you are finished, proofread carefully and correct all remaining errors.

¶ If you have ever invited guests to come into your home for an evening

of television, you have been given a chance to see televiewers at their

best and at their worst. ¶ At least one of these visitors may have been

the *restless* type of person who sprints from his chair to the video set to adjust

the controls for you.   The fact that he has no set of his own seems

to fill him with an uncontrollable desire to play with yours.   First

he experiments with the volume control.   The

(Do an Interim Save (F10), name the document TV.2)

mustic is just a little too loud or too soft for him and he is sure for the other listeners as well. having adjusted the dials so that every muted violin may be heard by all, he must leap forward again to diminish the volume because of a sudden and unexpected strength in the voice of the man giving the Commercial. Our diligent friend becomes so intoxicated with his power over the machine that he also works with the image. He even takes it upon himself to hunt for programs that may be more pleasing than the one you have selected. The result of his apt and unfailing devotion to duty is a jumble for the eys and an assault on the nervous systems of the other viewers.

(Do an Interim Save (F10), TV.2)

Or perhaps you have been so unlucky as to include in your circle the noisy, jovial type of person. His talk is loud and endless. He prides himself on his powers of sparkling oral discourse. He will allow no dull moment to dim the luster of the evening. He has not the slightest awareness of the fact that moments of silence are more eloquent and more pleasing to overtaxed ears than is a constant flow of meaningless words. Your more subdued guests must take their video salted and peppered with his witty comments.

(Do an Interim Save (F10), TV.2)

Moving Through the Text a Page or a Screen at a Time

You have already learned how to use the Arrow keys and the Home key to move around in your text. But it is often necessary or desirable to move through the text of a document a screen or a page or more at a time. Since a page of text with normal sized type contains about 54 single-spaced typewritten lines (66 total, minus 6 each for the top and bottom margins), and a screen can display only 25 lines, there is quite a difference between the amount you can see on the screen and what is actually on the page. A little mental arithmetic will tell you that you can see a little less than half a page of actual text at a time on the screen.

On your keyboard, you will see the PgUp, PgDn, Screen Up (or – minus) and Screen Down (or + plus) keys.

◻ With TV.2 on the screen, press each key and watch the status line as you do.

As you can see, the cursor jumps from page to page when you use the PgUp and PgDn keys, showing you only 24 lines of each page (25 with the status line). When you press Screen Up or Screen Down, the line indicator shows that the cursor moves down the page in 24-line jumps. It takes a little more than two screens to see an entire page.

Each of these features is suited to a particular circumstance. If you wish to move through your text quickly, and do not need to see every line, you would use the PgUp and PgDn keys. In the process, however, you would miss seeing about half of the text.

On the other hand, if you were reading through the text or searching for a particular word or line, you would want to see everything even if it took a little longer. In this case, you would use the Screen Up (–) and Screen Down (+) keys. This is faster than scrolling line-by-line, but not as fast as jumping a page at a time.

The diagram on page 49 illustrates the difference between Page Down and Screen Down.

When you proofread, use the Screen Up (–) and Screen Down (+) keys so you will see the entire text of your document.

To get acquainted with the way these keys work, spend some time experimenting with them. Notice what appears on the screen in response to each one.

Page down from page 2 to page 3   Screen down within page 2

To Review

The PgUp key will move up ___________ lines of text.

The PgDn key will move down ___________ lines of text.

The Screen Up key will move up ___________ lines of text.

The Screen Down key will move down ___________ lines of text.

Cursor Movement With Go To, End, Tab, and Esc

You have already learned how to move the cursor with the Left, Right, Up, and Down Arrow keys; you have also learned how to use the Home and Ctrl keys as well as the PgUp/PgDn and Screen Up/Screen Down keys to make bigger jumps so you can move around in your document quite well. There are four more commands that are helpful in moving around in the text. Follow along to see how they work.

Go To

The Go To command is activated by pressing Ctrl-Home. When you press those keys, the following prompt will appear in the lower left-hand corner of the screen:

```
Go to
```

From this point, you have several options.

You can press the Up Arrow key to cause the cursor to jump to the top of the page.

You can press the Down Arrow key to cause the cursor to move to the end of the page. If the top or bottom of the page is not currently displayed, the contents of the screen will also change.

You can move to any page in your document. To do this you would press the Ctrl and Home keys. When the words **Go to** appear on the screen, you would simply type in the page number you wish to go to and press Enter. The word **Repositioning** would appear in the lower left, and then the top of the page you requested would appear. As you can imagine, this is quite an aid in moving around quickly in a fairly long document.

You can move to the first occurrence of any single character (letter, number, punctuation mark), providing it can be found within the nearest 2000 characters. For instance, if you typed Ctrl-Home J, the cursor would move to the character following the nearest J within 2000 characters.

■ You do not yet have a document long enough to move from page to page, but you can use the Up Arrow and Down Arrow keys with the Go To command. You can also move to specified characters in your document. Try them once or twice to see how they work. Then remember to use the Go To command to move from page to page when your document is longer.

End

The End key can be used to send the cursor to the right-hand end of the line. It does not work going left, but can be very helpful in moving along a line.

Tab

As you know, pressing the Tab key moves the cursor (and text to the right of it) to the next tab stop. And, although you can't see it, a [Tab] command is inserted in your document so that the printer will know what to do.

However, when Ins is Off and **Typeover** shows in the lower left-hand corner of your screen, the Tab function works differently: the cursor moves but the text does not, and no Tab command is inserted in your document. In other words, when Ins is Off, the Tab key can be used to move the cursor from one tab stop to another without affecting your document.

■ Try using the **Tab** command with Ins both On and Off (watch the lower left-hand corner of your screen for the word **Typeover**) and see the difference.

To Review

When Typeover is showing on your screen, Tab commands (will or will not?) be inserted.

Esc

In addition to many other functions, the Esc key is also a repetition-counter. This means that it will repeat some functions a specified number of times. The default for this command is 8, meaning that the function you specify will be performed 8 times, unless you indicate otherwise.

The Esc command works with all the Arrow keys and the PgUp/PgDn keys.

■ To see what happens, position your cursor at the bottom of the screen and press **Esc**. Immediately you will see the following in the lower left-hand corner of the screen:

```
Repeat Value = 8
```

If you do not type in another number, WordPerfect will use 8 as the default.

TIP: Don't press Enter after typing in a Repeat value number. Doing so will abort the command so it will not work. It also will change the Repeat value default to the number you entered.

■ For now, type in **10**.

■ Then press the **Up Arrow** key. Notice that the cursor jumps upward 10 lines.

■ Now press **Esc** again.

■ When Repeat value = 8 appears, type in **5** and press the **Down Arrow** key.

The cursor will move downward five lines. To see how the default works, do the following:

■ Press **Esc**. Do not type in another number.

■ Press the **Up Arrow** key.

■ Press **Esc** and **Up Arrow** twice. The cursor should jump upward eight lines each time. If the document were longer, the cursor would continue to move upward with each command.

You can move sideways the same way by simply typing in the number of characters you would like the cursor to move and then press the Right or Left Arrow, or by moving the cursor 8 spaces at a time with the default.

It is also possible to move forward or backward a specified number of pages. To do so, you would press Esc and type in the number of pages you would like to move. Then press either the PgUp or PgDn keys. The cursor would immediately jump forward or backward the specified number of pages.

TIP: If the Repeat value = 8 prompt appears and you do not want to move the cursor, then press the Cancel (F1) or the Enter key to stop it.

The Esc command will also do something else, unrelated to moving the cursor but still a very useful tool.

▣ To see what this is, move the cursor to a blank space at the end of your document.

▣ Then press **Esc**.

▣ When the Repeat value = 8 prompt appears, press **any letter** on the keyboard.

Immediately you will see that letter printed eight times on your screen.

▣ Press **Esc** again and then **another letter**. WordPerfect will print the second letter eight times as well, beginning at the cursor.

▣ Press **Esc** again and the **underline (F8)**. WordPerfect will print a line 8 spaces long.

You can also change the number of times the letter is printed by entering a new amount for the repeat value and then pressing the key you want repeated. Using the Esc command, you can print a character a specified number of times without having to type it in each time individually. This is nice for drawing lines.

TIP: All of the following can be used with the Esc command: Arrow keys, Delete, Delete to End of Line, Delete to End of Page, Delete Word, Macro, Page Up/Down, Screen Up/Down, Word Left/Right.

▣ Now clean up your document. Proofread it and correct any errors. Then resave it as TV.2 and print it.

▣ When you are finished, **Exit (F7)** to clear the screen.

To Review

What does a repetition-counter do?

What is the default for the Esc command?

If you pressed Esc and then PgDn, what would happen?

If you pressed Esc and then the letter R, what would happen?

Summary

In summary, to use Esc as a repetition-counter:

a. Position the cursor.

b. Press Esc.

c. Indicate the number of times the action is to be performed or use the default of 8.

d. Press the appropriate key or command.

Using The Print Menu

There are a number of other commands on the Print Menu that will be useful to you. You have already seen some of them in Chapter 1. Let's review those and take a look at the rest.

◻ Press **Print** (**Shift-F7**) to bring up the following menu.

```
Print

      1 - Full Document
      2 - Page
      3 - Document on Disk
      4 - Control Printer
      5 - Type Through
      6 - View Document
      7 - Initialize Printer

Options

      S - Select Printer              IBM PC Graphics Printer
      B - Binding                     0"
      N - Number of Copies            1
      G - Graphics Quality            Medium
      T - Text Quality                High




Selection: 0
```

Printing from the Screen

Options 1 and 2 will print either the full document on the screen (1) or the page the cursor is on (2). You have already used these commands. Both are, however, limited to printing the document you are currently working on.

Printing from the Disk

Option 3 will print any document on the disk. This is new. Let's see how it can be used.

- Select Document on Disk **(3)**. Immediately you will be asked to enter the name of the document you would like to print.

- Type **TV.2** and press **Enter**.

- The next prompt will ask which pages you want printed.

```
Page(s): (All)
```

Specifying the pages to print

There are a number of ways you can indicate to WordPerfect what you want to print.

If you want to print the entire document, press Enter to accept the default (All).

If you want individual nonconsecutive pages printed, type page numbers separated by commas like the following: 1, 3, 5

If you want a range of pages printed, type the beginning page, a hyphen, and the ending page, like this: 21-28

If you want to print from a certain page to the end of your document, enter the beginning page followed by a hyphen: 34-

If you want to print from the beginning of your document to a certain page, enter a hyphen followed by the last page to be printed: -16

If some of your pages are numbered with Roman numerals, such as ii or iv, simply show them in that format.

If you want to use more than one of the commands described above, simply enter them in sequence, separated by a comma. For example, ii, 2, 5-9, 34- will print pages ii, 2, 5 through 9, and 34 to the end of your document.

TIP: You should not insert any spaces between numbers in any of the above entries.

- ◼ If TV.2 had only two pages, you could type either 1 or 2. Since it only has one page, type **1** to print page 1.

- ◼ Press **Enter** to begin the printing process

- ◼ When you are finished, label your document **PgPrnt.2**.

TIP: It is also possible to queue, or stack, several print jobs using Option 3. As soon as one job is entered, simply select 3 again, indicate a filename and the pages to be printed and press Enter. WordPerfect will remember the command and when it has finished printing the first document begin the next.

Printer Control

The fourth option provides information on the status of the current job that is printing as well as any that are waiting to be printed. In additon it allows you to cancel a print job, insert a rush print job ahead of others waiting to be printed, and stop or start the printer again.

- ◼ Select **Printer Control (4)** to bring up the menu shown on page 57.

Most interaction with the printer takes place through this menu. As you can see, you can monitor what is happening with the job that is currently printing.

If you have entered commands for several jobs to be printed, one after another, the *Job Number* indicator will tell you which one is currently being printed.

The *Status* indicator will report whether the job is printing or not.

The *Paper* indicator will show the size of paper being used. For instance, it may show Standard 8-1/2 x 11, which is the default, or some other size depending on what you may have specified in the forms menus.

The *Location* indicator reports where WordPerfect expects to find the paper. This could be continuous feed, sheet feed, a bin number, etc.

```
Print: Control Printer

Current Job

Job Number: 1                                    Page Number:   1
Status:      End of job                          Current Copy: 1 of 1
Message:     Printer not accepting characters
Paper:       None
Location:    None
Action:      Check cable, make sure printer is turned ON


Job List

Job  Document                 Destination            Print Options
 1   B:\TU                    LPT 1




Additional Jobs Not Shown: 0




1 Cancel Job(s); 2 Rush Job; 3 Display Jobs; 4 Go (start printer); 5 Stop: 0
```

This menu also tells you which *Page Number* is currently printing such as 2 of 5 which means page 2 of 5 total pages is being printed. In addition, the *Current Copy* keeps track of how many copies have been printed when multiple copies have been specified.

Finally, the *Message* and *Action* lines will often give you information about the print job, problems that may be occurring, instructions on what you should do, etc. For instance, you may see a message such as "Printer not accepting characters." and an action statement such as "Check cable. Make sure printer is turned ON." or "Give printer a (G)o to start printing."

TIP: If your printer does not respond after you have entered a command to print, it is a good idea to check the printer control menu to see if WordPerfect has a message telling you what the problem might be.

You can also see a *Job List* of all jobs waiting to be printed, which printer they have been directed to (if more than one is being used), and any options indicated. Up to three jobs waiting to be printed may be shown in the job list. Additional jobs will be indicated at the bottom of the menu and can be listed by pressing D for Display Jobs.

Finally, the menu line across the bottom will allow you to do several other things to control the printer and change the way jobs are printed.

You can *Cancel* print jobs that are in process or in line for printing if you press **1** or **C**. More about this later.

You can insert *Rush* jobs into or ahead of others already in line for printing if you press **2** or **R**. If you should interrupt a job currently printing, it will resume at the top of the page on which it was interrupted when the rush job is completed.

You can *Display* a list of all print jobs lined up to print if you press **3** or **D**.

You will give the printer a *Go* or reset command if you press **4** or **G**. If you use one of the commands shown on this menu to stop the printer for any reason, you must then give it the go-ahead to begin again by pressing G.

You can *Stop* the printer if you press **5** or **S**. You may then abort the printing process altogether or restart the printer and continue. More on this later.

Type -Through

One of the shortcomings of word-processing programs in the past has been their inability to handle things like envelopes and fill-in forms. Now that WordPerfect has type-through capability, many of those problems are resolved. This feature allows you to send text directly to the printer, bypassing the internal-memory function. In other words, you can now use your word processor like a typewriter.

To see how this feature works, suppose you want to print your name and address at the top of a form.

■ **Position the paper in the printer** so that the print head is on the first line you want to type. Let's assume you want to start seven lines down from the top of the page. Do not allow extra space for the top margin; the printer will not automatically add it when using this feature. Insert the paper so the top of the page is under the print head. Then turn on the printer and **press the line-feed button** seven times.

■ Then press **Print (Shift-F7)** to bring up the Print menu. (Since the menu is already on your screen, you will not need to do this at this time.)

■ From the print menu, choose **Type Through (5)**. The following message will appear at the bottom of the screen:

```
Type Through by: 1 Line; 2 Character: 0
```

NOTE: Some printers, including most lasers, do not allow the Type-through feature since they print by page rather than line or character. If so, you may see a message at the bottom of the screen that says "Printer not ready" or "Feature not available on this printer." If that happens, you will not be able to do the following exercise. However, you should read and study the information so you will be familiar with this command when you are working with a different printer.

If you choose **Line (1)**, you can type a line of text up to 200 characters long that will then be printed all at once when you press Enter. The word wrap function does not work in type-through mode. You can, however, use the cursor-movement keys and space bar to edit the line of text before sending it to the printer.

If you choose **Character (2)**, the text will be sent to the printer character-by-character as you type it. As a result, you cannot change the text once it is typed and printed.

■ For practice, choose **Line (1)**. The following will appear on your screen:

```
Line Type-Through Printing

Function Key                    Action

Move                            Returns the previous line for editing
Print Format                    Do a printer command
Enter                           Print the line
Exit/Cancel                     Exit without printing
```

■ Make sure the printer is on line and ready to accept text from your machine.

■ Type your name and press **Enter**. Then type your street address and press Enter. Type your city and state and press **Enter**.

Notice that only two lines of text are displayed at a time. You can recall a previous line by pressing Move (Ctrl-F4).

■ Edit the line of text you recalled by adding the ZIP code after the state, and again press **Enter**.

■ Hold down the **Space Bar** to move the cursor to the middle of the screen. Then type your name again and press **Enter**. Notice that the printer prints the text in the middle of the page.

Another trick you can do in type-through mode is to move down the page with the printer.

■ Press the **Down Arrow** key a few times. The paper in the printer moves down one line each time you press the key. Try it for a line or two. Slick, wouldn't you say?

TIP: Some printers also allow you to move the paper backward using the Up Arrow key. Do not use this key, however, if your printer does not support it as you may cause damage to the printer and/or ruin your document. (Check the printer manual or ask your instructor for information on the capability of your printer.)

■ When you are finished, press **Exit (F7)** or **Cancel (F1)** to leave type-through mode. Reset the top of the paper in the printer before going on to the next exercise.

View Document

As you know, you can see less than half of each page of your document on the screen at a time (80 spaces x 24 lines or 8" by 4"). There are times, however, when it would be helpful to see an entire page at once so you could check things like placement, where the page numbers will appear, any footnotes you may have added, how graphics will look on the page as a whole, spacing, etc. When this is the case, you will want to see the entire page at once in WYSIWYG (What You See Is What You Get) fashion.

■ For some practice with this command, retrieve the document named TV.2 if it is not already on your screen. Position the cursor on page 1.

■ From the Print menu (Shift-F7) select **View (6)**.

WordPerfect will generate the first page as it will appear when it is printed and then display it on the screen in full page format. Because the size must be reduced in order to display the entire page, it is difficult to read the text. However, this view does give you a better overall picture of the page as a whole, including parts that do not normally display. For instance, if you had inserted page numbers, footnotes, footers, and the like, they would also be displayed even though you could not normally see them on the regular editing screen of your monitor.

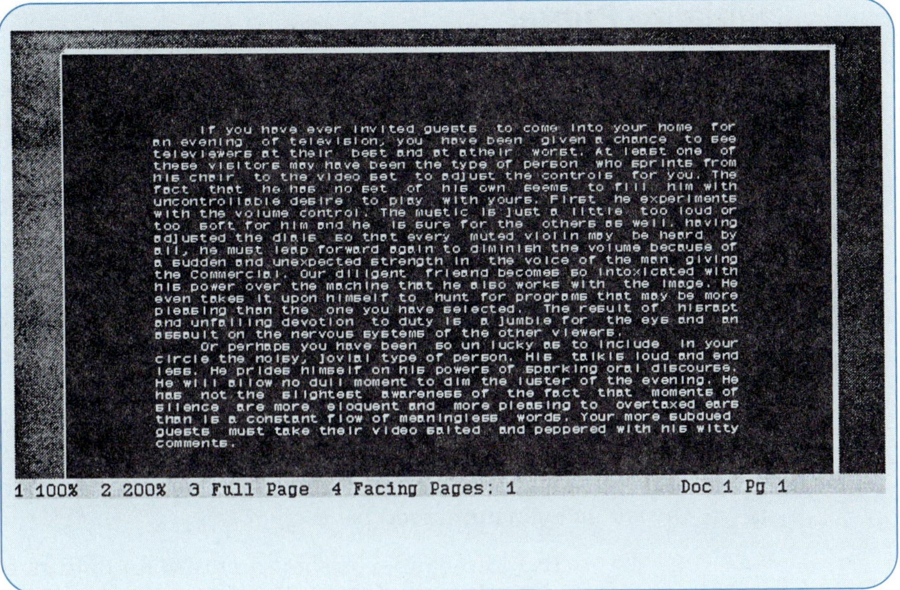

Several other options are listed across the bottom of the screen. First you can see the document at 100% or full-size such as 8-1/2" x 11". Second, selecting 200% will display the document twice as big as normal (printed appearance). Third, you can display the full page (default); or fourth, you can look at facing pages.

TIP: Facing pages are somewhat unique. When WordPerfect displays two pages, it puts the even numbered page on the left and the odd numbered page following it on the right. To make this command work, therefore, you must have at least three pages in your document. WordPerfect will not display pages 1 and 2 this way.

It is also possible to see additional pages if you wish. You can use the PgUp and PgDown keys to move forward or backward a page at a time; and when your document is displayed in 100% or 200% size, you can use the Up and Down Arrow keys to scroll the document on the screen.

- Move to page 2 of your document. To do this, you can either move the cursor to that page and select View, or you can use PgDn.

- When you have finished looking at the view screen, press **Exit** (**F7**) to return to your document.

TIP: Using the View command does not affect your document in any way. You cannot make changes, add, or delete from the View screen. It is useful, however, to help you see what parts of your document that do not normally display will look like and to see how the page will look when printed.

Initialize Printer

This command blanks the printer memory and allows you to download soft fonts that have been marked with the cartridges and fonts feature. You will work with this command more later.

You have already used the Select Printer command. So let's look ahead to the remaining items on this menu.

Changing the Binding Width

It is unlikely that you will have frequent need to change the binding width, but if you should want to allow a little extra room on the left side of the paper for such things as holes or other binding on two sided copies, WordPerfect will shift the text slightly to the right on odd numbered pages and slightly to the left on even numbered pages.

To use this command, you should press **B** for Binding and enter the width you would like WordPerfect to shift on each page. When you Exit, WordPerfect will adjust the pages slightly to the right or left to provide the extra room you need.

Specifying the Number of Copies to Print

If you would like to print more than one copy of a document, you can specify that and have WordPerfect do it automatically. For some practice, let's print two copies of TV.2.

■ Retrieve the document named TV.2 if necessary.

■ With the Print menu on the screen, select **Number of Copies (N)** and type in **2**, which is the number of copies you want printed. Then press **Enter**.

■ Now print the document using any print method. WordPerfect will remember that you have specified two copies and will print them one after the other.

■ Label the printout **Copies.2**. When you are finished, reset the number of copies to 1.

Graphics and Text Quality

Depending on the capability of your printer, you can specify the quality of the printout as High, Medium, or Draft. Draft quality text and graphics can be printed much faster than high quality, and this setting is often used for quick copies or when lower quality is acceptable. You can also tell WordPerfect not to print graphics and/or text with this option. This might be useful when the printer you are using does not have full capability, or you do not want to wait for the graphics to print.

To Review

Which pages would the following command print? 23–30, 34, 40–49

If a binding width has been set, where will extra room appear?

Printing Problems

Occasionally, WordPerfect cannot print the document you specify. To let you know there is a problem, you may get one of the following messages across the bottom of the screen.

```
ERROR: Document was Fast Saved -- Must be retrieved to print
```

```
Document not formatted for current printer. Continue? (Y/N) N
```

Wrong printer

With the first message, WordPerfect is telling you that a different printer was in use when the document was saved. Since many codes, fonts, and other settings are printer specific and saved with the document, you may encounter difficulty if you try to print the document with a printer other than the one already specified in the file. If you elect to continue, WordPerfect will convert the codes in the file to match the printer in use as closely as possible and print the document. In most cases, this is satisfactory; but if you have inserted codes for features that are not available on the second printer, your document may not turn out as you intend.

Fast saved

The second message is telling you that your document was fast saved in unformatted manner. This is sometimes done to reduce the time needed to save a document. Since a document cannot be printed from disk unless it is formatted, you must retrieve the document, press Home, Home, Down Arrow to cause it to be formatted, resave it, then print. You may also retrieve it to the screen and use options 1 or 2 to print it without formatting and resaving. You will learn how to change the default and turn the Fast Save feature off in Chapter 10.

Stopping the Printer

At one time or another you will probably encounter problems with the printer and wanted to stop printing. There are three ways to stop the printer: (1) Cancel the job, (2) use the Stop Printing option, and (3) Ctrl-Num Lock. Each of these is explained below.

TIP: Many printers have buffer memories that will continue to send data to the printer for a short time even after you have given the command to stop. If this is the case, you must wait until the buffer memory is empty before the printer will stop printing. How long this will take depends on the size of the buffer memory in your printer.

Cancel

This option should be used only when the printer is working correctly but you want to stop the printing of a specific document. Cancel can be used during the printing of a document to interrupt and terminate a job, or it can be used before a job is printed to prevent its being started.

1. First, bring up the Printer Control menu. Then press **Cancel** (**1**) to Cancel Print Job(s). When asked Cancel which job? (*=All jobs) 1, do any of the following:

   Press the Enter key to cancel the *job currently being printed* (indicated by the number).

   Type in an asterisk (*) and press Enter to *cancel all jobs waiting to be printed.* When you are asked if you want to Cancel all print jobs (Y/N), type Y.

   Type in the number of the job (see Job List for its number) and press Enter to cancel the *printing of a particular job not currently being printed.*

2. Then press **G**(o) (**4**) to reset the printer so it will be ready to print again. WordPerfect will cancel the print job completely.

Stop Printing

This option will stop the printer without eliminating the command to print the document. When the printing is resumed, however, the printer will start again from the beginning of the document.

1. To use this command, retrieve the Printer Control menu. Then press **Stop** or (**5**) to stop the printer. Fix whatever the problem is and realign the paper.

2. Send the printer a G(o) by pressing **4** or **G** to start the same job again from the beginning.

TIP: It is important to remember that the printer will not begin to print again until it has received a G(o) command. You should also remember to adjust the paper and reset the top-of-form button on the printer so that your document will be printed correctly on the page. If you do not want to continue printing, cancel the print job and give the printer a G(o).

Ctrl and Num Lock

You can tell the printer to pause without starting over by doing the following:

1. Press Ctrl and Num Lock at the same time. (It is not necessary to bring up the Printer Control menu to use this command.)

2. When you are ready to resume printing, press Enter. The printer will begin again where it left off.

TIP: If all else fails, and your printer does not stop fast enough, you can always use the On/Off switch on the back or side to turn it off. It is better to use one of the commands described above, but if the paper is jamming, and/or damage is being done the equipment, use the On/Off switch rather than allow printing to continue.

To Review

To stop the printer, you can:

1. ____

2. ____

3. ____

Troubleshooting the Printer

If you are having problems getting the printer to work, there are several steps you can take to try to locate the problem.

1. Check to be sure the correct printer is selected by pressing Print (**Shift-F7**), Select Printer (**S**). Make any necessary adjustments and try to print again.

2. Check to be sure the printer is turned on, that there is paper in the printer, and that it is aligned properly. Some printers have a sensor that will not allow printing to occur if there is no paper in the paper path or it is jammed. If you share a printer with others, check to be sure the dial on the printer switch is turned to accept commands from your machine and that the appropriate on-line lights are on. Check to be sure the connections at the back of the computer and printer are completely plugged in.

3. Next, check the status by looking at the Printer Control Menu. You will be told either that the print queue is empty (waiting to receive commands to print); printing (printing--or thinks it is printing); or Waiting for a Go (waiting for your command to begin printing again).

If the printer reports that it is printing when it isn't, there could be a problem with the communication between the computer and the printer. Stop the printer (press S), turn the printer off and then back on, and send the printer a (G)o.

If the printer reports that it is not accepting characters, check to be sure the printer settings are correct, that there is paper in the printer, that the on-line lights are on, and so on. Give it a (G)o to see if printing will begin.

4. Sometimes a print job at the front of the line has a problem and creates a bottleneck that will not allow subsequent jobs to print. Cancelling that or all jobs and entering new commands to print may free the printer.

5. Finally, if the printer still does not begin, again check the status. If it still reports that it is printing, again stop the printer, cancel the print job(s), turn the printer off and back on, check the status to see if the print queue is empty or Waiting for a Go, and send it a (G)o if necessary.

If none of the above actions resolves the problem, ask your instructor or the lab assistant for help.

To Review

What is the printer status when each of the following is displayed?

1. The print queue is empty. _______________________________________

2. Printing _______________________________________

3. Waiting for a Go _______________________________________

4. Printer not accepting characters _______________________________________

Changing Printer Definitions

Occasionally you may want to delete a default printer definition that has already been saved with your document and insert another in its place. To do this, change the default printer setting to the new printer you want to use with Print (Shift-F7, S). Then clear your screen and space once, which will start a new document.

■ Press **List Files** (F5), highlight the file you wish to change and Retrieve (1) it to the screen. WordPerfect will ask if you want to retrieve this file into the current document. Answer Y(es).

■ Then **Backspace** to delete the blank space you inserted at the top of the file and resave the document. The old printer definition will be gone and the new one will be saved with the document.

Activities

You should have completed the following.

Nowis.2	*Now is . . . 10 times*
TV.2	*Complete document*
Pgprnt.2	*Page 1 of TV.2*
Copies.2	*Two copies of TV.2*

Chapter Review

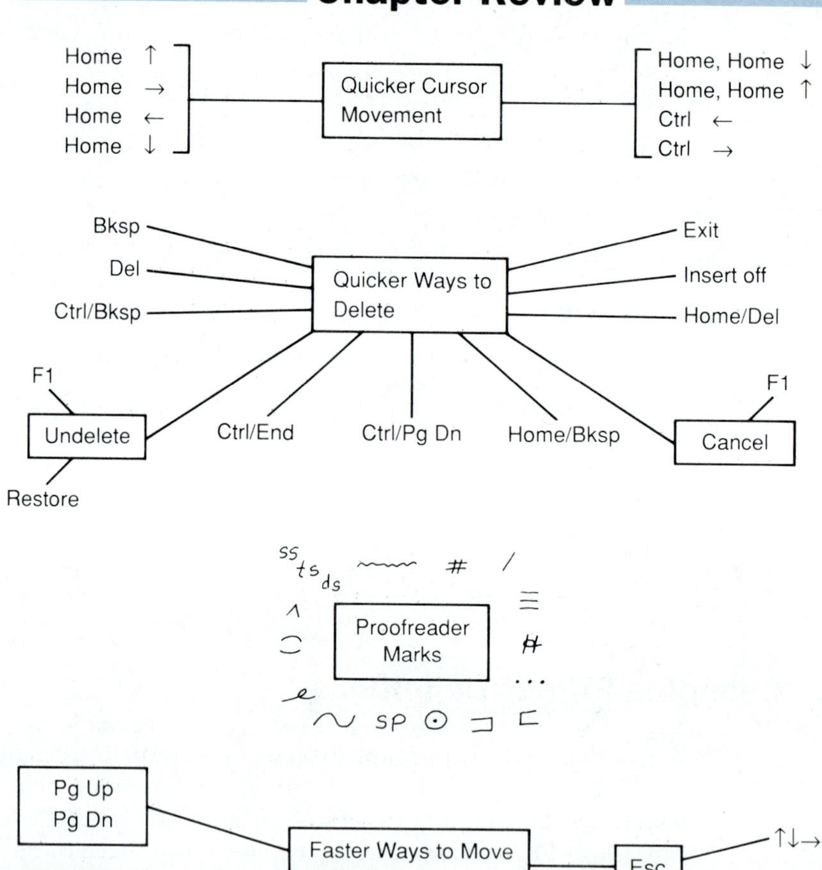

(continued on next page)

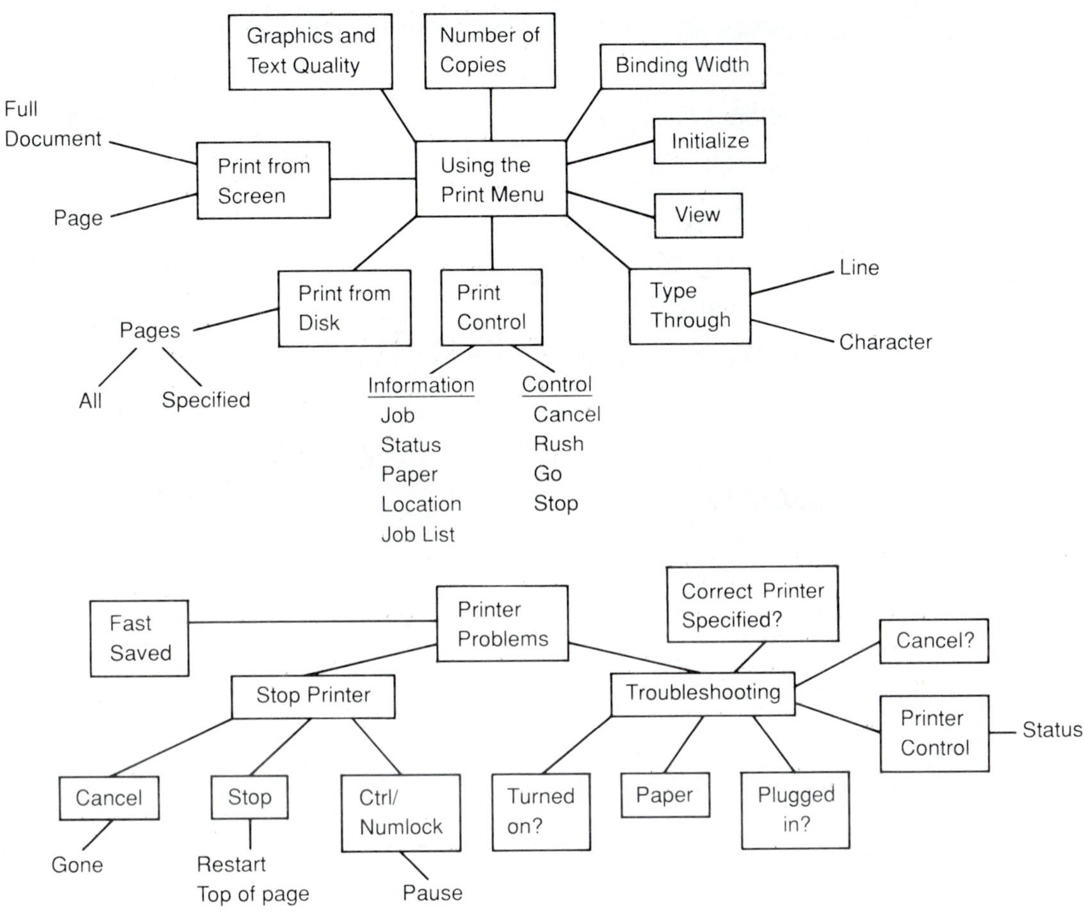

Self-Check Quiz 2

1. What effect will each of the following commands have on the cursor?

    a. Home, Up Arrow ________________________________

    b. Home, Right Arrow ________________________________

    c. Home, Left Arrow ________________________________

    d. Home, Down Arrow ________________________________

    e. Ctrl-Left Arrow ________________________________

(continued on next page)

    f. Ctrl-Right Arrow _______________________________________

    g. Home, Home, Up Arrow _________________________________

    h. Home, Home, Down Arrow _______________________________

    i. PageUp ____

    j. PageDn ____

    k. Screen Up ____

    l. Screen Down ____

2. Describe the effect of each of the following commands:

    a. Backspace (held down) _________________________________

    b. Del (held down) _______________________________________

    c. Ctrl-Backspace _______________________________________

    d. Ctrl-End ____

    e. Ctrl-PgDn ____

    f. Home, Backspace _____________________________________

    g. Home, Del ____

    h. Home, Del (Typeover On) ______________________________

3. What key stroke should you use to back out of a menu or status line prompt?

4. Why should you always have a clear screen before you retrieve a document?

5. What keystrokes will clear your screen?

6. How can you remove the Repeat value n= prompt from your screen?

7. What keys are used with the Go To command?

8. Distinguish between how the Tab command works with Ins (Typeover) On and Off.

9. What does the Repeat value n= or repetition-counter do?

10. How many previous deletions are saved for recall?

11. What must you do to print more than one copy of a document?

12. List two methods you can use to print a particular page of your document.

13. List three different commands you can use to print.

14. What happens when you cancel a print job?

15. What commands would you use to cancel ALL print jobs?

16. What command would you use to start printing again from the beginning of your document?

17. After stopping the printer, what command must be given to start printing again?

18. If the printer doesn't work, what should you do first?

    a. ____

    b. ____

    c. ____

19. What do the "Action" and "Message" options on the Printer Control menu tell you about the printer?

20. Which pages would be printed in response to the command -4, 9, 12-21, 40- ?

21. Write a command to print pages 3 through 8, page 11, 14, and pages 33 to the end of your document.

22. How can you tell which page is currently printing?

23. List at least five items of information about the current print job that you can get from the Printer Control menu.

24. Write the appropriate proofreaders' mark for each of the following.

Close Up __________

Move Right __________

Capitalize __________

Move Left __________

Delete __________

Ignore Correction __________

Underline __________

Add a space __________

Spell out __________

Use lower case __________

Single space __________

Delete and close up __________

Transpose __________

Bold __________

New Paragraph __________

Comma __________

Insert __________

Period __________

25. What can you see when you view a document?

26. What happens when you specify a binding width of .5"?

27. List three commands that can be used to stop printing?

28. If you wished to pause printing without starting over, what command could you use?

Extra Practice

For extra practice on the material covered in this chapter, do the following:

a.   Type the following sentence ten times and save it as Pract2.

The quick brown fox jumped over the lazy brown dog.

b.   Use the commands for quick cursor movements to move around in your document until you can use them easily.

c.   Print a copy and use proofreader marks to indicate any corrections. Then follow them to edit your document.

d.   Use the Esc (repetition counter) function to draw a line 20 spaces long two lines below the sentences. (Hint: Press Esc, type 20, press Underscore). Then enter another symbol and create a line 10 spaces long with it.

e.   Use the view command to see your document. Enlarge it to 100% and 200%.

f.   Delete a word, part of a sentence, to the end of the line, to the bottom of the page, etc. Then use the Undelete function to recall part of what you have deleted.

g.   Save your document as Pract2a and print it using the Printer Control menu.

h.   Change the print options so that two copies of each document will be printed. Then print two copies of Pract2 and Pract2a. When you are finished, be sure to reset the print option back to 1 copy.

i.   Type the text of one of your assignments for another class. Edit it carefully and make any necessary corrections. When you are finished, save it as Pract2b and print it.

3

Margins, Spacing, Tabs and Other Format Settings

Now that you know how to create a document, the next step in the document-creation cycle is formatting, or arranging the appearance of your text. In this chapter you will learn a number of ways to change the format. After completing this chapter, you will be able to:

- change margins.
- adjust spacing.
- set and change tabs.
- change hyphenation and hyphenation zone settings.
- turn justification and wordwrap on and off.
- use Reveal Codes to locate format commands.
- get onscreen help.

Line, Page, Document, and Other Format Functions

Once you have entered the text of your document, you will likely want to change the form, arrangement, or appearance of all or part of its contents. This is called formatting. There are a number of commands that will help you do this. For purposes of organization, WordPerfect distinguishes among them as line, page, document, and other format options.

Line format characteristics deal with commands that can affect one or several horizontal lines in the text. These items would include, among others, margins, spacing, and tab settings. These commands may be changed several times on the same page. For instance, you may have several different margin settings or change the spacing several times on the same page if you wish. You will work with many of these features in this chapter.

Page format commands affect the entire page as a whole and include such things as top and bottom margins, and page numbering. Only one setting for each of these commands is allowed per page.

Document format commands affect the entire document. Even though they can be changed within the text, their purpose is to govern the way specified items are handled for the document as a whole. For instance, if you wanted to change some of the defaults for your whole project, a document format command would allow you to do this.

Other options include several commands that affect the way a number of features that are not specific to other categories are used or displayed. These include how some items are printed on the line and whether spaces are underlined, among others.

You will learn to use all these features as you progress through this text. To start with, let's try the line format commands.

Changing Margins and Line Spacing

Some of the more common format settings that you will use frequently are those for margins and spacing. Let's use the document named TV.2 to work with these commands.

☐ Clear your screen and retrieve the document named **TV.2**.

Changing Margins

For some practice, change the margins on this material from the defaults (1 inch left and right) to $1^1/2$ inches left and right.

☐ Any margin changes will work forward from the cursor position when they are set. Therefore, in order to change the margins on the entire document, the cursor must be at the beginning of the document. Press **Home, Home, Up Arrow**.

☐ Then hold down the **Shift** key (because the command is printed in green) and press **Format (F8)**. The menu shown below will appear:

```
Format

    1 - Line
                Hyphenation                 Line Spacing
                Justification               Margins Left/Right
                Line Height                 Tab Set
                Line Numbering              Widow/Orphan Protection

    2 - Page
                Center Page (top to bottom)  New Page Number
                Force Odd/Even Page          Page Numbering
                Headers and Footers          Paper Size/Type
                Margins Top/Bottom           Suppress

    3 - Document
                Display Pitch                Redline Method
                Initial Codes/Font           Summary

    4 - Other
                Advance                      Overstrike
                Conditional End of Page      Printer Functions
                Decimal Characters           Underline Spaces/Tabs
                Language

    Selection: 0
```

Looking over this menu, you can see that it contains quite a number of commands that affect the format of a document and that the commands are identified by their relationship to the line, page, or document categories.

◼ Since Margins Left/Right is shown as a line format option, press the **1** or **L** key to enter that part of the menu. The following submenu will appear:

```
Format: Line

        1 - Hyphenation                          Off

        2 - Hyphenation Zone - Left              10%
                               Right             4%

        3 - Justification                        Yes

        4 - Line Height                          Auto

        5 - Line Numbering                       No

        6 - Line Spacing                         1

        7 - Margins - Left                       1"
                      Right                      1"

        8 - Tab Set                              0", every 0.5"

        9 - Widow/Orphan Protection              No


    Selection: 0
```

Scanning down the list, you can see that the Left and Right margins are currently set at 1 inch.

◼ To change the margins, select **Margins (7)**. The cursor will immediately jump to the setting beside the Left Margin listing.

◼ Type **1.5** and press **Enter**. Notice that you do not need to type the " symbol to indicate inches. WordPerfect automatically assigns an appropriate mark.

◼ When the cursor moves to the right margin indicator, again type **1.5** and press **Enter**.

◼ Then press **Exit (F7)** to leave the menu and return to your document.

Notice that the margins have already been changed, and that the text has been shifted to the left to keep the new margin at the left edge of the screen. If you watch the **Pos** indicator on your status line, you will see that the left margin generally moves to be aligned with the left edge of the screen.

TIP: If the margins do not automatically change, use the Down Arrow key (or Home, Home, Down Arrow) to run the cursor through the text. The margins will change as you do. If your margins still do not change, be sure the cursor is to the right of the previous settings before entering the new commands.

- Return the cursor to the top of your document and change the margins again, this time to **1/2** or **0.5** inch on the left and **1 1/2** or **1.5** inch on the right.

- Then change them one more time to **1.75"** Left and **1.0"** Right. Pretty easy, don't you think?

- Now save your document as **TVA.3,** with the new margins, using **Save** (**F10**).

TIP: You may wonder how to convert margin settings that you are familiar with, such as 10 and 75 or 12 and 90, into inches, or how to know what settings a 1 inch or other margin represents. Making these conversions is really fairly easy.

For the left margin, you need only remember how many characters there are to the inch and then multiply by the number of inches. For instance, with a 10 pitch font, there are 10 characters to the inch and 85 characters across the page. Therefore, a 1 inch left margin is the same as space 10.

Determining the setting represented by a 1 inch right margin is a little trickier, but still quite easy. Simply subtract 10 spaces (1 inch) from the total possible. Therefore, 85 minus 10 results in a margin setting of 75. As you can see, 1 inch left and right margins is the same as settings of 10 and 75.

If you were using 12 pitch type with a total of 102 spaces across the page, 1 inch margins would equate to 12 and 90.

Summary

In summary, to change margins:

a.   Position the cursor to the left of the text that the new margins will affect. (This could be at either the beginning of the document or a point within it where you want to change the margin settings.)

b.   Press Format (Shift-F8).

c.   Choose Line (1).

d.   Select Margins (7).

e.   Enter the new left and right margin settings as you are prompted.

f.   Press Exit (F7) to leave the menu and return to your text.

Adjusting Spacing

The Format (Shift-F8) key is also used to change the amount of space between lines in a document. Again, the cursor must be to the left of the text you wish the new spacing command to affect. Therefore, if you want to change the spacing throughout your document, the cursor must be at the beginning when you enter this command.

◼ Press **Home, Home, Up Arrow**.

◼ Now press **Format (Shift-F8)** to reveal the format menu again.

◼ This time, press **Line (1)** and then **Line Spacing (6)**. The cursor will jump to the 1, beside Line Spacing.

   This message means that your document is currently set for single-spacing.

◼ Type a **2** to indicate double spacing and press **Enter**. Then press **Exit (F7)** twice to return to the text of the manuscript on the screen.

   WOW!

```
    If you have ever invited guests to come into your home

for an evening of television, you have been given a

chance to see televiewers at their best and at atheir

worst. At least one of these visitors may have been the

type of person who sprints from his chair to the video

set to adjust the controls for you. The fact that he has

no set of his own seems to fill him with uncontrollable

desire to play with yours. First he experiments with the

volume control. The mustic is just a little too loud or

too soft for him and he is sure for the others as well.

having adjusted the dials so that every muted violin may

be heard by all, he must leap forward again to diminish

C:\WP50CPTS\VIEW.WP                        Doc 1 Pg 1 Ln 1" Pos 1.75"
```

If you inserted an extra line between paragraphs in your original single-spaced text, when you changed to double spacing the blank lines between the paragraphs were also doubled; and you will now have four lines between paragraphs. Since this is too big a gap, you will need to delete the extra lines with the Backspace delete key.

■ If you need to delete extra lines, position the cursor on the blank line and press **Backspace**.

TIP: In the future, do not insert an extra line between paragraphs if you intend to change the spacing from single to double.

On a document of several pages, WordPerfect always starts subsequent pages on Ln 1. Even if you had inserted extra lines following the last line on the previous page, WordPerfect would ignore them and begin at the top of the page.

Notice, too, that the spacing command (like most others) works forward from the cursor. This is so because the printer is unable to back up and change something once it has been printed. Therefore it will not accept commands that would require it to alter something that is already on the paper.

TIP: If you should want a portion of a double-spaced document to be printed single-spaced (or some similar configuration), you would need to insert a single-spacing command just before the affected text. At the end of the passage you want single-spaced, you would need to insert another command to instruct WordPerfect and the printer to revert to double-spacing.

■ Now resave your changed document as **TVA.3,** and clear your screen.

Line Height

Another command on the Line Format menu that affects spacing is the line height option. Line height is the amount of space assigned to each line computed from the bottom of one line to the bottom of the next.

Line 1

Line 2 _____

Line 3 _____ | = line height

As you know, some type sizes are larger or smaller than others and take up correspondingly more or less room on a page. Normal sized type has six lines per inch. Larger type may allow only 3 or 4 lines per inch and smaller type may have room for 8 or 10 lines per inch.

It could be quite a chore to remember the differences and make appropriate adjustments every time you changed fonts. But again, WordPerfect comes to the rescue with a built-in table that automatically assigns a "leading" line height to each font.

- To see how this works, again press **Format (Shift-F8)**.

- Select Line Format (**L**) and then choose the Line **Height** (**4**) option. Notice that Auto is the default, meaning that WordPerfect will make whatever adjustments are necessary for the font you specify.

  Immediately the prompt **1 A**uto; **2** Fixed: **0** will appear at the bottom of your screen.

- Since Auto is the default and you already know what that will do, select Fixed (**2**). Immediately the cursor will jump to the Line Height option and the word Auto in the menu will change to 0.16. Since you already know that there are six lines to the inch, dividing 1 by 6 results in .1666666, which may round to 0.17.

TIP: Recall that earlier you learned that sometimes the Ln indicator on the status line reports a decimal number such as 9.75 instead of an even 9 or 10. The rounding up of numbers such as .1666666 to .17 is what causes the uneven number to occur. This can vary depending on the printer and font in use.

When WordPerfect determines how much distance it should move from line to line for single, double, or other spacing, it simply multiplies the line height setting by the number of lines specified. Therefore, if the line height is .17, WordPerfect allows .17 of an inch for each line and there is room for approximately six lines per inch. If the line height is set at .25, WordPerfect allows .25 of an inch for each line and there is only room for four lines in each inch on the page. As a result, even though the size of type does not change, the number of lines that will be printed per inch does.

TIP: As you can see, the spacing of your document is affected by both the line spacing and the line height commands working together. It is not likely that you will want to change the line height often for normal word processing. However, if you were doing some desktop publishing functions or wanted to create a special effect, this command would be useful.

- Now, because you do not want to change this setting right now, press **Cancel** (**F1**), and the setting will immediately change back to Auto. Then press **Cancel** (**F1**) twice more to return to the blank screen.

Setting, Changing, and Deleting Tabs

The Line Format (Shift-F8, 1) command also controls the setting and changing of tabs for your document.

■ Position your cursor to the left of where you wish to insert the first tab command. Since you do not have a document on your screen, the cursor should be in the upper left-hand corner.

■ Press **Format (Shift-F8)** to again bring up the menu and select Line Format (**1**).

■ When the Line Format menu appears, select **T**ab Set (**8**). Notice that Word-Perfect indicates that the tabs currently begin at 0" and are set every 0.5" (or half inch).

At the bottom of your screen, you will see something like the following:

```
L....L....L....L....L....L....L....L....L....L....L....L....L....L....L....L...
!    ^    !    ^    !    ^    !    ^    !    ^    !    ^    !    ^    !    ^
1"        2"        3"        4"        5"        6"        7"        8"
Delete EOL (clear tabs); Enter Number (set tab); Del (clear tab);
Left; Center; Right; Decimal; .= Dot Leader
```

Each L is a Left Tab setting. As you can see, tabs have been preset every half inch. Using **Home, Right Arrow**, move the cursor along the tab line. Notice that the screen scrolls sideways. The default for paper size is 8 1/2 by 11 inches. Therefore, tabs are only set from 0 to 8 1/2 inches along the tab line. It is possible, however, to set tabs for paper up to 54 inches wide and have a maximum of 40 tabs.

As the bottom line of text indicates, WordPerfect allows you to set several different types of tabs. The left-justified tab—the default—is the most familiar kind. But you can also set tabs that would right-justify your text, center it, align the decimals (or any other character you specify) or add leaders (. . . . .) to left, right or decimal tabs.

Sound interesting? Let's give it a try.

Setting Tabs

There are several ways to set a tab. Right now you will learn two of the most common. Before beginning, it is always a good idea to clear out all tabs you do not want so they will not be in the way and cause problems later.

◪ To clear out tabs, start with the Tab Menu on the screen. Position the cursor to the left of the tabs you wish to delete (usually at 0). Notice that you can use most of the cursor control keys to move along the tab line. These include Home, Home, Left Arrow; Home, Home, Right Arrow; Home, Right Arrow; etc.

◪ For now, move the cursor to 0 with **Home, Home, Left Arrow**. Then press **Ctrl-EOL** (End/1).

All(the tabs (L's) to the right of the cursor disappear. Now you are ready to set new tabs for your document.

To set a tab, you can do either of the following:

1. Simply type in the position number (such as, 2.5) you wish to use for a tab stop and press the Enter key. By default this will add a left-justified tab.

2. Using the Arrow keys, move the cursor to the position number you wish to use for a tab stop (in this case, 2.5), and press **L, R, C,** or **D,** depending on which kind of tab you want to set. This is the only way you can insert Right, Center, Decimal, and Leader tabs. To cause leaders to precede the tab, enter a period (.) over an L, R, or D on the tab line.

TIP: | To avoid having to move the cursor to each tab stop before setting it for Right, Center, and Decimal tabs, you can set the tab as a Left tab as explained above. The cursor will jump to that position and you can then simply type R, C, or D to change the type.

When you have set all the tab stops you want, press Exit (**F7**) twice to return to your document.

TIP: | It may help to note that with 10 pitch (Pica) type, space 15 is 1.5 inches. Space 32 is 3.2 inches. Therefore to set tabs at 21, 43, and 55, you would enter 2.1, 4.3, and 5.5.

◪ For practice, and to see how each kind of tab works, set the following tabs at the places indicated. Before you begin, remember to clear out all existing tabs with Ctrl-End.

2.1 (L)   3.5 (R)   4.8 (C)   5.7 (D)   7.0 (R.)

You may use either method to set the Left tab at 2.1. For the others, however, you must move the cursor to the correct position and type the appropriate letter. For the tab at 7.0, position the cursor first, type an **R,** and then type a period (.) over the R. When the period is typed, the R will appear boxed. Your settings should look like the following:

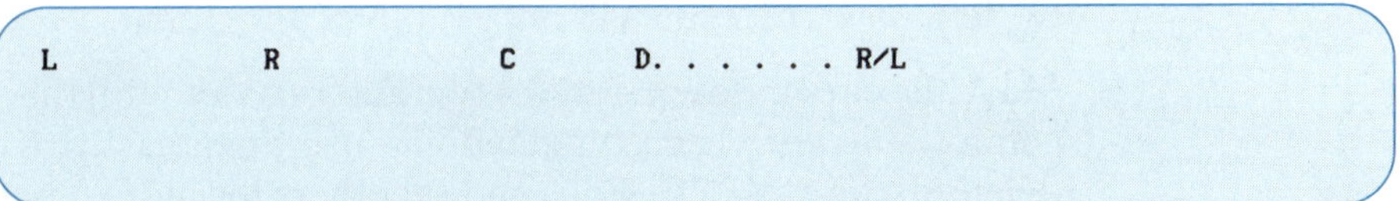

◼ Then press **Exit (F7)** twice to leave the Tab Menu and save the tab settings you just entered.

◼ To see what happens when each of these tabs is used, press **Enter** once to move down the screen a line.

◼ Let's label each tab so you can tell what kind it is. Press **Tab** and type L. Then press **Tab** again and type **R**. Press **Tab** three more times, typing **C**, then **D**, then **R/L**.

◼ Then press **Enter** twice more. Your screen should look like the following:

Now **Tab** to the first setting (2.1") and type the word **LOOK. Tab** again and type **LOOK** once more. Notice how the right-justified tab is handled. **Tab** again (to 4.8") and type **LOOK** another time. Watch as WordPerfect centers the word over the tab stop.

◼ **Tab** again, to the decimal tab at 5.7". A message will appear in the lower left-hand corner of your screen informing you that the alignment character is a period. This means that all the characters you type before you type the alignment character will appear to the left of the tab stop; subsequent characters will appear to the right of it. This feature is usually used to align the decimals in numbers. Type **456.00.**

◼ **Tab** one more time. Wow! WordPerfect has inserted leaders from the last character you typed to the new tab stop.

◼ Now type **LOOK** again to see what will happen.

```
   L              R              C          D . . . . . . R/L
   LOOK         LOOK           LOOK       456.00 . . .LOOK
```

Very impressive. You can have fun with all the possibilities available with these tab options. As you can see, they can make many word-processing tasks much simpler.

One word of caution. As you probably noticed, all characters that precede the period in a decimal tab are pushed to the left, and all characters that follow it appear to its right. This has quite an impact on where you should set the tabs.

For other kinds of tab settings, you would position them to accommodate the longest line (or number) in the column. To line up the decimal points, you would simply indent shorter numbers using the space bar. With the decimal tab, however, you must set your tabs so that the cursor will stop at the decimal. Then when WordPerfect pushes the numbers preceding the decimal point to the left, your columns will not get out of alignment.

◼ Move the cursor down a line or two and practice with these tabs until you feel comfortable with each type and can use them easily. If you wish, you can delete all the tabs (Ctrl-End) and set others for more practice.

TIP: If you want to set evenly spaced tabs, there is a quick way to do it. Bring up the Tab Menu and clear out all tabs you do not want. Then enter the location of the first tab stop, a comma, and the distance you want between tabs. For instance, if you wanted tabs set every seven tenths of an inch beginning at 1.8 inch, you would type **1.8, 0.7** and press **Enter.** WordPerfect would then insert tabs every seven-tenths of an inch from 1.8 inches forward. If you do not specify otherwise, WordPerfect will set left justified tabs. If you want one of the other kinds (D, R, C, etc.) used, enter it in the 0 position before entering the command outlined above.

If you wished to revert to the defaults, you would first press Home, Left Arrow to return to 0 on the tab line. Next, press Ctrl-End to delete all tabs. Then type 0,0.5 and press Enter, then Exit. Tabs would be set every half inch beginning with 0.

When you have finished, move ahead to the next exercise to learn how to delete tabs one at a time.

Deleting Tabs

Because you do not need to be concerned with the different types of tabs when deleting them, it is a much simpler process than entering them.

To delete individual tabs, you can do either of the following:

1. Type in the position number of the tab you wish to delete. Then press the Enter key, then Backspace.

2. Using the arrow keys, move the cursor under the tab you wish to delete. Then press Del or Backspace. Press Exit (F7) to return to your document.

◼ For practice, delete two tabs using each of the methods outlined above.

TIP: Occasionally you will find that the tabs you set don't work. First check to be sure that they are inside the margins. For instance, if you have a tab set at 1.0 and your margin is at 1.5, the cursor will stop at 1.5 and fail to engage the tab set at 1.0. Even though the tab is set correctly, it will not function. If this is the case, you must change either the margin or the tab so that the tab is between the right and left margins.

```
        Left                                                     H-        Right
        Margin                                                   Zone      Margin
T---------- | ---------------------------------------------------- | -------- |  1.0"
1.0       1.5"                                                    6.3"       7.0"
```

To Review

The Line Format commands are found on the _________________ menu.

List the defaults for:

     Margins _______________________________________

     Tabs _______________________________________

     Spacing _______________________________________

Summary

In summary, to Set and Delete Tabs:

a. Position the cursor to the left of where you want to insert your first tab command.

b. Press Format (Shift-F8).

c. Choose Line Format (1).

d. Select Tab Set (8).

e. Clear out all unwanted tabs (Ctrl-End).

f. Change tabs as desired, using the methods listed below.

g. Press Exit (F7) to return to the document.

To Set Tabs:

1. Type the position number of the tab stop you want to set and press Enter (for left-justified tabs only).

2. Move the cursor to the position where you want to set a tab and type in the appropriate letter for the type of tab desired (L, R, C, D). For leaders, type in a period with L, R, C, and D tabs. (You may also enter an L tab and then strikeover the L with a C, R, or D.)

3. For evenly spaced tabs, type the position of the first setting, a comma, and the distance between tabs (for example, 0,0.5).

To Delete Tabs:

1. Move the cursor to the position of the tab you want to delete, and press Backspace or Del.

2. Type the position number of the tab you want to delete. Then press Enter and Backspace or Del.

3. Press Ctrl-End to delete all tabs forward from the cursor.

Hyphenation and the Hyphenation Zone

You may have wondered how WordPerfect knows when to end a line of text and begin a new one. Well, it's magic... Actually, WordPerfect has some help, called the Hyphenation Zone.

The Hyphenation Zone is an area at the end of the line that signals WordPerfect when it is near the right margin (like the bell on a typewriter). The hyphenation zone is preset to begin ten percent before and four percent after the right margin. When a line of text moves into the hyphenation zone, WordPerfect will begin to watch for a space. When a space is typed, it will end the line and wrap (carry) the next word to the following line.

If no space is typed within the hyphenation zone, WordPerfect has three options:

1. It can move back to the last space typed, end the line there and carry the rest over to the new line, thus avoiding hyphenation.

2. It can use some built-in rules for hyphenation and automatically hyphenate the word within the hyphenation zone based on those rules.

3. It can ask you where the word should be divided by displaying it in the lower left-hand corner of the screen with the message:

```
Position hyphen: Press ESC (sampleword)
```

If this message appears, you can use the Left and Right Arrow keys to move the hyphen to an acceptable place within the hyphenation zone to divide the word. Then press Esc.

TIP: The Arrow keys will not move outside the hyphenation zone when in this mode. If you are not sure where the word should be divided, refer to a dictionary or word-division guide. If you do not want to divide the word, you may press Cancel (F1). WordPerfect will then carry the entire word over to the next line.

The default for hyphenation is Off, which means that WordPerfect will not divide words. Except in extreme cases, it will always end the line at a space. This is a nice feature, but it can occasionally create some problems, particularly if WordPerfect decides to wrap a long word over instead of putting it on the previous line. Then, if the printer stretches the short line to make the right-hand margin even, large gaps may appear between words and/or letters.

If you would rather have some words divided at the end of the line so this will not occur, you can turn the hyphenation feature to Manual or Auto. Then WordPerfect will still end the line with a space wherever possible; but if a long word extends through the hyphenation zone and no spaces appear, Word-Perfect will ask for your help in deciding where to divide it (Manual), or use its built-in dictionary (Auto) to determine an appropriate place to divide.

◼ Press **Format (Shift-F8)**, Line (**1**) to bring up the Line Format Menu, which you have used before.

◼ Select **Hyphenation** (**1**). Note that the default is Off.

As you can see, Hyphenation is set to Off and the hyphenation zone is set to begin 10 percent before the right margin, and to end at 4 percent after the right margin. The Off default, means that WordPerfect will not ordinarily hyphenate words. If a blank space does not appear within the hyphenation zone, the entire word will be carried over to the next line.

You can turn hyphenation to Manual or Auto, or give it new hyphenation zone settings from this menu. The following choices are available:

```
1 Off; 2 Manual; 3 Auto: 0
```

Manual (**2**) means that, if a word must be divided at the end of the line, WordPerfect will ask you to decide where to divide it. WordPerfect will help you by suggesting where to divide the word, based on a set of hyphenation rules within its program. To confirm WordPerfect's division of the word, press Esc. You may also use the Right and Left Arrow keys to move the hyphen elsewhere and then press Esc.

If you choose **Auto** (**3**), or automatic hyphenation, WordPerfect will automatically divide the word, based on its rules. You do not need to confirm.

When hyphenation is **Off** (**1**), WordPerfect will avoid dividing words, preferring instead to wrap long words to the next line. This can result in substantial gaps between words on the printout. With hyphenation On, WordPerfect will divide words either manually or automatically, as you specify. Hyphenating some words this way may give a more condensed look to your text.

TIP: If it becomes necessary, and you would like to specify in advance where a word is to be divided, you can insert a soft hyphen by pressing Ctrl- (Ctrl-Hyphen). This hyphen will not display on the screen; it will only be used if the word must be divided. The soft hyphen can be inserted while typing the word or later if you have a line that leaves too many blanks between words when printed.

For some practice, let's turn the hyphenation feature to manual mode.

■ With the Line Format Menu on the screen, press Hyphen (**1**), then Manual (**2**). Notice that the prompt immediately changes from **Off** to Manual. That's all there is to it. Press **Exit** (**F7**) to return to your document.

Now, if WordPerfect encounters a word that extends beyond the hyphenation zone, or no spaces are typed to let WordPerfect know where to end the line, it will flash the message at the bottom of the screen. Based on its internal hyphenation rules, WordPerfect will place the hyphen either in a possible place to divide or at the right margin. You will be asked to make the final decision.

Your choices are as follows:

1. If the hyphen is in an acceptable place to divide the word, simply press Esc.

2. If it is not, use the Left or Right Arrow keys to move the hyphen to an acceptable division point and then press Esc.

3. If you do not want to divide the word at all, press Cancel (**F1**) to carry the entire word over to the next line.

WordPerfect will treat the word as you specify, and you can go on typing.

For some practice, move to the end of the text.

■ With the hyphenation zone on **Manual** (**2**) (the word Manual will appear in the menu), type the sentence shown below. Use default margins. (Do not type the hyphens. Type the words without dividing to force hyphenation.) When the hyphenation zone message appears, use the **Arrow** keys to move the hyphen to a point where the word can be divided. Then press **Esc**.

TIP: WordPerfect will aid you by suggesting an appropriate place to divide the word. If you agree, confirm with **Esc**.

My subordinates indicate several extremely difficult unsubstantiated procedures were incorporated with the previous requalifications resulting in problems with the text.

- To see the difference between Auto and Manual, again press **Format (Shift-F8)**, Line **(1)**, and Hyphenation **(1)**.

- This time, select Auto **(3)**.

- Then retype the sentence, observing the difference in how WordPerfect responds. Notice that some words are automatically hyphenated; for others, you must still make the decision.

- Save the two versions of the sentence as **Hyphen.3** and print them.

To Review

The hyphenation zone works only on the _________________ margin. It is preset to start _____________ percent from the right margin and to end _____________ percent after the right margin. The default setting is

_________________________ .

TIP: Occasionally, a line of text may overhang the right margin of your printout. This occurs when the word overrides the hyphenation zone and the printer cannot squeeze it onto the line. To overcome this problem, position the cursor at the beginning of your document and reset the hyphenation zone defaults to 9 percent left and 3 percent right, using Format **(Shift-F8)**, Line **(1)**, Hyphenation Zone **(2)**.

Changing Justification and Word Wrap

As you know, your text is automatically justified (aligned at the right margin) when it is printed. However, you may, for one reason or another, not want that to happen. Some instructions on how to change these commands follow.

Justification

Let's start with the justification command. Again using the Line Format menu **(Shift-F8, Line 1)**, you can turn this feature off. This will cause the text to be printed as you see it on the screen, with a ragged right hand margin.

◾ To see how this works, clear your screen and press **Format (Shift-F8)** to bring up the Format menu.

◾ Select **Line (1)** and **Justification (3)**.

◾ To turn the Yes beside justification to No, simply press **N**. Then **Exit (F7)** to return to the document screen. If you wish to return to the Line Format screen to make additional changes, press Enter.

◾ Then type the first paragraph of **Charlie.1** again.

◾ Save it as **Justioff.3** and print it. Notice the difference in the right margin when justification is not on.

TIP: If you wished to turn justification off on a document you had already entered, you could simply move the cursor to the top and press Format (Shift-F8), Line (1), Justification (3), and N(o). When the document was printed, it would have a ragged right margin, as you saw it on the screen.

You might also want to change the hyphenization mode to get a more even right margin when justification is turned off.

TIP: To justify a line, WordPerfect normally expands or compresses the spacing between words as needed. You can adjust the limits used to do this if you wish. Then when the specified limit has been reached, the spacing between characters will be adjusted if necessary. The command to set these limits is reached by pressing Format (Shift-F8), Other (4), Printer Functions (6), Word Spacing Justification Limits (4). From this menu you would enter the percentage you wish and press Exit (F7). The change will affect all text from that point on in your document.

Word Wrap

Another way you can alter the way the lines end is to adjust word wrap, or the automatic returning of the cursor at the end of each line. Since there is no way to turn this feature off, you must outsmart it.

You can do this by making the right margin very small (such as 0" or .01") and then pressing Enter yourself when the line gets as long as you want it to be. (Watch the Pos indicator in the status line.) The printer will always honor the [HRt], or hard return new line command, over word wrap, or a [SRt] (soft return). When the document is printed, the end of each line will be at the places where you returned the cursor. The fact that the margins were very small will not show.

If you wish, you can try doing this with the first paragraph of Charlie.1 to see how it works.

Reveal Codes

Sometimes you change the margins, spacing, and tabs repeatedly in a document. Let's find out how WordPerfect keeps track of all of this.

- Clear your screen and retrieve **TVA.3**.

- Move the cursor to the beginning of your document.

- Press the Reveal Codes (**Alt-F3**) keys to bring up the hidden commands WordPerfect is using for the seven or so lines around the cursor. You will see something similar to the following:

```
[HRt]
[HPg]
[L/R Mar: 1.5", 1.5"][L/R Mar: 0.5", 1.0"][L/R Mar: 1.75", 1.0"][Ln
Spacing: 2][Spacing: 1][Tab Set: 2.0", 2.5", 3.0"]
```

What's all that? If you look closely, you will see that WordPerfect has divided the screen in two, with a ruler line that displays the current margin and tab settings. Above the ruler line is your text, as it appears on the screen. Below the ruler line is your text as WordPerfect sees it, with all the embedded (hidden) printer and format commands that you have inserted.

Notice that every set of instructions you gave about the margins, spacing, and tabs is still there. As you can see, WordPerfect does not erase commands when they are changed. New ones are simply added at the cursor position, and the last command in line is used to format your document. The codes preceding it are ignored.

As you look over the contents of your screen, you will see several of the following codes. (A complete listing is included in the appendix.)

Code	Meaning
[^]	Cursor position
[BOLD][bold]	Text between the upper-case and lower-case word is bold.
[Cntr][C/A/Flrt]	Text between the first and second command is centered.

[UND][und]	Text between the first and second command is underlined
[Spacing:]	Indicates spacing set (single, double, etc.)
[L/R Mar:]	Indicates margin settings
[Tab]	Indicates a tab
[142Indent]	Indicates indentation (F4 key)
[SRt]	Soft Return: a carriage return entered by WordPerfect at the end of a line. Changes as the text expands or contracts.
[HRt]	Hard Return: a carriage return entered by pressing the Enter key. Does not change.
[HPg]	Hard New Page: a page break created by pressing Ctrl and Enter. Does not change. (Appears as ==== on screen.)
[SPg]	Soft New Page: a page break created by WordPerfect. Changes as lines are added or deleted. (Appears as ---- on screen.)
[Just Off] [Just On]	Justification off or on

Sometimes you will see that duplicate commands have been entered. Duplicate commands can create problems like the following:

1. Since the last command in a string is the operative one, it is important for the most recent one to come last. This may not be the case if several similar commands are inserted at the same point, such as multiple margin settings. Sometimes WordPerfect gets confused when more than one command of a particular kind appears at the same place. For instance, suppose you change the setting to double spacing, but nothing happens. Why? You may have inadvertently inserted the double-spacing command before a single-spacing command. Or WordPerfect may simply be unable to respond to multiple commands in the same place.

2. Sometimes part of the text you are typing will not be displayed on the screen. Part of a line will show, and the rest just disappears. When this happens, it is likely that WordPerfect is overloaded with multiple, repetitious commands.

3. The commands may not work. If there are a number of commands being pushed along ahead of the cursor, they will interfere with the operation of other settings and must be deleted.

To prevent or solve these problems, it is a good idea to delete all but the few commands you want WordPerfect to use. WordPerfect will allow you to move the cursor around in the Reveal Codes text, using either the Backspace or the Del key to eliminate any commands you do not want to retain.

▣ For some practice, move the cursor to the right of the margin setting for 0.5", 1.0".

▣ Then press **Backspace** to delete it.

You can delete any other commands or text you wish the same way. You will notice that changes you make in the text in the bottom half of the screen are instantly made in the top half of the screen as well. You can edit, add to, and delete commands and text this way to make your documents appear as you want them to.

▣ When you are finished, press **Reveal Codes** (**ALT-F3**) to Exit and WordPerfect will return to where you were in the document.

TIP: The Reveal Codes command displays the text and commands for the two lines above and seven lines below the cursor in the bottom half of the screen. To find a particular command, or to see what commands are located at other places in your document, simply scroll the text, using the regular cursor-movement keys, to display what you want to see.

▣ Delete all but the last commands you inserted, leaving only double spacing, 1.75", 1.0" margins, and the tab setting. This will help you avoid problems like those described above.

TIP: It is always a good idea to clean out unnecessary commands from a long document, or one you've been working on for a long time, so you will be less likely to have a problem when you print. It is also important to check Reveal Codes occasionally to see what commands are in use, and that they are in the right place.

Help Menus

Now that you have covered quite a few commands in WordPerfect, you may have forgotten some of them. If you would like some help remembering, it is available in the Help feature.

▣ To access the Help feature, press the **Help** (**F3**) key. The following message will appear:

```
 Help                                               WP 5.0   05/05/88


      Press any letter to get an alphabetical list of features.

          The list will include the features that start with that letter,
          along with the name of the key where the feature is found.  You
          can then press that key to get a description of how the feature
          works.


      Press any function key to get information about the use of the key.

          Some keys may let you choose from a menu to get more information
          about various options.  Press HELP again to display the template.

      Press Enter or Space bar to exit Help.


      WPHELP.FIL not found.  Insert Learning Diskette and press drive letter.
```

NOTE: If you are working with a hard disk, you will not need to change disks. However, if you are working with a dual disk system, do the following:

◼ Remove your data disk. Replace it with the WordPerfect 1 disk and press **B**.

As the menu explains, you may press any letter of the alphabet, function key, or arrow key, as well as the Tab key, the Print key, Home, Esc, or Enter, to see information about that particular command or key.

After you have read the material that appears on the screen, you can try another key or press **Enter** or the Space Bar to return to your document. An illustration of what you would see if you pressed the Cancel (**F1**) key is shown on page 98.

◼ For practice, check the help section on the Right Arrow, the Esc, and the Home keys. You can also review any other keys that are of interest to you before moving ahead.

◼ Press the **Spacebar** or **Enter** to exit Help. Then remove the WordPerfect 1 disk from Drive B and replace it with your data or Student Exercise Disk.

◼ To complete this exercise, resave your document as **TVA.3** with the **Exit (F7)** option. It should have the new margins you set (1.75–1.0), be double-spaced, and contain no errors.

> Cancel
>
> 1. Cancel:
>   Cancels the effect or operation of any function key which displays a prompt or menu. It will also stop the operation of a macro or merge before it is finished.
>
> 2. Undelete:
>   When no other function is taking place, this key undeletes up to three deletions. A deletion is any group of characters erased before the cursor is moved. The most recent deletion is inserted temporarily in reverse video. You can then restore the text or display the next deletion.

Summary

To Set	Press
a. Margins	Format (Shift-F8), 1, 7 or M
b. Line Spacing	Format(Shift-F8),1, 6 or S
c. Tabs	Format (Shift-F8), 1, 8 or T
d. Hyphenation Zone	Format (Shift-F8), 1, 1
e. Justification	Format (Shift-F8), 1, 3 or J
f. Word Wrap	Adjust right margin
g. Reveal Codes	Reveal Codes (Alt-F3)
h. Help	Help (F3)

You're getting to be quite proficient with WordPerfect. You can give yourself a big pat on the back. You've covered quite a bit in the first three chapters. You can now create text, correct errors, move the cursor on the screen, save your document two ways, retrieve from the disk, print from the screen, change the margins, adjust the spacing, set several kinds of tabs, move around in your document, and exit from the program. In addition, you can use the help menus, work with the hyphenation zone and use several special function keys.

You're doing great!

Review Project

Before going on to additional commands, take a breather and review what you've covered so far. The following project should give you an opportunity to practice all the things you've learned up to now.

Type the exercise below, (or you may retrieve the file named Jobs.3 from the Student Exercise Disk) making the corrections and changes indicated by the proofreaders' marks as you go. Use the Interim Save (F10) command at least twice as you go along, using the name **Jobs.3** for the filename.

a.   Use the default settings for spacing, margins and paragraph tabs.

b.   Use whatever tab settings you wish for the list of job requirements.

c.   Use the Interim Save command (F10) at least twice as you type.

One of the most inexpensive and easiest ways to learn about job opportunities is to consult the classified section in the newspaper. Many of the jobs are listed there and often you are led right to the best company. That names there is no agency fee involved. Some of the ads require you to write to a box number in care of the local newspaper. The letter you write should encourage the firm to call you and ask you to come in for an interview.

As the very first step in answering a help-wanted ad, it is essential to know exactly what the prospective employer wants. An easy way to do this is to make a check list of all the job requirements listed in the ad like that shown below. This list will make it simple to cover the points in your letter. It will also prevent its being eliminated because some vital point is missing.

Good References   Degree
Computer Background   Experience
Knowledge of Co.   Good Worker
Gets Along With Others   Dependable

Apply for a specific job. many firms place ads in papers for different types of jobs on the same day. When they pick up their mail at the news paper office, they may have 2 or 3 hundred applications for the Different positions. Naming in the first paragraph of your letter the specific job for which you are applying will accomplish two ends. it will make it easy to classify your application, and it will put you in step with the person reading your letter. Next list the requirements mentioned in the ad. In this way the employer knows that you have a clear under standing of the job. In addition you make it easy for him or her to see how well your qualifications measure up to the company's needs and how you will be able to serve the firm.

The very last paragraph is one of the most common stumbling blocks in a letter of application. The close is most important because it is the last picture left with the potential boss. Good applications letters end in an easy, sure way that brings quick action. beating around the bush about what the letter is for is a sign of waekness. Asking for an interview is one good way of ending on a positive note.

When you have finished typing the entire document, save it as **Jobs.3**, using Exit (**F7**). Then Retrieve it using (**Shift-F10**), and make the following changes:

a.   Change the margins to 1.5" left and right.

b.   Change the spacing to double spacing.

c.   Indent paragraphs .8" from the left margin.

d.   Single-space the table.

e.   Turn justification off.

f.   Save the revised document as **JobsA.3.**

g.   Proofread carefully to be sure you have corrected all your errors, and resave if necessary.

h.   Then print **Jobs.3** from the disk and **JobsA.3** from the screen.

Activities

You should have completed the following:

TVA.3	*Double-spaced*
	Margins at 1.75 and 1.0
Hyphen.3	*Hyphenation exercise*
Justioff.3	*Justification exercise*
Jobs.3	*Review project*
JobsA.3	*Revised review project*

Chapter Review

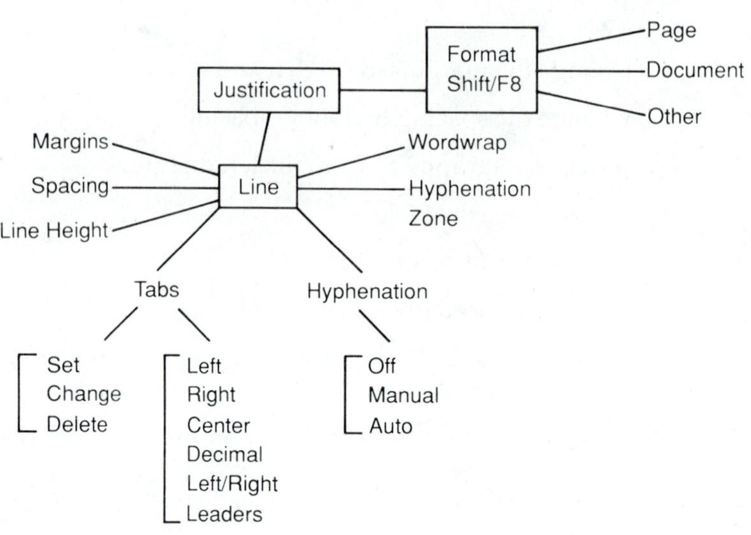

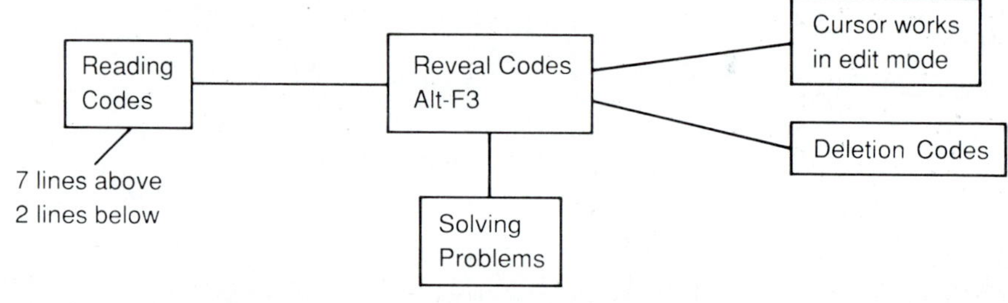

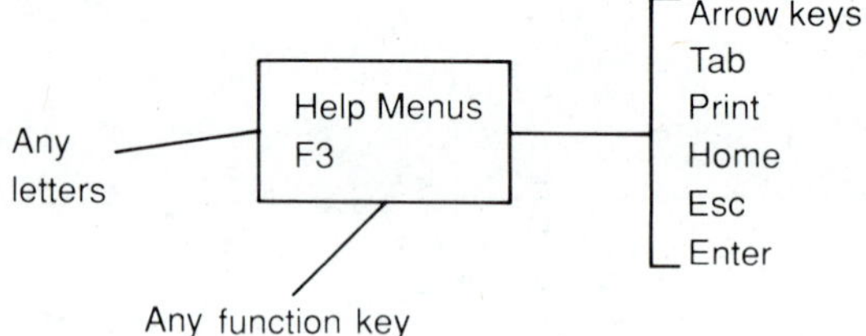

Self-Check Quiz 3

1. Write the sequence of commands you should use to change the margins from 1" Left and 1" Right to 2" Left and 2" Right.

2. Write the sequence of commands you should use to alter the spacing from single spacing to double spacing.

3. Write the sequence of commands you should use to add and delete tabs.

4. Write the sequence of commands that will return your tabs back to the defaults.

5. When you are proofreading your text, which keys should you use to move through your document and see every line?

6. If you are reformatting your document and it is not necessary to see every line, which keys can you use?

7. If you need help with a command, which key should you press to bring up a help menu?

8. Which commands or keys have help menus?

9. How wide is the default hyphenation zone? What function does it perform?

10. What keys should you press to see the commands embedded in your document?

11. What command should you use to save text without clearing the screen?

12. When setting tabs, what will happen when each of the following types of tabs is used?

>   Left-Justified
>
>   Right-Justified
>
>   Centered
>
>   Decimal
>
>   Leaders

13. What do Auto and Manual mean for hyphenation?

14. How can you set a soft hyphen?

15. With a 10-pitch font, what should you type to set evenly spaced tabs, 7 spaces apart, beginning two inches from the left margin?

Extra Practice

For extra practice on the material covered in this chapter, do the following:

a. Retrieve the file you named **TV.2** and resave it as **Pract3**. (Hint: Press Save (**F10**), enter the new name, and press **Enter** to cause the program to save.)

NOTE: This procedure will enable you to work on the material in **TV.2** without affecting the original, which you will need in future chapters. Simply make a second copy of the original file under a different name. Then use the new (duplicate) file for these exercises. When you are finished, you can delete the practice file if you wish without affecting the original.

b. Using **Pract3**, make the following changes (shown in **bold**) to the practice file:

Or perhaps you have been so **unfortunate** as to include in your circle the noisy, jovial type of person. His talk is loud and endless. He prides himself on his powers of sparkling **conversation**. He will allow no **quiet** moment to dim the luster of the evening. He has not the slightest awareness of the fact that moments of silence are more eloquent and more pleasing to overtaxed ears **and nerves** than is a constant flow of meaningless **chatter**.

c. Change the margins to 1-1/2 inches left and right. Set spacing to double spacing. Set tabs at 1.0, 3.2, and 5.8. Save your document as **Pract3a**, print it, and clear the screen.

d. Change the hyphenation mode to Auto. Retype the paragraph given above. See what effect this has on the ends of lines. Then change it to Off and type the paragraph again.

e. Choose and set appropriate tabs. Then add the following paragraph at the end:

some of his favorite programs are:

Wild & Wooly	Monday	Detective
Brave Jungle	Wednesday	Adventure
Car Bash Capers	Thursday	Sports
Friday Fights	Friday	Sports

f. Save the table as **Pract3b**.

g. Use WordPerfect to write a short story, your autobiography, a diary, or some personal correspondence. Use appropriate margins, spacing, and tabs. Print a preliminary copy and use proofreaders' marks to mark editing changes. Then make the changes on the computer. When you are finished, save your document and print it.

4

More Format Tips, Including Centering, Bolding, and Underlining

Now that you can enter, edit, save and print text, let's get a little fancier with the format. Using WordPerfect, you can do a number of things to make your text more readable. In this chapter you will learn to:

- center text on a line.
- underline.
- bold.
- flush right.
- tab align (or right align) and change the alignment character.
- insert a page break.
- use the conditional-end-of-page command.
- protect against widow/orphan lines.
- use the block protect feature
- retrieve and print a second way.
- number the pages of your document.

Centering

Centering headings and captions is easy with WordPerfect.

- Find the **F6** key. Notice that the word **Center** appears in **green** on the template beside it.

- Activate this function by pressing Center (**Shift-F6**). The cursor will jump to the middle of the screen.

- **Type your name** and watch what happens. Wasn't that easy!

- Now press **Enter**. The centering function will be deactivated.

- Press **Enter** again, press Center (**Shift-F6**) again and **type your address**.

- Press **Enter** again to deactivate the centering. (If your name was Mary Jones and your address was 425 Main Street, your screen should resemble the following:

Mary Jones

425 Main Street

That's all there is to centering. Simply press Center (**Shift-F6**) and type whatever you want centered. When you are finished, press the Enter key and the cursor will go back to the regular mode.

There are a couple of things you will need to remember:

1. You must press Center (**Shift-F6**) for each line you wish to center. The Enter key deactivates the command each time it is pressed. You can, however, center several lines at a time by marking them as a block and then centering the block. You will learn how to do this later.

2. WordPerfect centers between the margins, whatever they may be. If your margins are 1 inch left and right and you are using pica type, the center point will be 4.2 (the middle of the page). If your margins are 0.5" and 2.0", (one-half inch left and 2 inches right) however, the center point will be 3.5 (which is not the middle of the page). Note the difference in where things appear with different margins:

(Margins: 1 inch left and right)   (centered at 4.2")
WordPerfect

(Margins: 2.5" - 0.5")   (centered at 5.2")
WordPerfect

Be careful. If you are not careful, what you enter will not appear centered on the page, where you expect it. You cannot assume that whatever you type will be centered from 5.1" or 4.2" or any other point, only from the point that is halfway between the left and right margins.

TIP: You can also center anywhere on a line by placing the cursor in the middle of where you want to center and then pushing the center command. You will learn more about how to use this function when you work with tabulation.

If you need to determine where center point will be with different margins, do the following:

a. Add the left and right margins together.

b. Subtract that from the total spaces across the page (shown in inches).

c. Divide the remainder by 2.

d. Add that amount to the left margin.

e. The result will be the new center point.

For instance, if you had margins of 1.5" and 1.0" and wanted to know the center, you would do the following:

$$1.5 + 1.0 = 2.5$$
$$8.5 - 2.5 = 6.0$$
$$6.0\ /\ 2\ \ = 3$$
$$1.5 + 3\ \ \ = 4.5 \text{ or } 45 \text{ (center point)}$$

◼ For some practice, see if you can determine the center point with margins of 0.8" and 1.2", assuming you have 10 pitch pica type with 85 characters across the page. Then compute the center point for elite type with 102 spaces across the page. (Did you get a center point of 40 pica and 49 elite?)

To Review:

WordPerfect will center from a point that is ___________________________.

To turn the centering function Off, press the _____________ key.

Underlining

Now let's try underlining. Underline is printed in **black** on the template beside the **F8** key.

◻ Press the **Underline** (**F8**) key and type your name. Notice that each letter is underlined as it is typed. If you delete, both the letter and the underline disappear.

TIP: Some monitors display underlined text in reverse video or another color, rather than as an underscore under the words. Whichever way it is displayed on your monitor, the printer will underline the words.

◻ Press **Enter** and type some more. The underlining function stays On.

This key is a toggle switch, which means that it will continue to function until it is turned Off.

◻ To deactivate the underlining, simply press the **Underline** (**F8**) key again and it quits.

◻ Now press **Underline** (**F8**) a time or two, to turn it Off and On. Meanwhile, watch the number beside **Pos** on the status line. When the underline function is **On**, the number is underlined. When it is **Off**, no underline appears.

TIP: If you are not at the end of whatever is on your screen, you can also press the Right Arrow key once to move the cursor past the underline code (which you cannot see right now) and deactivate the underline mode. Try this a time or two and watch Pos in the status line to see what happens. (If necessary, move the cursor up on the screen a line or two so this command will work.)

If you wish, you can both Center and Underline at the same time.

◻ Press **Center** (**Shift-F6**) and then the **Underline** (**F8**) key. Then **type your name**.

◻ To deactivate the centering function, press **Enter**. To stop the underlining, press **Underline** (**F8**). (Or you can use the **Right Arrow** to move past the code in your document and deactivate either or both commands if you are not at the end of the text on the screen.)

Mary Jones

◻ Experiment a little with these keys, using them separately and together, to get acquainted with their use. Type your birthday, your address, the name of your school or your city and state.

Bolding

Now let's see how to emphasize headings and other items by printing them in boldface. Text in boldface is typed over twice by the printer, making it darker.

The Bold function is in **black** beside the **F6** key. It, too, is a toggle switch; simply press the F6 key to activate it, and press F6 again to turn it Off when you are finished.

TIP: The Right Arrow key will also move the cursor past the bold command, thus turning it off, if you are not at the end of the text on the screen.

◼ For practice, press the **Bold (F6)** key and again **type your name**. Notice that it appears brighter on the screen than the other characters.

TIP: If the bolded characters do not appear brighter on your screen, then adjust the brightness control on your monitor.

◼ Now press **Bold (F6)** again to turn bolding OFF, and type your name again. Compare the two:

Mary Jones

Mary Jones

◼ Press the **Bold (F6)** key several times, and observe the change in the brightness of the number beside **Pos** on the status line. This is WordPerfect's way of letting you know whether the Bold feature is activated.

Again, you can combine this feature with others, such as centering and underlining. Try various combinations with a few lines of practice text.

Flush Right

Another special function in WordPerfect's repertoire is right alignment. To see what this feature will do, look at the F6 key again.

◼ Since Flush Right is printed in **blue**, press **Flush Right (Alt-F6)**. Notice that the cursor immediately jumps to the right margin.

◼ Now type your name.

◼ Press **Enter**. Like the centering function, pressing Enter causes Flush Right to turn Off.

- Press **Flush Right** (**Alt-F6**) again, and type the name of your school or business. Then press **Enter**; the cursor returns to the left margin. As with other commands, you can also use Right Arrow to turn Flush Right Off when you are not at the end of the text on your screen.

Mary Jones
Valley Business Supply

Tab Alignment

WordPerfect will also align the decimal points (or any other character you specify) in lists of numbers or words. Decimals can be aligned either by setting a decimal tab, as you did previously, or by using the Tab Align feature at other tab settings. Since we have already set decimal tabs, let's try Tab Align. Tab Align is also on **F6**, printed in **red**.

- Press **Tab Align** (**Ctrl-F6**) to activate this command. Notice that the cursor jumps to the first tab.

- This time, type the following two-column list. (Note: Don't type Ctrl-F6. Simply press that key.) Press **Enter** at the end of each line.

(Ctrl-F6) **23.45** (Ctrl-F6, Ctrl-F6) **words**.

(Ctrl-F6) **1000.498** (Ctrl-F6, Ctrl-F6) **IBM.PC**

(Ctrl-F6) **5.5** (Ctrl-F6, Ctrl-F6) **type.34**

Tabs are pre-set every one-half inch, so the align key will move the cursor one-half inch each time. Remember, though, that the decimal will be printed at the tab setting. If you to need to change the tab settings, use the Format (Shift-F8), Line (1), Tabs (8) function. The Tab Align key (Ctrl-F6) will then jump the cursor to the tab settings you specify.

When you press Tab Align (Ctrl-F6), a message similar to the following will appear at the bottom left of your screen:

```
Align char: = .
```

This message tells you that the character WordPerfect will use to align with is the decimal point, or period. In the next section you will learn how to specify a different alignment character. But for now, since the period is the most commonly used alignment character, it is the default. WordPerfect will use it unless you specify otherwise.

TIP: Remember that you must set any tabs, that you wish to right align on, at the decimal (or other alignment character).

You can use the Tab Align (Ctrl-F6) feature, like Flush Right (Alt-F6), to right-align entries at positions other than the right margin—but you must be careful not to select alignment characters that will appear in your text. Simply set the tab one space to the right of the position where you want to right-align your entries. Then Tab Align to that position and type in your first entry. The entry will back up to the left, awaiting the alignment character. When you are finished typing in your entry, press Tab or Enter and the cursor will jump to the next tab stop or line. WordPerfect saves the extra space for the alignment character. However, since you never enter an alignment character, the space is left blank. The following is an example:

Christmas	December 25
Independence Day	July 4

To Review:

To activate the Center function, press the ______________ and ______________ keys.

To turn Underline On and Off, press the ______________ key.

To turn Bold On and Off, press the ______________ key.

To Tab Align, press the ______________ and ______________ keys.

Changing the Decimal/Alignment Character

WordPerfect's defaults save you from having to set margins, spacing and the like every time you enter text. Sometimes, though, the defaults are not suited to what you want to do. And sometimes you can adapt the defaults to help you do a job quickly. Changing the alignment character is one of those adaptations.

For lists of numbers, aligning on the decimal is usually appropriate. But other kinds of items may share a different characteristic that can be used to line them up. For instance, if you were typing a table that included times of day (such as an itinerary or a meeting schedule), you could align on the colon between the hours and the minutes. Or you could use a comma, a slash, a hyphen or any other symbol. Try the following:

▣ Start with a clear screen (Exit/No Save).

▣ Then press **Format (Shift-F8)** to bring up the Format menu.

▣ Select **Other (4)** to bring up the following menu:

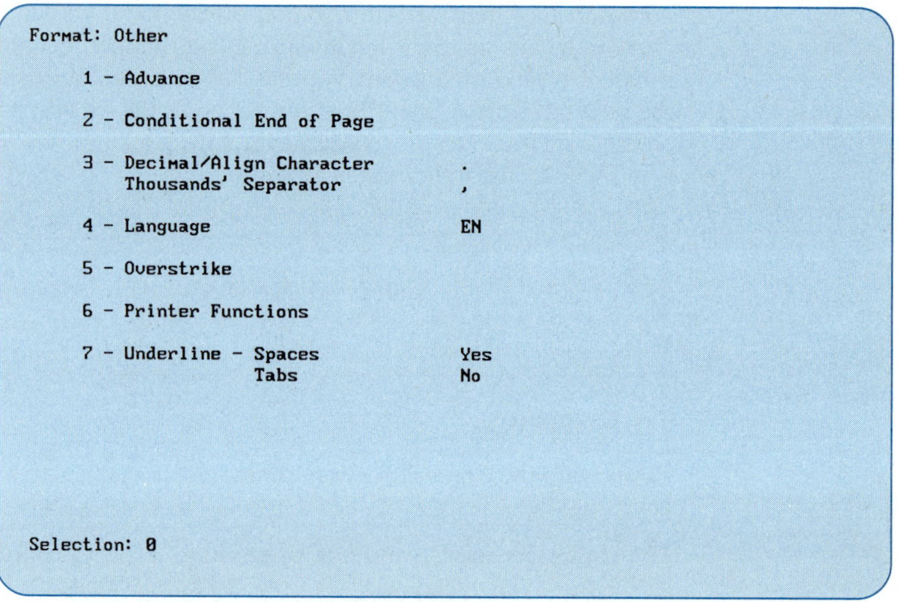

▣ Select **Decimal/Align Character (3)**. The cursor will jump to the . (period) beside the description.

▣ Now, simply type in whatever character you wish WordPerfect to align on. Then when you press the Tab Align (**Ctrl-F6**) keys and type, the new character will be used to align on.

▣ For now, type in a colon (:) and press **Enter**. The cursor will jump to the Thousands' Separator. Leave the Thousands' Separator as a comma (,) by pressing **Enter** again. Press **Exit (F7)**.

■ Then type in the following list, using Tab Align (**Ctrl-F6**), and watch what happens:

>   2:30
>
>   3:45
>
>   10:45
>
>   12:00

With a little imagination, it's not hard to see the possibilities of this feature. You could also use a slash (/), a hyphen (-), or any other key.

■ Now, change the alignment character back to the decimal point (period) before moving on.

TIP:

The defaults always reappear when WordPerfect is restarted. However, if you change a default but do not want the change to affect the rest of your document, you must change it back. Otherwise, WordPerfect will retain the new settings until you alter them or exit from the document.

Also, if you want the change to be permanent for your document, you must remember to save. If you make a change, enter text, and then exit without saving, WordPerfect will come up with the defaults when you restart, and the changes you made will be lost.

If you have made quite a few changes in defaults and want to erase them all at once, just exit WordPerfect and restart.

To Review:

To revert to the defaults, you can:

1. ____

2. ____

■ Clear your screen. Then type the following text (or you may retrieve the file **Acting.4**, from the Student Exercise Disk), using these specifications:

  a. Double-space (except where single spacing is specified).

  b. Bold all headings.

  c. Use the default settings for margins and paragraph tabs.

  d. Use whatever tab settings you wish for tables and lists within the text.

IT'S Only MAKE BELIEVE

Everyone at one time or another has dreamed of acting in an amateur theatrical, and some have even found themselves doing just that. While acting, they have made Some very interesting discoveries.

Make-Up *underline*

Make-up is necessary for even the ruddiest complexion. Without it or with too little, any actor will have a ghostlike appearance. this is due to the blinding klieg lights which tend to wash out all but the most soldi colors. The make-up commonly used is either a garish orange or a dull gray, and either seems unnatural when seen at a distance of a only few feet. However from the audience this will looke perfectly normal.

Movement *underline*

Actions must be rehearsed just as often as speeches. They can not be left to chance. Even professional actors and actresses benefit by having a director point out suitable motions. Selecting the actions beforehand and rehearsing them for timing helps prevent awkward or inappropriate movements

Voice *underline*

Speech on stage should be clear and distinct. Each syllable should be given its full value. Most performers insure this by playing to the balcony, directing both words and acts to the highest point in the audience. To do this, performers must often project their ovices several hundred feet in order to be heard as cam be seem in the following listing of distances in feet from the stage to the back row for several of the alrger theaters:.

Downtown Playhouse   408.40

Orpheum   650.5

Blue Belle   480.75

Ritz   546.

Stage Manners

An old theater rule said no performer should ever turn his or her back on the audience. When a speech must be delivered, this rule is only intelligent. Where movement alone is involved, the case is somewhat different. In order to make the actions of the people on stage seem natural and real, the old rule sometimes must be violated. Can you imagine someone backing off a stage instead of turning gracefully and walking into the wings?

Forcing another performer to turn his or her back on the audience when a line is spoken is called "up-staging." This is done simply by standing behind the person so that he or she must turn around to address the words to their proper place. Up-staging is a cardinal sin of the theater, seldom forgiven by other performers. Other tricks used by players in minor parts to get the attention of the audience are to wiggle a foot or drop an object or look for some thing in a jacket or Purse. Recognizing that those with real talent do not need to use such devices, most players never resort to such trickery.

of the theater, seldom forgiven by other performers. Other tricks used by players inminor parts to get the attention of the audience are to wiggle a foot or drop an object or look for some thing in a jacket or Purse. Recognizing thatthose with real talent donot need to use such devices, most players never resort to such trickery.

Character Analysis

In order to play a part well, a thorough knowledge of the character to be portrayed is necessary. The way in which Even a 2-word reply is said will depend on the type of person the part calls for. however, it is not enough to speak lines correctly and with feeling. To create his part, a performer must also listen carefully and respond as the character being played would respond to the lines and actions of others. Imagine the different behavior patterns that would be required for each of the following:

Annie	Annie
Scarlet O'Hara	Gone with the Wind
Buttercup	HMS Pinafore
Moses	Ten Commandments
Butch Cassidy	Sundance Kid
Liza	My Fair Lady
Darth Vader	Star Wars
Superman	Superman II

> Summary *underline*
>
> It is easy to see that there are many aspects to be considered and mastered if one is to become successful as a performer. Acting talent alone will not guarantee success. The techniques of make-up, movement, *and* voice are also important. Proper character analysis and stage presence will lend credibility and realism to a performance. It's apparent that what goes on behind the scenes is as important as what goes on on stage!

■ Save your work, under the name **Acting.4**.

Page Break

In the document you have just typed, you will probably notice a line of hyphens running across the page like this:

This is a page-break marker. It is WordPerfect's way of letting you know where the page will end. If the page break is in an acceptable place, you need do nothing. If not, you will want to change it.

To change the location of the page break, you would move the cursor to the point where you want the page to end (this must be above the page break showing on the screen).

Then you would press Ctrl-Enter. A line of double hyphens would appear, and the pages would break at the new position. You will notice that WordPerfect shows its own page breaks as a single line of hyphens and those you insert as a double line of hyphens.

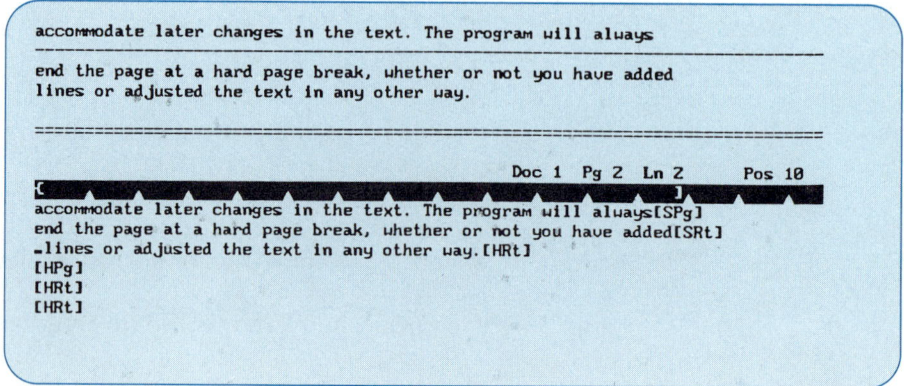

The single dashed line indicates a soft page break, the double dashed line a hard page break. The codes, [SPg] and {HPg], will appear in Reveal Codes mode.

TIP: Since, by default, WordPerfect is limited to 54 lines of text per page, you cannot include more than 54 lines without changing the default. If the page break is unacceptable, you will need to find an alternative location above the current page break, since WordPerfect will not allow you to locate a page break below the default. This means that you cannot squeeze one more line onto the bottom. Instead, you will need to carry an extra line over from the previous page to avoid having a widow/orphan line or heading alone at the bottom or top of the page.

■ Try inserting a hard break into your document. Move the cursor to the point just above the final paragraph, and press **Ctrl-Enter**.

A double line of hyphens should appear on your screen where the cursor was, and the single line of hyphens should have disappeared.

Hard/Soft Page Breaks

There is another difference between the page breaks the program inserts and those you insert. The program's page breaks, called soft page breaks [SPg], will adjust themselves if you add lines or change the spacing of your document. Those that you insert are called hard page breaks [HPg], and they will not change to accommodate later changes in the text. The program will always end the page at a hard page break, whether or not you have added lines or adjusted the text in any other way.

This feature is useful because you can be sure that something starts on a new page. But it can be troublesome because it is inflexible. If you change your text and would like the bottom of the page to be automatically adjusted, you must delete the hard page break.

TIP: To delete a hard page break, position the cursor near the page-break line on the screen. Press Alt-F3 (Reveal Codes). Move the cursor to the immediate right or left of the [HPg] symbol, and use the Delete or Backspace key to remove it.

Conditional End of Page

Now let's try one more way of controlling how your document will appear on the printed page. This one is called Conditional End of Page. It tells WordPerfect to test for a specified number of lines at a certain point.

For example, suppose you are typing a table and are nearing the end of the page. You are concerned that your table will be split, with part appearing on one page and part on the next page. To prevent such a separation, you can tell WordPerfect that it must keep a specified group of lines together. If they cannot all fit on one page, the entire group must be carried over to the next page.

To do this, you should move your cursor to the line immediately above the text you want to keep together. Activate the Format Menu by pressing **Shift-F8**. Select Other (4) to bring up the following menu:

```
Format: Other

     1 - Advance

     2 - Conditional End of Page

     3 - Decimal/Align Character            .
         Thousands' Separator               ,

     4 - Language                           EN

     5 - Overstrike

     6 - Printer Functions

     7 - Underline - Spaces                 Yes
                     Tabs                   No




     Selection: 0
```

When the Conditional End of Page (2) is selected, the following message will appear at the bottom of your screen:

```
Number of Lines to Keep Together:
```

You are being asked to specify the number of lines that must be treated as a unit.

Count the number of lines in your table (including blank lines) and type in that number. Then press the **Enter** key. When the document is printed, those lines will remain together.

◼ For practice, move the cursor to the end of the line just above the two-column list beginning with Annie. (The cursor must be positioned a line above where the conditional end of page break is to begin.)

◼ Then press **Format (Shift-F8)** and select **Other (4)**. When the Other Format menu appears, select Conditional End of Page (2).

◼ Since there are 9 lines in your list (don't forget the blank line on the top), enter the number **9** and press **Enter**. Press **Exit (F7)** to leave the menu.

Nothing will show on the screen, but these 9 lines will not be separated if they should fall at the end of the page. If you would like to verify that the command is in fact recorded, press Reveal Codes (**Alt-F3**). You will see the printer command [Cndl EOP:9] that will not allow those nine lines to be separated.

◼ Now check back through your document to see where the side headings fall. If a heading has fewer than two lines of text following it on the same page, use the conditional end of page command to carry the heading over to the next page with the paragraph that follows it.

To Review:

List two ways you can use to control where a page will end:

1. ____

2. ____

____

Widow/Orphan Lines

There is another way to control what happens at the bottom of the page. It is generally considered undesirable to begin a page with a partial line ending a paragraph (a widow) or to end a page with a single line beginning a paragraph (an orphan).

```
insert are called hard page breaks [HPg], and they will not
change to accommodate later changes in the text. The program will
always end the page at a hard page break, whether or not you have
----------------------------------------------------------------
added lines or adjusted the text in any other way.


                        WIDOWS AND ORPHANS

Widow                             Orphan
Short line at end of paragraph    Short line at beginning of paragraph
Occurs at top of page             Occurs at bottom of page


     There is another difference between the page breaks the
program inserts and those you insert. The program's page breaks,
called soft page breaks [SPg], will adjust themselves if you add
lines or change the spacing of your document. Those that you
insert are called hard page breaks [HPg], and they will not
change to accommodate later changes in the text. The program will
always end the page at a hard page break, whether or not you have
added lines or adjusted the text in any other way.


     There is another difference between the page breaks the
program inserts and those you insert. The program's page breaks,
B:\TEST                                     Doc 1 Pg 2 Ln 20     Pos 10
```

This illustration shows a page with a widow at the top of the page.

To help you avoid these situations, WordPerfect has a built-in function called Widow/Orphan protection.

- ◼ To activate this feature, position the cursor at the beginning of your document and press **Format (Shift-F8)** to bring up the Format menu.

- ◼ As you can see, Widow/Orphan Protection is a Line Format command, so enter **1** or **L**.

- ◼ Select **Widow/Orphan Protection (9)**. The default is No, meaning that the protection feature is not On.

- ◼ To change the command to Yes, and thus have Widow/Orphan Protection On, type a **Y**. Immediately the word Yes will appear beside the item on the menu. Then press **Exit (F7)**.

That's all there is to it. WordPerfect will not allow one line of a paragraph to appear at the bottom or top of a page.

```
always end the page at a hard page break, whether or not you have
added lines or adjusted the text in any other way.


                        WIDOWS AND ORPHANS

Widow                              Orphan
Short line at end of paragraph     Short line at beginning of paragraph
Occurs at top of page              Occurs at bottom of page


          There is another difference between the page breaks the
_________________________________________________________________
program inserts and those you insert. The program's page breaks,
called soft page breaks [SPg], will adjust themselves if you add
lines or change the spacing of your document. Those that you
insert are called hard page breaks [HPg], and they will not
change to accommodate later changes in the text. The program will
always end the page at a hard page break, whether or not you have
added lines or adjusted the text in any other way.

          There is another difference between the page breaks the
program inserts and those you insert. The program's page breaks,
called soft page breaks [SPg], will adjust themselves if you add
lines or change the spacing of your document. Those that you
B:\TEST                                     Doc 1  Pg 3  Ln 7       Pos 60
```

This illustration shows a page with an orphan at the bottom of the page.

TIP: As helpful as this feature is, it will not prevent widowed side headings at the bottom of the page, or paragraphs of only three lines. You will need to use the conditional end of page command, block protect, or a hard page break to avoid such situations.

Block Protect

You can also prevent a block of text from being split with a soft page break by blocking it (which you will learn in Chapter 6) and pressing Format (**Shift-F8**). Instead of the regular Format menu which you have been working with, a prompt will appear at the bottom of the screen similar to the following:

```
Protect block? (Y/N) No
```

If you respond with **Yes**, WordPerfect will not allow a page break to occur within the block. If there is not enough room on the current page for the entire block, it will be carried over to the next page.

Retrieving and Printing from the Disk (List Files)

- ▣ You're now ready to print this document. Check it over one last time to be sure all the errors have been corrected, including the proofreaders' markings and you have followed instructions carefully.

- ▣ Save it as **Acting.4**, with the **Exit (F7)** function, and return to WordPerfect.

    You are about to learn a different way to retrieve and print, using the List Files command. In the past, you have been printing documents from the screen and temporary memory. This time you will be printing from the disk.

- ▣ Press **List Files (F5)**. At the bottom of the screen you will see the message:

```
   Dir B:\*.*                                      (Type = to change default Dir)
```

    This message offers you access to a directory, or list of all the files on Drive B. You can get access to another drive by pressing = (equal sign) and the drive letter. (More about this later.)

- ▣ For now, press **Enter** to bring the B directory to the screen.

    As you can see, all the files you have created are listed. You can highlight any file by using the arrow keys to move the highlighter. Try it.

    Notice that the following prompt appears at the bottom of the screen:

```
   1 Retrieve; 2 Delete; 3 Move/Rename; 4 Print; 5 Text In;
   6 Look; 7 Other Directory; 8 Copy; 9 Word Search; N Name Search: 6
```

Retrieving from the Disk

Several operations can be performed from this menu. For now, we will use the Retrieve and Print options; you'll learn about the others in Chapter 8.

- ▣ Highlight the **Acting.4** file, and **Retrieve (1)** it to the screen. Answer Yes if you are asked if you want to retrieve. Pretty impressive, isn't it? If your file was saved with a different default printer, you may also see a message at the bottom of the screen indicating that the printer commands are being converted to your current printer.

TIP: When retrieving files this way, be sure that you always begin with a clear screen and memory (use Exit (F7)). If you already have a document on the screen, you will end up with a file composed of the two documents mixed together. To help you avoid accidentally combining files this way, WordPerfect will ask if you want to retrieve this file into the current document. Respond with Yes or No as appropriate.

Printing

Now let's use the same command to print. It is not necessary for a document to be showing on the screen for it to be printed from the directory. It is even possible to print one file while you are working on another. Commanding WordPerfect to do two things at once sometimes slows it down, but it can handle both projects if you are patient.

■ Just to clean things up, **Exit** (**F7**) from the document. Since you haven't changed it, it is not necessary to save it again.

■ Press **List Files** (**F5**) to bring up the directory indicator.

■ Then press **Enter** to bring the directory to the screen.

■ Turn on the printer, if necessary, and check to be sure it is selected and ready to accept your document.

■ Use the Arrow keys to highlight **Acting.4**, then press **Print** (**4**).

■ A prompt asking which pages of this document you want to print and indicating the default as (All) will appear at the bottom left of your screen. You can use any of the methods previously outlined in Chapter 2 to tell WordPerfect which pages it is to print.

```
Page(s): (All)
```

■ For this activity, you will print the entire document, so press **Enter** to accept the default.

In a few seconds, the printer should begin to print your document.

TIP: You can use this method to queue (or stack) several print jobs. They would then be printed one after another until they were all finished. To do so, you would highlight one file and press Print (**4**). The red disk light would come on, indicating that WordPerfect is setting up the print job, and printing would begin. Then the prompt would reappear at the bottom of the screen. At this point, you could highlight another file and again press 4 or P. WordPerfect would begin printing the second file immediately after finishing the first. Several jobs can be lined up this way. CAUTION: It is not a good idea to make the list too long, or to leave the printer unattended for any length of time. If the paper should jam or some other problem occur while you are away, damage could be done to the hardware and/or the data on your disk.

■ When the printing is finished, remove the printed copy from the printer, separate the pages and staple them in order.

Numbering Pages

Before ending this chapter, let's add page numbers to this document. When doing so, there are three things to consider:

1. Where the numbers are to appear on the page.

2. What the beginning page number should be.

3. The style (Arabic or Roman) the numbers should be printed in.

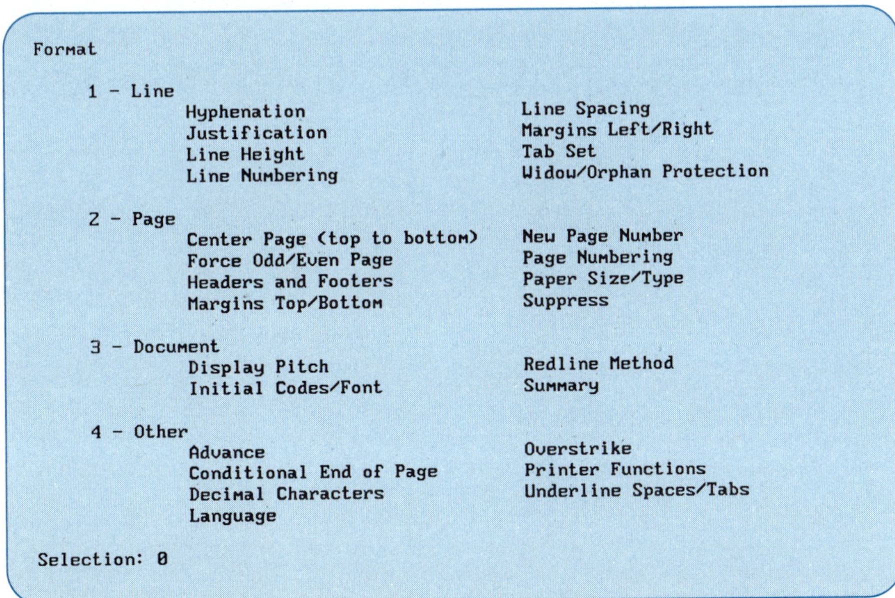

■ Clear your screen and memory (do not save) and retrieve **Acting.4** if it is not already on your screen. Let's identify position first and put the page numbers at the bottom center of each page.

■ Press **Home, Home, Up Arrow** to move to the beginning of your document.

■ Then press Format (**Shift-F8**) to bring up the Format Menu shown on page 127.

■ As you can see, New Page Number and Page Number Position are on the **Page Format (2)** menu. Select **Page (2)** to bring up that menu.

■ From the Page Format menu, select **Page Numbering (7)** to identify where the numbers are to be positioned on the page. The following menu will appear:

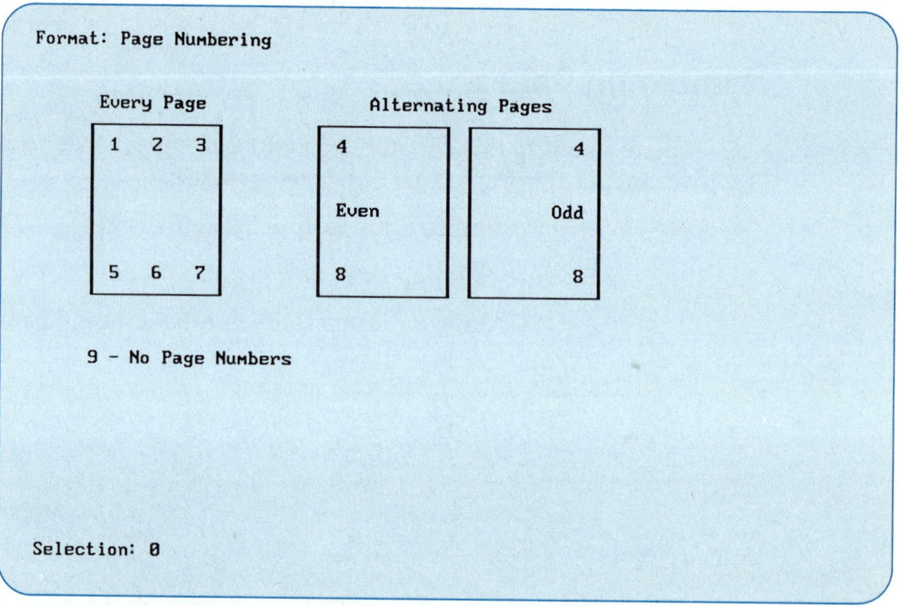

As you can see, page numbers can be printed in the following eight positions:

1. Top left corner

2. Top center

3. Top right corner

4. Top left corner for even pages and top right corner for odd pages

5. Bottom left corner

6. Bottom center

7. Bottom right corner

8. Bottom left corner for even pages and bottom right corner for odd pages

◼ To have the page numbers appear at the bottom center of every page of your document, select **6**. Then press Exit (**F7**).

Even though the page numbers do not show on the screen, you can be assured they will appear on the page when it is printed. If you want to see how they look prior to printing, use the Print (Shift-F7), **View** (6) command to see the pages with numbers displayed.

TIP: If you do not specify otherwise, WordPerfect will begin with page number 1 and automatically number the pages forward. If you wanted to specify a different beginning page number, you could select **New Page Number (6)** on the Page Format menu and enter it in. WordPerfect would then number the pages forward beginning with the number you specified.

In addition to numbering pages in Arabic order (1, 2, 3, 4), WordPerfect can also number them in Roman numerals (i, ii, iii, iv,). As you can see on the menu, all you need to do is enter the beginning number in the style that you want WordPerfect to use. Therefore, if you want to begin with page number 4 in Arabic, enter 4. If you want the numbers printed in Roman numerals beginning with 4, enter iv. It's as simple as that.

You can also have both Arabic and Roman numbers in the same document. If, for instance, you wanted the Table of Contents and Preface numbered in Roman at the bottom center of the page, but the body of the text numbered in Arabic in the upper left corner, you would enter the commands for Roman number i on the first page of the document to be printed at the bottom center. Then on the first page of text you would enter another command showing Arabic number 1, together with a command to have it printed in the upper left corner. WordPerfect would print the numbers where you specified, numbering the pages i, ii, etc., until it encountered the new numbering command. At that point, it would begin again with the new instructions and start numbering the pages 1, 2, 3, etc.

TIP: When you change a page number, the new number will appear on the status line and all subsequent pages will be numbered in consecutive order.

◼ Finally, WordPerfect locates page numbers on the first or last line of the page. Thus when you add page numbers, one line of text at the bottom of each page will shift to the top of the next page. Check through your document to be sure each page still ends satisfactorily. Use Widow/Orphan On and/or Conditional End of Page commands where necessary. Also check to be sure there are no problems with spacing, capitalization, and the like, and fix any that appear.

◼ Save your document as **PageNum.4** and print it.

If you like, you can experiment with other page numbering options. (If you use the same file, you will need to delete the previous page number command first. Use Reveal Codes, and delete the command [Pos Pg#].)

Summary

Command	To Turn On	To Turn Off
Center	Shift-F6	Enter
Underline	F8	F8
Bold	F6	F6
Flush Right	Alt-F6	Enter
Tab Align	Ctrl-F6	Alignment Character
Change Alignment Character	Shift-F8, 4, 3, New Character	
Page Break	Ctrl-Enter	
Conditional End of Page	Shift-F8, 4, 2, number of lines	
Widow/Orphan	Shift-F8, 1, 9, Y(es)	
List Files	F5, Enter	
Print from Disk	F5, Enter, Highlight file, 4, pages to print	
Retrieve from Disk	F5, Enter, Highlight file, 1	
Number pages	Shift-F8, 2, 7, (position)	

Activities

You should have completed the following:

Acting.4	*It's Only Make Believe*
PageNum.4	*Acting.4 with pages numbered*

Chapter Review

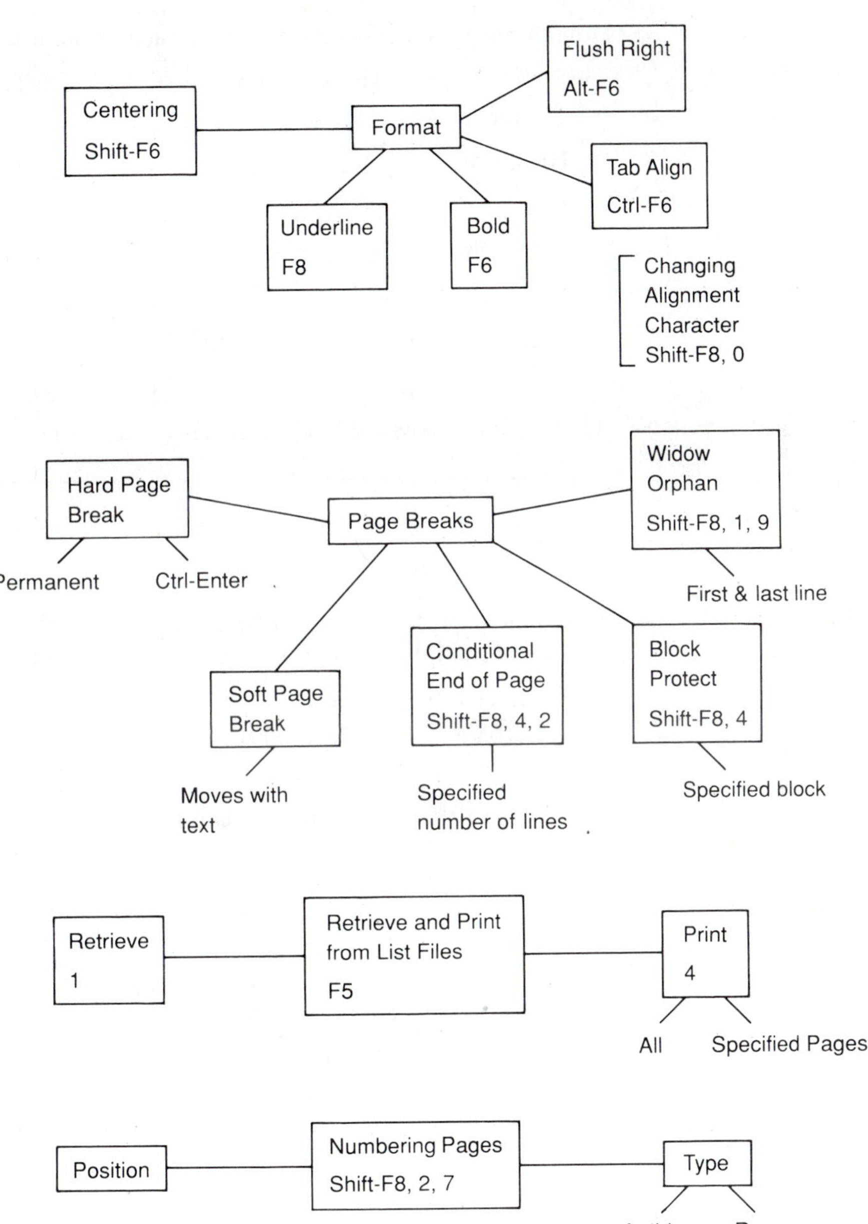

Self-Check Quiz 4

1. How do you activate and deactivate each of the following functions?

	To Turn On:	To Turn Off:
Center	_____________	_____________
Underline	_____________	_____________
Bold	_____________	_____________
Flush Right	_____________	_____________

2. If your margins are 1.0" and .5", what point will WordPerfect center from?

3. What do the following lines signify?

   ===

4. When using the Tab Align function, where should you locate the tab stop for each of the following? (Use ^ to indicate the tab stop.)

   $15,400.03   5.3%

   TXT.FIL   28.999301

5. Circle any of the following that can be used in combination with other commands.

Center	Underline	Bold
Tab Align	Page Break	Flush Right

6. What will happen when you press Ctrl-Enter? What does it mean?

7. If you were typing a table 15 lines long, how could you insure that it would all print on the same page?

8. How can you tell if the Bold and/or Underline commands are On?

9. What is the difference between a hard and a soft page break?

10. How can you clear the screen to start another document?

11. What does Widow/Orphan protection do?

12. Indicate the sequence of steps you should follow to number pages at the top center.

Extra Practice

For extra practice on the material covered in this chapter, do any or all of the following exercises:

a. Center and bold the following title at the beginning of the document: INTERVIEWING TIPS

b. Insert the following paragraphs two lines below the title.

One of the major hurdles you must face when searching for a job is the interview. If an employer feels that your qualifications and experience fit the position that is available, he or she will likely want to talk to you personally.

Your personal appearance can be a major factor in whether you are selected or not. Therefore, it is very important that you prepare carefully for the interview so that things will go well and you can make the best possible impression.

You should always be sure that you are neat and clean and that there is no noticeable odor on your body or clothing. Bathe often and hang your clothes out to air frequently to eliminate stale odors.

Women should remember to be sure their makeup is not overdone and that their hair style is not extreme. What may be acceptable at a social function or with your peers may not be appropriate for business. Men should have their hair neatly trimmed. Remember that you will be expected to conform to business standards on the job and that your employer may prefer more subdued attire.

Clothing, too, is generally more conservative in a business setting. Garments that are overly casual, such as jeans and shorts, are usually out of place. Depending on the environment, men may be expected to wear ties and women dresses. It is best to appear at the interview as you would dress for work.

Your accessories also can influence the impression you make at an interview. Other items that you will want to give attention to include:

> Hat (if worn)
> Belt
> Briefcase
> Shoes
> Watch
> Jewelry

These items should match the rest of your outfit and be appropriate for business. Gaudy jewelry and unshined shoes can be the worst offenders.

c. Move to the beginning of your document and turn Widow/Orphan protection On.

d. Save your document using Exit (**F7**) under the name **Pract4a** and clear your screen.

e. Use List Files (**F5**) to retrieve your document. Then change the spacing to double. Keep the listed items (hat, etc.) single-spaced.

f. Add the following side headings before the paragraphs indicated. Bold and underline all headings.

> **Personal Hygiene**
>
> (before 3rd paragraph)
>
> **Clothing**
>
> (before 5th paragraph)
>
> **Accessories**
>
> (before 6th paragraph)

g. Number the pages at the top left of every page.

h. Check your document to be sure all pages end correctly. Use Conditional End of Page to make sure that each heading is followed by at least two lines of text. Also use Conditional End of Page to make sure the list of accessories is kept together on the same page.

i. Add the following paragraphs just before the last side heading, Accessories. Bold and underline the headings.

Style.   **Unless you are working in a situation where style is part of the business, the cut, line, or other aspects of your clothing should not call undue attention to themselves.**

Color.   **Color also has an impact on your appearance. Learn the colors that look best on you and build your wardrobe around them.**

---

j. At the very end of the document, create a new page using Ctrl-End to insert a hard page break. Prepare a cover sheet for your document with the title, your name, and today's date arranged attractively on the page.

k. Save again using **F7** (Save-Clear Screen), under the name **Pract4b**, and use **F5** (List Files) to print one copy of your revised document.

l. Enter the following table. Center and bold as indicated. Use a center tab for the second column and a right tab with leaders for the third column. Use whatever settings you wish. When you are finished, save it as **Pract4c** and print it.

FALL MUSIC GUILD FESTIVAL

Young Artists Section
October 1, 19--
6:30 p.m.

Piano Duet	Rhapsody in A	Bill & Jim Simms
Flute Solo	Spring Breezes	Kris Andrews
Vocal Solo	Prelude	Ann Evans

m. Enter the following table. Center the lines as indicated. Use a right tab with leaders for the last column. Change the alignment character to a colon (:) and use it for the third column. When you are finished, save it as **Pract4d** and print one copy using List Files (**F5**).

APPOINTMENT SCHEDULE

Bill Wilson President	Ajax Company. . . . . . . .9:30 a.m.	
Darren Shaw Sales Manager	R. S. Mfg. . . . . .10:00 a.m.	
Emily Howe Manager	Home Arts. . . . . 11:30 a.m.	
Mark Mason Manager	B. E. Builders. . . . . .1:45 p.m.	
Sheri Hall Owner	Make-ur-Own. . . . . 3:30 p.m.	

n. Create a program or announcement for a group or organization you belong to. Center the headings, use the bold and underline functions, and include tabs with leaders to make it attractive and easy to read. Save and print your document.

5

Using the Speller and Thesaurus

WordPerfect's ability to help you check the spelling in your documents is a very helpful tool. The Thesaurus is also very helpful for locating the right word to convey your meaning in writing. When you have completed this chapter, you should be able to:

- use the Speller to check a single word, a page, or an entire document.
- add words to the supplementary dictionary.
- look up the spelling of a word in a variety of ways.
- identify things the Speller cannot check.
- use the Thesaurus to find synonyms and antonyms for words in your document.

The Speller

Before you can use the Speller, you will need a document to check.

◼ Type the following material on Boosters, as instructed. Do not correct your errors yet. You may, if you wish, retrieve the file named **Boosters.5** from the Student Exercise Disk.

    a. Use default settings for margins, paragraph tabs, and single spacing.

    b. Center the title.

    c. Capitalize and bold the word **Boosters** throughout.

    d. Use whatever settings you wish for the tab-aligned list of subscribers. Include leaders.

HOW MUCH MONEY WILL YOU MAKE THIS YEAR?

This is a special invitation for you to join a group of businessmen who recently subscribed to the new business service called Business BOOSTERS...a monthly booklet containing ideas to increase sales and profits.

BOOSTERS is for businessmen who see business opportunities in the future and a chance to move ahead. Boosters is for the smaller business firm that is determined to increase profits. Some of our subscribers are:

Boosters is tied to your future . . .

Ideas to increase sales and profits This service that have been tested, that work, that show a profit under today's conditions.

No office reading time To fit your busy schedule, BOOSTERS is put up in the exact size of a rail road timetable. Slips into your coat pocket. Ideas are pictured and illustrated with a brief description of how yu can turn the ideas to profit.

Now you can quickly find out for yourself how much BOOSTERS can mean to you by accepting this invitation to join the 10,000 new readers. If you will mail the enclosed order form, we will send you immediately and free of charge 6 previous issues of BOOSTERS containing scores of profitable ideas you can use write now. That is a bonus just for trying BOOSTERS. Then, for only $3.68 we will extend to you the special Introductory Rate of 18 months of BOOSTERS.

Mail in your order today!

◼ Save your document as **Boosters.5**, using the **Save (F10)** command.

TIP: It is always a good idea to back up your document by saving it before beginning the spell check process.

Activating the Speller

To check the spelling in your document, the cursor must be positioned on the word, page, or in the document you want to check. The WordPerfect speller disk (which you can obtain from your instructor or the lab assistant) must be in Drive B.

NOTE: If you are using a hard disk or network system, your speller dictionary should be stored in the same directory as your WordPerfect program and you will not need to change disks. If the speller files (SPELL.EXE and WP{WP}EN.LEX) are stored in a different directory, you will need to indicate that in the SetUp menu under Auxiliary Files, Main Dictionary. Ask your instructor for help if you need it.

◙ First, position the cursor at the beginning of your document (Home, Home, Up Arrow).

◙ Open the door of Drive B and **remove your data disk**. Since the document you wish to check is now stored in the computer's memory, you can take this disk out without fear of losing your document. Remember, though, that you must **never** remove a disk when printing is in progress or the disk drive red light is on.

◙ If necessary, insert the WordPerfect Speller disk in Drive B.

◙ Press **Spell (Ctrl-F2)** to activate the Speller. The following prompt will appear:

```
Check: 1 Word; 2 Page; 3 Document; 4 New Sup. Dictionary; 5 Look Up; 6 Count: 0
```

TIP: If the message **Main Dictionary Not Found** should appear, enter **B:LEX.WP** and press Enter. Then move ahead.

Option 1 will check a single word.

Option 2 will check the page showing on the screen.

Option 3 will check the entire document.

Option 4 will move you to a supplementary dictionary.

Option 5 will let you look up the spelling of a word.

Option 6 will count the number of words in your document.

You may press any other key to exit the menu.

TIP: The Speller can also check a block of text. Define the block with the Block (Alt-F4) command before activating the Speller with Spell (Ctrl-F2). See Chapter 6 for information on defining a block.

◾ Select **D**ocument (**3**) to check the entire document.

The prompt ***Please Wait*** will appear in the lower left-hand corner of your screen while WordPerfect is checking the spelling of the words.

TIP: You can stop the spelling process at any time by pressing Cancel (F1).

WordPerfect has two dictionaries containing a total of more than 100,000 words. One is a smaller list of frequently used words and the second is a longer list of commonly used words. To speed up checking, the smaller list is reviewed first. If a match is not found, the second list is checked. Checking takes longer if WordPerfect must go to the second list.

TIP: WordPerfect can also check spelling in several other languages such as Spanish and Danish. To activate this feature, you must identify the language on the Format, Other, Language menu (Shift-F8, 4, 4). WordPerfect would then substitute the appropriate Speller, Thesaurus, and Hyphenation files for the language you specify. Check your WordPerfect reference manual for additional instructions on how to access these files for other languages.

WordPerfect matches the words in your document, one by one, with those in its dictionaries. If it finds a match, it assumes the word is correct (which may not be true).

If the word being checked does not match one in either of the dictionaries, is a double word, or a word with a number, WordPerfect will highlight the word at the top of the screen in reverse video, divide the screen in the middle, list words in its dictionary similar in spelling to the highlighted word, and display the following menu asking what it should do next.

```
Not Found: 1 Skip Once; 2 Skip; 3 Add Word; 4 Edit; 5 Look Up:  0
```

Suppose the word **ahead** had been misspelled as **ahed** in the material you just typed. The following is what you would see when the Speller menu was displayed. Note that six or so lines of text are displayed above the double line, the misspelled word is shown in reverse video, and several alternatives for correct spelling are given:

```
This is a special invitation for you to join a group of businessmen
who recently subscribed to the new business service called Business
BOOSTERS...a monthly booklet containing ideas to increase sales and
profits.
BOOSTERS is for businessmen who see business opportunities in the
future and a chance to move ahed. Boosters is for the smaller
business firm that is determined to increase profits. Some of our
subscribers are:
Reed Hansen         Hansen Auto Parts
J. L. Crandall      Downtown Office Supply
Shauri Wilson       Fashion Boutique


================================================================================

     A.  abed              B.  aced              C.  ached
     D.  adhed             E.  aged              F.  ahead
     G.  ahem              H.  aped              I.  awed
     J.  axed              K.  aphid




Not Found: 1 Skip Once; 2 Skip; 3 Add Word; 4 Edit; 5 Look Up:  0
```

This is WordPerfect's way of letting you know that it could not find a
match for the highlighted word (ahed) in its dictionaries and asking you what
it should do next.

TIP: Occasionally a word is listed more than once because WordPerfect finds it in
more than one dictionary. When this is the case, you may select either letter
to replace the misspelled word. Also, if the list extends beyond the screen, you
may press Enter to see the additional words in the replacement list.

Using the Speller Menu

If the correct spelling of the word is displayed with a letter beside it, you can
simply type the letter that corresponds to your choice. WordPerfect will
replace the highlighted word in your text with the new word.

For instance, the correct spelling of *ahead* is listed as F. You could simply
type an F, and WordPerfect would do the rest. It can't get much easier than
that!

If the correct spelling is not displayed, the menu offers you some other
options:

If you choose Skip Once (1), WordPerfect will skip over the word without
requiring you to change it. If it encounters the same word or spelling
again, it will stop again.

If you choose Skip (2), WordPerfect will skip over the word. It will also remember the word and not stop at it again.

If you choose Add Word (3), WordPerfect will add the word to its supplementary dictionary and won't stop for it again.

TIP: Using the speller utility, you can edit words in the supplementary dictionary or add them to the regular dictionary. You can also create new supplemental dictionaries if you wish. Check your WordPerfect Reference Manual for further instructions on how to do this. Since these are permanent changes, check with your instructor before adding words to the dictionaries or before creating supplemental dictionaries on disks that are shared by others.

If you choose Edit (4), WordPerfect will allow you to edit the spelling of the word, using the regular Edit functions.

If you choose Look Up (5), WordPerfect will look up and display all the words in the dictionary that match a pattern you provide. You will work with this command later.

For now, choose either the letter beside the correct spelling if it is displayed, or Edit (**4**) to correct and make the necessary changes in the word.

TIP: There will be times when WordPerfect stops at a word that is spelled correctly. This happens because the word is not found in the dictionary, and Word-Perfect does not have anything to compare it with. When this occurs, check the spelling of the word yourself, make any necessary corrections, and press Enter to continue. The speller will advance to the next misspelled or not-found word.

Edit

When you choose Edit (**4**), (or press Right or Left Arrow) the prompt **Press EXIT when done** appears at the bottom of the screen. Correct the word and then press the Enter key to continue with the spelling check.

Look Up

If you do not know the spelling of a word, choose Look up (5). The following prompt will be displayed in the lower left-hand corner of the screen.

```
Word or word pattern:
```

WordPerfect is asking for a clue to the spelling of the word. You can type in the first two or three letters followed by a hyphen (-) or you can type in the parts of the word you're certain of and indicate what you're not sure of with a hyphen (-). For instance, you could enter accom-*date* or embar-*as*- if you were not sure of their correct spellings.

WordPerfect will also respond to your request using a question mark or an asterisk. These are special commands that give you more flexibility in helping WordPerfect.

A question mark (?) can be used to substitute for a single letter. For instance, the pattern *wor?s* would produce works, words, worms, etc., but would not show workmen.

An asterisk (*) can take the place of a group of letters. For instance, if you typed in *wor*s* WordPerfect would show you all the words with multiple letters where the asterisk was. You'd get words like worthless, words, workshops, etc.

You may also combine question marks and asterisks in the same pattern if you wish. What would you expect the difference in result between the following two patterns to be? w?rd* w*rd?

After supplying the pattern, press the Enter key. WordPerfect will display all the words in the dictionary that match the pattern. (If the screen fills up, press the Enter key to see if there are more words on a second or third screen.) If any of the words you see is the correct one, type the letter beside it and WordPerfect will automatically substitute it for the one highlighted in your text. How's that for effortless?

TIP: If the word you are looking for does not appear in the list, type 0 to continue or the space bar to enter a new word pattern. If the screen is blank, WordPerfect did not find any matches.

Of course, the more help you can give WordPerfect and the more specific you can be about the correct spelling of the word in the word pattern, the fewer words WordPerfect will have to find for you. So it's a good idea to provide as much of the word as you can. This is a great way to check spelling if you're not sure whether a letter should be doubled, whether "i" comes before "e", and so on.

TIP: If you enter a word pattern without a ? or *, WordPerfect will list all the words in its dictionary that sound like the pattern.

Caution! Things the Speller will not check: Keep in mind that WordPerfect will not check the accuracy of abbreviations, numbers, or words with numbers in them. You must do this manually to ensure their accuracy.

Double Words

The Speller will also scan for double words. Occasionally, you may type the same word twice, usually by accident but sometimes on purpose (e.g., Walla Walla, Washington, or hip hip hooray). If a word is repeated, WordPerfect will display the following message:

```
Double Word: 1 2 Skip; 3 Delete 2nd; 4 Edit; 5 Disable Double Word Checking
```

Using these options, you can either skip the double word, delete the second one, edit them, or tell WordPerfect to quit checking for double words.

Numbers

When the Speller encounters a word containing a number, such as LSN2, the following prompt appears:

```
1 2 Skip; 3 Ignore words containing numbers; 4 Edit: 0
```

You can skip over the word, add it to the dictionary; edit it, look up other spellings; or tell WordPerfect to ignore words containing numbers. Obviously, it is impossible for WordPerfect to know if the numbers are correct, since it has nothing to match them with. It simply points them out for you to act on if you need to.

Homonyms and Misused Words

Even after the Speller has gone through your document, you cannot be certain that it contains no misspelled (or misused) words since it may contain words that are incorrect but nevertheless match words in the dictionary. For instance, if you type **It is two late to call** or **I cannot here you** WordPerfect will not find the errors (*two* should be too and *here* should be hear) because both pairs of words make a match in the dictionary. Therefore, it is always wise to read through your document after the speller has checked it to catch errors in numbers, usage, and other things that WordPerfect does not find.

Count

When the speller has finished scanning the document, it displays the number of words it has checked, together with the prompt **Press any key to continue**, as shown below. Pressing the Enter key, or any other key, will exit from the spelling function and return you to your document.

```
Word count: 258          Press any key to continue
```

TIP: WordPerfect will check the contents of headers and footers as it works through your document. However, if you should want to check a header or footer apart from the rest of the document, retrieve the header/footer into the editing screen (Format, Page, Header/Footer, Edit), then select the Speller (Ctrl-F2) and follow the prompts.

Exiting from the Speller

When spell-checking is complete, do the following:

- Press the **Space Bar** (or any other key) to exit from the Speller. Then remove the Speller disk from Drive B and replace it with your data disk. Otherwise, when you save your corrected document, it will be saved on the Speller disk instead of your data disk.

- Then resave your corrected document as **Boosters.5**, using **Exit** (**F7**), and print it.

TIP: If you are using a hard drive, you will not need to change disks. However, be sure to save your work in a directory other than the one containing your WordPerfect program and Speller files.

To Review

List the types of errors WordPerfect is not likely to find.

How do you create a pattern to use with the Look Up function?

What will the Speller find if the pattern has a ? (question mark) in it? an * (asterisk) in it?

Summary

In summary, to use the Speller:

a. Enter your document and save it.

b. Position the cursor at the beginning of the text to be spell-checked.

c. Remove your data disk and insert the Speller disk in Drive B (if necessary).

d. Press Spell (Ctrl-F2).

e. Specify whether to check a word, a page, or the entire document, or to take another action.

f. Perform the spell check.

g. Remove the Speller disk and return your data disk to Drive B (if necessary).

h. Save and print.

The Thesaurus

If you're dazzled by the Speller, hold onto your seat and take a look at the Thesaurus. Not only can WordPerfect help you check the spelling of the words you write; it can also help you find the right words to use in the first place.

A thesaurus is a special kind of dictionary that is a collection of **synonyms,** or words that mean the same thing. For instance, the words *done, completed,* and *finished* are synonyms; if you looked up any one of them in the thesaurus, the other two would be listed there as well.

In addition to synonyms, the WordPerfect Thesaurus supplies **antonyms,** or words that mean the opposite of the word you are checking. For instance, *near* is an antonym for *far*.

If you were writing a letter or report and wanted some help finding just the right word, the Thesaurus would be the tool to use.

◻ To see how the Thesaurus works, you will need something to try it out on. Clear your screen and type the following sentence:

Fools rush in where angels fear to tread.

Activating the Thesaurus

You will need to have the Thesaurus disk, which you can obtain from your instructor or the lab assistant, in Drive B.

NOTE: If you are using a hard disk or a network system, your Thesaurus file (WP{WP}EN.THS) should be stored in the same directory as your Word-Perfect program and you will not need to change disks. You may, however, need to identify its position in the SetUp menu under File Location.

- To find out what other words could be used in place of *rush*, position the cursor on that word.

- Since the Thesaurus is stored on a separate disk, remove your data disk Drive B and insert the Thesaurus disk in its place (if necessary).

- When you have done that, press **Thesaurus (Alt-F1)**. You will see something similar to the following on your screen:

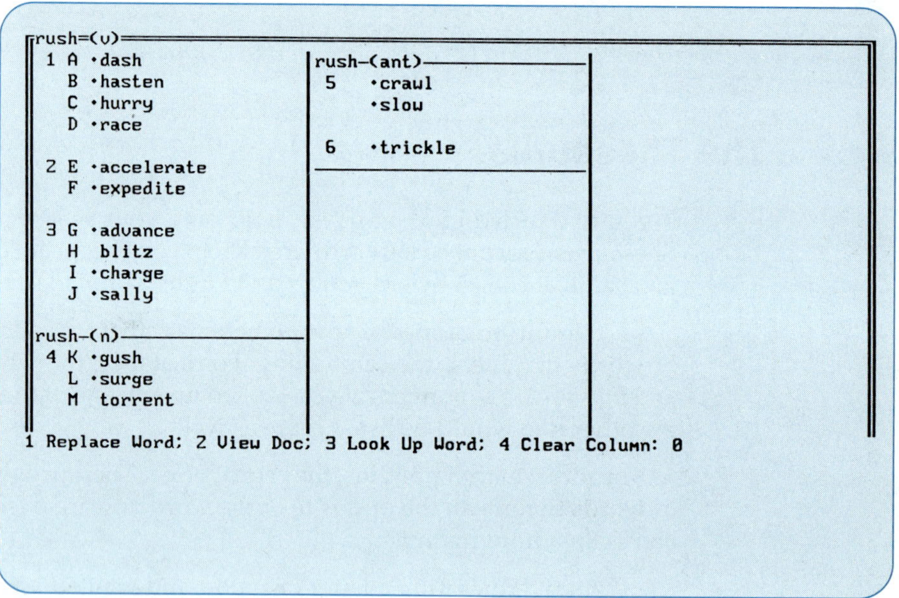

Using the Thesaurus Menu

Several synonyms for the word *rush* are listed below it, each with a letter beside it. The (v) beside the word means that it is being defined as a verb and the (n) beside the word *rush* further down the column means that those words are used as a noun. An antonym (ant) is also listed.

Notice also that some of the words have a dot (.) beside them. This means that they are **headwords**, and you can also get synonyms and antonyms for them if you wish. WordPerfect has identified over 10,000 words as headwords. Those without a dot are not listed separately in the Thesaurus.

The prompt at the bottom offers four options.

If you choose Replace Word (**1**), you can replace the word in your text marked by the cursor with one of the words shown. To do so, you would type a 1. The prompt **Press letter for word** would appear, and you would type the letter of the word of your choice. WordPerfect would then replace the word in the text with the word from the list.

If you choose View Doc (**2**), you would return to the text of your document. You could then scroll or move wherever you wished to review the content, check on context, or whatever you needed to do to help you decide which synonym to choose. You could also select another word for the Thesaurus to work with. You cannot enter text, edit or use other commands at this point. While you are in this mode, the prompt **Press EXIT when done** will be displayed across the bottom of your screen.

If you choose Look Up Word (**3**), you will be asked for a word to look up. When you type in the word of your choice and press Enter, synonyms and antonyms for that word will be displayed. If the word is not a headword, however, the message **Word not found** will flash across the bottom of your screen and you will be returned to the main prompt.

TIP: If the word you entered is not a headword, try using Look up Word to enter a similar word and move ahead from there.

If you choose Clear Column (**4**), you can step back (or clear) a column. But let's postpone that for a bit. Right now, let's see how the Replace Word (**1**) feature works.

Replace Word

Suppose you would like to replace the word *rush* with *charge*.

■ First select the **R**eplace Word option (**1**).

■ When you are asked for a letter, enter an *I* since the word *charge* is labeled I.

Zap!

Now the sentence reads **Fools charge in where angels fear to tread.**

Headwords

But that's not all the Thesaurus will do. It has other tricks as well. Follow along to see what they are.

■ Position the cursor on the word **angels**.

■ Then press **Thesaurus (Alt-F1)** to bring up the Thesaurus and the synonyms. This time, however, let's check one of the headwords on the list.

■ **Spirit** has a period beside it, so press the **E**.

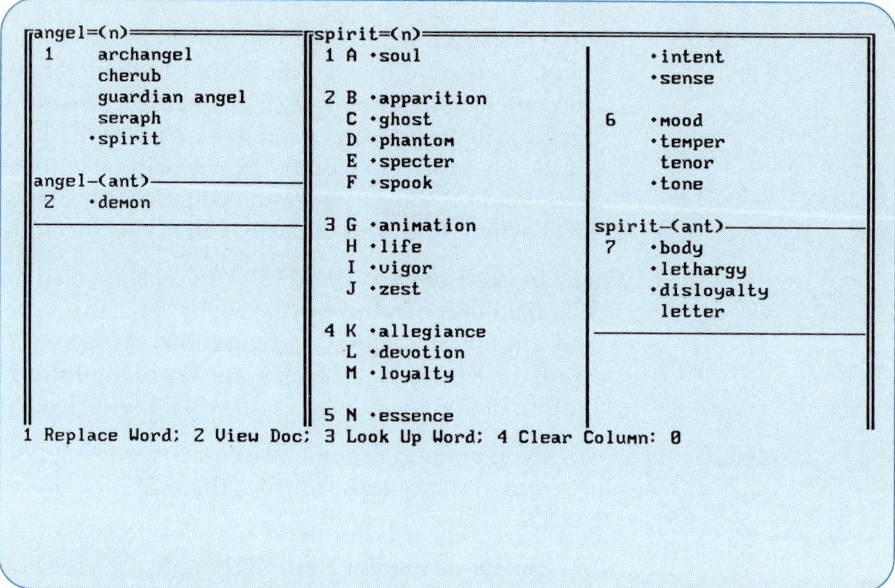

Can you beat that? Now you have all the synonyms and even an antonym for *spirit*. Notice that the alphabetic letters (or Reference Menu) have moved into the second column. You could use one of the words in column 2 simply by following the procedure you used earlier to replace.

If there were additional headwords for *spirit*, you could choose one of them, and WordPerfect would show you even more words to select from.

■ If you want to go back to one of the other two columns, you can simply press the Left or Right Arrow keys and the alphabetic letters will move in the direction you indicate. Try that a time or two.

TIP: You can also use Up Arrow; Down Arrow; Screen Up; Screen Down; Page Up; Page Down; Home, Home, Up Arrow; and GoTo to move around in the Thesaurus menu.

You can even go back and look up a different headword from one of the first two columns. Just move the letters to the column you want to select from, making it the active one, and type the letter beside the word you want. The synonyms for that word will appear in the next column. Isn't this fun?

Clear Columns

If you want to clear everything from one of the columns, simply make it the active one by using the Right and Left Arrow keys to move the letters to it. Then select Clear Column (4). You can also use Backspace or Del to clear the columns.

As you can see, you can choose any of the synonyms at any time by selecting Replace Word (**1**) and typing the letter of your choice.

Changing Words and View Doc

Finally, if you should want to see the synonyms for a different word altogether, there are two ways to do this.

First, you can select Look Up Word (**3**) and then enter the word when asked by the prompt. The Thesaurus will immediately jump to the new word and display the synonyms listed in its dictionary.

Second, you can select View Doc (**2**) and scroll to another word that you want to see synonyms for. With the cursor on the new word, again press Thesaurus (Alt-F1). The synonyms for the new word will appear.

Exiting from the Thesaurus

As you can see, choosing a word from any column will exit from the Thesaurus and return you to your document. If you do not wish to make a choice, you can return to the document at any time by pressing Cancel (F1).

■ When you are finished, remove the Thesaurus disk (if necessary) from Drive B and replace your data disk.

■ Then save your document, with changes, under the name **ThsaursA.5**. You may print it if you like. If you are using a hard disk drive, be sure to save your work in a directory other than the one containing your WordPerfect program and Thesaurus files.

■ Clear your screen. Then, for some practice, Retrieve **Nowis.2** and use the WordPerfect Thesaurus to change words in at least five of the sentences so they differ from the rest. As you do so, experiment with all of the commands and options in the Thesaurus until you feel comfortable using them.

◾ When you are finished, remove the Thesaurus disk, save your revised document as **ThsarusB.5** and print it.

To Review:

To choose words from the Thesaurus, you should type ______________ , ______________ , and ______________ .

Two ways to exit from the Thesaurus are:

1. ____

2. ____

____

Summary

In summary, to use the Thesaurus:

a. Retrieve to the screen the document you wish to check.

b. Position the cursor on the word to be checked.

c. Remove your data disk and put the Thesaurus disk in Drive B (if necessary).

d. Press Thesaurus (Alt-F1).

e. Use the Thesaurus.

f. Remove the Thesaurus disk and return your data disk to disk drive B (if necessary).

g. Save and print.

Activities

You should have completed the following:

Boosters.5	*Article with spelling checked and corrected*
ThsarusA.5	*"Fools Rush in..." with changes*
ThsarusB.5	*Nowis.2 with Thesaurus changes*

Chapter Review

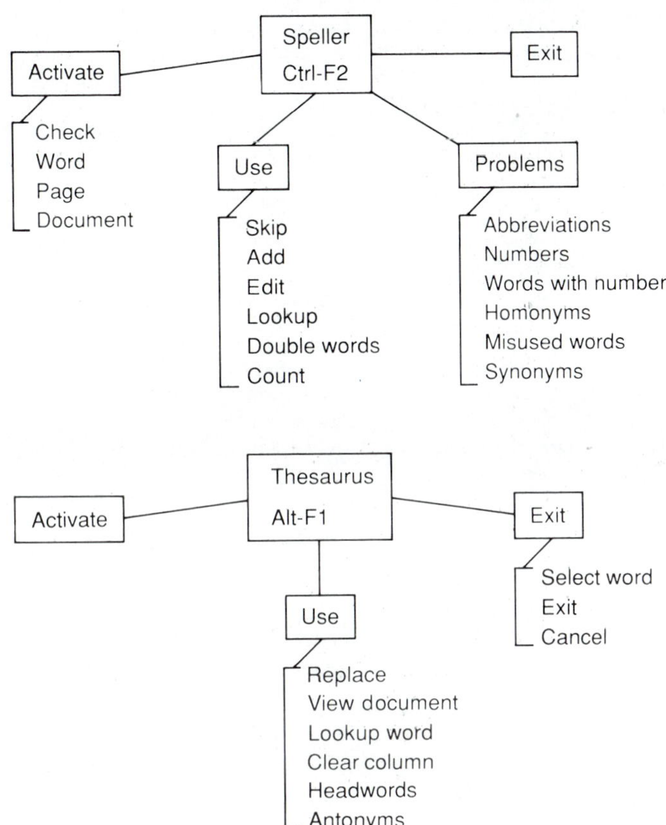

Self-Check Quiz 5

1. List at least two types of things the WordPerfect Speller will not check.

2. What does the term "Not found" mean when the Speller displays it?

3. Using the WordPerfect Speller, how would you look up the spelling of a word?

4. How does the Speller tell whether a word is spelled correctly or not?

5. How can you find out how many words are in your document?

6. What is a synonym? A homonym? Which of these will the Speller check?

7. What is a headword? How can you tell whether a word is identified as a headword?

8. How can you move to another word while using the Thesaurus?

9. What must you do to replace a word in your text with a word from the Thesaurus?

10. What does (a) stand for in the Thesaurus?

11. What is an antonym?

Extra Practice

For extra practice on the material covered in Chapter 5, do the following:

a. Type several paragraphs from this book, another book of your choosing, the newspaper, or a magazine. Save the text as **Pract5a**.

b. Then use the Speller to check your spelling. Correct any errors you find and resave the corrected version as **Pract5a**.

c. Using the Thesaurus, change several words in the text. Use a headword and the look up feature at least once. Then resave the changed version as **Pract5b**.

d. Enter the following sentence: **The miniature train with the miniature engine chugged up the long hill.** Then use the Thesaurus to change several of the words.

e. Use WordPerfect to enter an assignment or personal document. Use the Thesaurus as you go along to select appropriate words for the text. When you are finished, use the Speller to check your document. Make any necessary corrections and save and print your work.

6

Searches, Blocks, Windows, and Other Fun Things

Some of more exciting things you can do with a word processor are searching for specific items in a document, applying a variety of commands to a block of text, and working on two items at once. In this chapter, you will learn how to:

- use the forward and reverse search functions.
- use Search and Replace with and without confirm.
- do extended searches to include auxiliary parts of your document.
- work with blocks of text.
- do cut and paste functions in a variety of ways.
- move columns and rectangles
- work with two documents at once.
- create temporary margins.
- use the window function.
- create and use a ruler line.

Before you can do any of these things, however, you need some material to work with.

- Use List Files (**F5**) to retrieve the file you named **TV.2** (Hint: F5, Enter, highlight TV.2, 1)

Searching Your Documents

You are now going to search your document to find certain words. Notice that beside the **F2** key the template says **Search**, in both **green** and **black,** and that there are thick arrows pointing in different directions.

> The green arrow points left, signifying a backward (from the cursor to the left) search.

> The black arrow points right, indicating a forward (from the cursor to the right) search.

The Search function will proceed right or left (whichever you choose) from the position of the cursor. To search right, therefore, the cursor must be at the beginning of the text you wish to search. To search left, the cursor must be at the end of the text you wish to search.

Search Right

To begin, let's do a forward (or right) search.

- Position the cursor at the beginning of your document with **Home, Home, Up Arrow.**

- Press **Right Search** (**F2**). The following message will appear in the lower left-hand corner of the screen:

```
-> Srch:
```

WordPerfect is asking what you want it to search for.

- Type in the word **and.**

- Press the **Search (F2)** key again. (You could also press the Esc key.)

  The cursor will immediately jump just past the first **and** in your document, where it will stop.

- Press **Right Search (F2)** then **F2** or **Esc** again. The cursor will move right to the next **and** in your document. Continue through your document, stopping at each **and**, and moving forward by pressing Right Search and F2 or Esc.

TIP: If you capitalize the word(s) you are searching for, WordPerfect will stop only at instances that are capitalized. If you enter the word(s) without capitalization, WordPerfect will stop at all occurrences.

  When WordPerfect has completed its search and found all the instances of **and** in your document, the message ***Not Found*** will appear in the lower left-hand corner of your screen.

TIP: You can end a search or interrupt it to make changes in the text at any time. When you are ready to begin again, simply press Right Search (F2) and Esc to move ahead.

Search Left

Now do the same thing in reverse (or going left), searching for the word **for.** This time the cursor must be at the end of your document before you begin. Use Left Search (Shift-F2).

TIP: You can change the direction of either a Right or Left search by pressing Up or Down Arrow while the Srch: prompt is on the screen. Pressing the Up Arrow will change the search arrow to Left, and pressing the Down Arrow will change the search arrow to Right.

Code Searches

The search feature can also help you find codes. To see how this works, try the following:

- Move the cursor to the beginning of your document.

- Press **Right Search (F2)**. When the message → **Srch** appears in the lower left-hand corner of your screen, press **Enter**. A **[HRt]** code will appear beside the arrow.

- Press **Esc**. Immediately, WordPerfect will find the first [HRt] code in your document and stop beside it. Even though you can't see the code on the screen, you can be sure that it is there.

- To check, press **Reveal Codes (Alt-F3)**. Sure enough, there it is.

    If you wished to find additional instances of the [HRt] code, you could press Right Search (F2) and Esc again and WordPerfect would move right to the next [HRt] code in your document. Once the code has been located, you can then delete it, check its settings or location, or enter a different code. You will find this tool very helpful in finding elements of your document that are hidden from view on the screen.

- Now do another search, looking for the word **of.**

Summary

In summary, to Search:

  a. Position the cursor at the beginning or end of the text you wish to search.

  b. Press the Search key (F2 for Right Search, Shift-F2 for Left Search).

  c. Enter the word, code, or string to search for.

  d. Press Search (F2 or Shift-F2) or Esc.

  e. To continue the search, again press the appropriate search key or Esc.

Search and Replace Without Confirm

If you want to find a particular word, code or string of characters and replace it with something else, use Replace (Alt-F2).

- Move your cursor to the beginning of your document (**Home, Home, Up Arrow**).

- Then press **Replace (Alt-F2)** to display the following message:

```
w/Confirm? (Y/N) No
```

WordPerfect is asking if you want to confirm or approve each replacement before it is made. If you answer N(o), replacements will be made automatically throughout the text. If you answer Y(es), you will be asked to type Y or N each time WordPerfect finds the word or code that matches what you ask it to search for.

◼ Answer **N(o)**.

The next message will ask you to specify what you want to search for.

```
-> Srch:
```

TIP: Again, you can use the Up or Down Arrow to change the direction of the search if you wish.

◼ Type in the word **the** and delete the [HRt] code if it is there. Press **Esc** or **F2**. Next you will see the message:

```
Replace with:
```

WordPerfect is asking what it should insert in place of **the**.

◼ To make it easy to spot where changes have been made, type in the symbols **&&&** and press **Esc** or F2 again.

ZIP!!! WordPerfect will automatically make the changes. Isn't that remarkable?

You may notice that some strange things have happened. For one thing, the letters **t-h-e** have also been replaced in words such as they and these. WordPerfect did not distinguish between the word **the** and the same characters within other words.

To prevent this, you must be more precise about what you are searching for. If you specify spaces before and after the words you supply, only those instances preceded and followed by spaces will be replaced. In other words, if you enter **(space) the (space)** and **(space) &&& (space)**, WordPerfect will include the spaces in its search and pass over other occurrences of the letters **t-h-e** that are not free-standing.

- Now do a Search and Replace for **&&&,** replacing it with **the** to return your text to its original form.

- Then do another Search and Replace, again replacing **the** with **&&&,** but this time include spaces before and after. When the Search and Replace is completed, only the individual word **the** will be changed to **&&&.**

TIP: To remove something throughout your document, you can enter it as the item to search for and then not enter anything when asked for the replacement. (Just press F2 or Esc without entering anything at that point.) WordPerfect will then replace whatever it is to search for with a "nothing" and the search item will be gone from your document. You can also press the backspace delete key when asked for the replacement and WordPerfect will delete whatever is indicated in the search each time it finds it.

To Review

When using the Search and Replace function, you must sometimes remember to include ______________ before and after the words you specify.

Summary

In summary, to Search and Replace (Without Confirm):

a. Position the cursor at the beginning of the document or text you wish to search.

b. Press Replace (Alt-F2).

c. When asked if you want to confirm, say N(o).

d. Specify the word, code or string of characters to search for and change the direction of the arrow if necessary.

e. Press Esc, Search (F2 or Shift-F2), or Replace (Alt-F2).

f. Specify the word, code, or string of characters to use in replacement.

g. Press Esc Search (F2 or Shift F2), or Replace (Alt-F2).

TIP: The word you are searching for could be overlooked because it is followed by a punctuation mark or, in some other way, does not precisely match the configuration you specified. Since WordPerfect works on a matching process, it will not pick up anything except the exact duplicate of the word(s) or commands you specify. For example, a search for **word (word(space))** would not pick up **words,** or **word.** which is followed by a comma or period. You may want to do the search more than once, with variations, to be sure you find all occurrences.

Search and Replace With Confirm

Sometimes you will not want to change every occurrence of the word you are searching for. If you would like WordPerfect to check with you before making each change, you should say **Y**(es) when asked if you want to Confirm.

◼ Move your cursor to the beginning or end of your document and press **Replace (Alt-F2)**.

◼ When the message **w/Confirm (Y/N) No** appears, type **Y**(es). This will tell WordPerfect that you want to approve each replacement.

◼ When → **Srch**: appears, change the direction of the arrow if necessary. Then type in **(space) to (space)**, delete the word "the" if it is there, and press **Search (F2)** or **Esc.**

◼ Replace with **(space) Doc (space)** and press **Search** (F2) or **Esc.** The cursor stops at the first to in the text, and you are asked to confirm the replacement. If you type **Y,** the change will be made. If you type **N,** the cursor will jump to the next "to" without changing the word.

◼ Type **Y** to replace. The cursor will jump **to** the next "to" in the document, and ask again if you want to replace. Press **N.** Continue through the document, pressing Y or N as you choose, to see how this command works.

TIP: If you should want to stop the Search and Replace function before the cursor has moved completely through the document, you can end the operation at any time by pressing Cancel (F1).

Keep in mind the effect of spaces and other items that you cannot see or may not realize will affect the search command so the results you obtain will be those you want.

TIP: If you wanted to search and replace using a code such as Bold, Underline, Flush Right, or Margin or Tab Setting, you could simply press the appropriate key (Bold (F6), Underline (F8), Flush Right (Alt-F6), Format/Tab (Shift-F8-1)) when prompted for a search target or replacement.

■ When you have finished, clear your screen before moving on to the next section. (Hint: Use Exit (F7) but don't save your document.)

Summary

In summary, to Search and Replace (With Confirm):

   a. Position the cursor at the beginning or end of the text you wish to search.

   b. Press Replace (Alt-F2).

   c. When asked if you want to confirm, say Y(es).

   d. Change the direction of the search arrow if necessary.

   e. Specify the word, code or characters to search for.

   f. Press Esc, Search (F2 or Shift-F2), or Replace (Alt-F2).

   g. Specify the word, code or characters to use as a replacement.

   h. Press Esc, Search (F2 or Shift-F2), or Replace (Alt-F2).

   i. Confirm with Y or N, as appropriate, when asked.

To Review

Use the _________________ keys to perform search functions.

Extended Search

If your document includes footnotes, endnotes, headers and/or footers, and you want WordPerfect to search through them as well, you would need to use the Extended Search feature. This feature works exactly like the search commands you have just learned, except that it also searches the additional parts of your document. It is activated by holding down the Home key and pressing the appropriate search key (Right Search (F2), Left Search (Shift-F2) or Replace (Alt-F2)).

TIP: You can also press the (Home, F2), (Home, Alt-F2), or (Home, Shift-F2) keys to make this command. Doing so eliminates the need to hold three keys down at the same time.

Text Moves (Cut and Paste)

One of the most helpful editing functions of WordPerfect is its ability to move words, lines, sentences, paragraphs, and blocks of text to another place in the document.

Moving Sentences, Paragraphs and Pages

Moving sentences, paragraphs and pages is easily performed with the Move command.

- Retrieve **TV.2** again. Let's move the second paragraph down to the bottom of the page.

- Position the cursor within the text you want to move (the second paragraph).

- Press **Move** (**Ctrl-F4**). The following message will appear:

```
Move: 1 Sentence; 2 Paragraph; 3 Page; 4 Retrieve: 0
```

WordPerfect treats as a *sentence* any text between the previous period, colon, question mark, or exclamation point and the next terminal mark of punctuation occurring after the cursor.

It defines as a *paragraph* any text between the previous new-line command [HRt], activated by the Enter key and the next one following the cursor.

A **page** is any text between the previous and the next new-page (---------- or =========) command following the cursor.

Using these criteria, WordPerfect will find the text you wish to move and highlight it.

- To see how this works, select **Paragraph** (**2**). The paragraph where the cursor is will immediately be highlighted. You will then be asked whether you want to:

```
1 Move; 2 Copy; 3 Delete; 4 Append: 0
```

If you choose **Move (1)**, the material you mark will be cut (reMOVEd) from the text, and stored in a temporary file until you specify a new location for it in your document.

If you choose **Copy (2)**, WordPerfect will make a copy of whatever you designate and hold it in a temporary file until you specify where it is to go in your document. The original is not removed. Thus you will end up with two instances of the material—the original and the copy you just made.

If you choose **Delete (3)**, the designated text will simply be deleted from your document. It is not placed in the special temporary file area but can be retrieved with Undelete (F1).

If you choose **Append (4)**, you can add the blocked text to the end of another file on disk. Such blocks can be added to locked files, but blocks containing graphics cannot be appended. If the target file cannot be found, a message **ERROR: File Not Found** will appear and the block is not appended.

■ For now, indicate that you wish to make a copy by typing **2** or **C**. The message at the bottom of the screen will disappear and a new one will appear.

```
Move cursor; press Enter to retrieve.              Doc 1 Pg 1 Ln 2.3" Pos 3.21"
```

WordPerfect has made a temporary file of the material you wish to copy, and is waiting to be told where to put it in the text.

■ Move the cursor to the place where you would like the copy of the paragraph to appear (below the final paragraph), and press **Enter**. The text will immediately be retrieved from the temporary file and inserted at the cursor.

TIP: If for some reason, you did not want to retrieve the text immediately, you could press Cancel **(F1)** to remove the message at the bottom of the screen. WordPerfect would hold the sentence in the temporary file until you retrieved it later (as many times as you wished) by positioning the cursor, and pressing Move **(Ctrl-F4)**, Retrieve **(4)**, Block **(1)**.

To erase material from its present position and move it to a different location in your text, you would follow the same steps outlined above except for choosing the move option.

■ Try cutting a sentence from the text and moving it to another location in the document.

- Finally, mark a sentence and choose the Delete option. As you can see, the text disappears from your document (and cannot be retrieved with Move (Ctrl-F4)).

- If you would like additional practice, go back and move or copy several more sentences and paragraphs. You can even move a page if you like. Since you saved the original text on the disk, you can feel free to alter the copy on the screen any way you wish. Do not continue until you are confident of your ability to move, copy, and delete text in this way.

Summary

In summary, to Move, Copy, Delete, and Append sentences, paragraphs, and pages:

a. Position the cursor within the sentence, paragraph or page you wish to manipulate.

b. Press Move (Ctrl-F4).

c. Choose the sentence (1), paragraph (2), or page (3) option.

d. Choose the move (1), copy (2), delete (3) or append (4) option. If you choose delete, the text in question will simply disappear.

e. To move or copy, move the cursor to the point where you want the text to appear.

f. Press Enter.

g. Or press Cancel (F1). Then position the cursor, press Move (Ctrl-F4), Retrieve (4), and Block (1).

Moving Random-Length Blocks of Text

If you want to manipulate a block of text that does not fall into the category of a sentence, paragraph, or page, the procedure is essentially the same. First, though, you must identify the passage you want to change.

- Since you have mixed up the material you have been working on, clear your screen (Exit and do not save, F7, N, N) and Retrieve **Jobs.3**.

    On your keyboard, you will see the word **Block** printed in **blue** next to the F4 key. This is the command you will use to designate the block of text you want moved.

- Position the cursor under the first letter of the block you want to move or copy. For this exercise, let's move the last two lines of the third paragraph.

- Press **Block** (**Alt-F4**). The words **Block On** will flash in the lower left-hand corner of your screen.

- Move the cursor to the end of the block you want to cut or copy—for our purposes, the end of the paragraph. The block will be highlighted as you move the cursor. This identifies for WordPerfect which block of text you want to move.

- Press **Move** (**Ctrl-F4**). The following prompt will appear:

```
Move: 1 Block; 2 Tabular Column; 3 Rectangle: 0
```

- Choose **Block** (**1**) to indicate that you want to move a block of text. The next prompt will be familiar:

```
1 Move; 2 Copy; 3 Delete; 4 Append: 0
```

- Select **Move** (**1**) to erase the text from its present position and make it ready to be moved to another location. The block of text will disappear from your document. It is in a temporary file, and WordPerfect will put it wherever you want it to go. The prompt "Move cursor; press Enter to retrieve" will again display.

  At this point you can either position the cursor where you want the block moved to and press Enter, or you can press Cancel (F1) and later retrieve the text with Move (Ctrl-F4), Retrieve (4), Block (1).

- For now, move the cursor to the end of the document (**Home, Home, Down Arrow**).

- Press **Enter** to retrieve the text. It will immediately appear at the cursor position at the end of the document.

- Again, practice copying and moving blocks of text until you feel comfortable with these commands.

Summary

In summary, to Move or Copy a Block of text:

a. Position the cursor at the beginning of the block you wish to move or copy.

b. Press Block (Alt-F4) to turn Block On.

c. Move the cursor to the end of the block of text you wish to move or copy. (The text will be highlighted.)

d. Press Move (Ctrl-F4).

e. Choose one of the move or copy options.

f. Move the cursor to the position where you want the text to appear.

g. Press Enter.

To Review

After you Move, you will have _________ copy(ies) of the material.

After you Copy, you will have _________ copy(ies).

Append

The Append option on the Move/Copy Menu allows you to copy a block of text from one document to the end of another document. To use it, mark the block you want to copy and press Move (Ctrl-F4). When the Move/Copy Menu is displayed, select **Block** (**B**). Then select Append (4). The following prompt will appear:

```
Append to:
```

WordPerfect is asking for the name of the file you want the marked block appended to. Enter the name of the file. The red disk-drive light will come on, indicating that the block is being copied to the end of that file. When the append is complete, the prompt will disappear and you will be ready to continue your work.

Moving Columns

WordPerfect also allows you to move text or numbers arranged in columns. This command only works for columns separated by Tabs, Tab Align, Indent, or Hard Return codes; you should not use it to move columns created in newspaper or parallel style.

◻ To practice moving columns, position the cursor at the end of your document and enter the following short table. Use 1" left and right margins, and set left-justified tabs at 2.0", 3.0", 4.0", 5.0", and 6.0".

June	245	689	21
July	325	987	58
August	272	885	34

Now let's copy the first column of numbers (245, 325, 272) and move it to the right of the last column of numbers (21, 58, 34).

◻ Position the cursor within the first entry (245) in the column you wish to move.

◻ Turn on the Block function by pressing **Block (Alt-F4)**.

◻ Highlight the column. WordPerfect will highlight the entire block at this point, but the highlighted area should begin at the top and end at the bottom of the column you wish to cut or copy. Therefore, the highlighted area should extend from 245 to 272 in the second column.

◻ Press **Move (Ctrl-F4)**, and choose Tabular Column with a **2** or **C**.

◻ When the prompt asks if you want to move, copy, delete, or append select Copy (**2**).

◻ Move the cursor to the position (**6.0"**) where you want the column to be copied and press **Enter**.

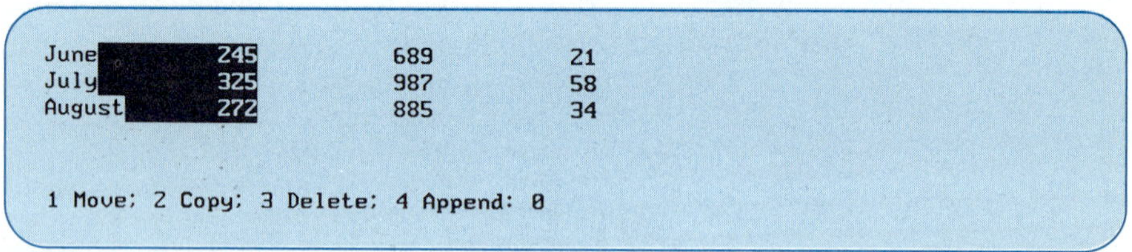

Bingo! The column should be copied to the new position. If the command does not work properly, try it again, making sure that you have preset a tab stop for it and marked the block correctly.

TIP: If you do not want to move the column immediately, you can press Cancel (F1) again. Later, when you are ready to retrieve the column, position the cursor and press Move (Ctrl-F4), Retrieve (4), and Tabular Column (2) to retrieve the tabular column.

■ Now try moving a column—choose any column you like. Follow the procedure outlined above, but choose option 1 to move. The marked column will disappear, and the remaining columns will move to the left to fill the space.

TIP: Because WordPerfect creates a temporary file for text you move and copy, it is possible to retrieve the material repeatedly. Simply position the cursor where you want the text to appear, press Move (Ctrl-F4) and choose option 1, 2, or 3 for Block, Tabular Column, or Rectangle as appropriate. Then reposition the cursor and repeat the steps outlined above as often as you like. This is a good way to fill a page with lines or other repetitive text.

Moving Rectangles

If you want to move a rectangular portion of your document that is not separated by tabs, tab align, indent, or hard return codes, you can use the Move Rectangle command. This feature is especially useful for moving statistical formulas or line drawings or other parts that cannot be classified as text, sentence, paragraph, page, or tabular material.

To mark a rectangle, you simply need to position the cursor at the upper left corner of the portion you wish to work with. Then move the cursor to the lower right corner of the material to be affected. Even though everything between the two points will be highlighted from margin to margin, Word-Perfect will know it is to use only that within the area defined by the upper left and lower right corners when you select Rectangle (3). You can Move (1), Copy (2), Delete (3), and Append (4) a rectangle. Practice with this command a little if you like.

■ Since your document is probably chopped up by now, do an **Exit (F7)** to clear the screen and memory. Do not save. Then retrieve **Jobs.3** again so you can use it for the next exercise.

Using Blocks

There are a number of other things you can do with blocks of text besides moving and copying. They include:

Bolding a block	Saving a block
Centering a block	Underlining a block
Printing a block	Deleting a block
Flush right a block	Protecting a block

First define the block of text you wish to work with by moving the cursor to the point where it begins. Press Block (Alt-F4) and move the cursor to the end of the block. Then simply press the appropriate key (Bold, Underline, Backspace Delete, etc.). The block will change accordingly.

■ Let's practice several of these using commands with the text on your screen. Block the first paragraph using **Alt-F4**. Then press **Bold (F6)**. The paragraph should be bolded immediately.

■ Underline a block of your choice, using the **Underline (F8)** key.

■ Experiment with the Delete, Center, Print, Save, etc., commands, until you can use them easily.

TIP: You may wonder what the difference between block protect, conditional end of page, and widow/orphan is: Block protect will keep a block of text together, conditional end of page will keep a certain number of lines together, and widow/orphan will protect against soft page breaks that fall on the first or last line of text. To some degree, their use overlaps.

Defining a Block

It is not always necessary to move the cursor or arrow keys to the end of the text you wish to mark. You can also use codes, characters, letters, and the like. For instance, you can use a period (.) to designate the end of a sentence, or Enter for the end of a paragraph.

Try this.

■ Position the cursor at the beginning of any sentence.

■ Press **Block (Alt-F4)** to turn Block On.

■ Press the period (.) key. Wow!

■ Then press any key you wish to use on this block of text, such as the Bold or Underline key.

■ Now try defining a paragraph with the Enter key. Put the cursor at the beginning of a paragraph and press **Block (Alt-F4)**, then **Enter**. Super!!! Do the same thing with the letter p. Position the cursor, press **Block (Alt-F4)**, and press **p**. Press **p** again. Any of the keys or commands will work the same way.

If you want to make more than one change to the same block, WordPerfect allows you to redisplay the block without having to redefine it. Let's see how this works:

■ Mark any block of text on your screen—a sentence, a paragraph, a line, or whatever you choose.

- ◼ Press **Bold** (**F6**) to bold the block. The text will appear in boldface, and the highlighting will disappear.

   Now suppose you also want to underline the same text.

- ◼ Press **Block** (**Alt-F4**) to turn Block On.

- ◼ Then press **Go To** (**Ctrl-7**) or (**CTRL-Home**), twice, and watch what happens. The previous block should reappear, ready for you to use again.

- ◼ Press **Underline** (**F8**) to underline it. It just gets easier and easier.

- ◼ When you have tried several of these commands, **Exit** (but do not save) from **Jobs.3**.

TIP: You will recall from Chapter 4 that it is possible to protect a block so that it will not be split with a soft return. To do this, mark the block and press Format (Shift-F8) and Y. And that's all there is to it. The block should begin with the first word of the passage and end with the last. Do not include hard return commands at the end in the block. Block protect is very useful for text that may be edited later since the number of lines can expand and contract within the block.

Summary

In summary, to use a Block function:

a. Position the cursor at the beginning of the block.

b. Press Block (Alt-F4) to turn Block On.

c. Move the cursor to the end of the block.

d. Press the appropriate function key (for instance, Bold (F6))

Switch

On the F3 key, you will see the word **Switch** printed in **green**. This key has two functions. One uses the block procedure to switch a block of text from upper-case, or capital letters, to lower-case or small letters, or vice- versa. This can be very handy when you need to change more than a word or two (such as when you accidentally leave Caps Lock on).

The other function allows you to work on two documents at the same time, switching back and forth between them. Let's practice both of these functions.

Using the Upper/Lower Case Switch

This command will help you change text that is entered in upper case to lower case and vice versa.

- Retrieve **Charlie.1**

- Position the cursor at the beginning of the first paragraph.

- Press **Block (Alt-F4)**.

- Move to the end of the paragraph.

- Press **Switch (Shift-F3)**. The following menu will appear in the lower right corner of the screen:

```
1 Uppercase; 2 Lowercase: 0
```

- Choose Upper case **(1)**, and watch what happens.

    If you want, change the paragraph back by using the same procedure.

TIP: WordPerfect will keep the capital letter at the beginning of a sentence if you include the final punctuation of the preceding sentence. However, the first letter in a paragraph may need to be capitalized manually if you switch from upper case to lower case.

Working with Two Documents at Once

If you want to work on two documents at the same time, simply press Switch (Shift-F3). When no block is defined, WordPerfect knows that you intend to use this function, not Upper/lower Case Switch.

- With **Charlie.1** on the screen, press **Switch (Shift-F3)**.

    The screen will clear, and you will see the prompt **Doc 2** in the status line. WordPerfect is ready to begin the second document. You can retrieve an existing document with List Files (F5) or you can create a new document if you wish.

    If you press Switch (Shift-F3) again, WordPerfect will jump back to the first document.

Not only can you work on two documents at once, but you can also move text back and forth from one document to the other if you wish.

▣ For practice, mark the first paragraph of Charlie.1 as a block and cut it. Then switch to Doc 2, and retrieve the block. How about that!

You can save the text in one document without affecting the other; retrieve files to one and not the other; exit from one without changing the other; choose different margin, spacing, and tab settings for each document, and so on. With a little ingenuity, you'll find this a very handy and useful feature.

One note of caution when using this function. If both documents are quite large, WordPerfect may run out of memory space to store them both. You may want to break up large documents into several smaller ones in order to avoid running out of memory.

To get out of Document 2 and back to Document 1, you must exit from Document 2. Do this as follows:

▣ With Document 2 showing on the screen, press **Exit (F7)**.

▣ When you are asked if you wish to save Doc 2, indicate **Y(es)** or **N(o)**, whichever is appropriate. Supply a filename if necessary.

▣ When you are asked if you wish to Exit Doc 2, answer **Y(es)**. You will immediately be returned to Document 1.

Windows

The Windows feature resembles the Switch function in that it allows you to work with two documents at once. The major difference is that you can see a part of both documents on the screen at once--one on top and one on the bottom.

▣ To activate this feature, press **Screen (Ctrl-F3)**. The following menu will appear:

```
0 Rewrite; 1 Window; 2 Line Draw: 0
```

▣ Select **Windows (1)**. The following prompt will appear:

```
Number of lines in this window: 24
```

WordPerfect is telling you that it is now devoting all 24 lines to the window (in this case, the full screen) you presently see. You can enter any number between 1 and 24, and WordPerfect will divide the screen at that point, allotting the number of lines you specify to the top part of the screen (or window) and leaving the remainder in the bottom part (or window). Keep in mind that there are 25 lines on the monitor. One line is reserved for the status line, leaving 24 for the window. When two windows are "open", there will be 23 lines remaining since two lines will be used for a status line in each window.

◼ For now, type **10** and press **Enter**.

With the Windows feature, two documents can be viewed at the same time. A ruler line separates them.

A ruler line will appear across the screen, leaving 10 lines above and the remaining 13 below. Notice that each window has its own status line, designating Doc 1 and Doc 2.

◼ To move from one window to the other, press **Switch** (**Shift-F3**).

Notice that the ruler line changes to indicate the margins and tabs of the window that is active. You can now work with documents in both windows, moving between them as you like and using a variety of commands. The windows can be used alone or together.

Ingenious!

◼ If you wish to exit from Windows and have only one document showing on the screen, simply bring up Windows with Screen (**Ctrl-F3**) and specify that you want **24** lines in the window. When you press Enter, your screen will return to single-document mode.

Ruler Line

You can also use this feature to keep a ruler line on the screen showing where the margins and tabs are set.

◼ To insert a ruler line, bring up the Windows option with **Screen** (**Ctrl-F3**), Choose **Windows** (**1**), and enter **23** when you are asked how many lines you want in the window. Then press **Enter**.

You can also use the arrow keys to move the ruler line. Instead of typing 23 (or any other number between 1-24) press the Up and/or Down Arrow keys to position the line. Then press Enter.

Since there are 24 lines available on the screen, the ruler line will appear on the bottom (24th) line, leaving 23 above it. You will not be able to use the second window, and will lose one line of your screen. But if you like a ruler line showing, it may be worth the tradeoff.

■ To eliminate the window on your screen, press **Screen (Ctrl-F3)**, **W**indow **(1)**. Specify **24** lines, or press the **Down Arrow** key and press **Enter**.

Summary

In summary, to create a Window:

   a. Press Screen (Ctrl-F3).

   b. Select **Window (1)**.

   c. Specify the number of lines in the top window (1-24).

   d. Press Enter.

   e. Use Switch (Shift-F3) to move from window to window.

■ Now that you have had an opportunity to try a number of new commands, clear your screen and type in the following text (or if you wish, retrieve the file named **Trips.6** from the Student Exercise Disk.). Use the Interim Save (F10) option at least twice as you go.

   a. Use the default settings for margins, spacing, and paragraph tabs.

   b. Turn Hyphenation On.

   c. Use any tab settings you wish for the table.

TRIPS ARE SUCH FUN

A goodly portion of the fun of any trip is the pleasurable anticipation and the planning. Although the trip itself may be a short one, the pleasant memories linger long after the travel is ended.

Come, take a trip with me. What fun to plan the itinerary, review the news to be recounted to friends upon arrival, and dream of the exciting sights we shall see! As we consider the route, it seems that the enjoyment of the trip might be increased by seeing unfamiliar country; perhaps we shall even make several stops along the way.

Travel Plans and Cost

Nowadays there are many ways to travel. The most common methods are by car, plane, bus, or train. The choice often depends on several factors such as time required, cost, availability of local transportation, and how much you expect to move around once you reach your destination. We have chosen to travel by train this time so we can see the scenery along the way. Our estimated costs are as follows:

Taxi	$ 19.00
Train Fare	285.93
Car Rental	150.75
Lodging	225.00
Food	200.00
Miscellaneous	75.00

With that decided, it's time to be off !

What to Take

We may plan the trip weeks ahead of time; but only as the time for departure draws near do we begin to think seriously about what to pack and, most importantly, what clothes we expect to take. You will be thankful if you follow a sage word of advice and take garments that do not muss easily. There will not be time or facilities for pressing out the wrinkles each place we stop. Knowing that your appearance is neat is good insurance against feeling a bit fidgety about your clothes. A suit is very appropriate for travel at almost any season of the year; whether it is one you wear or one you pack, you can be fairly certain that it will look well.

Appearance

You will not want to overlook the fact that the new synthetics or miracle fabrics are a boon to the traveler. They don't just shed wrinkles; they just don't get wrinkled in the first place.

Easy Care

In addition, the new fabrics simplify the problem of having an adequate supply of clean clothes and lingerie without taking many different items. With most, you can whisk them through the suds in the evening and find them dry and ready to put on in the morning, even with no ironing. It's easy as $1 + 1 = 2$.

Sightseeing Tips

Another thing to remember is that, when sightseeing, you will be very grateful for an extra pair of walking shoes. I concluded long ago,

> after doing a good share of sightseeing, that it makes little difference whether you are visiting historic shrines in the East, old mansions in the South, scenic spots in the West, or ski resorts in the North, two things are extremely essential: patience, or tolerance of others, and comfortable shoes for standing and walking. The shoes are easily acquired, even if the patience is not.

- Proofread carefully and correct all your errors.

- Save the document as **Trips.6** and print it using **Print (Shift-F7)**, Full Document **(1)**.

- Now make the following changes:

  a. Search your document for the word **pack**. Note in the upper left-hand corner of the first page how many times you found it. (Do not include variations like **packing, packed,** and the like.)

  b. Do a Search and Replace to change the word **trips** to **vacations**. Then do a Search and Replace w/confirm to change the word **trip** to **vacation**. Then capitalize the word **vacation** in the title, using Block and Switch/Upper Case.

  c. Move the sentence that begins "Knowing that your..." down to become the first sentence under the heading <u>Appearance</u>. Make sure the sentence is erased from its previous position.

  d. Delete the sentence **With that decided, it's time to be off!**

  e. After the last paragraph, create a new side heading called **Summary** and begin it with the phrase **As we said in the beginning.** Then move/copy the first paragraph to complete the Summary section. (Be sure to change the A in "A goodly portion" to lower case.)

  f. Change the spacing to double. However, leave single-spaced the "Come, take a trip. . ." paragraph and the six-item travel-cost list. Do not leave more than a double space between paragraphs, or above and below headings.

  g. Number the pages at the bottom center of the page.

- When you are finished, check your work for accuracy. **Save** your revised document under the name **Vacation.6**, and print it.

  You're moving right along!

Activities

You should have completed the following:

Trips.6   *Manuscript*
Vacation.6   *Trips.6 with changes*

Chapter Review

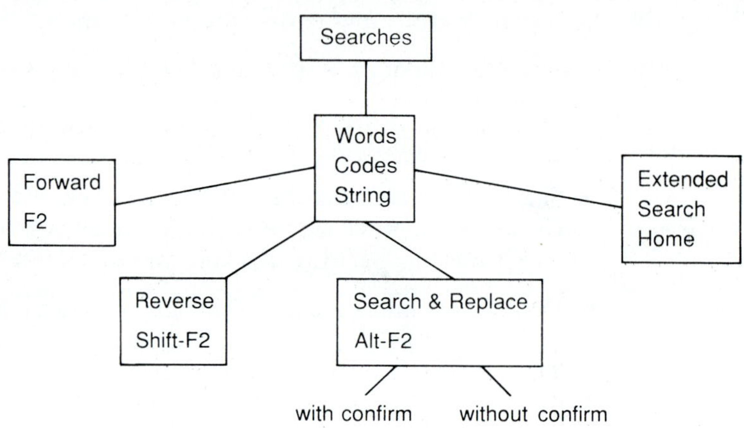

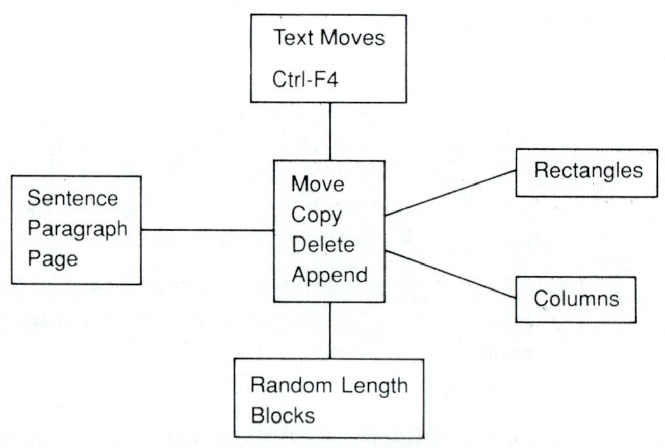

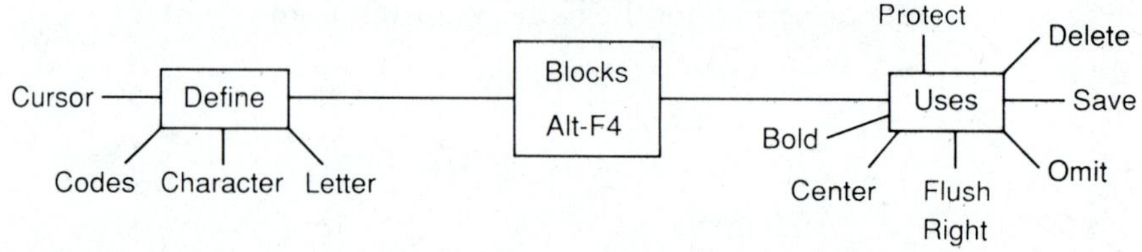

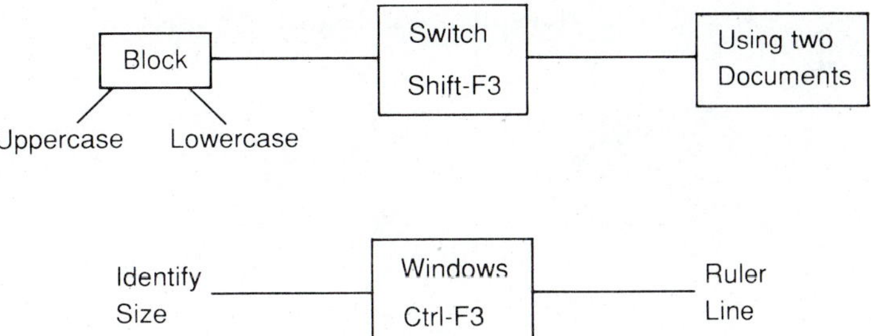

Self-Check Quiz 6

1. Where should the cursor be positioned before beginning a Search and Replace procedure?

2. How can you change the direction of a search operation?

3. Which keys may be pressed to execute any of the search functions?

4. Describe what will happen when you perform each of the following Block functions.

    a. Move

    b. Copy

    c. Delete

    d. Retrieve Text

5. How does WordPerfect define each of the following?

    a. Sentence

    b. Paragraph

    c. Page

6. What keystrokes do you use to insert a ruler line across the bottom of your screen?

7. List at least five functions that can be performed on a block of text.

8. What does the Switch function do?

9. What keys should you press to re-highlight a block of text?

10. What is the difference between Search and Replace with and without Confirm?

11. When would it be necessary to use the Extended Search feature?

12. What happens when a block is appended?

13. What must be present to move columns?

14. Which command should you use to move between two documents?

15. What is the maximum number of lines that may be used in a single window? In a double window?

Extra Practice

For extra practice on the material covered in Chapter 6, do the following:

a. Open a new document. Center the title **TRAVEL TIPS** at the top of the page. Space down twice, then enter the following text as the first paragraph:

> **When preparing for a trip, the question of what to wear is one of the more critical issues that must be addressed. Advance planning and careful selection can help you avoid problems along the way. Following are some tips to help make your trip more pleasant.**

b. Then use the Switch (Shift-F3) command to move to document 2. Retrieve **Trips.6** into Doc 2.

c. Block the sections titled **What to Take**, **Appearance**, **Easy Care**, and **Sightseeing Tips**. Use Move (Ctrl-F4), Copy (2), to copy them.

d. Then Switch back to Doc 1. With Move (Ctrl-F4), Retrieve (4), retrieve the sections you blocked and copied into Document 1. When you are finished, your document should consist of a title, the paragraph you entered, and the sections from Doc 2.

e. Change the Left and Right margins to 2.0" in Doc 1.

f. Add a command to number the pages in the new document. Have the page numbers appear at the top right.

g. Turn Widow/Orphan protection On.

h. Save the new document (Doc 1) as **Pract6a** and print it.

i. Exit from both Doc 2 and Doc 1 using Exit (F7). To avoid the possibility of altering **Trips.6** in Doc 2, **do not** save it again.

j. With a clear screen showing, retrieve **Pract6a** into Doc 1. (Do not confuse this with **Trips.6**.)

k. Create a window with 12 lines. Then move the cursor into the bottom window.

l. Using List Files (F5), retrieve **Pract6a** into the second window. You should now have two copies of this file active, one in each window.

m. With the cursor in the second window, move to the end of the paragraph headed **Appearance** and add the following:

Fabrics such as nylon, polyester, and Kodel are especially good for traveling.

n. Then Switch (Shift-F3) to the first window, move to the last section headed **Sightseeing Tips,** and block the first sentence about being grateful for an extra pair of good walking shoes. Use Move (Ctrl-F4), Copy (2), to copy this sentence.

o. Switch back to the second window and move the cursor to the end of the paragraph headed **What to Take.** Use the Move command to retrieve the sentence you blocked and copied from the other document so that it becomes the last sentence in that paragraph.

p. Use the Switch command to block the words **nylon, Polyester,** and **Kodel** and change them to upper case.

q. Save the new document in window 2 as **Pract6b**. It should contain the title, the paragraph you inserted, the material you copied from the first document, the sentence you added at the end of **Appearance,** upper case names for the fabrics, and the sentence about shoes that you copied from document 2.

r. Clear both windows and exit from the Windows feature. Then print **Pract6b**.

s. Retrieve **Jobs.6**. Resave it under the name **Pract6c**.

t. Using **Pract6c**, do a search with confirm for the word **ad**. Where appropriate, replace it with the word **advertisement**.

u. Again using **Pract6c**, do a search-and-replace with confirm for the word **job**. Replace it with **employment** where appropriate.

v. Resave the revised document as **Pract6c** and print it.

7

Using Temporary Margins, Date Commands, and Other Formatting Helps

Even though you've already learned quite a few formatting commands, WordPerfect still has some impressive tricks up its sleeve. In this chapter you'll work with some of the more unique commands including temporary margins, the date and time commands, advance and overstrike, and compose. You'll also learn how to use the line draw feature to create boxes, illustrations, and other graphic work as well as how to alter the way WordPerfect underlines text. Finally, you'll learn how to add hard spaces, hyphens, and dashes that will not be separated by line and page breaks.

When you have finished, you should be able to:

- use the temporary margins commands in a variety of ways.

- add commands to insert the date and time into your document.

- use the overstrike and advance line features.

- insert special characters with compose

Temporary Margins

A temporary margin is useful when you want to indent several lines in succession without having to press the Tab key each time you start a new line. There are two kinds of temporary margins.

One, called → Indent (Left Indent) indents the left margin as shown in this and the next three lines. The temporary margin will remain in effect until you press the Enter key; then WordPerfect will revert to the original left margin. The right margin does not change. This type of temporary margin is especially useful for lists and outlines.

The second type of temporary margin, → Indent ← (Left/Right Indent), indents from both the left and the right margins, as in this paragraph. The distance that will be indented is controlled by the tab setting on the left edge. The right margin will be indented an equal amount.

Left Indent (→ Indent)

The F4 key controls this procedure. Since the tabs are preset for one-half inch (.5" default), each time you press the Left Indent (F4) key the cursor will jump one-half inch inward (or to the next tab). After you press this key, additional lines will be lined up with the left margin until you press Enter. When Enter is pressed, the margin will return to the regular setting.

■ For practice, clear your screen and memory (do not save) and type the following using the Left Indent (F4) function instead of the regular Tab key. Remember that you must reset the temporary margin each time you press Enter. The code (F4) means to press the Left Indent (F4) key.

(F4)1. (F4)　When the end of this line is reached, the cursor will return to a position immediately under the word When.

(F4)2. (F4)　Each succeeding line will use the new temporary margin until the carriage is returned and the command is cancelled.

When you are finished, your screen should look like the following:

```
1.    When the end of this line is reached, the cursor will
      return to a position immediately under the word When.

2.    Each succeeding line will use the new temporary margin
      until the carriage is returned and the command is
      cancelled.
```

L/R Indent (→ Indent ←)

This function indents the line an equal number of spaces from both the left and right margins. It too is cancelled by the Enter key.

◼ To see how it works, press **Left/Right Indent (Shift-F4)** and type the following: Shift-F4 means to press those keys.

(S-F4)　The quick brown fox jumped over the lazy brown dog that was sleeping in the sun.

2(S-F4,S-F4)　The quick brown fox jumped over the lazy brown dog that was sleeping in the sun.

TIP: Material typed using this command may not appear indented on the screen. Do not be concerned. This is a printer command, and the printer will adjust the lines as they are printed.

To Review

The → Indent key indents the _____________ margin until the _____________ key is pressed.

The → Indent ← key indents the _____________ and _____________ margins an equal number of spaces until the _____________ key is pressed.

■ For some practice with temporary margins using the Left Indent and Left/Right Indent keys, clear your screen, retrieve **Vacation.6** and add the following section just before the text on Sightseeing Tips. Indent each of the numbered items one-half inch from the left margin. Use Left/Right Indent between the number and the item. Note the keys indicated below in number 1, which you can use as a guide.

How to Pack

Using a few simple precautions in the packing can help, too. For example:

(F4)1.   (Shift-F4)Try crushed tissue paper between the folds of skirts.

2.   Place heavier items in the bottom, and top, of your suitcase.

3.   Pack your bag sufficiently full so that the contents will not shake together—yet not too tightly.

4.   Do not put glass items into your bag. Transfer any liquids into plastic containers and wrap them in plastic bags.

■ Resave the file as **VacaIndt.7** and print it.

Summary

Tab	Single indent to next tab
→ Indent	Continuous indent from left margin until Enter key is pressed
→ Indent ←	Continuous indent from both left and right margins until Enter key is pressed

Date and Time

You will recall that you were asked to supply the beginning date and time when you started your work session. WordPerfect has an internal clock in its memory, and it has been keeping track of the current date and time since then. If you wish, WordPerfect will enter the current date and time in your document.

TIP: Some machines enter the date and time automatically when the WordPerfect program is started.

◼ To see how this command works, clear your screen and memory.

◼ Press **Date/Outline** (**Shift-F5**). The following prompt will appear:

```
1 Date Text; 2 Date Code; 3 Date Format; 4 Outline; 5 Para Num; 6 Define: 0
```

In the first three options, Word Perfect is telling you that it can insert either the text of the date, such as February 10, 1989 (option 1) or it can insert the date as a code (option 2). If you choose to enter a code, you will need to supply its format (option 3).

Date Text and Date Codes

You're probably wondering what a date code is. In this case, it means the format for displaying the date, the time or a combination of the two. If you select Date Text, WordPerfect will simply print the date as text. But if this format or arrangement isn't right for your needs, you can specify something different. Before going any further, let's see what will happen when you use Date Text (**1**) and Date Code (**2**).

◼ With the prompt on the screen, select Date Text (**1**). The date contained in your computer's memory should appear at the cursor position.

◼ Move the cursor down the screen several lines and again press **Date/Outline** (**Shift-F5**).

◼ This time choose Date Code (**2**) from the prompt.

The date will appear again. These commands seem to be alike on the screen, but there is more here than meets the eye.

◼ Press **Reveal Codes** (**Alt-F3**) to display the codes for the two versions of the date. You will see that, even though they look alike on the screen, WordPerfect sees them quite differently.

Differences between Date Text and Date Code

The first date is text, just as if you had typed it in. The second appears as a series of numbers (in this case, 3 1, 4). These numbers are a date code, representing a particular way to display the date and time. As it happens, the default date code you see (3 1, 4) displays the date the same way the text option does.

There is another important difference between these two commands. When you use Date Text (**1**), the date does not change; the date you see will be displayed whenever the document is retrieved or printed.

By contrast, the Date Code (**2**) command will display the current or updated date/time whenever the document is retrieved or printed. This could have an impact on which method you choose to display the date. Though the two versions of the date appear the same today, they will not be the same when you retrieve your document tomorrow.

TIP: Date Text (**1**) is best when you want the date on your document to stay the same. Date Code (**2**) is best when you want the date to change each time the document is retrieved or printed.

To Review

To have the date updated each time the document is used, select

______________________ .

To have the date remain the same each time the document is used, select

______________________ .

To change the way the date is displayed, use the ______________ option.

Date/Time Formats

Now let's take a look at the different formats that are available to display the date and time.

■ Press **Reveal Codes (Alt-F3)** and return to your document.

■ Again press Date/Outline (**Shift-F5**).

■ This time, choose Date Format (**3**). The following menu will appear.

```
Date Format

        Character    Meaning
           1         Day of the Month
           2         Month (number)
           3         Month (word)
           4         Year (all four digits)
           5         Year (last two digits)
           6         Day of the Week (word)
           7         Hour (24-hour clock)
           8         Hour (12-hour clock)
           9         Minute
           0         am / pm
           %         Used before a number, will:
                         Pad numbers less than 10 with a leading zero
                         Output only 3 letters for the month or day of the week


        Examples:   3 1, 4       = December 25, 1984
                    %6 %3 1, 4   = Tue Dec 25, 1984
                    %2/%1/5 (6)  = 01/01/85 (Tuesday)
                    8:90         = 10:55am


Date format: 3 1, 4
```

The cursor is blinking below the 3, waiting for your entry to specify how the date/time should be formatted.

If you wanted to use the format Tuesday, March 9, 10 p.m. (with the correct date and time drawn from the computer memory), you would enter 6, 3 1, 8 0 and press Enter. Then when you pressed Date/Outline (Shift-F5) and chose Date Code (2), the date and time would be displayed as you specified.

Also, adding a percent sign (%) before the month and day will cause them to be abbreviated to three letters. For instance: %3.1, 4 (%6.) will display Aug. 3, 1988 (Mon.).

TIP: Notice that you must enter any spacing or punctuation that should be included. You can also add words or other items in the format (up to a maximum of 29 characters). For instance, the format DATE: 2/1/4 would add the word DATE when the function was inserted.

■ Return the screen to the 3 1, 4 defaults before moving ahead.

To Review

Write the date command that would display each of the following:

9:30 a.m.

6-10-88

Mon. August 4

(03/10/1988)

January 3, 1989 -- 8:00 a.m.

Overstrike

There are times when you may need to put two characters into the same space, and WordPerfect makes it easy. Many foreign words such as Olé, manãna, and café require this and it is also a way to create special characters that are not on the keyboard, such as mathematical and chemical symbols.

Creating an Overstrike Character

For some practice, try the following:

- Type the following sentence: **It was a small caf**

- To overstrike the **e** in cafe with an accent ('), press **Format (Shift-F8)**, and select **Other (4)**.

- Then select **Overstrike (5)** and **Create (1)** from the menus as they appear.

- When you see the **[Ovrstk]** marker in the lower left corner of the screen, enter **e** and '. Then press **Enter** and **Exit (F7)**.

TIP: As you enter the characters, both will appear on the screen. However, when you return to the document editing screen, only the second character will display. Both will print and you can see them in Reveal Codes (Alt-F3) if you wish. For instance, Olé would appear as follows: Ol[Ovrstk:e'].

```
Format: Other

       1 - Advance

       2 - Conditional End of Page

       3 - Decimal/Align Character          .
             Thousands' Separator           ,

       4 - Language                         EN

       5 - Overstrike

       6 - Printer Functions

       7 - Underline - Spaces               Yes
                       Tabs                  No




  [Ovrstk]
```

▣ Then save your document as **OverStk.7** and print it.

Editing and Overstrike Character

If you wish to edit or change an overstrike character, you can do so easily by pressing Format (Shift-F8), Other (4), Overstrike (5), and selecting the Edit (2) option. Make whatever changes you need and again press Enter and Exit (F7) to save them.

▣ Try creating an overstrike character for several other words and symbols, such as José, résumé, ø, and ±.

Summary

In summary, to insert an Overstrike:

1. Position the cursor where the character is to appear.

2. Press Format (Shift-F8).

3. Select Other (4)

4. Select Overstrike (5) and Create (1).

5. Enter the characters.

6. Press Enter and Exit (F7).

Compose

Another feature you can use to create special characters is Compose (Ctrl-2). This command can be used to enter digraphs (two characters that represent one sound, such as Æ), diacriticals (a letter and a symbol to assist with pronunciation such as in café), and characters like ð, ⊦, §, ¥, °, ☺, ♪, Σ, from a variety of special character sets. (See listing in the Appendix.)

TIP: The Compose command resembles the Overstrike command in that it can put two characters in the same space. The Overstrike command, however, is limited to characters that are on the keyboard and it does not display both characters on the screen at the same time. The Compose command has a much broader selection of characters and symbols to choose from, including many that are not found on the keyboard. It will also display both characters in the same space on the screen. Not all printers have the fonts and/or the capability to print all of these special characters.

■ To use this command, press **Compose (Ctrl-2)**. (Note that this is the number 2, not F2.) Use the 2 key on the top of your keyboard. Your screen will not change, but WordPerfect has noted that you plan to send it a special command.

■ Type **A** and **E**. Immediately the digraph 146 will appear.

TIP: You can also press **Ctrl-V** to access the Compose command. When you do, the prompt "Key=" will appear in the lower left corner of your screen. The numbers or letters you enter will also appear.

■ Press **Tab** and then again press **Compose (Ctrl-2 or Ctrl-V)**. Type **s** and **s**. The digraph 98 will appear.

TIP: When creating digraphs with Compose, you must use both uppercase or both lowercase letters. You cannot mix them. Also, it does not matter which letter of the pair is entered first.

■ **Tab** again and press **Compose (Ctrl-2)**. Then type " and **o**. The diacritical 148 will appear. **Tab** again, then press Compose (**Ctrl-2**) and type **,** and **c** (,c) to see what will result.

TIP: For a partial listing of the digraphs and diacriticals that can be created, look in the WordPerfect reference manual.

In addition to digraphs and diacriticals, the Compose feature can use several special character sets that are built into the WordPerfect program. These range from languages such as Spanish, French, and German to Japanese, Hebrew, Greek, and Russian. They also include mathematical symbols, icons, and a variety of other figures that can be incorporated into your documents.

TIP: Not all printers can print all characters, so you will need to learn which characters in each of the 12 sets the printer you are using will print. Even though you may be able to see some characters on the screen, the printer may not be able to print them on the page.

■ To see a listing of the special characters available for your printer, move to Doc 2 with **Switch (Shift-F3)**.

■ Remove your data disk from drive B and insert the disk labelled Conversion.

TIP: If you are using a hard drive, you will not need to change disks. The contents of the Conversion disk should already have been copied into the same directory as your WordPerfect files.

■ The press **List Files (F5)** to see the files on this disk. Move the highlighter to and Retrieve (**1**) the CHARACTR.DOC file from the Conversion disk.

■ Then use **PgDn** or **Screen Dn** to scan through the list. The small black square beside some of the options means that it is not available for the printer currently defined.

TIP: If you wish, you can print a copy of the CHARACTR.DOC file for reference by selecting print (**4**) on the List Files menu.

Notice the number beside each option. To call up any of the available symbols, you should first press Compose (Ctrl-2). Then type the number as you see it—including the first number (which represents the character set), a comma, and the second number (which is the particular symbol within the character set). (See the Appendix for a listing of the character sets together with the number that accesses them.)

For practice, let's use character set 4 to do the following:

■ **Switch (Shift-F3)** back to Doc 1. Press **Compose (Ctrl-2)**. Then type **4,5** and press **Enter**. The symbol ¶ will appear at the cursor.

■ Press **Tab** to move the cursor, then again press **Compose (Ctrl-2)** and enter **4,1**. Immediately an **o** will appear on the screen.

■ Move back to Doc 2 and scan over the symbols available. You can see many that will be useful to you. Using Doc 2 for reference and Doc 1 to enter characters, experiment a little with several of them until you feel comfortable with this command.

TIP: You can also use the CHARMAP.TST file on the Conversion disk to see which characters are available on your printer. To use this file, make the printer you are checking the active one. Then retrieve the CHARMAP.TST file to see which characters are supported. If you have more than one font, you will need to check each font individually. If you wish, you can make a printout of these files also to use for reference.

☐ When you are finished, remove the Conversion disk and replace your data disk in drive B. Then save your document as **Compose.7** and print it to see which characters your printer will produce.

To Review:

What are digraphs and diacriticals?

What should you enter to insert character 14 from set 6.

Drawing Lines

Another nifty thing that WordPerfect will do is draw lines. You can use this to draw boxes, graphs, pictures, or whatever suits you—such as the following:

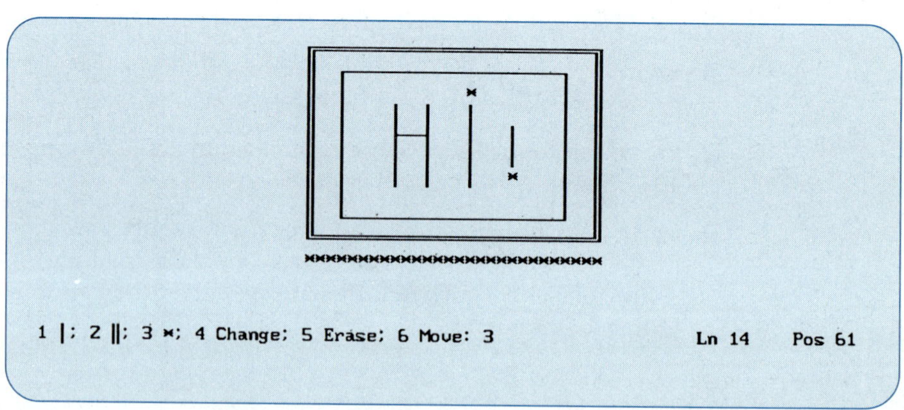

TIP: This feature is very handy for freehand items. The graphics command, which you will learn about later, is more limited in the shape and diversity of forms that can be produced.

- To activate this command, press **Screen (Ctrl-F3)**.

- When the following menu appears, choose Line Draw (**2**).

```
0 Rewrite; 1 Window; 2 Line Draw: 0
```

A second menu will appear.

```
1 |; 2 ||; 3 *; 4 Change; 5 Erase; 6 Move: 1                    Ln 1" Pos 1"
```

As you can see, you have the choices of three different line styles, changing to something that is not shown, erasing, or moving the cursor without drawing a line.

- For now, choose **Move (1)**.

- Then use the **Arrow Keys** to move the cursor a little.

    As you do, a line is created. You can go up, down, and across either left or right. Notice that WordPerfect inserts the corners when you change direction or intersect another line.

- Then select **Erase (5)** and delete part of a line.

- Now select **Move (6)** and move the cursor to a clear part of the screen.

- Then again press **1** and draw more of a line.

- To see what choices you have with the **Change** option, press **4** to get the following menu:

```
1 ▒; 2 ▓; 3 █; 4 ▌; 5 ▪; 6 |; 7 |; 8 ■; 9 Other: 0
```

◼ Wow! Look at all those line styles. Try a few for fun to see how they work.

◼ To see what WordPerfect is doing behind the scenes, **Exit (F7)** the Line Draw menu. Then press **Reveal Codes (Alt-F3)** and take a look. Notice, that among other things, [HRt] commands and spaces have been inserted in various places. Leave Reveal Codes with Alt-F3.

◼ Again bring up the Line Draw menu with **Screen (Ctrl-F3)**, Line Draw **(2)**, Change **(4)**. From this menu, choose Other **(9)** to see what else WordPerfect can do, and you will get the following menu:

```
Solid character:
```

What does that mean? Well, it means that you can enter any key from the keyboard, and WordPerfect will use that to draw lines with. You could use $, %, or even + for a fancy effect. Try it out.

◼ Type a **$**. Notice that the first menu reappears, but option 3 is now the $.

◼ Press **3** and then move the cursor.

Esc: You can even use the Esc and cursor arrow keys with this command. To see how it works, do the following:

◼ Press **Esc**. When the prompt **Repeat Value = 8** appears, press the **Right Arrow** key.

◼ Press **Esc** again. This time enter **16**, then press the **Down Arrow** key.

◼ Experiment with different Esc values and arrow keys.

Just think of the possibilities for designs, posters, and you name it.

◼ To end this command, all you need to do is press either **Cancel (F1)** or **Exit (F7)**.

Using some of the options on the Change menu, you can create borders and designs for a wide variety of uses. You can even draw pictures by combining various shadings.

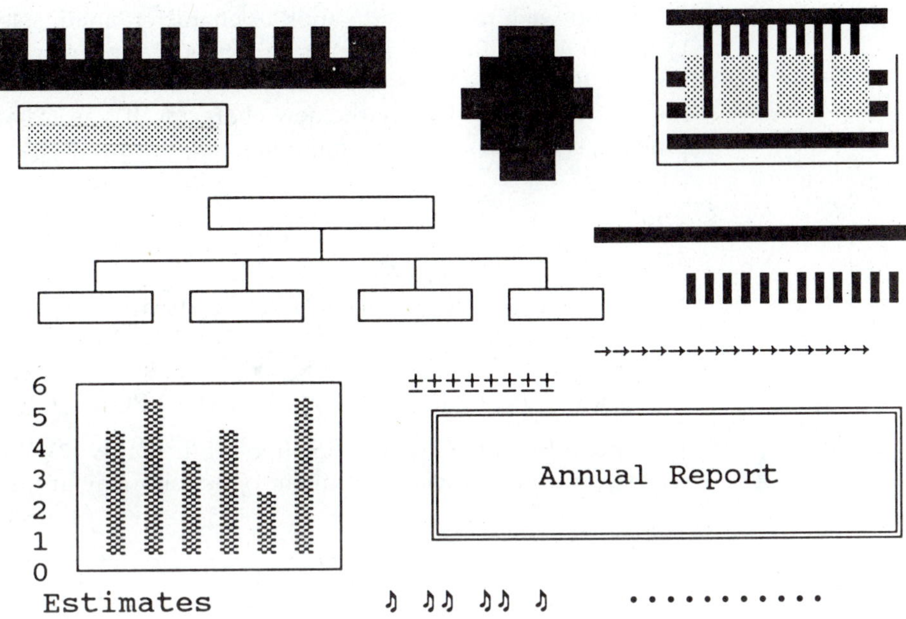

Using ASCII and Compose characters

You can also use the ASCII character set as well as any of the characters available with the Compose command. With these, you have access to a wide variety of symbols and characters.

- ◘ To see how these work, press **Screen** (**Ctrl-F3**), and select Line Draw (**2**).

- ◘ Then select **C**hange (**4**), and **O**ther (**9**).

  When the **Solid Character:** prompt appears, you can enter a Compose character using Ctrl-2 and the character set number. (Remember to use the keys on the top row enter ASCII character numbers.) For practice, let's add a happy face. That number is 5,7.

- ◘ With the Solid Character: prompt showing at the lower left corner of the screen, press **Ctrl-2**. Then enter **5,7**.

  Nothing will display on the screen, but do not be concerned. WordPerfect is recording your command. When you press Enter and return to the menu, notice that option 3 now shows a happy face.

- ◘ Select **3** and press any of the **arrow keys**. The happy face character will appear on your screen.

TIP: If you wish to vary the design, you can add spaces or delete parts of any of the lines after you exit the line draw command.

If you wish to change to another character, again select **Change (4)** and **Other (9)**. When the Solid Character: prompt appears, press Ctrl-2 and enter the ASCII or character set number for the symbol you want. Select 3 and use the Arrow keys to display the new character. It's as easy as that. For a little practice, see what any of the following will produce:

5,0	5,1	5,2	5,3	6,21	6,22	6,23	6,24	6,27	6,28
6,29	6,30	6,96	4,0	4,1	6,1	6,2	6,3	5,10	7,6
7,9	8,2	8,45	10,12	11,3	11,4	1,37	1,46		

Now that you've gotten a feel for how to draw lines, let's try something.

◘ Clear your screen.

◘ Come down several lines and type **FINAL REPORT** in the middle of a line.

◘ Then press **Screen (Ctrl-F3)** and choose Line Draw (2). Using any of the line styles you wish, draw a box similar to the following around the words.

```
┌──────────────────┐
│                  │
│   FINAL REPORT   │
│                  │
└──────────────────┘
```

TIP: You will find it easier to draw lines or boxes around text if you will enter the text first, then draw the lines. You may also want to use Typeover mode to keep things from moving when the lines are added.

◘ Save your document as **LineBox.7** and print it.

Summary

In summary, to Draw Lines:

a. Position the cursor where you want to begin.

b. Choose Screen (Ctrl-F3).

c. Choose Line Draw (2).

d. Choose line style with 1, 2, 3, or 4.

e. Move the cursor with arrow keys.

f. Use Move (6), Erase (5), or other selections as needed.

g. Press Cancel (F1) or Exit (F7) to end.

Advance

There are times when you may want text to be printed at a specific place on the page or somewhere other than the regular line. The Advance feature will allow you to designate that the text following it is to be printed a certain distance above, below, or to the left or right of the current cursor position. You can also advance to a specific line on the page or to a column. Then, to return to the original line, you must enter a second advance command in the opposite direction.

TIP: Since not all printers are capable of printing above and below the line, this feature may not work in all situations.

Advance Up/Down

This command is used to position characters above or below the line the cursor is currently on. To activate it, you must turn the command on and specify the distance the text that follows is to be advanced up or down, enter the text, then enter another advance command in the opposite direction to return to the original line.

For some practice, do the following:

▣ Start with a clear screen and press **Enter** twice to put the cursor on line 3 or 1.3" from the top of the page.

▣ Enter the following text: **Now is the time**

▣ Press **Format (Shift-F8)**. Choose **Other (4)** and **Advance (1)** from the menus as they appear. The following will display across the bottom of the screen.

```
Advance: 1 Up; 2 Down; 3 Line; 4 Left; 5 Right; 6 Position: 0
```

▣ Select **Up (1)**. Immediately the following will appear:

```
Adv. up: 0''
```

WordPerfect is asking how far it should advance the text that follows.

- Type **.25** to indicate one-quarter of an inch above the current line. Then press **Enter** and **Exit** (**F7**).

- Notice that the cursor did not move on the screen, but the new position is indicated on the status line. Check Reveal Codes (**Alt-F3**) to see the command that has been inserted.

TIP: The fact that the cursor does not move on the screen makes this feature a good way to enter items that are widely spaced when printed without creating a great deal of blank space on the screen.

- Then type the following: **for all good men**

- Again press **Format** (**Shift-F8**), choose **Other** (**4**) and **Advance** (**1**).

- This time, select **Down** (**2**) and enter **.25** to return to the original line. Press **Enter** and **Exit** (**F7**).

- Then type **to come to.**

- Again select **Format** (**Shift-F8**), **Other** (**4**), and **Advance** (**1**). Select **Up** (**1**) again and enter **.10**. Then press **Enter** and **Exit** (**F7**).

- Type **the aid of.**

- Select **Format** (**Shift-F8**), **Other** (**4**), and **Advance** (**1**) once more, Choose **Down** (**2**) and enter **.30**. Leave the menu with **Enter** and **Exit** (**F7**).

- Type **their country.**

When you are finished, save it as **AdvUp.7** and print it. The printout should look something like the following:

```
                                                    the aid of
    Now is the time                    to come to
                  for all good men                          their
    country.
```

TIP: One thing you will need to be aware of, particularly when using single spacing, is that characters or words that are printed in the advance up/down positions may print over those above or below them on the normal line.

Advance Left/Right

The Advance Left and Advance Right commands work very much like the Advance Up/Down commands. To use them, select Format (Shift-F8), Other (4), Advance (1), and Left (4) or Right (5). Enter the distance from the cursor you want the text printed, and press Enter and Exit (F7). Type in the text. Then enter a second command to return the cursor to the original line or position it somewhere else on the page.

Advance Line

The Advance Line command can be used to advance to a specified line on the page without inserting multiple hard returns. It is very useful for positioning text at an exact position on the page.

TIP: The Advance Up/Down and Left/Right commands move relative to the cursor position when they are entered, and the Advance Line and Advance Column commands measure from the top of the page, regardless of where the cursor is located.

■ For some practice with this command, press **Enter** five times to move the cursor down the page.

TIP: Before moving, note the current position of the cursor in case you want to return to the same line later.

■ Then press **Format (Shift-F8)**, **Other (4)**, **Advance (1)** and then **Line (3)**. The following will appear: (Note: The number displayed may vary.)

```
Adv. to line 2.34"
```

■ Type **4.25**, which indicates that you would like the cursor to move to the position on the paper that is 4 $1/4$ inches from the top. Press **Enter** and **Exit** (**F7**).

■ Then type **This is printed on line 4.25.**

■ Save the document as **AdvLine.7** and print it. You can now enter another command or return the cursor to its original position.

TIP: | This command could be used to fill in forms or to put addresses on envelopes beginning on a certain line.

Advance Position

The advance position command is used to move between and among columns. It works much like Advance Line in that it moves the cursor to an absolute position on the page. Once the cursor is moved, you must enter a second command indicating the original line value to return to the original place.

◼ Now type any sentence. Use **Adv Up** and **Adv Dn** for a part of it. Also try **Adv Ln** and specify a line that is one and a half inch or 10 lines down from where you currently are on the page. Watch the status line to see how it changes.

To Review

List the ways you can advance the cursor.

How can you turn the Advance commands off?

Summary

In summary, to use Advance:

1. Position the cursor.

2. Press Format (Shift-F8).

3. Select Other (4) and Advance (1).

4. Select Up (1), Down (2), Line (3), Left (4), Right (5), or Position (6).

5. Enter the distance to be advanced.

6. Type the text.

7. Turn Advance off by entering another command to return to the original line or some other place on the page.

Hard Spaces, Hyphens, and Dashes

When WordPerfect right-justifies lines with word wrap and manual hyphenation, some words that shouldn't be divided sometimes get split. Words that contain hyphens, like self-evident, can also run into trouble with word wrap.

To solve these problems, you can use what is called a hard or required character—one you insert with a special key or command, and that will always be remembered and honored by WordPerfect.

Of the several hard commands that you can enter, the most commonly used are those for the hard space, hard hyphen and hard page.

Entering Hard Commands

You have already learned how to enter Hard Page commands with Ctrl-Enter. The Hard Space and Hard Hyphen commands tell WordPerfect to treat the words joined by the hard space/hyphen as a unit and not to separate them.

Hard Space

The Hard Space command (Home, Space Bar) tells WordPerfect to retain the space exactly as you type it. This is important when you are typing things like mathematical formulas. For instance: $M + P / R = SB$. When the text is adjusted by the printer to right-justify the lines, this formula will always appear with precisely the spaces you entered between the letters and symbols. Also, the entire formula will be treated as one word; it will not be split if it should occur at the end of a line.

Hard Hyphen (and Dash)

When you use words that contain hyphens—such as mother-in-law or self-defense—you want to make sure that the hyphen won't be dropped or the two parts of the word separated. When you use a dash in a sentence—like this—you want to insure that it and the words on either side of it are treated as a unit. In these circumstances, you should use Home, Hyphen.

■ For practice, type the following lines using the Hard Hyphen and Hard Space commands:

<table>
<tr><td>first-class,</td><td>air-conditioning,</td><td>up-to-date,</td><td>self-esteem</td></tr>
<tr><td>I = P * R * T</td><td>A - L = OE</td><td>529-68-8845</td><td>18A-61-B4</td></tr>
</table>

A dash is handled the same way as a hard hyphen except that you press the hyphen key twice—Home, Hyphen, Home, Hyphen. (Remember that a dash used in a sentence should not have a space on either side of it.)

Soft Hyphen

The soft hyphen (Ctrl-Hyphen) is a way of controlling where you want an end-of-line hyphen to appear if the word falls at the end of a line. If the word does not appear at the end of a line, the hyphen will be ignored and will not appear in the text. You may want to use this command when Hyphenation is Off, and you need to divide a word at the end of a line to tighten up the spacing.

To Review

Write in the keys you should press to insert each of the following:

Hard Space: _______________________________

Hard Page: _______________________________

Hard Hyphen: _______________________________

Dash: _______________________________

Soft Hyphen: _______________________________

Underlining Tabs and Spaces

When you have used the underline feature up to this point, the text and spaces between words have been underlined. This is the default. However, Word-Perfect will also allow you to omit the underlining of spaces between words and/or underline the spaces skipped over by tabs as well.

■ To see the difference between these two settings, clear your screen and turn **Underline (F8)** On. Then press **Tab** twice and type the following sentence, using the defaults.

This example shows how the underline command will underline between words but not under tabs.

■ Then press **Tab** twice more and turn **Underline (F8)** Off.

■ Now, press **Enter** two or three times to move the cursor down the page a little. Then press **Format (Shift-F8)** to bring up the Format menu.

■ Select **Other (4)** and Underline Spaces/Tabs **(7)**.

  This option will allow you to specify whether spaces between words are underlined and/or whether the spaces skipped over by tabs displays an underline when underlining is turned On.

■ Reverse the settings by typing **N**(o) beside Spaces and **Y**(es) beside Tabs. Press **Exit (F7)** to return to the screen.

■ Turn **Underline (F8)** On. Then press **Tab** twice and type the following sentence.

This example shows how the underline command will underline between tabs but not between spaces.

■ Press **Tab** twice more, then turn **Underline (F8)** Off.

■ Save your document as **TabUnder.7** and print it.

  Notice the difference between the sentences, particularly where the tabs are shown at the beginning and end of each line. Your first sentence should have underlining beginning with the first word and ending with the last word of the sentence. Your second sentence should have an underline extending from the left margin to two tabs stops past the end of the sentence. There should also be no underlining of the spaces between words similar to the following:

This example shows how the underline command will underline between words but not under tabs.

This example shows how the underline command will underline between tabs but not between spaces.

TIP: Underlining under tabs is a quick and easy way to put a line across the page of a document. Simply select tab underline, turn Underline (F8) on, and TAB across your page. When the document is printed, you will have a single line across the page. The Tab underline is also handy for creating a line for totals in financial statements and other tabulated items.

To Review

What is the default for underline style?

Summary

To change underline styles:

1. Position the cursor.

2. Press Format (Shift-F8).

3. Select Other (4), and Underline Style (7).

4. Answer Y(es) or N(o) as appropriate.

5. Press Enter and Exit (F7).

6. Type the text.

7. Save and print.

8. Change style as needed.

Activities

You should have completed the following.

VacaIndt.7	*Vacation.6 with Indented margins added*
Ovrstk.7	*Text with overstrike characters*
Compose.7	*Various compose characters*
LineBox.7	*Line draw box with FINAL REPORT*
AdvUp.7	*Sentence with Advance up and down*
AdvLine.7	*Your name printed on line 4.25*
TabUnder.7	*Underlined tabs*

Chapter Review

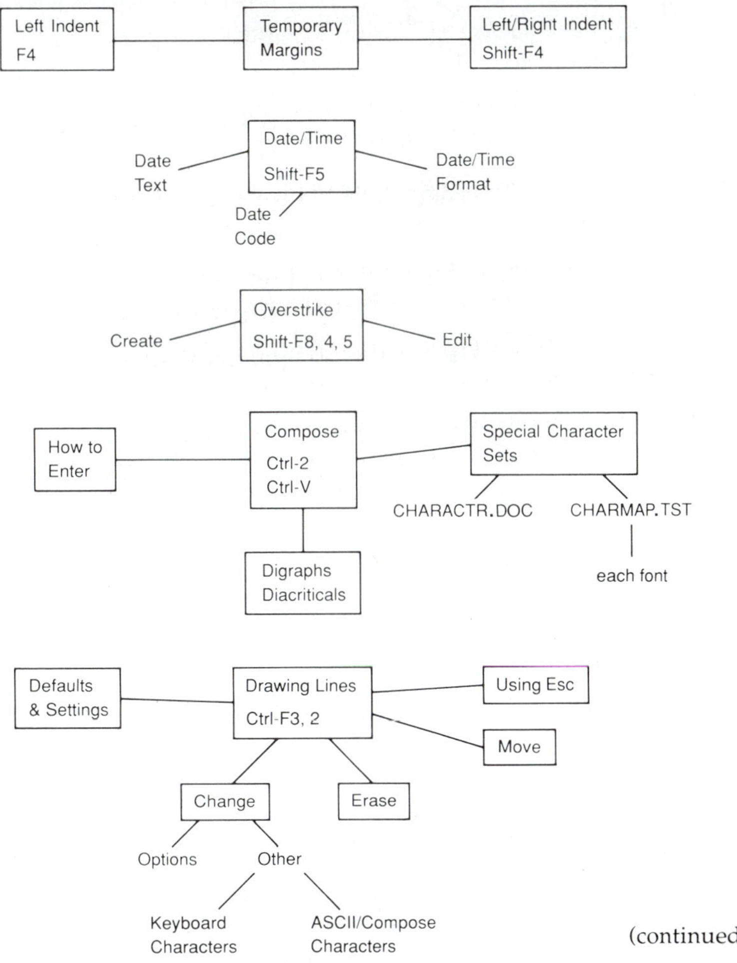

(continued)

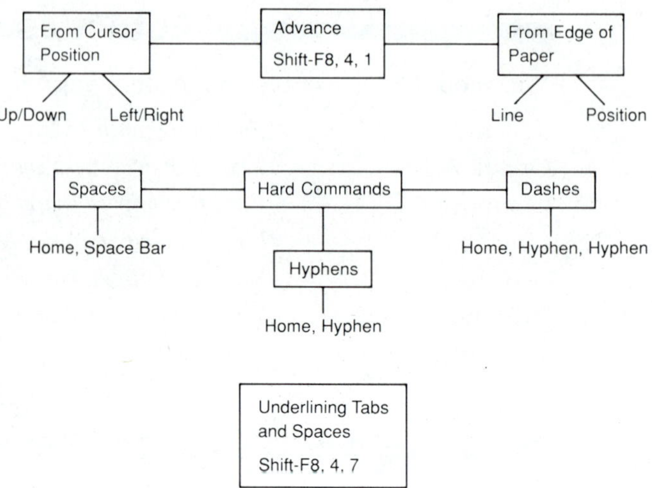

Self-Check Quiz 7

1. What are the differences in function among the Tab, Left Indent, and Left/Right Indent keys?

2. What key should you press to end Left Indent and Left/Right Indent and return to the original margin?

3. When using the Indent commands, what determines how far the left and right margins will be indented?

4. How do the Date Text and Date Code options on the Date command differ?

5. When defining date format, what happens when the percent sign (%) is inserted before the month or day?

6. If you wish to have the date updated each time your document is retrieved, which command should you use?

7. How does WordPerfect handle characters marked for overstrike?

8. What are the major differences between overstrike and Compose?

9. What is contained in the CHARACTR.DOC file?

10. Identify what the number 6,43 means when used with the Compose command.

11. How are the Advance Up/Down, Left/Right commands affected by the cursor position?

12. What must you do to turn the Advance commands off?

13. What is the starting point for determining distance when using the Advance Line command?

14. How are corners inserted with the Line Draw feature?

15. What keys can you press to Exit Line Draw?

16. How can you set a soft hyphen?

17. What is the difference between WordPerfect's reactions to a Hard and a Soft hyphen, space, or page?

18. How should a dash be typed?

19. What happens when the Underline Tabs command is set to Yes?

Extra Practice

For extra practice on the material covered in Chapter 7, do the following:

a. Enter the following text using temporary margin and date commands as indicated:

MEMORANDUM

TO: Faculty and Staff

FROM: Registration Office

DATE: (Date Code)

SUBJECT: New Student Enrollment Notes

As new students are enrolled for the coming session, please be sure they do the following:

1. Fill out the new student information sheet, completely listing both local and home address and phone numbers and return it to the Registration Office. Be sure this form contains today's date, which is (Date code to match sample: Mon. July 3, 1989).

2. Obtain a parking permit from the Campus Security office and affix it to the rear window of their car in the lower left corner.

3. Make an appointment to see their departmental counselor within one week to review their schedule and discuss any questions or concerns they may have.

4. Visit the bookstore, student center, and activities complex to become acquainted with the location and facilities available in each. Copies of a self-guide map are available in the lobby.

b. When you are finished, save your document as **Pract7a** and print it.

c. Use the line draw and advance up/down features to design an invitation to the fall social. It will be held Friday, September 24, at 6 p.m. and include a barbecue and dance. All students are invited. Save your document as **Practb**, and print a copy.

d. For additional practice with any of these commands, type some paragraphs from this text, including Dating Summary, Tip, and To Review sections. You can also enter text or notes from your schoolbooks or other sources if you like.

8

Doing File Management and DOS Functions with List Files and Shell Commands

Up to this point, you have been learning new ways to handle the text of your document. This chapter will focus on a different aspect of WordPerfect: how to perform special functions with the system of your machine using List Files commands. You will also learn how to exit to the DOS system for some commands and how to insert and use passwords to limit the access to your files.

When you are finished, you will be able to:

- use List Files commands to retrieve, rename, delete, print, and copy files.

- search your files from List Files in a variety of ways.

- look into files, do name searches, and change directories with List Files commands.

- save and retrieve files in DOS/ASCII format.

- save and retrieve locked files using passwords.

- convert WordPerfect 5.0 files into 4.2 files for use with that system.
- use Shell to go to the DOS system from within WordPerfect.

List Files

To begin, you will use the List Files command, which is located on the F5 key.

 The instructions in this section assume that the B drive is the active drive. If you are using a hard disk or network, the Drive you are working from will be shown instead of B and you will need to substitute the appropriate drive letter and/or path in place of the B. When that is done, the instructions will work as indicated.

- Press **List Files** (**F5**). You will see the following message:

```
Dir B:\*.*                                          (Type = to change default Dir)
```

This message tells you that you can call up a complete directory (list of files) of the contents of the disk in the default, or active, drive, (which in this case is B), and that if you want to change the default you should press the = (equal) key. Before moving ahead, let's try changing the default drive.

 If you simply enter the letter of a drive, without the = (equal) sign, the directory of that drive will list but the default will not be changed.

Changing the Default Drive

This command is used when you are in WordPerfect and want to change the default, or make another drive the active one. It is important to know which drive is serving as the default since WordPerfect will store to, retrieve from, and use the default drive for its functions unless it is told otherwise.

TIP: Under most circumstances, you will want someplace other than where your WordPerfect program is stored to be the default so that your working files will not be stored on the disk or directory that contains the WordPerfect program.

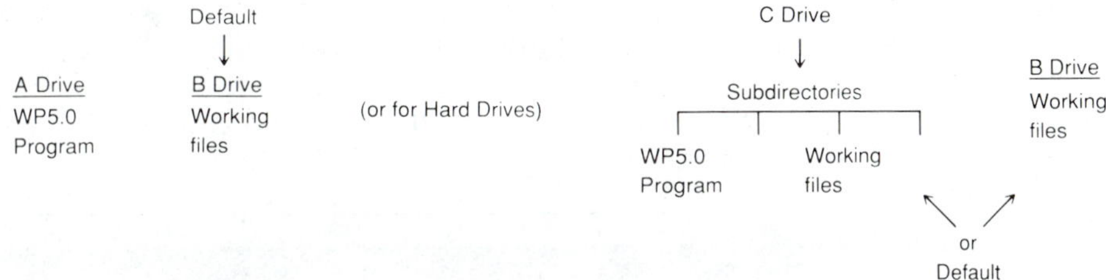

Assuming that B is the default, your working files should be stored on B. The WordPerfect program will probably be on a disk in the A drive, and you should not store files on the disk that contains the WordPerfect program. (If you are using a hard disk, the WordPerfect program will probably be in a subdirectory on the C Drive, instead of the A Drive, with your working files stored on B or another subdirectory in the C Drive. If that is the case, substitute C:\ and the subdirectory name for A and B in the following instructions.)

▣ To change the default drive, type = and the following message will appear:

```
New directory = B:\*.*
```

▣ Type **A:** and press **Enter**.

The indicated directory has now changed to A. Immediately WordPerfect will display a complete listing of the files on the disk in the A drive. Notice that none of your working files are stored on this disk.

▣ Press the **Space Bar** or **Exit** (**F7**) to return to the screen.

▣ Change the default drive back to B so you won't have problems later when you save your documents. To do so, press **List Files** (**F5**) again, and once more press =. Then type **B:** and press **Enter**.

▣ Check to be sure it worked by bringing up **List Files** (**F5**) once more. The message should read **Dir B:*.*** once again.

TIP: If you omit the = and type only B:\, the directory would be changed temporarily, and the next time you press List Files (F5) WordPerfect would go back to the original directory/drive. If you want the change to be permanent, you must type = first then, B:\. When you use List Files (F5) again, WordPerfect will use the new directory.

Directory

Now let's move on.

◼ With the B drive as the default, press **List Files (F5)** and then **Enter**. You should now have a screen full of files, showing a great deal of information about the contents of your disk resembling the following:

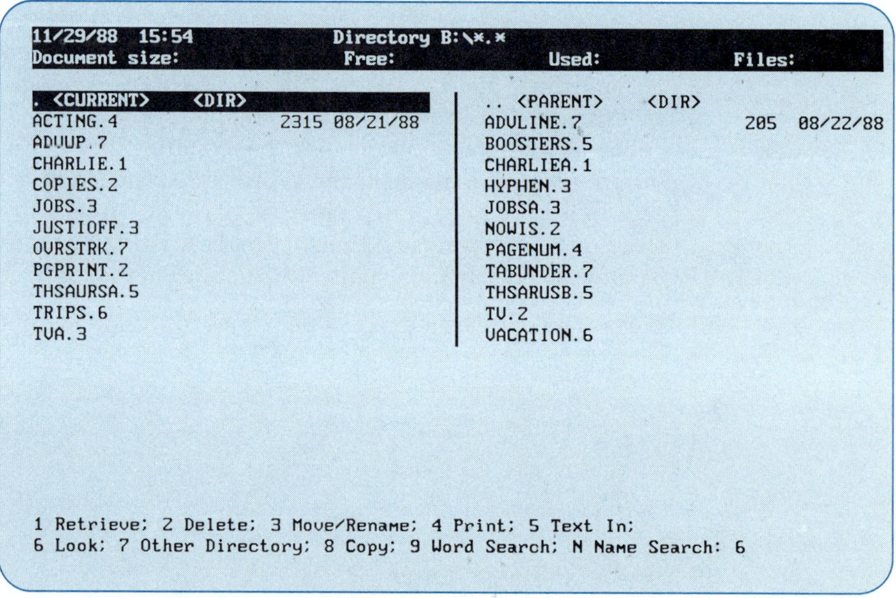

You will notice that .<CURRENT><DIR> is highlighted in reverse video. Use the arrow keys to move the highlighting through the filenames until the file you wish to work with is highlighted. Then choose one of the options at the bottom and press the corresponding number. The program will perform the function you select. Using this menu, you can retrieve text, delete files, rename files, print, import text from other programs, look at a file, change the directory (if you are using a hard disk or drive), copy a file, and search files for a specified word, term or name.

Checking Document Size and Available Disk Space

As you can see, you can learn many things from this menu. If you have a question about the size of the document you are working on, the number beside Document Size will tell you. If you suspect that your disk is getting full and may not have room for your current document, you can check Free Disk Space to see how much room is left. Compare that number to the size of your document before trying to save; otherwise you will risk losing what you have entered. You can also find out the date and time when each of the listed files was saved (if the correct date and time were entered when the machine was turned on). And you can tell the name, size, and type of each file.

To Review

List at least seven items of information you could obtain from the List Files directory.

Retrieving Files from List Files

You have already worked with this command, so you know that you need only move the highlighted area to the filename of the file you want and press **Retrieve (1)** and **Y**(es) to display it on your screen.

TIP: If you already have a document on the screen and attempt to retrieve a file this way, you will see the prompt "Retrieve into current document (Y/N) No". This is a reminder that what you retrieve will be added to the document on the screen at the cursor position.

Name Search

You can also do what is called a Name Search from the List Files menu. If you have many files, this is a quick way to find the one you want. Let's see how it works.

Suppose you would like to retrieve **JobsA.3**.

TIP: It is important to remember that you **must** begin with a clear screen and memory (use Exit/F7) before retrieving files this way to avoid mixing or doubling documents.

■ With the List Files directory on your screen, press **N** to select the Name Search option. Immediately the following prompt will appear:

> (Name Search: Enter or arrows to Exit)

■ Simply type the name of the file **JobsA.3**.

When you begin to type, the highlighter will jump to the first file that matches what you are entering. As soon as WordPerfect can tell exactly which file you want, the highlighter will move to and remain on that filename.

■ You must press **Enter** or an **Arrow Key** to return the menu to the bottom of the screen.

■ Then press **Retrieve (1)** and **Y** to retrieve the highlighted file.

■ Once again, clear your screen with **Exit (F7)** before moving ahead.

Changing to Another Disk Drive or Directory

There are two ways to change to another disk drive, and/or another directory on the same or a different disk drive. You have already used the first way—pressing List Files and keying in a different drive.

You also have a second option: you can use **Other Directory (7)**, to do the same thing.

■ With the directory listing displayed on your screen (press **List Files** and **Enter**) choose **Other Directory (7)**. The following message will appear:

> New directory = B:*.*

■ Type **A:** and press **Enter** twice.

In a second or two, The directory of the **A** Drive will replace the display of the B Drive on your screen.

TIP: If you are using a hard disk, which is usually designated as the C Drive, and the files are segregated by directory, you can also change directories on the C Drive by typing **C:\(directory name)** and pressing **Enter** twice.

- Once you have looked over the new directory, return to the B (or C) Drive and let's move ahead.

TIP: You can also highlight .<CURRENT> <DIR> and press Enter to activate the directory prompt at the bottom of the screen.

Printing From List Files

You may recall that you can print from the List Files screen by highlighting the file you wish to print, checking the printer and pressing **Print (4)**. It's as easy as that. Your printer will do the rest.

Renaming a File

Another trick you can do from the List Files menu is renaming files. Before using this command, you will need to create a small file to work with.

- First **Exit (F7)** to clear the screen. (You don't need to save **JobsA.3**, since a copy of it is already saved on the disk.

- Now type the sentence **This is file one.** and save it under the name **FileA.8**, using **Exit (F7)** to clear the screen.

- Then press **List Files (F5)** and **Enter** to bring up the Directory.

- Move the highlighter to **File A.8.**

- Choose the **Move/Rename (3)** option. The following prompt will appear:

```
New name: B:\FileA.8
```

WordPerfect already knows the name of the file you want to rename. You only need to type in the name you wish to change to.

- Type in **DocA.8** and press the **Enter** key.

The red disk-drive light will go on, and the name will be changed before your eyes. Like magic!

Deleting a File

You can also delete files from the Directory. For practice, let's delete the file you just created and renamed.

▪ With the Directory on the screen, move the highlighted area to DocA.8.

▪ Choose Delete (**2**).

WordPerfect will ask you to confirm that you wish to delete this file by displaying the following message:

```
Delete B:\DOCA.8? (Y/N) No
```

▪ Press the **Y** key. The red disk-drive light will go on. The filename you are deleting will disappear from the Directory, and the file will be gone from your disk.

TIP: As you work through this text, you are saving files as you complete exercises. One point to keep in mind is that DOS allows you to save only 112 files per disk. When this limit is reached, you will not be allowed to save any more files to that disk even if there is room on the disk to accept them. When the disk is full or has reached the maximum of 112 files, you will see an error message in the lower left corner of the screen indicating that the disk is full. When this happens, either use another disk or delete some of the existing files to make room for new ones on the present disk.

A WORD OF CAUTION: Deletion is permanent. You cannot recall these files once they have been erased. Be careful that you do not delete files you may want to use again.

To Review

Using List Files, how can you rename and/or delete files?

1. ____

2. ____

Text-in

This option allows you to import DOS and other files from other programs, such as Lotus 1-2-3, dBase, or another word processor, for use in WordPerfect. Since you do not have any such files on your disk, you cannot practice this command. You should simply be aware that this option is available, and review the procedures in your WordPerfect manual when and if you need to import files of this kind.

Look

If you've forgotten the name of the file you are searching for, or can't remember what is stored in a given file, you may want to glance into a file to see if it is the one you are looking for. **Look (6)**, allows you to do so.

◼ To see how this command works, activate the **List Files (F5)** command and display the list of your files on the screen.

◼ Highlight the file you wish to see.

◼ Select Look **(6)**.

TIP: Since 6 is the default for this menu, you can just press Enter to activate the Look command.

The first part of the document will immediately appear, together with a message across the top of the screen indicating the filename and file size.

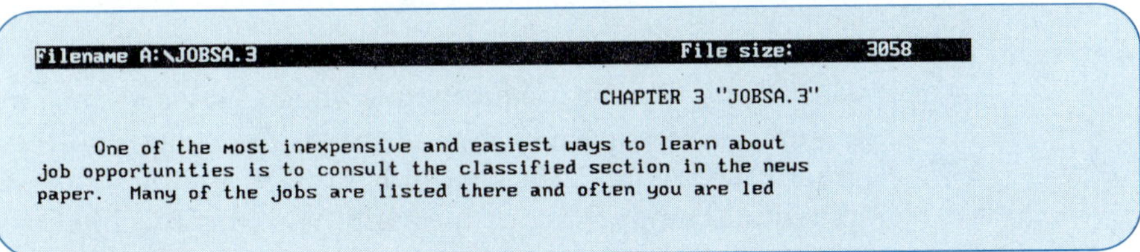

This text is not displayed in WordPerfect format. This means that you cannot edit or change the text in any way; you can only look at it. It also may not show formatting commands you have entered. You can, however, scroll downward through the text, using the Down Arrow, PgDn, or Screen Down keys. Pressing Exit, Enter or the Space Bar will return you to the List Files screen. If you did want to edit or change this file, you would need to retrieve it using option 1. Then you could revise it as you wished.

Copy

This command will allow you to:

1. make additional copies of a file on the same disk.

2. transfer copies of a file to another disk or drive.

3. change the name and/or transfer a copy of a file to another disk or drive.

To see how it works, do the following:

◻ Bring the List Files directory to the screen and highlight **Nowis.2**.

◻ Press **Copy (8)** and the following prompt will appear:

```
Copy this file to:
```

◻ Type in **NowCopy.8** and press **Enter**. You will see the red disk-drive light go on and off as the copy is being made.

When you retrieve the List Files directory again, you will see that the filename NowCopy.8 has been added.

◻ To see what this new file contains, press **Look (6)** to see into it. You will see that it is a duplicate of the original file. You can now retrieve, print, or edit this new file just like any of the others you have created.

TIP: If you wanted to transfer a copy of this file to a disk in the A Drive, you would select **Copy (8)**, and when the message **Copy To:** appeared you would type **A:Nowis.8**. If you were using a hard disk, you would type C:\Nowis.8. In either case, WordPerfect would transfer a copy of the file to the disk you specify and name the copy Nowis.8. You can also change the name of the copy when you transfer it to another disk, simply by typing in the new name you wish to use such as A:\Newname.

In sum, WordPerfect will make a copy of whatever file you have highlighted, and put it on whichever disk/drive you want, under whatever name you specify. You can't ask for much more than that.

A WORD OF CAUTION: Because this command allows you to make copies in a variety of ways, it is easy to lose track of which file is where, and what a given file is called. You can also end up with multiple copies of the same file under different names and on several disks. This wastes disk space and can be very confusing. Unless you have a reason to keep more than one copy of a file (or a backup), be sure to delete duplicates and/or keep a record of the copies you make and what they are named.

Marking Files

Another handy command available but not shown in the List Files menu is Mark Files. This is useful when you want to perform the same operation, such as printing, on several files, one after the other.

TIP: Some commands change when files are marked. For instance, the Move/Rename command renames files when no files are marked. If a file is marked, the command moves the marked files.

To see how this command works, try the following:

◻ Position the highlighter over the filename **CharlieA.1**.

◻ Type an asterisk (*), by holding down the Shift key and pressing the 8 key along the top of your keyboard. A bolded asterisk will appear to the right of the file size.

◻ Move the highlighter to the filename **Nowis.2** and again type an asterisk.

◻ Move the highlighter to the filename **NowCopy.8** and type another asterisk.

You should now have three files marked with an asterisk beside the filename. Now, let's say that you don't want the **NowCopy.8** file marked after all. To remove the asterisk:

◻ Move the highlighter to the filename **NowCopy.8** and type an asterisk again. That asterisk beside the filename will disappear.

Now let's print the remaining two marked files.

◻ Select **Print** (**4**). The following message will appear at the bottom left-hand side of your screen:

```
Print marked files? (Y/N) No
```

◻ Type **Y** and WordPerfect will print both files, one after the other.

TIP: You can also mark files this way for copying or for deletion from your disk.

◼ To avoid carrying this command forward to the next instruction, unmark any files marked with an asterisk in the List Files menu.

TIP: You can mark or unmark all files at once by pressing Alt-F5 or Home-*. In addition, all marks will automatically be deleted when you exit List Files.

Word Search

The Word Search command allows you to search through all the files on the disk for a particular word or pattern of words. If you should want to find the file or files that contain a particular word or name, you could use this command to locate it.

To see how this command works, suppose that you couldn't remember which files contained the material about Charlie, and you wished to search all the files to find them.

◼ With the List Files directory on the screen, select **W**ord Search (**9**). The following message will appear across the bottom of the screen:

```
Search: 1 Doc Summary; 2 First Page; 3 Entire Doc; 4 Conditions: 0
```

WordPerfect is asking what you want it to search.

If you select **D**oc Summary (**1**), it will search only the document summary of your documents.

If you select First Page (**2**), it will search only the first page of the documents.

If you select Entire Doc (**3**), it will search the entire documents.

If you select Conditions (**4**), WordPerfect will ask you to specify the criteria or conditions you want it to search for or use to search with.

◼ Choose Entire Doc (**3**) for this project.

◼ You will then be asked what to search for with the following prompt in the lower left corner of your screen:

```
Word pattern:
```

- Type in **Charlie**. Then press **Enter**.

TIP: If you want to quit the command at any point before performing the search, press Cancel (**F1**) or Exit (**F7**).

You will need to be patient; it will take WordPerfect several seconds to search through all the files on your disk. During the search, WordPerfect will keep you informed of where it is in the sequence of files by displaying the following message at the bottom of the screen:

```
Searching file  #  of  ##
```

When the search is completed, an asterisk will appear beside the name of the files containing the word(s) you specified. In this case, you should see the files for **Charlie.1**, **CharlieA.1**, and **Justioff.3** marked this way.

```
12/14/88  15:33                 Directory A:\*.*
Document size:           0  Free:    316416   Used:      1332        Marked: 1

.  <CURRENT>    <DIR>                      ..  <PARENT>    <DIR>
ACTING   .4       4851  12/07/88 11:58     CHARLIEA.1*       759  12/07/88 12:04
BOOSTERS.5        2417  12/07/88 11:58     CHARLIE .1*      1332* 12/07/88 12:04
TRIPS    .6       4020  12/07/88 12:03     TV       .2      2138  12/07/88 12:08
```

TIP: You can move the cursor from one marked file to another in List Files with Tab and Shift-Tab. If WordPerfect does not find any files matching your criteria, a "Not Found" message is displayed in the lower left corner of your screen.

You can then look at any of the files indicated, and retrieve or print, as you desire. This can be a real lifesaver when you need to find a special file.

TIP: If you want to search only specified files, you can mark them with an asterisk. When WordPerfect finishes searching those files, an asterisk will remain by the filename that contains the words you are searching for. All other asterisks will disappear. If you want to remark the original files, press List Files twice.

While this command is working, WordPerfect is pulling files from the disk into the internal memory of your machine one at a time and going through them to find a match for the word pattern you supplied. When it has checked one file, it will recall another, and so on. If you have many files, or the files are large, it may take several seconds to check each one. Even though this make take a little time, be assured that WordPerfect is working at the speed of light in its internal memory. Do not press other keys or commands while you are waiting, since WordPerfect cannot handle them until it is finished with this task, and you may cause an error. (Read ahead in your text while waiting, if you like.)

Using Word Patterns

There are a variety of ways you can identify what you want WordPerfect to search for. You have already used single words. You can also use multiple words, phrases, and number series. Other alternatives include using special characters (such as ? and *) and logical operators (like ; and ,). You can also enclose a word or words in quotation marks or use CtrlX if you want to search for an exact phrase.

TIP: WordPerfect does not distinguish between uppercase and lowercase characters in word patterns. Both are treated alike.

Special characters that you can use in these word patterns include the question mark (?) and the asterisk (*). The question mark represents a single character, and the asterisk represents any number of characters between it and the next hard return.

For instance, the word pattern *l?ke* would search for all of the following: *lake*, *like*, and *luke*. The word pattern *lik** would search for items such as *like*, *likely*, *liking*, *liked*, *likings*, *likable*, etc. If you combined these special characters into the combination *l?ke**, you would get files containing words such as *lakes*, *lukewarm*, *likewise*, and *liken*.

The search string *"computer equipment"* would yield only files containing those exact words. Terms such as *computerized equipment* and *computer equipment's* would not be recognized. However, if the search string were entered as *"computer* equipment"*, words such as *computerized equipment* would be included.

The semicolon (;) and comma (,) logical characters can also be combined with word patterns. A semicolon between two words tells WordPerfect to select files that contain both words (.AND.). The comma means that files containing one or the other of the words should be selected (.OR.). For instance, the word pattern Wilson;Hardy would select only files containing both Wilson and Hardy. The pattern Wilson,Hardy would select files containing either one or both of the words. These symbols can also be combined into patterns such as Wilson,Hardy;Smith. In this case, WordPerfect would select files containing either Wilson or Hardy together with Smith.

TIP: In determining the sequence for logical operators, WordPerfect always searches for them in left to right order.

You can also use the wildcard ^X to search with. This wildcard can be substituted for any character on the keyboard except a blank space. However, it cannot be used as the first character in a string or to locate a function code.

To enter this command, you must press the appropriate keys to initiate the search (F2, Shift F-2, Alt-F2). When the Srch 142 prompt appears, enter the first part of whatever you want to search for. Then you may enter the wildcard if you want. To do so, press Ctrl-V. The prompt Key = will appear in the lower left corner of your screen. Press Ctrl-X. A ^X will appear beside the search command. Press Esc and WordPerfect will stop at anything that matches the first part of your search statement.

For instance, if you wanted to find all instances of either "Company" or "Co." in your document, you could enter Co^X, using the wildcard. WordPerfect would find them both.

As you can see, you can be quite creative in specifying what WordPerfect is to search for.

Summary

In summary, the following codes can be used in specifying word patterns:

?   Replaces a single character

*   Replaces to the next hard return

;   Requires that both parts be found

,   Requires that either one or the other part be found

^X Wildcard

To Review

For some practice, write the word pattern in the space below each item that will search for the following:

a. all files containing the names Johnson, Johnsen, and Johns.

b. all files containing reference to either the Amherst or Willoby contracts.

(continued)

c. all files relating to the Spring Sale

d. all files written by Henry Day and Mary Jackson

e. all files containing data on contracts, contractors, and contracting.

Specifying Conditions

The last option on the search menu allows you to be even more specific about what files WordPerfect is to search through. Let's take a look at it.

◼ With the List Files Directory on the screen, select **Word Search (9)**.

◼ From the Search menu, choose **Conditions (4)** to bring up the following Word Search menu:

Option 1—Perform Search On—identifies how many files are to be searched. The default is all files. However, if you had previously marked some files with an asterisk (*), WordPerfect would show only the number of files that were marked here. In addition, if a previous word search had resulted in files being marked, the number of files "found" would be shown. Those files would then be used in the next search.

```
Word Search

    1 - Perform Search on                    All xx File(s)

    2 - Undo Last Search

    3 - Reset Search Conditions

    4 - File Date                            No
          From (MM/DD/YY):                   (All)
          To   (MM/DD/YY):                   (All)

                    Word Pattern(s)

    5 - First Page
    6 - Entire Doc
    7 - Document Summary                     <Filename>
          Creation Date (e.g. Nov)
          Descriptive Name
          Subject/Account
          Author
          Typist
          Comments

  Selection: 1
```

Option 2—Undo Last Search—will allow you to undo the last search, or step back one level. For instance, if you had searched all files for a word and seven files had been marked as a result. Those seven files would then be used in the next search (if there was one). If, however, you wanted to search all files again, you could press 2 to undo the last search and return the files to be searched to the previous number.

Option 3—Reset Search Conditions—allows you to reset or change the criteria for the next search. If a search for the word Charlie had resulted in four files being marked, you could now reset the conditions for the next search and look through those four files for a different criteria.

For the search to function, the criteria or pattern to search for must also be identified. Options 4, 5, 6, and 7 allow you to specify several different kinds of patterns.

Option 4—File Date—can be used both alone and with other criteria. It allows you to limit the files to be searched by date. The default is No, meaning that unless otherwise specified, WordPerfect will not distinguish by date. If you want to search only those files created between certain dates, you can indicate that with this option. To do so you would select 4, turn the function On by typing Y(es), and specifying the dates between which you wanted to search. The dates can be entered in a variety of formats. For instance, all of the following would be acceptable:

3/5/88

03/05/1988

3/05/88

3//88

//88

Option 5—First Page—will limit the search to the first page or first 4000 characters of a file, whichever comes first. When this option is chosen, you will also be asked to identify specific criteria in the form of a word or word pattern.

Option 6—Entire Doc—tells WordPerfect to search the entire document for whatever word pattern is specified.

Option 7—Document Summary—will limit the search to document summaries saved with the files on the disk. If you use the document summary to search, you can specify word patterns for several criteria, such as the date the document was created, identifying information like name or subject, the author and/or typist, or any comments that may have been included.

Some of these features are similar to those you have already seen and used from the Search (F2 and Shift-F2) menus. For instance, you can mark certain files with an asterisk (*) and then search either the first page or entire document for a word pattern. You can also search all or marked document summaries for a specified word pattern.

The F2 and Shift-F2 search commands, however, do not allow you to specify a range of dates, undo a search, reset the conditions, or be as specific about the document summary criteria.

For some practice with these options, let's search for the word "Charlie" in files created during the last week.

■ Press **List Files** (**F5**) and **Enter** to bring up the List Files directory.

■ Then select **W**ord Search (**9**) and **C**onditions (**4**) to display the Word Search menu.

■ Select **F**ile Date (**4**) and type **Y** to turn the date search On. Enter a date one week previous to today to search from and today's date to search to.

■ Then press **P**erform Search (**1**) and **Enter** to perform the search.

If you have created any files containing the word "Charlie" within the past week, WordPerfect will find them, place an asterisk (*) beside the filename in the List Files directory and display that directory as soon as the search is completed. If it does not find any files matching that criteria, it will display the message "Not Found" in the lower left corner of your screen.

■ Take a few minutes to experiment with this command until you feel comfortable with the menus and can specify word patterns that will yield the results you want.

To Review

List all the ways you can specify criteria for a search.

Summary

In summary, List Files can be used to:

   a. Retrieve files

   b. Delete files

   c. Rename files

   d. Print files

e. Import DOS files

f. Look into files

g. Change directories (two ways)

h. Copy files

i. Do word searches

j. Mark files

Text In/Out

You have already seen the List Files/Text In command, for importing a file into your document from another program. The Text In/Out command does some of the same things. However, because it will also convert your files to DOS text files, and allow you to lock and unlock files, it is really much more powerful than the List Files option. This command will also let you use WordPerfect as a text editor for programs that you write in computer languages.

Saving and Retrieving DOS Files

If you want to use a WordPerfect file in another program, such as Lotus 1-2-3, WordStar, Word, or dBase, you often must convert it to an ASCII or DOS text file before the other program will accept it. (ASCII [American Standard Code for Information Interchange] files are generic files that can be used by many different types of application programs.) You should be aware that, when you convert files to ASCII this way, many of the formatting commands (Underline, Center, Bold, and so on) may be deleted or modified. The way many of those commands are coded by WordPerfect is specific to its needs and may not be recognized correctly by other programs. Hard returns and tab commands will usually be preserved as they were typed; soft returns will often be changed to hard returns at the end of each line.

◻ To save a WordPerfect file as a DOS or ASCII file, you would press **Text In/Out** (**Ctrl-F5**) to bring up the following menu.

```
1 DOS Text; 2 Password; 3 Save Generic; 4 Save WP 4.2; 5 Comment: 0
```

If you choose 1, WordPerfect will display the following menu.

```
1 Save; 2 Retrieve (CR/LF to [HRt]); 3 Retrieve (CR/LF to [SRt] in HZone): 0
```

You are being asked whether you want to save or retrieve a DOS text file. If you choose to retrieve, you must specify whether you want the "carriage return/line feeds" in the original file to be converted to hard returns or soft returns in the new file. What you select will depend on what you plan to do with the file and the importance of word wrap capability in the new file.

If you select (Save) (1), you will be asked to supply a filename for the new file. When you enter the name and press Enter, the file currently in memory will be saved as a DOS file and listed in the List Files directory. This file may be retrieved with Text In/Out (**Ctrl-F5**). However, it will not come back in the same format, since many of the formatting commands will have been deleted in the conversion process. It is also likely to have strange characters scattered throughout, and it will not be usable as a normal WordPerfect file.

If you choose **Retrieve** (2), you can retrieve a DOS file from another program. WordPerfect will convert carriage returns and line feeds (commands that advance the paper) in the file to hard returns.

Choosing Retrieve (3) also retrieves a DOS file from another program. WordPerfect will convert carriage returns or line feeds in the H-Zone to soft returns.

Going back to the original menu, let's look at more options:

```
1 DOS Text; 2 Password; 3 Save Generic; 4 Save WP 4.2; 5 Comment: 0
```

Password (2) allows you to add, change, or remove a password. It is generally used when you need to lock a document. More about this later.

Save **Generic (3)** allows you to save a WordPerfect file in a generic format acceptable to another word-processing program, such as WordStar, Word, or Multimate.

Save **WP 4.2 (4)** will save a file created with WordPerfect version 5.0 in a format acceptable to WordPerfect version 4.2. If you use this option and later retrieve your file with 4.2, you will find that most of the new commands incorporated into the 5.0 revision (graphics, and others) have been stripped from the file. This is necessary because 4.2 cannot handle those commands. If you anticipate making conversions from 5.0 to 4.2, be careful not to enter commands that may cause difficulty in the transfer.

Comment (5) allows you to create, edit, or convert a comment to text.

▣ If you would like to experiment with any of these file-conversion options, create a new file to work with; you will not want to alter any of the files you are currently using. Type a paragraph or two, use some of the formatting commands, such as Tab and margin or spacing changes, and then save and retrieve the file in any of the formats available. Use a different filename each time you save, so you can keep them straight.

Using Passwords to Lock and Unlock Files

If you have documents or files that you do not want others to have access to because they contain confidential information or something else that limits their availability, you can lock them. Then a password is required to retrieve or print such a file.

Option 2—Password (2)—on the Text In/Out (**Ctrl-F5**) menu allows you to save and retrieve a locked file. For practice, let's lock the file you created for Chapter 2.

▣ First clear your screen and retrieve **Nowis.2**.

▣ Then press **Text In/Out (Ctrl-F5)**.

▣ When the menu appears, select **Password (2)**. The following menu will display:

```
Password: 1 Add/Change; 2 Remove: 0
```

■ Enter **Add (1)**.

You will then be asked to enter the password. For this exercise, type in **Pass** for the password. Then press **Enter**.

Notice that the password does not appear on the screen as you type it in. This is so it can't be accidentally learned by someone watching you. The password may be up to 25 characters long.

■ When you are asked to Re-enter the password, type it in again. You are being asked to enter the password twice to be sure you have not made any typing errors.

A WORD OF CAUTION: Choose and enter your password carefully, since there is *absolutely no way* to retrieve the document without it. It might be wise to write down and keep the password in a safe place since your document will be inaccessible to you as well as to others if you forget it.

■ Now save the file using **Exit (F7)**, under the name **Lockfile.8** The password will be automatically saved with the file.

■ To retrieve a locked document, you may use any of the normal methods. You must, however, also enter the password when asked.

If you enter the correct filename and password, the document will be retrieved. If you enter the wrong password, the message **ERROR: File is Locked** will appear in the lower left-hand corner of your screen, and you will be denied access to the file.

TIP: All files associated with the locked document are also locked and require a password to access. This includes backup files, move files, virtual files, etc.

Let's retrieve the file you just locked and saved:

■ Clear your screen and press **Retriev (Shift-F10)**. Enter **Lockfile.8** as the name of the document to be retrieved.

■ Then enter **Pass** as the password and Press **Enter**. The file will reappear on the screen.

TIP: You should be aware that, when retrieving a locked document this way, you must retrieve it to a clear screen and memory. Otherwise it will not remain locked when you use the Save or Exit keys later.

You can also retrieve a locked file using List Files. If you do, you must enter the password again before the file will be displayed. If you want to print a document that is locked, it is best to use the Print (**Shift-F7**) method.

Changing Passwords: To change a password, press Text In/Out (**Ctrl-F5**) and select **P**assword (**2**). Select Add/Change (**1**) and follow the prompts to enter and reenter the new password. When you save, print, or retrieve a document, you will find that you must supply the new password. The old password will no longer be accepted.

Removing Passwords

There are two ways to remove a password from a file. You can use the Remove command or you can retrieve the locked file into a file that is not locked. Then when the combined file is saved, it will not be locked.

TIP: Note that you must retrieve a locked file to a clear screen if you want to maintain its locked status. Otherwise, the password will be lost.

To unlock a document and remove the password, do the following:

■ With the locked document on the screen, press **Text In/Out** (**Ctrl-F5**), Password (**2**) and Remove (**2**). When you resave the document, it will no longer be locked.

Shell

Some functions (such as delete, copy, get a directory and others) can be performed using either DOS or List Files in WordPerfect. Others can only be done by exiting to the DOS shell. As a result, it is very helpful to be able to switch back and forth between WordPerfect and DOS. This is much more convenient than having to Save, Exit, bring up DOS, do your function and then go back into WordPerfect.

A number of the commands you have worked with up to this point interact with or use DOS, the disk operating system that controls many of the functions that your computer performs. DOS is a separate program that can be used to format disks, copy files, delete files, give you a directory of files on the disk, and the like. DOS must also be working before you can use Word-Perfect or other software programs. In other words, DOS performs some functions alone, and some with other programs.

■ To use DOS without exiting from WordPerfect, press **Shell** (**Ctrl-F1**). When you do, the following menu will appear:

```
1 Go to Shell: 2 Retrieve Clipboard: 0
```

■ Select **G**o to Shell (**1**), and a shell of DOS will be made available to you. You will see a message similar to the one that follows, indicating which version of DOS you are using and which drive is active. The actual words and format of your screen will vary depending on your particular version of DOS.

```
Microsoft(R) MS-DOS(R)  Version 3.21
          (C)Copyright Microsoft Corp 1981-1987


Enter 'EXIT' to return to WordPerfect
B:\>
```

■ From this point, you can activate many of the DOS commands. As an example, type **Dir** beside the B> prompt (or whatever prompt appears) and press **Enter**.

     You should see a directory of all the files on the active drive, together with information similar to what appears when you press List Files.

■ To get a printout from DOS of what appears on your screen, adjust the printer and press **Shift-PrtSc**. This command (which is often called a screen dump) can also be used from within WordPerfect to obtain a "quick and dirty" copy of what is on the screen.

■ When you are finished and wish to return to WordPerfect, type the word **EXIT** and press **Enter**. Do not press the Exit (**F7**) key.

     You will be returned to the point in WordPerfect where you were before pressing Shell (**Ctrl-F1**), and you can continue where you left off.

TIP: Because many of the functions found in DOS are duplicated in List Files, you may find less use for this command. However, it is extremely useful to format disks with basic DOS commands and perform other, more advanced, DOS functions when they are needed.

Summary

In summary, to use options available in Text In/Out:

To	Press
Save or retrieve a DOS file	Ctrl-F5, then 1, 2 or 3
Add, Change, or Remove Passwords	Ctrl-F5, then 2
Save a document created with WP 5.0 to be used by another word-processing program	Ctrl-F5, then 3
Save a document created with WP 5.0 to be used with WP 4.2	Ctrl-F5, then 4
Go to DOS without exiting from WP	Ctrl-F1

Activities

You should have completed the following.

NowCopy.8	*Copy of Nowis.2*
CharlieA.8	*Printout of Charlie A.1*
Nowis.8	*Printout of Nowis.2*
Lockfile.8	*Nowis.8 with password*

DOS screen dump of directory

Chapter Review

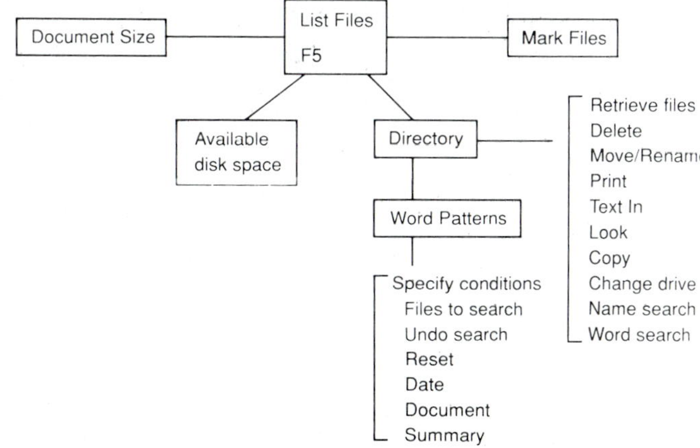

(continued)

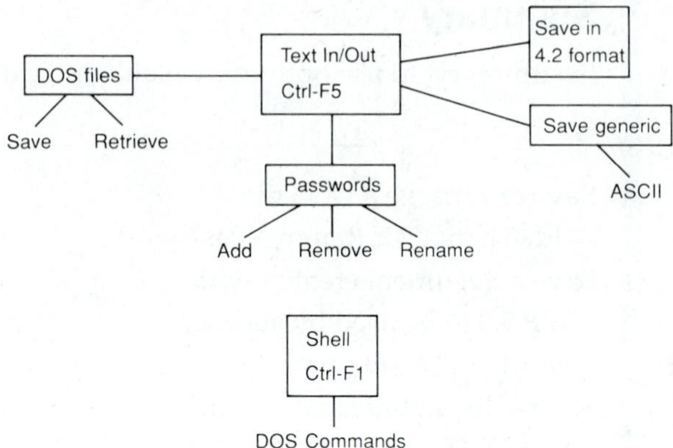

Self-Check Quiz 8

1. How can you tell how much space is left on the disk?

2. How can you find out if there is enough room on the disk to store your current document?

3. List the commands you can perform from List Files.

4. What does the term ASCII mean?

5. What will the Name Search command on List Files do?

6. What command will mark or unmark all files at once?

7. How can you find out what files are stored on your disk?

8. How can you rename a file? Delete a file?

9. What does it mean to "go to DOS" or use the Shell?

10. List the series of keystrokes required to print a locked document.

11. Why must you enter the password twice when lock/saving a document?

12. How can you mark files so that a single command will print, copy, or delete them?

13. What happens to commands in a file created with one program that cannot be transferred to another program?

14. Write a search command to find each of the following:
    a. All the files relating to the Harris contract.
    b. All files created during the last month.
    c. All files mentioning the name of William B. Jenks.
    d. All files referring to either the downtown or mall stores.

15. What will happen when you press Shift-PrtSc?

16. How can you delete a password?

17. What is the maximum length for a password?

18. What must you type to leave DOS and return to WordPerfect?

Extra Practice

For extra practice on the material covered in this chapter, do the following:

a. Retrieve **Trips.6** and resave it as **Pract8**. Use **Pract8** for the following exercises.

b. Use List Files to display a directory of all files on your work disk. Using the List Files Rename command rename all your Pract files to add a # to the file name. Therefore Pract1 will become **Pract#1**, Pract2 will become **Pract#2**, etc.

c. Use the List Files Look (6) command to review the contents of several of your files.

d. Use the List Files Copy (8) command to make another copy of Pract8. Give the new copy the name **Xpract8**.

e. Delete the new copy (Xpract8) you just made using the List Files Delete command.

f. Use the asterisk (*) to mark Pract#1 and Pract#2. Then print the marked files using the List Files Print command.

g. Use the List Files Word Search command to locate all files that contain the word **travel**.

h. Retrieve Pract#1 and lock it. Use the password **Lock** and resave the document under the name **Pract#8A**.

i. Retrieve and print Pract#8A using the password you assigned. Use any method you wish to print.

j. Check over your personal files on the disk. Good file management dictates that you should review and reorganize your files periodically. Rename as appropriate, or delete any that you do not wish to keep any longer. (Do not delete yet any files that have been created as exercises in this book.) Use Look to review any whose contents you do not recall. Add a password to any that you wish to keep confidential.

9

Using Styles and Creating Document Summaries and Comments

Now that you have learned a wide variety of commands for formatting your document, let's take a look at how to automate the process with styles, and create a style library. You'll also discover how to add document summaries to your files as well as insert notes and comments to yourself.

When you are finished, you should be able to:

- create and use styles to automate the formatting of your documents.
- create a style library.
- create and use document summaries.
- insert hidden comments into your text.
- convert comments to text and text to comments.

Styles

Although they can also contain text, styles are particularly useful for making format changes, including changing margins, setting tabs, and inserting font and printer commands. Adding format commands is easy with the style command in WordPerfect 5.0.

☐ Before moving ahead, enter the following text as shown. Use the defaults given and do not change margins, spacing, or other parts. You'll create several styles to help you do that later. When you are finished, save it as **Sumrfun.9** If you wish you may retrieve the file **Sumerfn.9** from the student exercise disk and move ahead.

SUMMER FUN

Introduction

When summer comes, most young people look forward to a variety of outside activities. Many of these require clothing or equipment of one kind or another. According to Harry White, a prominent recreational counselor: While it is possible to spend a great deal of money for the necessary items, unless one is working at a professional or training level such activities can be enjoyed with relatively simple, easily available, and inexpensive equipment.

To illustrate his point, Mr. White lists several of the more common activities together with basic equipment needed.

A. Fishing

Essential equipment for a day at the lake or stream is a pole of some kind, a reel, tackle or hooks, and bait. In addition, a little patience is a good thing to have. While the price of patience is unknown, the rest of the items can often be obtained for under $30.

> B. Bicycling
>
> A bicycle in good repair is really the only basic item needed if one wishes to spend time riding. Whether the bicycle is new or old, one speed or ten speed, there is ample opportunity to enjoy the outdoors. A tire pump and special clothing can also be added, but they are not required for an enjoyable afternoon.
>
> C. Swimming
>
> Aside from adequate clean water, all one really needs to enjoy a good swim is clothing that allows freedom of movement and is not harmed by getting wet. This is usually a swim suit, but shorts or other such items can easily be substituted for a fun day in the water.
>
> D. Baseball
>
> The great American pastime requires only a ball, a bat, a little outdoor space, and several people to share the fun. Gloves, hats, and protective clothing are also good to have to avoid accidents and injury.
>
> Conclusion
>
> There are many activities that can be enjoyed during the good weather of summer which require only minimal equipment that can be obtained at reasonable cost. The relaxation and fun are well worth the time and effort.

To see how styles work, let's create and use several for the text you have just entered.

TIP: You may feel, working with this short document, that it would be as easy to insert the commands manually as it is to create and use styles. And you would be right. Styles are really more useful for long documents or when you want to use the same format again and again. At this point, however, using a short document avoids the need to key in a lengthy manuscript and still provides an opportunity to work with the commands and see how they are used.

First, looking at the document, notice that the heading should be centered. Centering is a function that is frequently done and therefore setting a style for it would be helpful.

Let's say that you often create reports like this one and want to use the same margins, spacing, and other settings each time. Putting those in a style will eliminate the need to remember them. So a second style could be created for these reports that contains the left and right margins of 2" and double spacing.

Also like this one, many reports contain quotations, which should be single spaced and indented. A third style could be used to format quotations.

Finally, suppose you would like to single space and indent the comments following each of the activities five spaces from both the left and right margins. A fourth style can help you do this.

Let's create these four styles.

TIP: In this case, the text has been entered first, and the styles are inserted later. You may also create the styles, turn them on, type the text, and turn the styles off. The result will be the same.

Style Types

Styles can be created in two ways—open and paired.

The **open** type is similar to a macro because it affects the document from its location forward. For instance, a margin change could begin where it was inserted and continue to the end of the document or until it was changed by another code.

The **paired** type is different. It has a beginning and an end, with codes at both points. You could, with one style command, change the format for a paragraph, long quote, or another special part and return it back to the regular format at the end all with one style command. You can also use a paired styles type for commands like center, bold, and underline which insert a command before and after the items to be affected. A macro can change the codes at the beginning, but it cannot insert the codes at the end.

To Review

A style contains:

Paired styles are best for:

Open styles are best for:

Creating a Style

Looking at the first style to be created, remember that centered items have codes inserted at both the beginning and end of the text. (You can look at centered text in Reveal Codes (Alt-F3) to verify this.) As a result, the centering style will be paired. Let's create it now. The cursor may be anywhere in the document, and it is not necessary to have a clear screen.

☐ Press **Style (Alt-F8)** to bring up the following Styles menu:

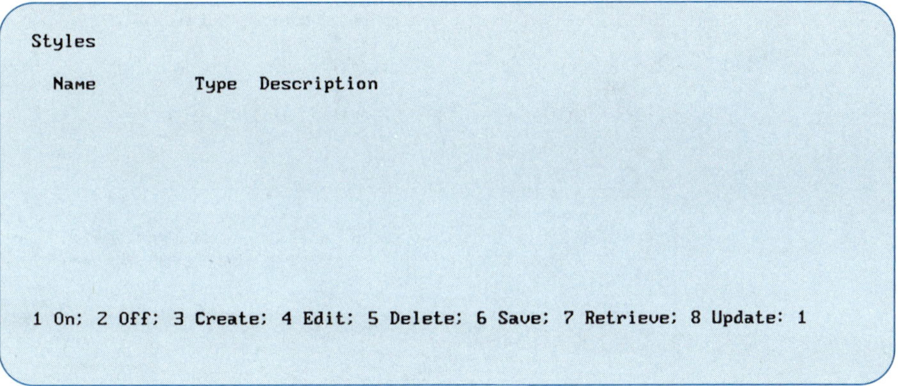

TIP: This screen will eventually display all the styles that are available. Since there have been no styles created yet, it is blank.

☐ Select **Create (3)** to display the next Styles Edit menu:

This menu will allow you to name the style, indicate the type (Open or Paired), record a description of what the style will do, enter the codes, and define the function of the Enter key (for paired styles).

■ Select **Name (1)**. Since this is a style to center titles, type **Centers** for the name and press **Enter**.

■ Select **Type (2)**. A prompt at the bottom of the screen will allow you to specify (1) Paired or (2) Open type. Note that paired is the default. Since there will be commands at the beginning and end of the text involved, this will be a paired style. Indicate that by typing **1** or **P**.

■ Select **Description (3)** and type **Centers a heading** and then press **Enter**.

TIP: | The description may be up to 54 characters long.

■ Select **Codes (4)** to bring up the following screen.

Notice that the cursor is at the top of the screen. WordPerfect is telling you to put the cursor above the box at the top while you enter any codes or commands that you want to come at the beginning of the text (Style On). The cursor should be below the box while you enter any codes or commands that should come at the end of the text (Style Off). You can use the Left and Right arrow keys to move the cursor back and forth from top to bottom. The commands themselves, similar to what you see in Reveal Codes, will be displayed in the lower half of the screen. The Style On codes will appear before the [Comment] marker and the Style Off codes will appear after it.

■ Since this is a style to enter centering commands, position the cursor at the top of the screen (above the box) and press **Center (Shift-F6)**. Note that the command **[Cntr]** has been entered near the middle of the screen.

■ Then tap the **Right Arrow** key a time or two. The cursor will jump below the box.

■ Press **Enter**. The ending command for centering will appear after the [**Comment**]. Your screen will look like the following:

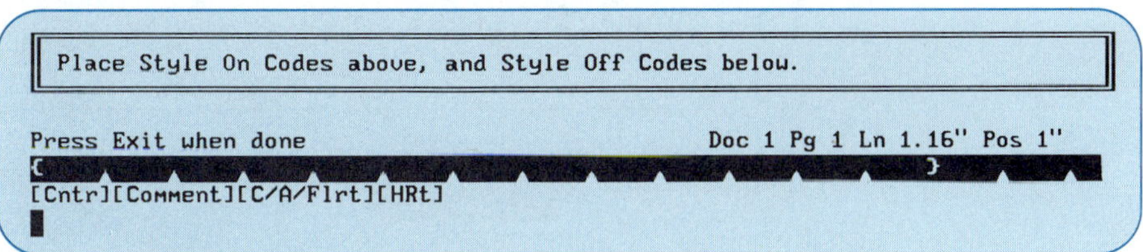

■ Press **Exit (F7)** to return to the previous menu.

The last option on the style menu, Enter, allows you to define the function of the Enter key when a paired type is indicated. This key can be set as a normal hard return, to turn the style off, or to turn the style off and back on. For this exercise, leave it at the default, which is a normal hard return.

■ Press **Exit (F7)** to leave the menu and return to the styles editing screen. Notice that the style you just created is now listed there.

TIP: You can also create styles by blocking existing codes (and enclosed text) in your document and pressing Style (Alt-F8) and Create (3). The codes at the beginning of the text will be inserted before the comment and those following the text after the comment. The text itself will not be saved. These styles can then be used with the Style On and Style Off commands.

■ To create the second style, press Create (3) again to return to the style creation menu.

■ Name this style **Docu Format**.

■ Since the commands to set margins and spacing will affect the entire document and really don't end until the end of the document, this will be an Open style. Enter that selection.

■ Type **1.5" Margins and Dbl Spacing** for the Description.

■ Select **Codes (4)**. Notice that the screen is a little different than that for the paired type. Since you do not need to indicate ending commands, that portion is missing.

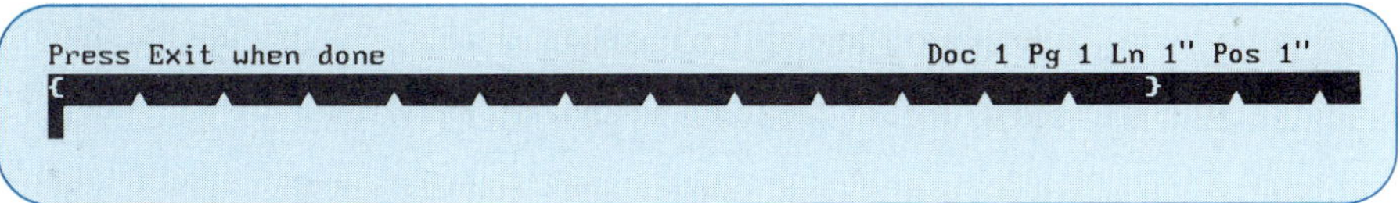

■ To enter the new margins, press **Format (Shift-F8)**, select Line (**1**), and **Margins** (**7**). Enter **1.5** for both left and right margins.

■ Select Line Spacing (**6**) and type **2** for double spacing then press **Enter** and **Exit** (**F7**) to return to the codes screen.

Those commands will now appear as follows:

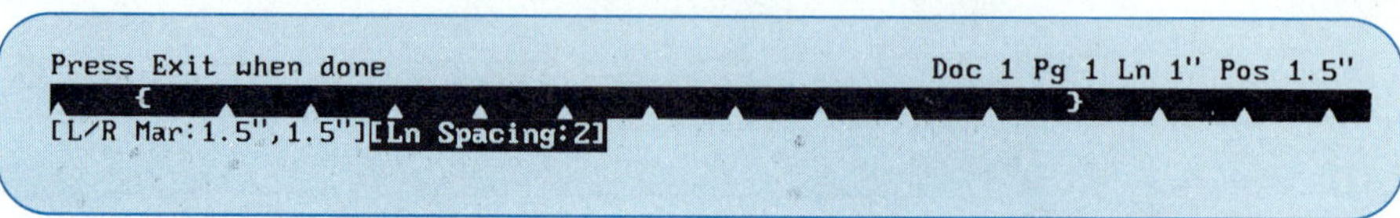

■ Press **Exit** (**F7**) twice to return to the styles creation screen.

■ Now create the third and fourth styles, with the following information.

<table>
<tr><td>Name:</td><td>Quotes</td></tr>
<tr><td>Type:</td><td>Paired</td></tr>
<tr><td>Description:</td><td>Single Spaced, L/R Indent</td></tr>
<tr><td>Codes:</td><td>Single spacing, margins 2" left and right above comment
Double spacing, margins 1.5" left and right below comment</td></tr>
<tr><td>Enter:</td><td>HRt</td></tr>
<tr><td></td><td></td></tr>
<tr><td>Name:</td><td>Indent Para</td></tr>
<tr><td>Type:</td><td>Paired</td></tr>
<tr><td>Description:</td><td>L/R Indented Paragraphs</td></tr>
<tr><td>Codes:</td><td>Single spacing, left/right indent 5 spaces above comment
Hard return, double spacing below comment</td></tr>
<tr><td>Enter:</td><td>HRt</td></tr>
</table>

When you are finished, the style editing screen should look like the screen shown on the next page.

■ Press Exit (**F7**) to leave the Styles screen.

```
Styles

   Name           Type  Description

   Center         Paired Centers a heading
   Doc Format     Open   1.5 Margins and DBL Spacing
   Ind Pars       Paired L/R Indent Para
   Quotes         Paired Single Spaced, L/R Indent




 1 On; 2 Off; 3 Create; 4 Edit; 5 Delete; 6 Save; 7 Retrieve; 8 Update: 1
```

Summary

In Summary, to create a style:

1. Identify the format to be included in the style.

2. Press Style (Alt-F8).

3. Select Create (3).

4. Provide the Name (1), Type (2), and Description (3).

5. Enter the Codes (4).

6. Exit (F7).

Using Styles

Let's use these styles to format the document on SUMMER FUN. To begin, we will set up the left and right margins and spacing.

- Move the cursor to the top of the document and press **Style** (**Alt-F8**). Highlight the style named **Format**. Turn it **On** (**1**).

   Quick as a wink, the margins will change and the text will appear double spaced. How's that for easy.

- Next, mark the heading SUMMER FUN as a block, using **Alt-F4**. Press **Style** (**Alt-F8**) and highlight the style named **Centering**. Then turn it **On** (**1**). The title will jump to the center.

TIP: Note that you do not need to turn the style Off since it is a paired type and the ending commands are included in the style itself. However, if you were entering text as you go, you would need to turn Style Off at the end, with Style (Alt-F8), Off (2).

- Now move the cursor to the beginning of the quotation by Harry White that begins, "While it is." Press **Block (Alt-F4)** to turn block on. Move the cursor to the end of the quotation following the words "inexpensive equipment." The entire quotation should now be highlighted on the screen.

- Press **Style (Alt-F8)**, highlight the style named **Quotes**, and turn the style **On (1)**. Immediately the block you had marked will change to single spacing with margins of 2 inches.

- Now block the paragraphs under each of the activities (Fishing, Bicycling, Swimming, Baseball) one at a time, and insert the style named **Indent Para** around each one.

- Then adjust any spacing that is out of order so the report looks neat and well done.

- When you are finished, see if you can create a style to underline and bold the two side headings **Introduction** and **Conclusion**. Use them on the headings.

- Then save your document as **Style.9** and print it.

Summary

In summary, to use a Style:

1. Block the text to be affected or position the cursor where the style is to begin.

2. Press Style (Alt-F8).

3. Highlight the desired style name.

4. Turn it On (1).

5. If necessary turn it Off (2) at end of text.

Editing Styles

One of the nice things about using a style to format a document is that you only need to change the master style to make changes. When the style is changed, the commands throughout your document will automatically be adjusted wherever the style is used. To see how this works, let's change the Indented Paragraphs style from Left/Right Indent to Left Indent only.

- Press **Style (Alt-F8)**, highlight the **Indent Para** style, and select Edit (4).

- When the style editing menu appears, select Codes (4). The editing screen will reappear.

- Move the cursor (highlight) to the Left/Right Indent code [INDENT] and delete it. Insert a **Left Indent** code [INDENT] in its place.

TIP: You may want to change the description to show that this style now indents from the left only.

- Then press **Exit (F7)** three times to return to the main screen. The change should already appear in the four paragraphs in the text where the **Indent Para** style is used. Can you imagine the time this feature can save?

- Save your edited document as **StyleA.9** and print it.

TIP: Styles can only be edited through the style menu and changes will be reflected in all places where the style is used. You cannot alter them individually or in any other way (such as using Reveal Codes). If you must vary the format somewhere in the text from that shown in the style, you may need to insert the commands manually or use a macro.

Deleting a Style

Deleting a style is quite simple. Just move to the style screen (**Alt-F8**), highlight the style you wish to delete, and select **Delete (5)**. The style will be gone from the screen and memory of your machine immediately.

Saving to, Retrieving from, and Updating Styles using a Style Library

The last three options on the style menu allow you to save a group of styles to a separate file, retrieve a file containing styles into your document, or bring styles from a style library into your document.

Since styles are saved (like other formatting commands) with the document, you must create or retrieve them into each new file in which they are used. If you wanted to use the styles you have just created in another document without having to create them all over again, you can save them for future use. You could create several small files, each containing a few styles, but it would be much more efficient and easier to find styles if they were organized into a library.

To make this easy, WordPerfect allows you to specify a file on the Setup Menu in which to save all styles in. Then, whenever you select **Save (6)**, **Retrieve (7)**, or **Update (8)**, it will go to that file to complete your command.

- To establish this file, press **Setup (Shift-F1)**, select Location of Auxiliary Files **(7)**, and Style Library Filename **(6)**.

- If you are working on a dual disk machine, enter **B:STYLLBRY** to save it on your data disk. If you are working from a hard disk, enter **C:\(directory name)\STYLLBRY**. Then press **Exit (F7)**.

TIP: If you are using a hard drive, you must enter a complete path and name for the file you wish to have the styles stored in.

- Now return to the style menu with **Alt-F8** and select Save (**6**). When you are asked for the filename, type **B:STYLLBRY** or **C:\(directory name)\ STYLLBRY** and press **Enter**. Your styles will be saved to that file as a regular WordPerfect file.

TIP: Because the styles file is an ordinary file, you must resave it if you make changes to a style that you want to keep.

- To retrieve styles from a file into your document, you simply select **Retrieve** (**7**), enter the path and filename of the file to be retrieved, and press **Enter**. The names of available styles will be quickly inserted into the style menus.

If styles with the same name as those being retrieved already exist in your document, you will see the message **Style(s) already exist. Replace? (Y/N) No** in the lower left corner of the screen. If you want those from the file being retrieved to overwrite those in your document, enter **Yes**. If you want only those styles that have different names retrieved, omitting those with names like those already in the document, enter **No**.

The Update (**8**) command retrieves the entire style library into your document. You can then select, edit, or delete from this group.

Styles can be very useful when there are a number of pages or a lot of text needing multiple changes that are repetitive. Using a style simplifies this process. Styles are also useful when uniformity is desired over a period of time, such as for letter or manuscript format. In addition, using styles relieves the writer of the need to remember all the settings that are to be used at various points in a document. Finally, styles are very useful when there are many or complex format changes to be made a number of times.

- Before moving ahead, if you are sharing equipment or using a hard disk, press **Setup (Shift-F1)** and delete the names of the Style Auxiliary Files and Style Library Filename so that others coming after you will not encounter the settings you have inserted.

To Review

List three uses for styles.

Describe a style library.

Now let's move on to another useful feature of WordPerfect.

Using a Document Summary

It is often helpful to be able to include information, such as the author's name, who typed the document, when it was last updated, and other such facts with the file when it is saved. This information will not be printed, but it is useful for reference. To insert such items, you can use the Document Summary feature.

◾ For a file to practice with, retrieve **StyleA.9**.

TIP: It is not necessary to pre-position the cursor because document summaries can be created at any time and any place in your document. WordPerfect will automatically insert them at the top of the file.

◾ Press **Format (Shift-F8)** and select **Document (3)**.

◾ Select **Summary (5)**. The following screen will appear.

```
Document Summary

    System Filename              Style2

    Date of Creation             (Today's Date)

1 - Descriptive Filename

2 - Subject/Account

3 - Author

4 - Typist

5 - Comments

┌──────────────────────────────────────────────────────────┐
│SUMMER FUN; Introduction: When summer comes, most young people look│
│forward to a variety of outside activities.  Many of these require│
│clothing or equipment of one kind or another.  According to Harold│
│White, a prominent recreational counselor: While it is possible to│
│spend a great deal of money for the necessary items, unless one is│
│working at a professional or│
└──────────────────────────────────────────────────────────┘
```

As you can see, WordPerfect has already inserted the previous filename and the creation date. It has also entered the first 400 characters of the document in the comments box.

TIP: The date of creation is the date on which you first created the file. It does not change with subsequent saves of the document on other dates. If the file had not yet been named, the prompt (Not named yet) would appear. This would be replaced by the filename when one was entered later. You may enter a Descriptive Filename (1) of up to 40 characters. WordPerfect will use the first 11 characters of the Descriptive Filename for a filename, if you do not enter a different one when you save.

You can enter the names of the author and the typist (up to 40 characters each), and you may change the comments by inserting up to 780 characters of text. The bold and underline functions will work within the comments section, but other commands will not.

◾ Enter the name of your teacher or employer as the Author and your own name as the Typist.

◾ Select **D**escriptive Filename (**1**) and enter **DocSmry.9** to change the name of the file in the menu.

◾ If WordPerfect finds the words you have entered as the subject search string (RE is the default) within the first 400 words, the subject will be automatically inserted beside this option. You may also enter a subject of your own.

◾ Change the **C**omments (**5**) to say:

This is a practice file for working with document summaries.

◾ Then press **Exit** (**F7**) twice to return to the document and use **Save** (**F10**) to save the file as **DocSmry.9**.

That's all there is to it. This document summary will be saved as a part of your file, and you may use it for reference or edit it at any time.

TIP: Document summaries are often used as a quick way to learn the contents of a document when using Look (**6**) on the List Files (**F5**) key.

If you want WordPerfect to prompt you for a Document Summary each time you save or exit a file, you can change the default on the Setup menu.

◾ To do this, press **Setup** (**Shift-F1**) and select Initial Settings (**5**). The following menu will appear:

```
Setup:   Initial Settings

     1 - Beep Options

     2 - Date Format  3 1, 4

     3 - Document Summary

     4 - Initial Codes

     5 - Repeat Value 8

     6 - Table of Authorities


Selection: 0
```

◼ Select Document Summary (**3**) to bring up the next menu.

```
Setup: Document Summary

1 - Create on Save/Exit  No

2 - Subject Search Text  RE:

Selection: 0
```

This menu will allow you to specify that a document summary is AL-WAYS created when you save or exit. You would not need to press **Format (Shift-F8)** to select it. The menu also allows you to change the **S**ubject Search Text (**2**) used to search the first 400 bytes (characters) of a document to locate the Subject/Account. For example: the default search text is RE:. Therefore, anytime RE is used in the first 400 bytes (characters) of a document the words between it and the next hard return would automatically be inserted in the document summary next to Subject/Account. This text would then be scanned by WordPerfect when doing Word Searches (9) from List Files.

◼ Do not make any changes in the settings on this menu right now since doing so would constitute a permanent change. Press **Enter** twice to leave the menu.

Whenever you would like to review the document summary, edit it, or use it for reference, you only need press Format (Shift-F8), Document (3), and Summary (5) to bring it to the screen.

◼ Before moving on, if necessary, return the Document Summary setting on the Setup menu to the default by pressing **Setup (Shift-F1)**, Initial Settings (**5**), Document Summary (**3**), and entering **N**o.

Summary

In summary, to create a Document Summary:

If Document Summary is already set to Yes

a. Press Format (Shift-F8) and select Document (3)

b. Select Summary (5)

c. Enter information as prompted.

To set Document Summary to Yes

a. Press Setup (Shift-F1)

b. Select Initial Settings (5)

c. Select Document Summary (3)

d. Select Create on Save/Exit (1) and Enter Yes

e. Press Enter and Exit (F7)

Document Comments

Now suppose you would like to insert some notes or comments to yourself in your document, as reminders of things to do, information to check on, follow-up dates and the like. Inserting these notes can be done with the Comment option. To see how it works, try the following:

TIP: These comments can be displayed on the screen, but they cannot be printed unless they are converted to text.

◻ With the **DocSmry.9** file on your screen, position the cursor after the second sentence.

◻ Press **Text In/Out (Ctrl-F5)** to bring up the following prompt:

```
1 DOS Text; 2 Password; 3 Save Generic; 4 Save WP 4.2; 5 Comment: 0
```

◻ Select **Comment (5)** to bring up the next menu:

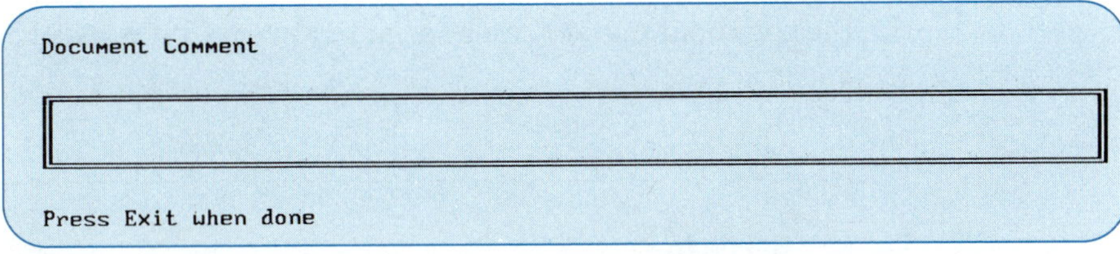

■ Select **Create** (**1**). The following will appear:

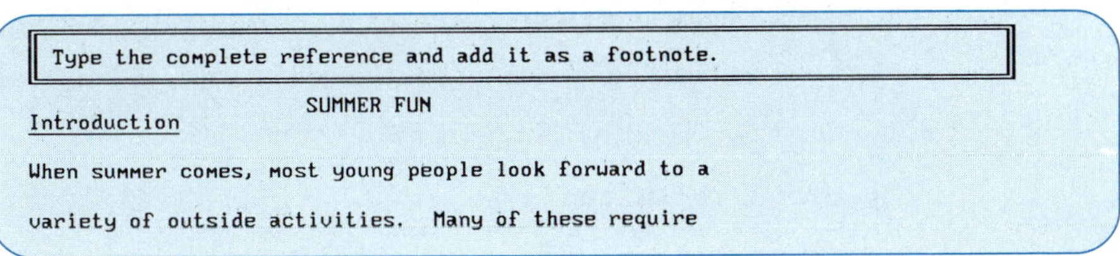

TIP: You may enter any comments you wish up to 1024 characters.. You may also use both the bold and underline commands as well as any Compose character.

■ For this exercise, type **Find the complete reference and add it as a footnote.**

■ Then press **Exit** (**F7**) to return to the text of your document.

Again, that's all there is to it. The comment will appear on your screen.

By default the document comments will display on your screen. If they do not, do the following:

■ To turn Document Comments Display On, press **Setup** (**Shift-F1**) and select **Display** (**3**).

■ If **Display** Document Comments (**3**) is set to **No** press **Y**(es) to turn it on. (If it is already **Yes** simply press **Enter** twice to return to the editing screen.)

Type the complete reference and add it as a footnote.

                    SUMMER FUN
Introduction

When suMMer coMes, Most young people look forward to a

variety of outside activities. Many of these require

TIP: Since this is a system setup command, the change is permanent until it is changed again. If you do not want the comments to display, you should enter No at the prompt.

You can enter as many comments as you like into your document. They can be very helpful in your work. If you wish, you may use the search feature to find hidden comments, and if you need to delete an entire comment, you can do so from Reveal Codes.

TIP: Document comments are not shown in the View Document mode. However, the comment marker can be seen in Reveal Codes (Alt-F3).

◼ Now add the following paragraph *as a comment* just above the Conclusion.

E. Hiking

Getting out in the fresh air to enjoy the outdoors on a hike requires only some shoes that are appropriate for the terrain and that provide support to your feet. Many people hike or walk daily for exercise.

TIP: Sometimes when a comment is added in the middle of a line, the text appears separated on the screen. Do not be concerned. This will not affect the spacing or placement of the text when it is printed.

Summary

In summary, to create Document Comments:

a. Turn Document Comments Display On (Setup (Shift-F1), Display (3), Display Document Comments (3) Yes) if necessary.

b. Position the cursor where the comment is to be placed.

c. Press Text In/Out (Ctrl-F5).

d. Select Comment (5).

e. Select Create (1).

f. Enter the text of the comment.

g. Exit (F7) to return to the editing screen.

Editing a Comment

If you should need to edit a comment, you must place the cursor AFTER the comment (to the right) and press Text In/Out (**Ctrl-F5**), then select Comment (**5**) to bring up the following menu:

```
Comment: 1 Create; 2 Edit; 3 Convert to Text: 0
```

Select Edit (**2**), and WordPerfect will search backward for the next comment and return it to the screen. Then you can use any of the editing commands to change, delete from or add to the existing comment. When you are finished, press Exit (**F7**) to return to your document.

TIP: It is often very helpful to be able to include this kind of commentary in your files. Remember, however, to update or edit the document summary and comments whenever changes are made, so your record will remain current.

Converting a Comment to Text

You can also change a comment to text so that it becomes a part of the document. To do this, you must position the cursor AFTER the comment before starting the command. For some practice, let's convert the comment on hiking into text.

◼ Position the cursor at the end of the document. Then press **Text In/Out** (**Ctrl-F5**) and select **Comment** (**5**).

◼ From the Comment menu, select Convert to Text (**3**).

Immediately the box around the comment will disappear. The text is now a part of your document.

◼ Use the style commands to format the paragraph to match the rest of the document.

Summary

In summary, to convert comments to text:

a. Position the cursor to the right of the comment to be converted.

b. Press Text In/Out (Ctrl-F5).

c. Select Comment (5).

d. Select Convert to Text (3).

Changing Text to a Comment

You can also convert text to a comment. For some practice, let's change the last sentence of **DocSmry.9** to a comment.

▣ Block the last sentence of the conclusion that reads "The relaxation and fun are well worth the time and effort."

▣ Press **Text In/Out** (**Ctrl-F5**). The following prompt will appear in the lower left corner of the screen:

```
Create a comment? (Y/N) No
```

▣ Enter **Yes**. Immediately, the text that was blocked has been converted and is now surrounded by a comment box.

▣ Finally, save the document as **Comment.9** and print it.

▣ For additional practice in creating comments, editing them, converting comments to text, and changing text to comments, experiment a little with the **Comment.9** file. When you are finished, **Exit (F7)** but do not save the document.

▣ Finally, return the Comment setting on the Setup menu to the default by pressing **Setup (Shift-F1)**, Display (3), Display Document Comments **(3), No**.

You're ready to move ahead.

Summary

In summary, to convert text to comments:

a. Block the text to be converted.

b. Press Text In/Out (Ctrl-F5)

c. Enter Y(es) at the Create a comment? prompt.

Activities

You should have completed the following:

Sumrfun.9   *Original document*
Style.9   *Sumrfn.9 with Left/Right Indented paragraphs*
StyleA.9   *Sumrfn.9 with Left Indented paragraphs*
DocSmry.9   *StyleA.9 with Document Summary*
Comment.9   *DocSmry.9 with comments*

Chapter Review

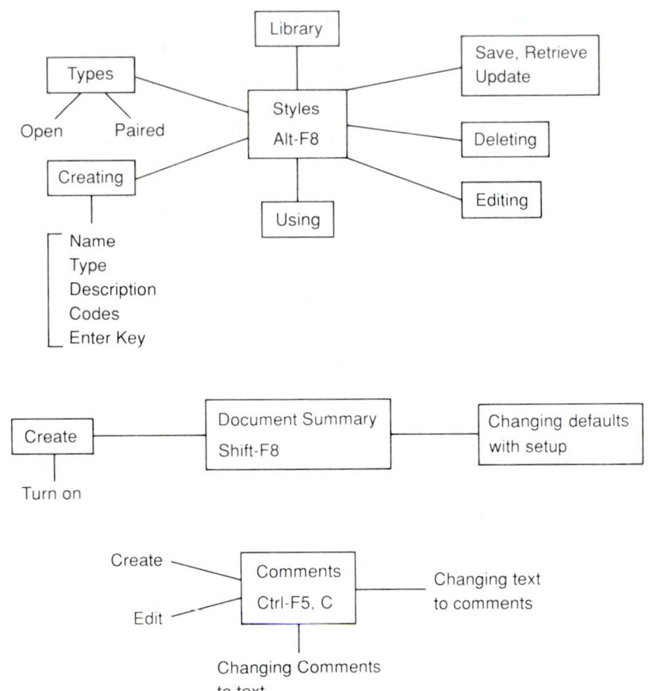

Self-Check Quiz 9

1. List several functions styles can be used for.

2. Identify the difference between open and paired style types.

3. Why should you save styles you have created?

4. How is a style library used?

5. When creating a paired style, which codes go above the box in the creation screen and which go below it?

6. How can you move the cursor from the top of the style creation screen to the bottom?

7. What happens to the styles already in your document when you edit or change the codes in a style?

8. What information is contained in the document summary?

9. How many characters can be included in a document comment?

10. Where must the cursor be placed when editing or converting comments to text?

11. Where can document comments be inserted?

Extra Practice

For extra practice on the material covered in this chapter, do the following:

a. Create a style to enter the margins and spacing for the following memo. Make it open type. Insert margins, spacing, tabs, etc. as appropriate.

b. Use the memo style and enter the following:

TO: Scheduling Office
FROM: Registration
DATE: (Today's Date)
SUBJECT: Space for New Student Orientation Meetings

As the fall session begins, meetings are being scheduled by the various colleges within the institution for new student orientation. This memo is to request rooms for the following:

College of Science

> **September 21, 10:30 a.m. Space needed for approximately 65 students. Auditorium in Science Building preferred.**

College of Business

> **September 22, 9:00 a.m. Space needed for approximately 120 students for general meeting. Two smaller adjoining rooms also needed for individual groups of around 40 at 10:00-- Refreshments to be served.**

College of Humanities

> **September 21, 10:30 a.m. Space needed for approximately 150 students. VCR and screen to be used. Podium requested.**

Please confirm as soon as possible if rooms can be scheduled for these meetings.

---

c. Save as **Pract9** and print.

d. Create a document summary for Pract9. Enter yourself as the typist and Harvey Wilson as the author.

e. Insert a comment following the heading **College of Business** that says "Check on arrangements for refreshments."

f. Create a style to bold and underline text. Use it on the following announcement.

It's our biggest Back-To-School Event

FALL FASHION HIGHLIGHTS

Main Floor Auditorium

Thursday, August 21, 19--

1:30 p.m.

g. Edit the style to remove the underline. Center the announcement on the page.

h. Create a document summary showing yourself as the typist and Monica Howard as author. Indicate in the comments that 250 copies are to be printed.

i. Save the announcement as **Pract9a** and print it.

j. Create a document summary and/or comments for any of the exercises in this book that you wish.

k. Return all Setup settings to the defaults.

10

Using Special Menus for Setup and Forms Definition

Since you've already worked with a number of DOS commands from both inside and outside Word-Perfect, let's explore some of the internal program commands and defaults that control how it functions. These include options for automatic backup of your files on a periodic basis; the manner in which various screen messages are displayed; initial format settings; special settings for keyboard and screen functions and displays; and the way margin, tab, screen locations, and other points are measured. We'll also work with the commands for identifying forms for the printer.

When you have finished, you should be able to:

- set a backup time for automatic backup of your document.

- change the cursor speed.

- define how various items are displayed on the screen.

- change the defaults for fast saved, unformatted files.

- **identify initial settings and codes for several WordPerfect defaults.**
- **identify the location of auxiliary files.**
- **work with several units of measure options.**
- **change the way units of measure are displayed on the status line and in other menus.**
- **add forms definitions to the printer settings menu.**
- **use forms setups to control printer functions.**

Changing Defaults with Setup

Setup is another new feature of WordPerfect 5.0 that makes it much easier to customize the defaults and other settings of a variety of commands. You have already worked with some parts of Setup menus in previous sections of this text. Now let's take a more in-depth look at what this feature offers.

A WORD OF CAUTION: Since the changes made with the Setup menus are semi-permanent and will be saved and used by WordPerfect each time the program is started, alterations you make to Setup options can affect the program for those who use the disks after you. If you are working in an environment where disks and other equipment are shared, check with your instructor or lab assistant to obtain instructions on how to work with it *before* starting this material. In particular, you will need to know which exercises you should do and the settings your disks should have when you are finished with this section. Unless you are instructed otherwise, return all settings to the defaults before quitting.

☐ To begin, press **Setup (SHIFT-F1)** to bring up the main Setup menu.

```
Setup

    1 - Backup

    2 - Cursor Speed                30 cps

    3 - Display

    4 - Fast Save (unformatted)     No

    5 - Initial Settings

    6 - Keyboard Layout

    7 - Location of Auxiliary Files

    8 - Units of Measure




Selection: 0
```

Backup

Backup means to make an extra copy of your document to protect against the possibility of data loss if there should be a power failure, equipment malfunction or other accident. Sometimes the backup is temporary, intended only for use until a permanent final copy is made. Other times the backup is a permanent file copy to guard against other types of loss. The **Backup (1)** option allows you to set backup in two ways. The first is an automatic periodic backup of your document as you are working on it. The second is a backup of the original document whenever you replace it with Save or Exit.

■ To see what these functions do, press **Backup (1)** to bring up the Backup menu.

Timed Backup

The first option on this menu will allow you to determine (1) whether backups are to be made, and (2) if backups are made, how often that will occur. The backup directory referred to is the directory that the backup files are to be stored in if you are using a hard drive on your machine.

The backup files created with this option are temporary and will be deleted when you exit WordPerfect normally. However, if you should have a power or equipment failure, the backups will be retained. They can then be retrieved, renamed, and used when you start WordPerfect again.

```
Setup: Backup

        Timed backup files are deleted when you exit WP normally.  If you
        have a power or machine failure, you will find the backup file in the
        backup directory indicated in Setup: Location of Auxiliary Files.

        Backup Directory

    1 - Timed Document Backup                   No
        Minutes Between Backups                 30


    Original backup will save the original document with a .BK! extension
    whenever you replace it during a Save or Exit.

    2 - Original Document Backup                No














    Selection: 0
```


Even though the backup feature can be a safeguard against losing large amounts of data, it is *not a substitute* for regular backups on separate diskettes. You should always make independent backup copies of important files on a regular basis and store them in a secure place.

◼ Select **T**imed Document Backup (**1**) to set a timed backup.

◼ When the cursor appears beside "Timed Document Backup", type **Y**(es).

◼ Then type **15** for the minutes between backups, and press **Enter**.

That's all there is to it. When you Exit (**F7**) the Setup menu, the timed backup settings will be saved, and WordPerfect will immediately begin to save your files automatically every 15 minutes. When this occurs, WordPerfect will pause for a few seconds and you will see the message "***Please Wait***" in the lower left corner of the screen.

It is important to note that if you are working on two documents at the same time, only the document currently on your screen will be backed up.

These backups will be saved in files called {WP}BACK.1 and {WP}BACK.2 for documents 1 and 2. When you exit WordPerfect normally, the files are deleted. However, when problems occur and the normal exit process is not followed, the files remain on your disk. When WordPerfect is restarted, you are notified that they are there with the message "Old backup file exists. 1 Rename; 2 Delete:".

TIP: If you wish to use the backup file, you must rename it before retrieving. To do so, select 1, give the file a new name, and retrieve the renamed file with the regular commands. If you select Delete, the file will be erased.

Original Backup

The second option creates an **Original Document Backup (2)** which is useful when you make changes, save them, and then decide you want to return to the original version of the document. As you know, when a file is replaced on the disk, the original is destroyed. The original backup feature allows you to overcome the potential loss of that file.

Files created with the original backup option have the same filename as the original plus a .BK! extension. They remain on your disk even when WordPerfect is exited properly, and they may be retrieved in the normal manner.

TIP: The .BK! file contains the file that existed on your screen before the last save. As repeated saves (or timed backups) of your document are made, the .BK! file is also updated to contain the last version of the previous file.

A WORD OF CAUTION: WordPerfect does not distinguish among files with the same name but different extensions such as Contract.1, Contract.2, etc. In these cases, both or all files would share one backup file, which would contain the last file saved. If you want backup files created for each file, use individual names such as Contr1. and Contr2. to avoid this problem.

■ Press **Enter** to return to the main Setup menu.

TIP: When working with the Setup menus, pressing Enter will step you back through the menus one at a time. Pressing Exit (F7) will usually return you to the main editing screen immediately.

To Review

What is contained in each of the following backup files?

{WP}BACK.1 ____

{WP}BACK.2 ____

.BK! ____

Which of the above backup files is temporary and which is permanent?

____

Cursor Speed

The second option on the main Setup menu is **Cursor Speed (2)**. When a key is held down, WordPerfect normally repeats a character 10 times every second. If you wish, you can increase this up to 50 times per second.

■ Press **2** to display the following menu across the bottom of the screen:

```
Characters Per Second: 1 15; 2 20; 3 30; 4 40; 5 50; 6 Normal: 0
```

Selecting 1, 2, 3, 4, or 5 will cause WordPerfect to repeat characters on keys held down a number of times corresponding to that shown. Normal speed (option 6) is 10 characters per second.

TIP: Increasing the speed on this option also increases scrolling speed for the Arrow keys.

■ Press **6** to select normal speed. Then press **Enter** to return to the document editing screen.

■ Press **Setup (Shift-F1)** to bring up the Setup menu again.

Display

Option 3 on the Setup menu is Display. This feature controls how several items are shown on the screen.

■ Press **3** to bring the Display submenu to the screen which should be similar to the one on the next page.

Options 1, 3, 4, 8, and 9 are questions that can be answered with a Yes/No response. They ask whether you want the screen to be automatically updated as changes in text and settings are made, whether document comments are to be displayed, whether you would like the filename shown in the bottom lower left corner of your screen, and whether columns should be shown side-by-side on the screen as they are being entered. Your responses will customize these features according to your personal preferences. Do not change any of the defaults at this time.

```
Setup: Display

      1 - Automatically Format and Rewrite    Yes

      2 - Colors/Fonts/Attributes

      3 - Display Document Comments           Yes

      4 - Filename on the Status Line         Yes

      5 - Graphics Screen Type                Hercules 720x348 mono

      6 - Hard Return Display Character

      7 - Menu Letter Display                 BOLD

      8 - Side-by-side Columns Display        Yes




Selection: 0
```

Option 2—Colors/Fonts/Attributes--allows you to set the color and style of various features on your monitor. Exactly what your monitor will display can vary widely and will depend on whether it is a color monitor, monochrome monitor, EGA monitor, or another type.

The **Graphics Screen Type (5)** option allows you to specifically identify the hardware in your machine by selecting from a list of several graphics boards. Do not make changes in this menu without first consulting your instructor.

The **Hard Return Display (6)** option will enable you to specify a character to display on the screen when a [HRt] character is pressed. Normally, no character is shown, but some users like to see where hard returns exist in the file. Some of the more popular characters used for this are the period (.) and the right angle (>).

■ To see what this looks like, select **6**, type **>**, and press **Exit (F7)**. You will immediately see a > on your screen any place the Enter key has been pressed.

■ Return to the Display menu by pressing **Setup (Shift-F1)**, Display (**3**), Hard Return Display Character (**6**) and remove the > with backspace delete so that no character shows.

The **M**enu Letter Display (7) controls the appearance of the highlighted letter on the screen in many menus. This command is most useful with a color monitor or one that displays various shades of amber or black. The actual appearance of the letter on the screen will be determined by the setting established for each characteristic (Fine, Vry Large, Italc, etc.) in the Colors/Fonts/Attributes menu. For instance, if Fine is set to display in red on that menu, selecting Fine on this menu will cause the menu letter to display in red. If you do not have a color monitor, many of these options will appear alike. If that is the case, you will probably want to select various forms of bolding and reverse video to provide contrast. If you make changes, return the setting to BOLD before proceeding.

Fast Save (unformatted)

The default for the Fast Save (unformatted) (**4**) option on the Setup menu is No or Off which means that, unless changed, WordPerfect will save files in formatted form. For the time being, do not change this setting.

TIP: If the setting were changed to **Y**(es), or unformatted form, WordPerfect would save your files faster. It would not have to deal with the formatting codes. However, using fast save and thus creating unformatted files has one major drawback. Unformatted files cannot be printed from the disk, and if you wanted to print those files, they would need to be retrieved to the screen and printed from there.

If you wanted to format files before saving with fast save, you could move the cursor to the beginning of the document and press Home, Home, Down Arrow to run the cursor completely through the text. Doing so will cause the formatting codes to be entered and allow you to print documents saved with fast save from the disk command.

Initial Settings

Option (5) on the Setup menu allows you to set different initial or default settings to be used by WordPerfect when it is started. If you wanted margins, tabs, or settings other than those originally set with the program, you could use this command to change them.

■ Press **I**nitial Settings (5) to retrieve the following menu and see the items that can be affected.

```
Setup: Initial Settings

     1 - Beep Options

     2 - Date Format                    3 1, 4

     3 - Document Summary

     4 - Initial Codes

     5 - Repeat Value                    8

     6 - Table of Authorities

Selection: 0
```

The **B**eep Options (**1**) on the Initial Settings menu will permit you to set the bell to ring when an error is encountered, when words must be hyphenated, and/or when a search fails.

As you know, the **D**ate Format (**2**) of 3 1, 4 displays the date in standard order (Month Day, Year). If you want the default for this order changed, this option will allow you to make that adjustment using the date format menu.

The third option on the Initial Settings menu, Document **S**ummary (**3**), gives you an opportunity to indicate whether you want to create a document summary whenever a document is saved or exited.

The Initial Codes (**4**) option allows you to change the defaults for several of the beginning codes in effect when WordPerfect is started.

A WORD OF CAUTION: Be very careful to distinguish between the Initial Codes option on the Format menu (Shift-F8, 3, 2) and the Initial Settings/Codes option on the Setup menu (Shift-F1, 5, 4). Even though both deal with format commands, they affect different things. The Setup options are permanent and become defaults for all documents unless changed. The Format options affect only the document with which they are saved.

Option (**5**), **R**epeat Value, allows you to change the default for the Esc key, which determines the number of times a command is repeated. It is currently set at 8.

Finally, the Table of Authorities option (6) on the Initial Settings menu deals with a specialized type of legal bibliography. You will work with this feature in Chapter 19. This option controls whether dot leaders are displayed, whether underlining is allowed, and whether blank lines are inserted between individual entries in a Table of Authorities.

■ Press **Enter** to return to the main Setup Menu.

To Review

What is the difference between the Initial Codes on the Format menu and Initial Codes on the Setup menu?

Keyboard Layout

The Keyboard Layout (6) option on the main Setup menu allows you to change the keyboard assignments (keys to press to activate the command) for most of WordPerfect's features. There are several built-in keyboard definitions that you may use or edit to suit your needs. You can also use a macro command to assign commands to certain keys. You will learn more about this later.

Location of Auxiliary Files

If you are using a hard disk or a network, it is possible that several files (see menu below) used by WordPerfect may be stored in directories other than where the WordPerfect program is located. If this is the case, WordPerfect will not be able to find them unless you tell it where they are. The Location of Auxiliary Files (7) menu item will help you identify their location for Word-Perfect. If you are using a dual disk machine, all files will be stored in the A or B Drive.

■ Press **7** to display the Location of Files menu shown on the next page.

As you can guess, **B**ackup Directory (**1**) indicates where backup files are to be stored.

TIP: If no other directory is listed for an option, the currently active (or default) directory is assumed. If you are not using a hard disk or network, all options will be either A or B. You may also need to insert special disks for the printer, speller, and thesaurus options.

```
Setup: Location of Auxiliary Files

     1 - Backup Directory

     2 - Hyphenation Module(s)

     3 - Keyboard/Macro Files

     4 - Main Dictionary(s)

     5 - Printer Files

     6 - Style Library Filename

     7 - Supplementary Dictionary(s)

     8 - Thesaurus




Selection: 0
```

Hyphenation Module(s) (2) allows you to indicate where files relating to hyphenation are stored.

Keyboard/Macro Files (3) allows you to use a different directory if you do not want keyboard layout and macro files stored on the current one.

Main Dictionary(s) (4) and **Supplementary Dictionary(s) (7)** tell Word-Perfect where the main and supplementary dictionaries used by the speller are.

Printer Files (5) indicates where the printer definitions are stored. These are used when you want to add or change a printer setup to your system.

Style Library Filename (6) allows you to store styles in a separate directory.

Thesaurus (8) tells WordPerfect where to find the Thesaurus files.

TIP: Information on any of these file locations can be changed simply by entering the number of the item you wish and typing in the correct information beside the cursor.

◼ Again, do not change any of the settings. Press **Enter** to return to the Setup menu.

Units of Measure

The last item on the main Setup menu, Units of Measure (8), is perhaps one of the most revolutionary for WordPerfect. Prior to version 5.0, all positions on the screen and page were identified by horizontal spaces across and vertical number of lines up and down.

As you know, in Version 5.0 the default for position measurement is inches. In addition to inches, however, it is also possible to identify position in centimeters and points.

◼ Press **8** to display the following Units of Measure menu:

```
Setup: Units of Measure

     1 - Display and Entry of Numbers          "
           for Margins, Tabs, etc.

     2 - Status Line Display                   "


Legend:

     " = inches
     i = inches
     c = centimeters
     p = points
     u = WordPerfect 4.2 Units (Lines/Columns)










Selection: 0
```

The options allow you to identify:

1. How you want to display the numbers used for margin, tab, and other settings in menus and other places.

2. The kind of measurements you want used for display on the status line.

TIP: Recall that the Ln measurement on the status line is vertical distance from the top of the page down. The Pos figure indicates horizontal distance measured from the left to the right side of the page.

Using the legend, you can see that it is possible to display measurements in inches (two methods), centimeters, and points. In addition, you can use line and column positions similar to those used in Version 4.2. It is not necessary to use the same measurement type for both the menu displays and the status line.

TIP: Inches are counted in 1/12 of a foot, centimeters in 1/100 of a meter, and points in 1/72 of an inch. To determine size, it is helpful to remember that the larger the number, the wider the distance.

Because of the many different fonts now available, the current vertical measure (Ln) will change according to the line height and the current horizontal measure (Pos) will change according to the pitch required for any given font. For example: larger fonts will have fewer characters per inch across the page and fewer lines per inch going down the page; smaller fonts will be just the opposite.

This large font is more spread out.

This small font takes less space across the page.

You should not try to use current horizontal measure with proportionally spaced fonts since the width of all characters is not equal. Doing so would **TIP:** result in an inexact measurement.

Even though you may have identified a particular style for displaying measurements in the Setup menu, it is not necessary to enter all measurements in that style. For instance, if centimeters were the default, you could still enter 1", and WordPerfect would automatically convert the inches to centimeters and display the measurement in centimeters in the menus and on the status line.

Finally, once you have identified a measurement style in the Units of Measure menu, WordPerfect assumes that any measurement you enter without accompanying changes is intended to be in that style.

☐ To see what these differences look like, select **D**isplay and Entry of Numbers for Margins, Tabs, etc (**1**). Type **c** to change the display of measurements in menus to centimeters.

☐ Select Status Line Display (**2**) and type **p** to change the display of measurements to points on the status line.

☐ Then press **Exit** (**F7**). Note the change on the status line.

▣ Press **Format (Shift-F8)**, Line **(1)** to bring up the Line Format menu. Note the way measurements are displayed in the menu.

▣ Press **Cancel (F1)** and return to the screen. Then press **Setup (Shift-F1)** again. This time, change the settings to another option. Make at least one of them **u** for Lines/Columns. Remember to press **Exit (F7)** to save the changes.

The example shown below illustrates the differences among the various settings for the same point on the screen.

Inches = "	Doc 1 Pg 22 Ln 3.58" Pos 3.7"
Inches = i	Doc 1 Pg 22 Ln 3.58i Pos 3.7i
Centimeters	Doc 1 Pg 22 Ln 9.09c Pos 9.39c
Points	Doc 1 Pg 22 Ln 257.7p Pos 266.4p
Lines/Columns	Doc 1 Pg 22 Ln 16.48 Pos 37

▣ Again note the status line and take a look at the Line Format menu. When you are finished, return all settings to inches and the defaults.

TIP: Remember that if you are sharing equipment or disks you should return the Setup options to the defaults or whatever settings your instructor or lab assistant directs at the end of each work session.

To Review

List the default for each of the following:

BackUp
    Timed Backup
    Original Document Backup

Cursor Speed

Display
    Automatically Format and Rewrite
    Colors/Fonts/Attributes
    Display Document Comments
    Filename on the Status Line
    Graphics Screen Type
    Hard Return Display Character
    Menu Letter Display
    Side-by-side Columns Display

Fast Save
    Initial Settings
    Beep

Using Forms Definitions For Printer Commands

As you work with a variety of documents, you will likely find that you use several different types quite often. These might include envelopes, labels, letterhead, different forms, and others. Because their size varies, you likely will need to change the paper size often.

In addition, you may have several bins on your printer, each containing a different item and you must let WordPerfect know which bin contains the form you wish to use at any given time.

Some items may need to be hand fed into your printer and some can be automatically fed. Most will be printed with the shorter edges of the paper at the top and bottom and the longer ones at the sides (portrait orientation), but others may need to be printed with the long side of the paper at the top and bottom (landscape orientation).

Entering all these commands each time you change a print job can be quite a chore, so WordPerfect has come up with a way to allow you to do it once and then store the commands to be reused again and again whenever you need them.

To use the forms command requires two major steps. First you must create a forms definition containing the size, location, orientation, and other information about each form you plan to use and store it with the printer definitions. To do this you will use the printer definition keys found on Print (**Shift-F7**).

Second each time you enter a print job, you must let WordPerfect know how to find the correct forms definition for that particular item. This is done using the Format (**Shift-F7**), Page (**2**) commands.

Creating a Form Definition

To see how this works, let's create a forms definition and use it in a print job.

■ To begin, press **Print (Shift-F7)**, Select Printers (**S**) and Edit (**3**). Notice Forms (**4**) on the following menu:

```
Select Printer: Edit

        Filename                        HPLASEII.PRS

    1 - Name                            HP LaserJet Series II

    2 - Port                            LPT1:

    3 - Sheet Feeder                    None
      .
    4 - Forms

    5 - Cartridges and Fonts

    6 - Initial Font                    Courier 10 pitch (PC-8)

    7 - Path for Downloadable
          Fonts and Printer
          Command Files




Selection: 0
```

■ Select Forms (**4**) to bring up the forms selection menu. (Note: the default forms can vary from printer to printer. As a result, what you see may not look exactly like the example.)

```
Select Printer: Forms
                                           Orient  Init              Offset
   Form type                  Size          P  L   Pres  Location   Top      Side

   Envelope                   4" x 9.5"     N  Y  Y  Manual  0"      0"
   Standard                   8.5" x 11"    Y  Y  Y  Contin  0"      0"
   [ALL OTHERS]               Width ≤ 8.5"        N     Manual  0"        0"



   If the requested form is not available, then printing stops and WordPerfect
   waits for a form to be inserted in the ALL OTHERS location.  If the requested
   form is larger than the ALL OTHERS form, the width is set to the maximum width.

   1 Add; 2 Delete; 3 Edit: 3
```

This menu contains several predefined forms that can be used to specify print requirements. Notice that it displays form type and size. Whether a form is portrait or landscape orientation is identified, and whether the form is initially present (in a bin or tray) is also defined. Where the form will be fed from is shown with manual meaning hand fed and continuous meaning the paper is in a tray or bin or is continuous feed paper.

If the defined printer has more than one bin, the bins will be listed on this menu. Finally an offset that affects where the first line of printing begins is identified. This offset is used to compensate for differences in the way the paper is loaded into the printer. The offset of 0" 0" shown assumes that the top left corner of the paper is positioned immediately under the printhead when printing begins. If that is not the case, you will want to adjust the offset. More about that later.

When WordPerfect begins a print job, it will go to this menu for a form definition that matches the type and size of paper for the job it has been given. If it finds a match, it will use the remaining parts of the form definition to set the printer up. As a result, it will "know" what the orientation should be, whether the paper is already present, how the paper will be fed, and whether there is an offset.

If WordPerfect does not find a match, it will default to the [ALL OTHERS] option and use that. The message at the bottom of the screen indicates that when this happens, WordPerfect will stop and wait for you to insert a form (sheet of paper) before moving ahead.

TIP: When the printer stops this way you will hear a beep. To restart it, you must insert a sheet of paper into the printer, press Print (**Shift-F7**), Control Printer (**4**), and **Go**.

Let's assume that you often need to print on letterhead that is 7" wide by 8.5" high and create a form definition for that.

▣ To begin, select **Add (1)**. The following menu will display:

```
Select Printer: Form Type

     1 - Standard

     2 - Bond

     3 - Letterhead

     4 - Labels

     5 - Envelope

     6 - Transparency

     7 - Cardstock

     8 - [ALL OTHERS]

     9 - Other




  Selection: 1
```

This menu offers you a selection of widely used form types to choose from. If options 1 - 7 do not meet your needs, you may use 8 [ALL OTHERS]. However, since ALL OTHERS is the one WordPerfect will default to if it does not find a match otherwise, it is usually best to have that one quite generic. You may also define one that is not on the list as Other if you wish.

TIP: It is also possible to have more than one definition for each type, such as two or three for labels. As long as their sizes are different, WordPerfect will be able to distinguish among them. If it cannot, it will prompt you for a choice.

▣ Since this is for a letterhead, select **3** or press **H**. The menu shown at the top of the next page will appear.

```
Select Printer: Forms

        Filename                    Printerfile.PRS

        Form Type                   Letterhead

1 - Form Size                       8.5" x 11"

2 - Orientation                     Portrait

3 - Initially Present               Yes

4 - Location                        Continuous

5 - Page Offsets - Top              0"
                   Side             0"




Selection: 0
```

■ Select Form Size (**1**) to display the Form Size menu shown below. As you can
see, it lists a number of predefined commonly used forms as well as allows
you to set one of your own with Other.

```
Select Printer: Form Size
                                Inserted
                                Edge

     1 - Standard                8.5"    x    11"

     2 - Standard Wide           11"     x    8.5"

     3 - Legal                   8.5"    x    14"

     4 - Legal Wide              14"     x    8.5"

     5 - Envelope                9.5"    x    4"

     6 - Half Sheet              5.5"    x    8.5"

     7 - US Government           8"      x    11"

     8 - A4                      210mm   x    297mm

     9 - A4 Wide                 297mm   x    210mm

     0 - Other

Selection: 1
```

■ Because the size for the form you wish to define is not listed, select **Other** (**O**).
A prompt like the following will display at the lower left corner of the screen.

```
Width:0"  Length:
```

- Type **7** for the width and press **Enter.** Then type **8.5** for the length and press **Enter.** WordPerfect will insert the size you have specified and return to the previous menu.

    Since the orientation of the paper for this new form is portrait (or short edges at top and bottom), you will not need to change this option. If you needed to, however, you could specify that the form was portrait, landscape, or both.

- Let's assume that you will use continuous feed paper for print jobs using this form so select Initially Present (**3**) and type **Y**(es). (If you were going to hand feed the forms, you would enter No.)

- Select Location (**4**) to see what options you have available. A prompt like the following will appear across the bottom of your screen.

```
Location: 1 Continuous; 2 Bin Number; 3 Manual: 0
```

    You may tell WordPerfect that the paper is continuous fed or that you will manually insert it when needed. In addition, if your printer has several bins, you may indicate which one contains this particular form.

- Since the form you are defining is continuous fed, select **Continuous** (**1**). (If you were going to hand feed it, you would select Manual to let WordPerfect know that you would supply it when needed.)

    If the paper you are using allows the printhead to be positioned on the upper left corner of the first line of printing on the page as it is fed in, you do not need to set a page offset. However, if it has any unusual characteristics such as an extra wide margin, tractor feed holes on the sides, binding at the top, or other variations to compensate for, you would want to identify that as an offset.

TIP: You might also use the offset option if your printer setup were different than normal. For instance if your printer was set to advance the paper $1/2$ inch from the default starting position, you would need to specify that.

The offset is identified in inches, with positive measurements (such as .25) used for forms with a top edge that extends above the printhead and/or a left edge that extends to the right. Negative numbers are used for forms with a top edge positioned below the printhead or a left edge that is left of the printhead.

TIP: When changing offsets at the top of the page, remember that unless the top margin is changed, WordPerfect will insert a one-inch top margin before beginning to print. This will be in addition to any offset you specify.

▣ Press **Exit (F7)** to save the settings and return to the printer select menu. As you can see, the form you just defined has been added.

▣ Since you also use letterhead that is 8.5" wide by 11" long frequently, create a second letterhead form definition for that size.

TIP: If you wanted to add another form, delete one of the settings, or edit an existing form definition, you could do so from this menu. You cannot, however, select a form for use from here. This, and its related menus, is used only to identify the form specifications.

▣ When you are finished, press **Exit (F7)** four times to save the form definitions and return to the document editing screen.

Selecting a Form for Use

With the forms already defined, let's select one for use.

▣ Press **Format (Shift-F8)** and since the Paper Size/Type option is under **Page (2)**, select that.

▣ From the Page Format menu select Paper Size/Type **(8)**. The Paper Size menu will appear.

▣ Since the size you want to use is not shown, select **Other (0)**.

▣ Enter the width of **7"** and height of **8.5"**.

▣ The Paper Type menu will appear. Select Letterhead **(3)**.

WordPerfect will automatically match the Paper Size/Type code you have just entered to a form definition and use the form from that point on. If you should have more than one form defined at the same size, WordPerfect will display them all and ask you to select the one you want.

Using forms this way provides a great deal of flexibility and solves many problems with the printer. It also allows you to identify the printer criteria (landscape vs. portrait, special size paper, offset, location, etc.) once and then reuse the settings over and over without having to enter them each time you print.

Now that you've learned how to create several automatic settings to customize WordPerfect to your needs, let's move ahead.

Activities

Return all settings to the defaults. No files saved.

Chapter Review

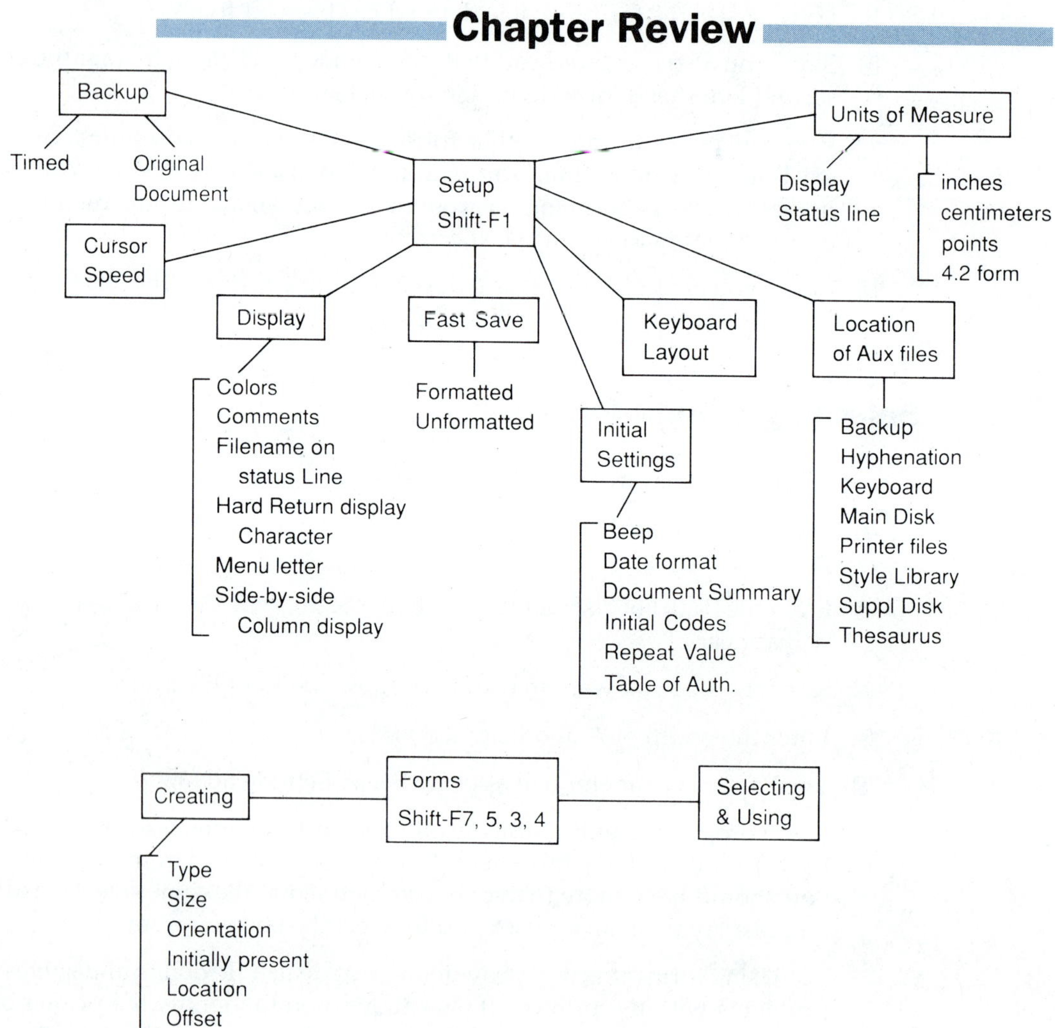

━━━━━ Self-Check Quiz 10 ━━━━━

1. What is a backup file?

2. What does the timed backup do?

3. What does the original document backup do?

4. What does it mean that Setup menu changes are semi-permanent?

5. What must you do to format a document saved with fast save?

6. Identify the default for date format.

7. List the default for units of measurement.

8. Why are inches, centimeters, or points a better way than spaces and columns to show position on the line?

9. List four ways units of measure can be displayed.

10. Why is the current horizontal measure not a good indicator of distance when using proportional spaced fonts?

11. What information must you supply to create a forms definition?

12. What keystrokes should you use to create a forms definition?

13. What keystrokes should you use to use a forms definition?

14. How does WordPerfect use the forms definitions you create?

15. When is the ALL OTHERS form definition used?

16. What does Initially Present mean in a forms definition?

17. Describe the difference between portrait and landscape orientation.

18. When should you use the Page Offset command?

11

Automating Your Work with Macros and Keyboard Layouts

You're ready to learn some new tricks using macros and keyboard layouts to make things you do frequently easier. These are very useful functions and will save you a great deal of time by eliminating the need to re-enter commands for tasks that you do often. When you have completed this lesson, you should be able to:

- create and use macros to do a variety of tasks.
- edit macros.
- use repeating and chained macros.
- create and use several special keyboard layouts.
- change the command assignments for keys and other functions.

Creating and Using Macros

A macro is a group of words, lines, sentences, codes, functions, or a combination of all of these that can be saved and recalled by WordPerfect and used again and again. Macros can be used for either a process (such as SAVE, PRINT, or the commands to set up a letter) or some special text (such as the date, the company address, a name, a special paragraph, and the like).

Creating a macro is similar to recording on a tape recorder. You turn the recorder on, talk, and turn it off. Then any time you want to hear what is on the tape, you simply play it back. With a macro, WordPerfect asks you to provide a name and description to distinguish this macro from others it may have. Then you turn the macro recorder on, enter the macro, and turn the recorder off. To use the macro again and again, you need only provide the name, and WordPerfect will find the macro and "play it back." Sound easy? It is. Here are the steps to follow.

To create a macro, you must:

1. Tell WordPerfect to begin the macro definition (where the macro begins) by positioning the cursor and pressing **Macro** (**Ctrl-F10**).

2. Give the macro a name and description when prompted.

3. Type the macro in.

4. Tell WordPerfect to end macro definition (end the macro) and save it by pressing **Macro** (**Crtl-F10**) again.

TIP: The commands included in the macro (such as margin changes, etc.) are actually entered by WordPerfect at the cursor position as the macro is being created. Therefore, if you do not want them to appear in your document at that point you should move to Doc2, use a clear screen, or use a document you do not intend to save while they are being created.

Define and Name Macro

To see how macros work, try the following:

- Clear your screen and press **Macro Def (Ctrl-F10)** to begin defining your macro.

- When the prompt "**Define Macro:**" appears, give your macro a **name** and press **Enter**. You can name your macro in one of three ways:

    a. You can enter a word between one and eight characters long.

    b. You can hold down Alt and press one letter (A-Z).

    c. You can simply press Enter.

TIP: Either of the first two options (a and b) create separate macro files on your disk and are saved permanently. The third option creates only a temporary macro that is lost when you EXIT WordPerfect.

- For now, let's use option **a**. Type in **NameMac** and press **Enter**.

- When you are asked for the description, type **Name and address** and press **Enter**.

TIP: The description is sometimes used in advanced macro operations. It can be up to 60 characters long.

The following words will begin to flash in the lower left corner of the screen.

```
Macro Def                                              Doc 1 Pg 1 Ln 1" Pos 1"
```

- Enter your macro. For this exercise, **center your name, street address, and city and state on separate lines**. Be sure to end the last line with **Enter**.

- Press **Macro Def (Ctrl-F10)** again to turn off the macro definition. The macro will be saved automatically. It is not necessary to use any of the other saving functions.

TIP: If you would like to make sure your macro has been saved, press List Files (**F5**) and look for the file with the .WPM extension. You will see that it has been saved as NameMac.WPM.

Start or Use the Macro

Now you are ready to use the macro you have created.

◪ Return to your document screen. Move the cursor to the place you want the macro to appear. (In this case, press **Enter** twice to move the cursor down the screen a little.)

◪ Press **Macro (Alt-F10)**. You will see the following prompt:

```
Macro:
```

◪ Type in the name of the macro you wish to use. (In this case, **NameMac**) and press **Enter**.

TIP: If you had named your macro with the Enter key (option c), you would press Macro (**Alt-F10**) and the Enter key to retrieve it.

Can you see the possibilities of this command? (You could create one for your name, class number, time, or lesson number to use with each assignment.)

TIP: Macro files with the .WPM extension can only be retrieved with Macro (Alt-F10). You cannot retrieve them with Retrieve (Shift-F10) or via List Files (F5). If you try, you will get an error message saying "Incompatible file format," or "File not found."

◪ Following the last three steps, start (or retrieve) the macro twice more.

TIP: If you should need to stop a macro while it is running, you can press Cancel (F1) to interrupt it.

Repeating Macros

You can also use the ESC key Repeat Value command to make the macro repeat itself a certain number of times. To see how this works, try the following:

■ Move the cursor down the page several lines and press **Esc**.

■ When the **Repeat Value =** prompt appears, type **3**.

■ Press Macro (**Alt-F10**) and type **NameMac**. Then press **Enter**.

How's that for a surprise! There are many possibilities for reusing macros with this option.

TIP: If you plan to use macros this way, you will likely want to add lines before and after the text of the macro so there will be space between each occurrence.

To Review

What would have happened if you had not ended the last line of the macro with Enter to insert a [HRt]?

Using Macros to Format

Macros can be used to set up special formats for documents that you type often. For instance, if you wanted to create a macro that would change margins, spacing, top margin, and the like, automatically, you would follow the same procedure outlined above. However, instead of typing your name or other text, you would change the margin settings, etc., and store them in the macro. Then, when you used the macro, these commands would replace the defaults or whatever was on your machine.

TIP: Using a macro to enter format commands is similar to an open style, which you learned about in Chapter 9. Even though both a macro and a style can be used to enter a format, there are differences in the way the commands function.

For some practice with a formatting macro, try the following:

■ Clear your screen and press **Macro Def (Ctrl-F10)** to begin defining your macro.

■ Enter **Ltrfmt** as the name and **Letter format** for the description.

■ When the **Macro Def** signal begins to blink, press **Format (Shift-F8)** to bring up the Line Format menu.

- Choose Line (**1**) and Margins (**7**).

- Enter left and right margins of **1.5"** and **Exit** with **F7**.

- Press **Macro Def** (**Ctrl-F10**) again to turn macro definition off.

- Move down the screen two or three lines and press **Macro** (**Alt-F10**).

- When you are asked for the macro name, enter **Ltrfmt** and press **Enter**.

  Immediately WordPerfect "plays back" the series of keystrokes you recorded and, in the process, changes the margins to the new settings.

- Then press **Reveal Codes** (**Alt-F3**) to see what the macro has done. You should see the changed margin settings listed twice, similar to that shown below. One was inserted when you entered the macro, and one was inserted when you used the macro.

> [L/R Mar: 1.5", 1.5"]
> [HRt]
> [L/R Mar: 1.5", 1.5"]

Each time you use this macro, the margin settings stored in it will be inserted at the cursor. This makes it very easy to change margins. You could place several commands that would change margins, spacing, tabs, fonts, etc., in the same macro. Then, using the macro, you could enter them into a document all at once.

Styles vs. Macros

You may notice that some macros function very much like styles. There are some differences, however, that you will find of interest when deciding whether to use a macro or a style for a particular application.

1. To change the commands in a style throughout your document, you need only change the master style. All changes made there will be automatically inserted wherever the style is used in the text. To change a macro, you may need to search for and alter each occurrence.

2. Styles can only be edited from within the style menu. Once a style is changed, all occurrences throughout the document are changed at the same time. In contrast, when a macro is changed, the changes are shown only in future uses. In addition, macros already inserted into the document may be changed individually, without affecting the same macro in other places.

3. Styles are most useful for format applications, with margins, tabs, fonts, centering, indenting, and the like. They are not intended for things like printing, doing merges, or performing searches. For those applications, macros work better.

The macro command is a very powerful feature and can be used in many other ways. Some of these include sending documents to the printer, inserting function codes, chaining macros, and executing merges. There are also other ways to name and use macros. If you wish to learn more about these advanced uses, refer to the WordPerfect Reference Manual.

To Review

List the four steps in creating a macro:

1. ____

2. ____

3. ____

4. ____

What are the three ways a macro can be named?

1. ____

2. ____

3. ____

What keystrokes should you use to start or use a macro:

1. ____

2. ____

3. ____

For the time being, let's do a little exercise using macros. To complete this, you will need to create two macros and type a letter.

■ First, clear your screen and remove Reveal Codes from it if necessary. (Do not save your document.)

Pretend that you work for the Anderson Cleaning Company, and that you send out many letters with the same return address and closing lines.

To avoid retyping these items each time, let's create some macros that will do the work for you.

◾ Press **Macro Def** (**Ctrl-F10**) to begin defining a macro for the following address. Name it **Address1** and provide an appropriate description. Then center each line as you type it.

ANDERSON CLEANING COMPANY

6808 Main Street

Richfield, UT 84701

◾ Press **Enter** at least once after the ZIP code. Then press **Macro Def** (**Ctrl-F10**) to end the definition and save it as a macro file.

◾ Now, create a second macro for the following closing lines. Call it **Name1** and indicate that it goes with the sales letter for the Spring sale. (NOTE: Since this is for a modified block letter, begin on position 4.2--or the center point between the margins. If you have forgotten what modified block means, ask your instructor to review this information with you or look in the appendix in the back of this book.)

> **Yours very truly**
>
> **(Press Enter 4 times)**
>
> **(Your Name)**
> **Sales Division**

◾ **Clear your screen**. Since the macros have already been saved, you do not need to save them again.

◾ Type the following letter and start the macros as indicated. You may retrieve **Letter.11** from the student exercise disk and finish it from the interim save if you wish.

a. Use the left and right default margins of **1"**.

b. Type the letter in modified block style with open punctuation.

c. Center the letter on the page.

d. Proofread carefully and correct all errors.

(Use Today's Date, start at center point)

(Press Enter 4 times)

Mrs. Louise Smith
158 West 2300 North
Woodland, UT 84653

Dear Mrs. Smith:

Now that spring is here, you're no doubt thinking of Spring Cleaning. In addition to the work you do around the yard and in your home to get ready for the coming summer months, you're likely going through your wardrobe, too.
Before putting those winter clothes away, why not let us clean and repair your coats, suits, and other cold weather items. You'll be especially interested to know that all items brought in before the end of the month will receive a 25 percent discount.

(Do an interim SAVE here. Name it Letter.11).

In addition, if you will attach one of the enclosed coupons to your garments, you will receive an extra 5 percent reduction at our new location. The address is:

(Start Address1 macro)

You'll receive the same fine, prompt service you've come to expect. We're looking forward to seeing you soon.

(Start Name1 macro)

(Press Enter twice)

(your initials as typist)

Enclosure

◼ Use **Ctrl-Enter** to force the printer to begin a new page for the next part.

◼ Save your document as **Letter.11** using the regular Exit (**F7**) method to save.

The coupons mentioned in the letter will be printed with the address, as shown in Address1. We will prepare a sheet with four coupons to be enclosed with the letter.

◼ To do this, start with a **clear screen**, and use the macro **Address1** four times on the page. Use the **Repeat Value** command to automate the macro. Remember that the macro will begin on the line where the cursor is located when you start it. Center the coupons on the page and draw lines (or a design) around each one if you wish.

◼ Save your document as **Insert.11**. Then print two copies.

Editing Macros

As you work with macros, you may find that occasionally you need to change one, or you may make errors during macro creation that should be deleted. For some practice, let's change the Address1 macro so that everything is in uppercase letters.

◼ **Clear your screen**, then press **Macro Def** (**Ctrl-F10**). When you are asked for the name of the macro to define, type **Address1** and press **Enter**.

WordPerfect will give the following prompt to report that you already have a macro named Address1:

```
ADDRESS1.WPM is Already Defined.   1 Replace; 2 Edit: 0
```

◼ Press Edit (**2**) to edit, and the screen shown on the next page will appear:

◼ Select **Action** (**2**), and the cursor will jump to the text and code inside the box.

◼ Change **Main Street** and **Richfield** to uppercase characters.

◼ Then press **Exit** (**F7**) to return to your document. If you wish, call the macro to see if the changes have been made.

It is possible to add, delete, and change most text and codes as you edit your macros. You cannot, however, insert an Enter command. It is often helpful to add an extra one when the macro is first created, if you suspect that you will need another one later on.

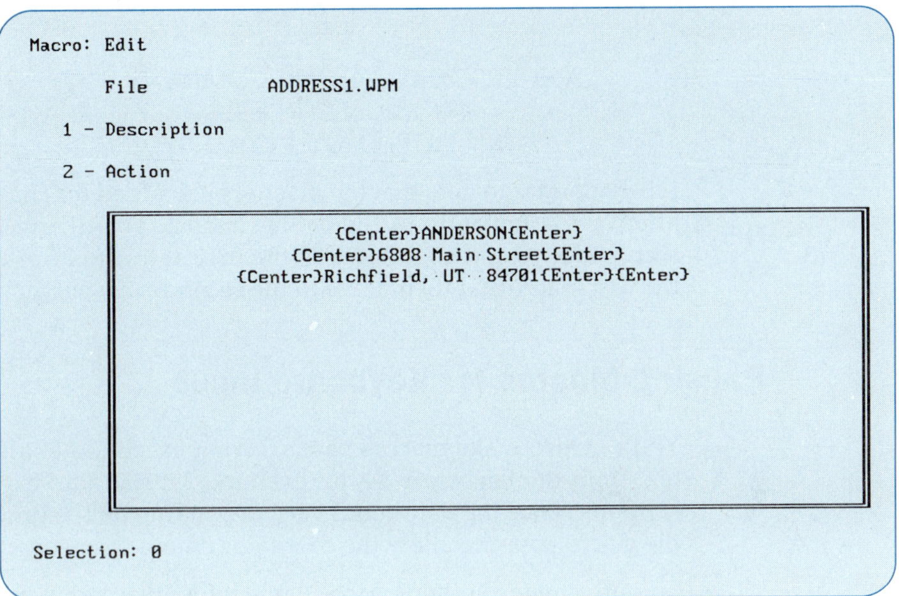

Chaining Macros

Now let's try something a little more challenging. WordPerfect will allow you to chain macros so that as soon as one has finished, another automatically starts. For some practice with this command, let's create a new macro to print the word COUPON and chain it to the Address1 macro.

- First, define a new macro called **Coupon**. Then, press **Enter** to move the cursor down one line from the top and center the word C O U P O N. Type it so there is a space between each letter in the word.

  Now you are going to insert the Address1 macro into the Coupon macro so that as soon as the word COUPON is printed, WordPerfect will move to the Address1 macro and begin to execute it. To make this happen, do the following:

- Press **Enter** twice and then **Macro** (**Alt-F10**).

- When the **Macro**: prompt appears, type **Address1** and press **Enter**.

- Then end macro definition for the Coupon macro by pressing **Macro Def** (**Ctrl-F10**).

  You have told WordPerfect to display the word C O U P O N, then to get the Address1 macro and execute it. When the Coupon macro is run, the result will look like the following. Try it to see if you get the same result. You can even use the repeat value command to print multiple copies.

C O U P O N

ANDERSON CLEANING COMPANY
6808 MAIN STREET
RICHFIELD, UT 84701

TIP:

It is important to note that the macro being added (or chained) must be listed after any commands in the calling macro. WordPerfect cannot execute a second macro and come back to the first. It must perform the commands of the first macro and then move to the second.

Pausing Macros for Keyboard Input

You can also make macros pause during execution to allow the addition of text from the keyboard. As an example, let's add an expiration date to the coupons. Since the date could vary depending on the promotion, we'll make the macro pause to allow the date to be entered as needed.

■ To start, create another macro. Name it **EXPIRE** and when you are asked for a description, you can indicate that it adds an expiration date.

■ When **Macro Def:** begins to flash in the lower left corner, center the following, but *do not* press Enter: **Expiration date:** Press the space bar twice after the colon.

■ To insert the pause command, press **Ctrl-PGUP** to display the following menu:

```
1 Pause; 2 Display; 3 Assign; 4 Comment: 0
```

■ Select **Pause (1).** Then press **Enter** twice.

■ To end macro definition, press **Macro Def (Ctrl-F10)** again.

Before moving ahead, let's review the rest of the options. You already know that Pause stops the macro temporarily. Selecting the Display option will turn on the display of the commands and you will see them zip by on the screen as they are executed. The Assign option allows you to assign values to variables that are used in macro execution. The Comment option allows you to make comments about the macro as it is executing. When the macro is run, the comments are ignored.

Now, use the macro to see if it pauses and waits for you to enter the expiration date.

- ■ Press **Macro** (**Alt-F10**) and type **EXPIRE** when you are asked for the name of the macro.

- ■ The words **Expiration date:** will display. Notice that the cursor is at the end.

- ■ Type **January 31, 19—** and press **Enter**. You will see the following on your screen:

Expiration date: January 31, 19—

Chaining Macros

Now, for an extra challenge, let's chain this macro to the Address1 macro to see what will happen. Do the following:

- ■ Press **Macro Def** (**Ctrl-F10**) and type **Address1**, then press **Enter**. When WordPerfect indicates that Address1 already exists and asks if you want to replace or edit, select Edit (**2**).

- ■ Then select **2** again for **Action** and move the cursor just to the left of the last {Enter} command at the end of the macro.

TIP: It is important that at least one {Enter} command come after the name of the macro being chained (in this case EXPIRE). Otherwise, the macro may not function completely.

- ■ Press **Macro** (**Alt-F10**) to insert a Macro command code and type **EXPIRE**. The commands displayed on your screen should look similar to the following:

```
{Center}Anderson Cleaning Company {Enter}
{Center}6808 Main Street{Enter}
{Center}Richfield, UT 84701{Enter}{Enter}
{Macro}EXPIRE{Enter}
```

- ◘ Then press **Exit** (**F7**) twice.

- ◘ Now press **Macro** (**Alt-F10**) and execute the **Address1** macro. You should get the name and address followed by the expiration notation.

- ◘ Supply an appropriate date when the macro pauses.

- ◘ Then, execute the **Coupon** macro. WordPerfect will execute all three macros, one after the other. Coupon will call Address1, and Address1 will call Expire.

```
                C O U P O N

        ANDERSON CLEANING COMPANY
             6808 MAIN STREET
           RICHFIELD, UT  84701

    Expiration date: January 31, 19--
```

As you can see, you can be quite creative with macros. You can even cause them to repeat themselves and use them to make decisions. These particular commands are especially useful with different types of searches. If you would like to learn more about them, consult the WordPerfect manual.

To Review

What steps should be followed to do each of the following?

a. Edit a macro

b. Repeat a macro a specified number of times

c. Chain macros

d. Pause a macro

Summary

In summary, to create and use Macros:

a. Press Macro Def (Ctrl-F10) to begin macro definition.

b. Type in the macro name and definition.

c. Enter the text, commands, etc., that you wish to store in the macro.

d. Press Macro Def (Ctrl-F10) to end macro definition.

e. Position the cursor where you wish to use the macro.

f. Press Macro (Alt-F10) and enter the macro name.

g. Press Enter and the macro will be executed.

Keyboard Layouts

A new feature of WordPerfect 5.0 is the ability to change the location of commands on the keyboard or to assign new commands with a keyboard definition.

For instance, the F3 key currently causes the Help menus to appear. If you want that command assigned to another key, you can easily change it. In addition, if you want to create a new function and assign it to a particular key or keys, that can also be done. You can even assign a macro and execute it simply by pressing the specified keys. And to top it all off, WordPerfect already has some keyboard layouts and macros built in that are ready to use.

NOTE: Because these files depend on many other parts of the WordPerfect program to work, this function can only be used from a hard disk. Such a disk can store the contents of all 12 of the WordPerfect disks in the same place and make them accessible as needed. A dual floppy disk computer cannot provide this availability. If you are using a dual disk machine, do not try to do the following exercises. However, you should read and study them carefully so you will be familiar with and able to use them when you have an opportunity.

▣ To see what is available, press **Setup (Shift-F1)**.

▣ When the Setup menu appears, as shown on the next page, select Keyboard Layout (**6**):

NOTE: If you are using a hard drive and the supplementary keyboard names do not appear as shown above, return to the Setup menu (Shift-F1) and select Location of Auxiliary Files (7). Then select Keyboard/Macro Files (3) from the next menu and specify the drive/directory where the Conversion Disk files are stored. This will probably be the location for your WordPerfect program files. Then try the command again.

```
Setup: Keyboard Layout

   ALTRNAT
   ENHANCED
   MACROS




1 Select; 2 Delete; 3 Rename; 4 Create; 5 Edit; 6 Original; N Name search: 1
```

Supplementary Keyboards

WordPerfect is telling you that there are already three keyboard layout definitions available. Notice that you can select, delete, rename, or edit an existing keyboard layout. You can also create a new one, return to the original keyboard, or search for names.

ALTRNAT Keyboard

To see what this keyboard definition contains, do the following:

◻ Move the highlighted bar to **ALTRNAT** and choose Select (**1**).

◻ When you return to the Setup Menu press Keyboard Layout (**6**) again. Then select Edit (**5**). The screen shown at the top of the next page is what you will see:

Selecting this keyboard layout will change the F1 key to Help, the F3 key to Escape, and the Esc key to Cancel.

◻ Press **Exit** (**F7**) to return to the Keyboard Layout menu.

ENHANCED Keyboard Layout

This keyboard definition is designed to use the extra F11 and F12 keys found on an enhanced keyboard. It also has several other commands that can be activated with that keyboard. If you are not using an enhanced keyboard, the commands on this layout will not work on your computer. You can, however, select the definition and take a look at what is available.

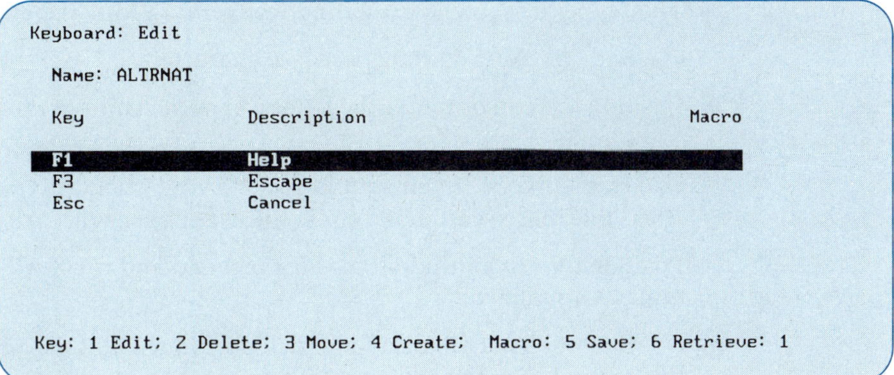

MACRO Keyboard Layout

The third layout contains some interesting pre-defined macros.

- To take a look, highlight MACROS, and choose **Select** (**1**). Again choose **Keyboard Layout** (**6**), and **Edit** (**5**) to bring up the following menu:

- To see how a few of these macros work, press **Exit** (**F7**) twice to return to the main editing screen.

◼ Then type the sentence: **A sunny weekend in May is perfect for a holiday.**

Let's try Alt-T to transpose two characters.

◼ Position the cursor under the letter **c** in perfect and press **Alt-T**.

Quick as a wink, the two characters immediately to the left of the cursor will trade places. If you should make errors, such as typing "teh" instead of "the," this macro could be very helpful. Let's see what Alt-C does.

◼ Position the cursor under the **w** in weekend and press **Alt-C**. In a flash the W will be capitalized.

But that's not all this macro will do. Notice that the cursor has jumped to the beginning of the next word.

◼ Again press **Alt-C** and the first letter of that word is also capitalized, with the cursor again jumping to the next word. This command could be very useful for creating headings or other items that require capitalization.

Using Macros to Address Envelopes

Notice that Ctrl-E will allow you to print a name and address on an envelope. Before this feature can be used, be sure that your printer is selected correctly, and that an envelope form is identified. Then enter the following name and address. When you are finished, be sure to insert two [HRt] commands following Tulsa, OK 74157.

Mr. Jack Winters
Manager
Acme Lumber & Hardware
235 Merchant Blvd.
Tulsa, OK 74157

◼ Position the cursor at the top left of the first line of the address (on Mr.) Then press **Ctrl-E** and follow any prompts. Soon WordPerfect will print the name and address as if it were an envelope.

Calculator

One of the macros is "Calculator."

◼ Press **Ctrl-C** and immediately a calculator overlay like the following will appear on the left side of your screen:

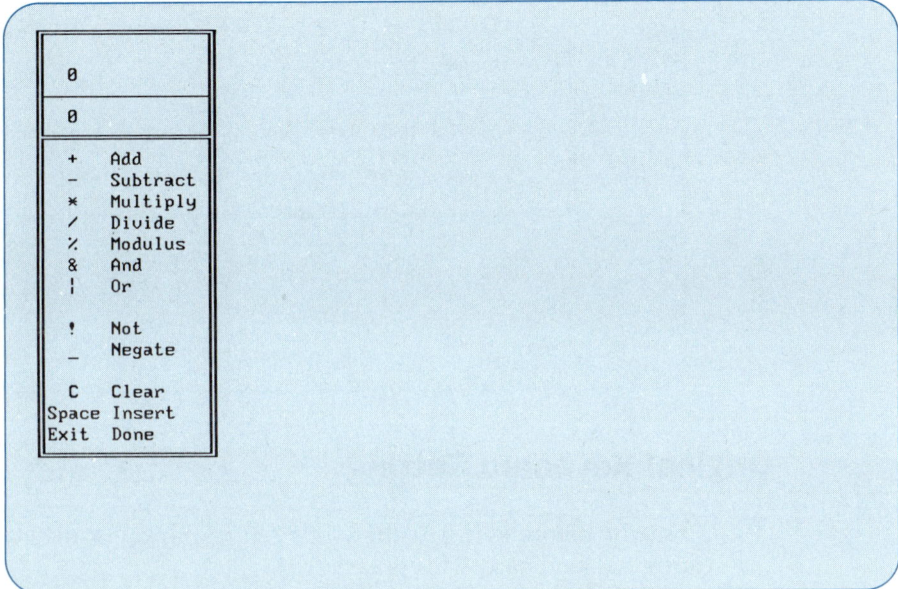

◼ Try entering several numbers to see how the calculator works. When you are finished, press **Exit** (**F7**) to return to your document.

Programming Macros

There are a number of programming commands that can be used with advanced macros. This text does not cover them in any detail, but take a look at one to see what it is like. Many programming commands have been used to create the macros you have just seen.

◼ Enter the commands to bring up the MACROS keyboard layout screen showing the list of macros. Highlight the macro to print an envelope and press Edit (1). At the edit screen, enter Action (2). **DO NOT MAKE ANY CHANGES IN THIS FILE.** If you wish, you may scroll the cursor through the commands to see more at the bottom.

◼ When you are finished, press **Exit** (**F7**) to return to the previous menu.

If you wish to learn more about how to use these programming commands, consult the WordPerfect manual for further instructions.

```
Key: Edit

        Key             Ctrl-E

  1 - Description       Print Name & Address on an Envelope

  2 - Action


        ┌─────────────────────────────────────────────────────────────┐
        │ {IF}{STATE}&4              {;}Only editing screen-           │
        │ {ELSE}                                                       │
        │ {RETURN}                                                     │
        │ {END IF}                                                     │
        │ {DISPLAY OFF}                                                │
        │ {ON NOT FOUND}{GO}prompt-    {;}Try to find location         │
        │ {Home}{Home}{Home}                                          │
        │ {Search}{Math/Columns}2{Math/Columns}3{Esc}                 │
        │ {GO}have it-                                                 │
        └─────────────────────────────────────────────────────────────┘



  Selection: 0
```

Original Keyboard Setting

Finally, before going further, let's return the keyboard layout settings to the original keyboard. This is easy to do.

- ■ Press **Setup (Shift-F1)**, and select Keyboard Layout (**6**), and Original (**6**).

Creating Keyboard Layouts

You can create a definition to be added to an existing Keyboard Layout, or you can create a new Keyboard Layout with a whole new set of separate definitions. Let's create a new keyboard layout first and then add some definitions to it.

TIP: Creating new layouts this way can allow you to set up specialized keyboards for different applications.

- ■ To begin, press **Setup (Shift-F1)**, and select Keyboard Layout (**6**).

- ■ At the Setup menu, choose **Create (4)**. When you are asked for a Keyboard filename, type **TRIAL** followed by your initials. For instance, if your name were Mary Jane Smith, you would enter **TRIALMJS**.

    WordPerfect will immediately establish a new Keyboard Layout file ready to receive instructions on how you want special keys defined.

Creating Keyboard Definitions

For something to practice with, let's say that you would like to assign the Reveal Codes function to the Ctrl-R keys, since it is easier to type than Alt-F3, and then add this definition to the Keyboard Layout Menu you just created.

◘ With the **TRIAL(your initials)** Keyboard Layout menu on the screen, select **Create (4)**.

The word **Key**: will appear at the lower left corner of your screen. WordPerfect is asking you which key(s) you wish to assign the command to.

TIP: It is generally a good idea to assign keys that will not ordinarily be used for other functions. You must also watch that the combination of keys you select has not already been used for another definition. In most cases using Ctrl, Alt, and Shift with a letter key will produce good results. You can also use keys like < and | that are not often used in other ways.

◘ Press **Ctrl-R**. The following menu will appear.

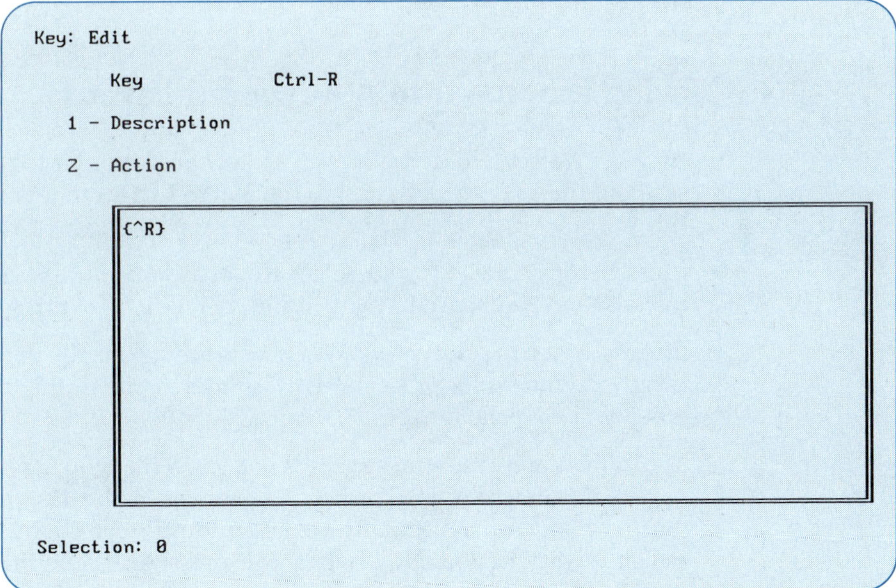

◘ Enter Description (**1**). Then type **Reveals Codes** and press **Enter**.

■ Select **A**ction (**2**). The cursor will jump inside the box. Notice the Ctrl-R. This is the beginning of the command for WordPerfect. You MUST use the arrow keys to move the cursor to the right of this command before entering the next keystrokes. Do that now.

■ Press the **Reveal Codes (Alt-F3)** keys. Then press **Exit (F7)** four times to return to the main editing screen.

■ Now test your new command. Press **Ctrl-R**. Immediately the Reveal Codes screen will appear. Press **Ctrl-R** again and it will disappear. Wonderful!

You can use this command to customize all kinds of functions. It has many possibilities.

Entering Text

It is also possible to assign text to a key. For instance, you may want to be able to press a key and have your company name entered on the screen. If so, simply assign a key(s) and type in whatever you want the key to enter inside the action box when requested.

Retrieving Macros Into A Keyboard Layout

Another way to add definitions to a keyboard layout is to retrieve a macro. To see how this is done, let's assign the macro **Ltrfmt** that you created earlier in this lesson, to the keys Alt-L.

■ Press **Setup (Shift-F1)** and select Keyboard Layout (**6**). Select **TRIAL(your initials)** and Keyboard Layout (**6**) and then Edit (**5**) to bring up the Edit screen.

■ Choose **M**acro Retrieve (**6**). When you are asked for the keys you wish to assign the macro to, press **Alt-L** and **Enter**. Type in the macro name **Ltrfmt** when you are asked.

Immediately the editing screen will show that you have assigned the Alt-L keys to this macro. WordPerfect will even insert the description you gave the macro when it was originally created and number the macro in the order in which it was entered. Now when you press Alt-L, the macro **Ltrfmt** will be executed.

Saving Macros

This option allows you to create (or save) a macro from a keyboard definition. All you need to do is highlight the definition you wish to copy to a macro, select Macro Save (5), provide a macro name, and press Enter. Immediately WordPerfect will create a new macro file that contains the instructions from the keyboard definition. It can then be used like any other macro you have created with the Ctrl-F10 keys.

Moving Key Definitions

You may change your mind about the keys to be pressed for a particular function and want to use something other than what was originally defined. If so, you can use the Move command on the Keyboard Layout Edit menu. WordPerfect will simply ask you for the new keys. Press them and the change will be made before your eyes.

Experiment with several more key assignments and keyboard layouts until you feel comfortable with what this command will do and you can use it efficiently. When you are finished, return the keyboard layout to the original settings. You're doing well.

Activities

You should have completed the following.

| Letter.11 | *Smith letter* |
| Insert.11 | *Two copies of coupons with lines* |

Chapter Review

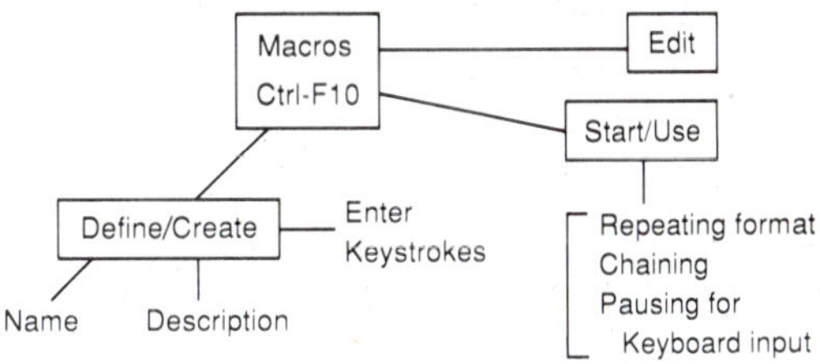

(continued)

Self-Check Quiz 11

1. What is a macro?

2. What are the steps to follow in creating a macro?

3. How do you get a macro from the disk into your file?

4. List the three ways you can name a macro.

5. List at least 10 things, other than text, that could be stored in a macro.

6. Which keys should you press to cause a macro to repeat more than once?

7. What should you do to edit a macro?

8. How can you chain macros?

9. What are keyboard layouts used for?

10. What is the difference between a keyboard layout and a keyboard definition?

11. What information must you supply to define a key for a keyboard layout?

12. What steps should you follow to retrieve a macro into a keyboard layout?

Extra Practice

For extra practice on the material covered in Chapter11, do the following:

a. Create a macro named Memo11 with the following settings; margins of 1.5" and left tabs at 2.0, 2.5, and 4.5. Set justification off.

b. Use the date function (Shift-F5), option 3 so the current date will automatically be inserted each time the form is used.

<table>
<tr><td colspan="2" align="center">MEMORANDUM</td></tr>
<tr><td>TO:</td><td>DATE: (Date Function)</td></tr>
<tr><td colspan="2">FROM:</td></tr>
<tr><td colspan="2">SUBJECT:</td></tr>
</table>

c. Use the macro form to create the following memos. Use your name in the FROM line.

TO: Bill Western

SUBJECT: Schedule Change

Our meeting in the Conference Room scheduled for 3 p.m. Monday has been changed to 10 a.m. Tuesday. Please let me know ASAP if you cannot attend at the new time.

TO: May Anderson

SUBJECT: Supply Order

The supplies I ordered for the demonstration next week have not yet arrived. Would you check the status of PO#4877 to see if there is a problem with delivery?

---

d. Save the memos as **Pract11a** and **Pract11b**. Then print both memos.

e. Create a keyboard layout named **PRACTICE**. Enter a keyboard definition that will bold a letter. Also change the key assignment for the List Files command to Shift-L. Add both key definitions to the PRACTICE keyboard.

12

Using Merge Commands

The merge command is most commonly used to send the same letter to many people, but it also has many other uses. It allows you to create a list with the names and addresses or other data in one file, the letter or other information you wish to send to each of them in another, and then combine (or merge) the two so that you do not have to retype the same material again and again.

This command, like the Macro command, is a very powerful WordPerfect feature and can be used for a great number of things, such as filling in forms, generating reports and lists, filling in contracts, creating memos, and using boilerplate. It also allows you to enter information from the keyboard during the merge process, change primary files, and use it with macros. When you have completed this chapter, you should be able to:

- merge letters and lists in a variety of ways.
- use the date function in merge files.
- set up merge files that include keyboard input.
- merge files directly to the printer.
- use merge to create lists.
- fill in forms with merge commands.
- perform document assembly with merge files.

Sounds interesting. Let's get started.

For some practice with the merge function, let's begin by sending a letter to several people. Before starting, however, become acquainted with some new concepts and function keys on the keyboard.

Merge Commands

Look at the F9 key. Notice that it has the commands Merge/Sort, Merge Codes, and Merge R on it. All of these functions are used with merge operations.

Fields and Records

To execute the merge operation, WordPerfect uses fields and records to identify position. A record is a group of fields relating to one thing. A field is a category of information within a record. A record can have many fields. If necessary, a field can be several lines long. In the address below, there are four fields and one record.

```
Mr. Joseph Green^R          (Field 1)
2245 Wilson Avenue^R        (Field 2)
Salt Lake City, UT 84108^R  (Field 3)
Dear Joe^R                  (Field 4)
^E                          (End of Record)
```

Notice that each field ends with the symbol ^R. The first ^R is field 1 to WordPerfect, the second ^R is field 2, and so on. The ^E signals the end of one record (or group of related lines) and the beginning of another.

TIP: If you will think of the Merge R (^R) command as meaning "MERGE R(eturn)" and the Merge E (^E) command as being "MERGE E(nd) of record," it will help you remember their functions.

The ^R and a Hard Return code are entered when you press Merge (F9). The ^E and a Hard Page code are entered when you select E from those offered when you press Merge Codes (Shift-F9). (However, on some machines you can also use Ctrl and the appropriate letter key. When you use this method, you must enter the Hard Return and Hard Page codes separately.)

To Review

What do each of the following mean?

^R ____

^E ____

▣ For some practice, press **Merge R (F9)** and **Merge Codes (Shift-F9)**. The Merge R (F9) key will insert a ^R followed by a [HRt] command. The Merge Codes (Shift-F9) command will bring up the following menu from which you can select E:

> ^C; ^D; ^E; ^F; ^G; ^N; ^O; ^P; ^Q; ^S; ^T; ^U; ^U:

Merge Codes

Briefly, these codes will do the following. You will work with many of them in the exercises that follow.

^C Temporarily stops the merge and waits for keyboard input before proceeding.

^D Inserts the date from the system.

^E Indicates the end of a record in a secondary file.

^F Merges information from the appropriate field in the secondary file (file with names and addresses) into the primary file (file with letter to be sent).

^G Starts a named macro at the end of a merge.

^N Goes to the next record in the secondary file.

^O Displays a message on the status line.

^P Inserts a named file.

^Q Stops the merge from either the primary or secondary file.

^S Causes the merge to change to another secondary file.

^T Sends all merged text to the printer.

^U Updates the screen.

^V Allows transfer of merge codes into the new document.

Blank Fields

Another thing to remember when creating the address list is that since WordPerfect finds information to insert into the letter by position, all like items in different records (such as name, city and state, etc.) must be in the same field in each record.

If for some reason a record does not have anything in a field, a blank line with the ^R character must be left in its place so that WordPerfect can count down to the correct line (field) and use the right information as an insert when requested. For example, the city and state in any records used with the list previously shown would always need to be in field 3 similar to the following.

```
1  Ms. Sara Smith^R
2  ^R
3  Provo, UT 84601^R
4  Dear Sara^R
5  ^E
```

It is also important to design your lists carefully based on how you intend to use them. For instance, if you needed to use only the name of the city or a person's last name in a merge file, the listing shown above could not supply that. You would need to show those fields separately, similar to the following.

```
FName^R
LName^R
Title^R
Street^R
City^R
State^R
ZIP^R
```

In any event, you should give thoughtful consideration to how your lists will be used and design the format accordingly.

Now let's get started.

Merge List (Secondary File)

The first thing you need to do is create an address list (Secondary File)

■ **Clear your screen** and type the following address list using the **Merge R (F9)** and **Merge Codes (Shift-F9)** keys (or Ctrl-letter) as appropriate at the end of each line. Do not leave any blank lines between groups or any spaces between the last word in a field and the ^R. You may, if you wish, retrieve the **Address2.12** file from the student excercise disk and add the last two names.

```
Mr. Warren Wilson^R
Department Manager^R
Wilson Sports Shop^R
255 Main Street^R
Payson, UT  84651^R
(801) 556-3321^R
Warren^R
^E
==================================================
Mrs. Verl Somerville^R
Buyer^R
Milady Dress Shoppe^R
3680 University Way^R
Salt Lake City, UT 84102^R
(801) 377-7034^R
Mrs. Somerville^R
^E
==================================================
Mr. Mark R. Thomas^R
Manager^R
Master Career Center^R
355 Center^R
St. George, UT 84770^R
(801) 436-7850^R
Mark^R
E^
==================================================
```

```
Mr. Allen F. Johnson, CPA^R
Accounting Department^R
Mills Department Store^R
^R
Orem, UT 84057^R
^R
Allen^R
^E

===================================================================
```

- Save the address list as Address2.12 and use the **Exit** (**F7**) key to clear your screen.

Merge Letter (Primary File)

Now you need to create the letter that you will use to merge with the address list. Within this letter you must tell WordPerfect where you want to put the information from the address list. The Merge Codes (Shift-F9) command will help you do this. Notice that there are seven fields in the address list.

As you enter the letter, you should position the cursor where you want a field of information to appear in the merged document and press Merge Codes (**Shift-F9**) to bring up the following menu:

```
^C; ^D; ^E; ^F; ^G; ^N; ^O; ^P; ^Q; ^S; ^T; ^U; ^U:
```

- Since you wish to identify a field to merge, type **F**. The next prompt to appear will be:

```
Field:
```

At this point you could type the number corresponding to the field you wish to bring into the letter from the address list. (For example, 6 would cause the phone number to be printed in place of ^F6^ in the letter.)

When you press the Enter key to end the process, **^F6^** (or whatever number you specify) will appear on the screen in the place where the cursor was. Now give it a try.

■ Type the following letter. Remember to use the Merge Codes (Shift-F9) key to specify the field codes. You may retrieve **Letter 2.12** from the Student Exercise Disk.

   a. Use 2" left and right margins.

   b. Center the letter on the page.

   c. Type the letter in full block style with open punctuation.

(Type Today's Date or use the DATE function)

    (Press Enter four times)

^F1^
^F3^
^F4^
^F5^

Dear ^F7^

You will be pleased to know that our new line of sportswear will be on its way to you within the next two weeks. This is one of the most exciting collections we have ever presented and it should be a big seller for you in the months ahead.

You are guaranteed delivery before Easter on orders placed before the 15th of February. Because we anticipate a great demand for these new fashions, ^F7^, we encourage you to place your orders early.

Sincerely

    (Press Enter 4 times)

Arlene Andrews
Sales Department

> (Press Enter 2 times)
>
>
> (your initials as typist)

- ☐ Save this letter as **Letter 2.12** using **Exit (F7)** and clear your screen.

Merging Files

You are now ready to Merge the two files together.

- ☐ Make sure you have a clear screen and press the **Merge/Sort** command (**Ctrl-F9**) to obtain the following prompt:

```
1 Merge; 2 Sort; 3 Sorting Sequences: 0
```

- ☐ Select **Merge (1)**. You will then be asked for the name of the primary file. The primary file is the file with the ^F ^ commands in it (your letter).

```
Primary file:
```

- ☐ Enter the name of the letter file **Letter2.12** and press **Enter**.

   You will then be asked to enter the name of the secondary file. A secondary file is the file with the ^R and ^E commands in it (the one with the names and addresses or other variable information).

```
Secondary file:
```

▣ Enter the name of the address list file **Address2.12** and press **Enter**.

The message ***Merging*** will appear in the lower left corner of the screen while the letter and address list are being merged. When the Merge is complete, the last page of the merge will appear on the screen. You have now created a new file that contains the merged letters.

▣ Save this new file under the name **MrgltrsA.12** using **Exit (F7)**.

▣ Print the new file (**MrgltrsA.12**) using any method.

A WORD OF CAUTION. If the secondary file is very large and you create a great many letters (etc.) during the merge, you may find that there is not enough memory in your machine to store them all. If this should happen, you can break the secondary file into several smaller files and then do a separate merge for each one, or use the ^T command to send items to the printer while the merge is in process.

To Review:

What is the name of the file with the names and/or addresses in it?

What is the name of the file with the letter to be sent to each person on the list?

Missing Information in Merge Files

Occasionally you may find that you do not have the information for one or more of the fields in your secondary file. Perhaps you do not know the telephone number or street address (as is the case with the last record in your secondary file for Allen Johnson) or some other item. As you know, you must leave space for these items and indicate their position with a ^R. However, if you look at the letters you have just merged, you will see that the letter to Mr. Johnson has a blank line where the street address should be. Since this looks a little strange, let's see what can be done to get WordPerfect to close up the space in situations like this.

Take a look at the revised section of the primary file letter (**Letter2.12**) shown on the next page. Notice that there is a ? following the field number in the inside address. This ? will tell WordPerfect that if there is no information available for that field, it should not leave a line or space, but simply move on to the next item. Therefore, the address on the letter to Mr. Johnson would look like the example shown.

Revised Primary File	Merged letter with blank lines closed up.

^F1?^	Mr. Allen F. Johnson, CPA
^F3?^	Mills Department Store
^F4?^	Orem, UT 84057
^F5?^	
	Dear Allen
Dear ^F7^	

To insert the ? following the number, press Merge Codes (Shift-F9) and choose F (for field). When you are asked for the field number, type the number followed by a question mark (e.g. 1?) and press Enter. If you type 1? you will see ^F1?^ appear at the cursor.

Now let's go back and change the primary file for this letter so that it will print the letter to Mr. Johnson correctly.

- Clear your screen and retrieve **Letter2.12**.

- Delete the field codes for the inside address (^F1^, ^F3^, ^F4^, ^F5^).

- Position the cursor for field 1 at the left margin four lines below the date.

- Press **Merge Codes (Shift-F9)** and choose **F**.

- Type **1?** and press **Enter**.

- Put the cursor on the next line and repeat these steps for fields 3, 4, and 5 until your file looks like the example shown above.

- Merge the files again following the same steps you used previously.

- When you are finished, save again as **MrgltrsB.12** and print the letters.

Merge Applications

Using the Date Function

Because you may use the same primary file (letter) at another time, the date will need to be changed to keep it current. You could, of course, simply delete the old date and type in the current one each time. But there is an easier way that will not require you to do anything at all.

You will recall that you were asked to enter the current date (and time) when you turned on your computer and began your work session. (Or your computer entered it for you from its internal clock.) Since then, your computer has been keeping track of the date and time in its memory. With a special merge code in WordPerfect, you can insert that date in your letters. Sound interesting? Let's see how it works.

■ Again retrieve your primary merge file, **Letter2**.

■ Using **Ctrl-END**, delete the entire line at the top with the date on it.

■ Make sure the cursor is positioned after the document format commands (**Reveal Codes**).

■ Since this letter is in full block style, position the cursor at the left margin on the line where the typed date was. (If the letter were in modified block style, you would position the cursor at the center point of the page.)

■ Press **Merge Codes (Shift-F9)**.

■ Choose **D** from the menu.

You will see a ^D appear in your letter. And that's all there is to it. Now, when WordPerfect encounters this code during a merge, it will insert the date in the computer's memory where the ^D is. Therefore, if the current date is entered before you do the merge, it will be used in your letter and automatically changed as needed.

If you would like to see this happen, resave **Letter2.12** and do the Merge again. Notice that the date is inserted at the ^D in each letter. If you would like to see what happens on another day, change the date in your computer's memory and do the Merge again. WordPerfect inserts the changed date. Pretty nice!!!

Pausing for Keyboard Input

Two other features you can incorporate with a Merge are commands that will display a prompt or message at the lower left of the screen and cause the merging to stop at a specified place so you can enter information from the keyboard. This is handy when it is difficult or impractical to add the information to the secondary file. A case in point might be for sending out monthly billings to customers. The name, address, etc., could be kept in the secondary file, but since the amounts owed would change each month, it might be easiest to enter that information directly from the keyboard as each letter is merged.

To do this, you would use the ^O and ^C codes from the Merge menu. The ^O code allows you to display a prompt or message on the screen, indicating the information that should be inserted. The ^C code stops the merging until you restart it by pressing Merge R (F9) again.

To see how this works, let's use **Letter2.12** again.

◘ Clear your screen and retrieve **Letter2.12**.

Assume that your company allows a discount based on total purchases for the year. The more a company purchases, the greater the discount. You use sales to date to determine the discount for each customer. As a result, each of the people on your list will receive a different rate, which you will need to add as the letters are merged.

Based on a formula, you have determined that discounts should be given to each customer as indicated below:

Wilson Sports Shop	32 percent
Milady Dress Shoppe	28 percent
Master Career Center	22 percent
Mills Department Store	45 percent

Because these discount percentages may change from month to month, it is easier to add them as the letters are merged rather than to put them in the secondary file. Therefore, you will want WordPerfect to stop as each letter is merged and allow you to type in the appropriate percentage.

Let's add a sentence to the letter that contains a merge code. This will:

1. stop the merge.

2. display a prompt on the screen indicating what information should be supplied.

3. allow you to type the information in before continuing with the merge.

◘ With the primary file (Letter2.12) on the screen, move the cursor to the end of the second paragraph.

◘ Type in **A discount of** for the beginning of a new sentence.

◘ Then press Merge Codes (**Shift-F9**) and choose **O**. An **^O** will appear in your text.

◘ Type **Enter discount rate:** as the prompt or message that will display on the screen during the merge. Be sure to space twice after the colon.

- Press **Merge Codes (Shift-F9)**, choose **O** again. Another **^O** will appear at the end of the message. These ^O codes indicate O(nscreen) information.

- Press **Merge Codes (Shift-F9)** and choose **C**. A **^C** will appear after the second ^O. This ^C code will allow you to enter data from the C(onsole) or keyboard.

- Finish the sentence by spacing once and typing **percent is available on all purchases.**

  When you are finished, the second paragraph in your primary file letter should look like the following:

```
You are guaranteed delivery before Easter on orders placed
before the 15th of February.  Because we anticipate a great
demand for these new fashions, ^F7^, we encourage you to place
your orders early.  A discount of ^Oenter discount rate^O^C
percent is available on all purchases.

Sincerely
```

  That's all there is to setting up the letter to pause during the merge for input from the keyboard.

- Resave **Letter2.12** (your primary file) and let's merge one more time to see how it works.

- Clear your screen. Press **Merge/Sort (Ctrl-F9)**, Merge (**1**), (Primary file) **Letter2.12, Enter**, (Secondary file) **Address2.12, Enter**.

- Type in the discount rates from the table for each customer as you are requested. Press **Merge R (F9)** to restart the merge and move to the next letter. Wonderful!

- When you are finished, save the letters as **MrgltrsC.12** and print them.

Merging to the Printer

If you wanted to send the merged letters directly to the printer, you could include a ^T command at the end of the primary file. Then WordPerfect would send each letter to the printer as it was merged. This is a good way to avoid overflowing the RAM memory in your computer when you are doing large merges.

- To try this command, modify the **Letter2.12** file by adding a ^T at the end.

- Then make sure you are attached to the printer and do the merge again. Printing should begin before the merge is completed.

To Review

Which file contains the list of variable information?

Which file contains the ^F#^ codes? (# = field number)

Indicate what each of the following will do when used as a merge code:

    ^F#^
    ^F#?^
    ^D
    ^O... ^O
    ^C
    ^T

Creating Lists with Merge

If you wanted to generate a list using selected fields from your secondary file, you can use the merge function and the ^N ^P^P commands.

The ^N command tells WordPerfect to go to the next record in the secondary file. As you know, WordPerfect automatically does this with a regular merge. However, it also generates a hard page return and begins the next item on a separate page. This is not appropriate for a list, since you want as many items as possible on the same page. To make this arrangement, you must use the ^N to override the command to create a new page each time and to step the merge to the next record until it reaches the end of the file.

The ^P^P command allows you to insert a different file into the merge at that point. If no file is specified, WordPerfect will use the current one.

◼ For this list, create a new primary file like the following:

        ^F1?^
        ^F2?^
        ^F3?^
        ^F4?^
        ^F5?^

        ^N^P^P

◼ Save it as **MergList.12**.

◼ Now do a merge, using **MergList.12** as the primary file and **Address2.12** as the secondary file. The result will look similar to the following:

Mr. Warren Wilson
Department Manager
Wilson Sports Shop
255 Main Street
Payson, UT 84651

Mrs. Verl Somerville
Buyer
Milady Dress Shoppe
3680 University Way
Salt Lake City, UT 84102

Mr. Mark R. Thomas
Manager
Master Career Center
355 Center
St. George, UT 84770

Mr. Allen F. Johnson, CPA
Accounting Department
Mills Department Store
Orem, UT 84057

TIP: If the spacing between entries does not look right, edit the primary file. Use Reveal Codes to check the [HRt] commands and adjust them as necessary. Then do the merge again.

▣ Try the following to see what it will produce. Set a tab at 4.0 and create a new primary file with the codes shown below. Merge with the **Address2.12** file.

^F1?^   [Tab]   ^F6?^
^N^P^P

TIP: You have not yet worked with columns, but you can also use this concept to merge for labels. Adjust the left and right as well as the top and bottom margins. Set tabs as necessary. Then using the Columns feature (Alt-F7) define the columns and merge.

Forms Fill-In

The merge commands can also be used to fill in forms and other specialized formats. You must first determine the exact position on the page where each item is to be placed. Then you can use a combination of commands to accomplish the task. Can you tell what the following primary file named DATA would generate?

^F3?^

^F4?^

^F5?^

^OMethod of shipment?^O^C

^OEnter the quantity^O^C   ^OEnter the amt^O^C

^N^T^PData^P

Notice that data is pulled both from the secondary file and from the keyboard. The ^N^T^P Data ^P command will tell WordPerfect to step to the next record in the file (^N), send the pages to the printer as they are generated (^T), and reuse the primary file until the end of the secondary file is reached (^PData^P). F9 must be pressed to advance the cursor from prompt to prompt.

TIP: You can also use Advance Up and Advance Down if necessary to get exact placement of your printout on the page.

Math Merges

It is also possible to generate reports using WordPerfect's merge commands. Fields containing numeric data can be extracted, calculated and printed quickly. You simply create a primary file with tab settings and math column definitions, turn math on, enter the field codes, add ^N^P^P, and save. Then merge the two files, calculate, save, and print.

Document Assembly

WordPerfect's merge feature will also help you do document assembly. The following example is simple, but it will help you to see how this procedure is done.

First of all, you will need to create a number of small files, so do that now.

◼ Enter the following and save it as **Main.12**. This will be the primary file. Notice that the commands are followed by a hard page break and a command to cause the merge to loop to the end of the file.

```
^F3?^
^F4?^
^F5?^

Delivery time and credit rating:
^N^U^OEnter quantity ordered (100, 150, 200):^P^C^P^O
=======================================================
^PMAIN^P
```

☐ Enter the following and save it as **100**.

> **Delivery scheduled in one week**
> [TAB] ^U^OEnter Credit Rating (E, G, P):^P^C^P^O

☐ Enter the following and save it as **150**.

> **Delivery scheduled in two weeks**
> [TAB] ^U^OEnter Credit Rating (E, G, P):^P^C^P^O

☐ Enter the following and save it as **200**.

> **Delivery scheduled in three weeks**
> [TAB] ^U^OEnter Credit Rating (E, G, P): ^P^C^P^O

☐ Enter the following and save it as **E**.

> ^U^OCredit rating: Excellent
> ^U^OEnter Credit Limit (5000, 3000):^P^C^P^O

☐ Enter the following and save it as **G**.

> ^U^OCredit rating: Good
> ^U^OEnter Credit Limit (3000, 1000):^P^C^P^O

☐ Enter the following and save it as **P**.

> ^U^OCredit rating: Poor
> ^U^OEnter Credit Limit (0, 1000):^P^C^P^O

☐ Enter the following and save it as **5000**.

> **Credit limit: 5000**

☐ Enter the following and save it as **3000**.

> **Credit limit: 3000**

- Enter the following and save it as **1000**.

  Credit limit: 1000

- Enter the following and save it as **0**.

  Credit limit: 0

  Now you're ready to define the merge.

- Clear your screen and press **Merge/Sort (Ctrl-F9)** and select **Merge (1)**.

- Enter **Main.12** as the primary file and **Address2.12** as the secondary file.

- Watch the prompts at the bottom of your screen and supply the following data when requested. Press **Enter** if necessary to move to the next item.

	Wilson Sports	Milady Dress	Master Career	Mills Dept.
Quantity ord:	150	200	200	100
Credit Rating:	Poor	Excellent	Excellent	Good
Credit Limit:	0	5000	3000	1000

TIP: If you wish to stop this merge before it is completed, press Merge Codes (Shift-F9). You should also be aware that there are no error checks to guard against typing mistakes. In addition, entering an unknown filename at one of the prompts may abort the merge.

- Save the result as **Credit.12** and print.

As you can see, this type of merge is similar to creating many small files that could be selectively retrieved into a master document and then saved as one.

There are 14 different merge commands, including others that will allow you to start a macro at the end of a merge, change to another secondary file, and allow transfer of merge codes into a new document. Consult the Word-Perfect manual for additional practice with any of them.

To Review

What do each of the following merge codes tell WordPerfect to do?

^N
^T
^P^P
^Q

Summary

In summary, to do a Merge:

a. Prepare the address list (or other variable information) using ^R and ^E codes and save.

b. Prepare the letter (or other document for fill-in) using merge codes (^F#^, ^F#?^, ^D, ^O ...^O, ^C, ^T^N,^P, ^P) and save. Clear the screen.

c. Press Merge (Ctrl-F9).

d. Specify the primary file (document with ^F, ^D, ^O and other merge codes) and press Enter.

e. Specify the secondary file (list with ^R and ^E codes) and press Enter.

f. Save the new file with merged information. Use a different name than either of the other merge files.

g. Print.

Congratulations! You've become acquainted with most of WordPerfect's merge commands. Use them to make your work more efficient and productive. As you do, you'll find it easier to remember how they work and to think of many new ways to use them.

Activities

You should have completed the following:

Address2.12	*MergeList*
Letter2.12	*MergeLetter*
MrgltrsA.12	*Four copies of merged letter*
MrgltrsB.12	*Four copies of merged letter*
	Lines closed up
MrgltrsC.12	*Merged letters with keyboard input*
MergList.12	*MergeList available to someone*
Main.12	*Primary file for document assembly*
Credit.12	*Document assembly project*

Chapter Review

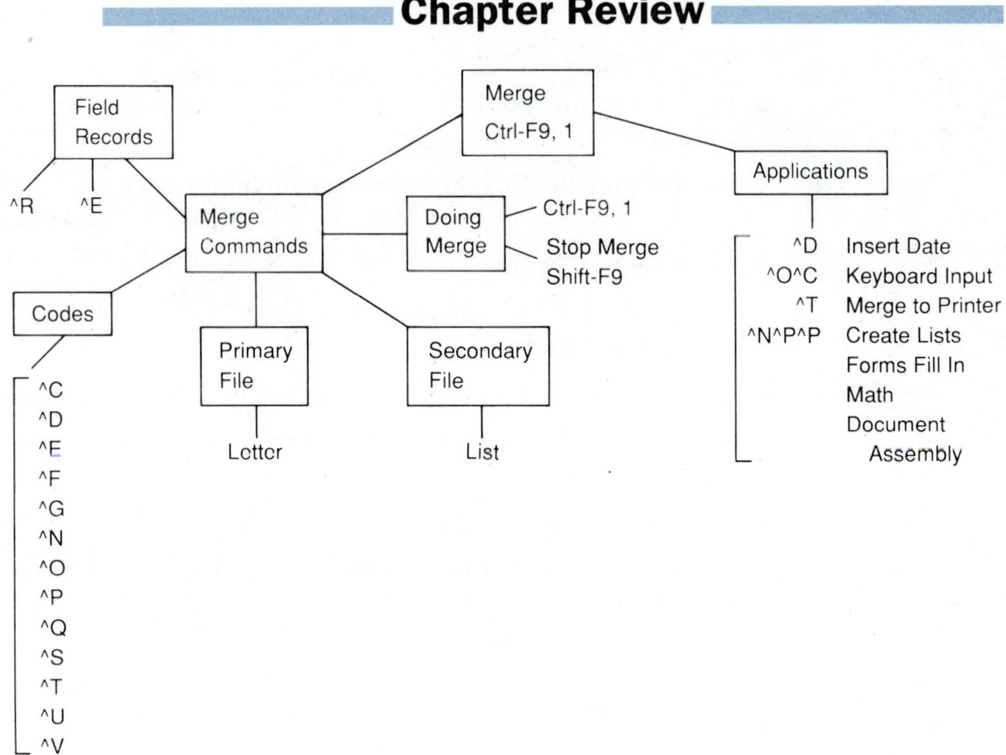

Self-Check Quiz 12

1. What does open punctuation style mean?

2. What is a merge field?

3. What is a merge record?

4. What must you do when you do not have any information for a merge field?

5. What is contained in the primary merge file?

6. What is contained in the secondary merge file?

7. What do ^R and ^E mean when you are creating merges?

8. What will happen when ^D is used in a primary file?

9. Which merge code will display a message on the screen during a merge?

10. Which code should you use to pause a merge for keyboard input?

11. Which key should you press to restart a merge following keyboard input?

12. What will the ? do in a merge?

13. What is the advantage of using the date function (^D) in a merge?

14. Which command will send merged items directly to the printer?

15. What will happen when the ^N^P^P command is used in a merge?

Extra Practice

For extra practice with the material contained in Chapter 12, do the following:

a. Create a merge list of at least six names and addresses of your friends, relatives, and/or schoolmates. Write a short letter telling them about your most recent vacation. Merge the letter and the list and send a copy of the letter to each of them.

b. Enter the following list. Insert the appropriate merge codes. Save as **Eplist.12.**

<table>
<tr><td>NAME</td><td>ITEM REQUESTED</td></tr>
<tr><td>Mr. Samuel Young
General Manager
8823 Misty Drive
Denver, CO 80201</td><td>Office furniture</td></tr>
<tr><td>Mr. William Bracken
Vice President
2462 Adams Court
Arvada, CO 80001</td><td>Executive desks</td></tr>
<tr><td>Mrs. Peggy Sue Jones
Branch Manager
23 Old Mill Road
Denver, CO 80201</td><td>Filing cabinets</td></tr>
<tr><td>Ms. Kathy Bills
2358 Riverside Drive #12
Denver, CO 80201</td><td>Carpets</td></tr>
<tr><td>Mr. Joseph Cole
Arcadia, CA 91006</td><td>Office supplies</td></tr>
</table>

c. Enter the following letter. Include the appropriate merge codes to add the inside address at the top. Use the date function and insert codes that allow keyboard input as indicated. Save it as **Epltr.12.**

Dear (Mr/Mrs last name)

If you've been looking for (enter item requested) now is the very best time to buy.

For the next 30 days all our regular and designer stock will be marked down for clearance. These items will be on display on our showroom in (city of residence). Why not come in this week and see for yourself.

Sincerely

(Your name)

enc

d. Merge the files. Save the result as **Pract12A** and print it.

13

Sorting and Selecting Techniques

It's difficult to top the tricks you've learned up to now, but WordPerfect isn't finished yet. It can also sort lists in a variety of ways, select specified items from a list, and present them either sorted or unsorted. This chapter will introduce you to the basics of these features. When you have completed this chapter, you will be able to:

- use the Sorter to do line, paragraph, and merge sorts.

- sort on alphanumeric and numeric fields, in ascending or descending order.

- sort on several keys or criteria at once.

- select items from a list by various criteria.

- use the logical operators to perform select functions.

The first step in learning to sort and select is to prepare a list of items for WordPerfect to work with. This list could consist of names, addresses, telephone numbers, classes, products, or anything you want to arrange in alphabetic or numeric order.

WordPerfect can sort using up to nine criteria (or keys) at a time, though you are unlikely to use that many very often. In other words, you could arrange your list alphabetically by last name, then alphabetically by first name for people with the same last name, and then by a third criterion, up to nine levels or keys.

For instance, WordPerfect would sort your list so that all the Jacksons were listed together (Key1). Then it would sort all the Jacksons by first name, so that Jackson, Andrew would be listed before Jackson, David (Key2). If there were more than one David Jackson, you could sort by middle initial so that Jackson, David B. would precede Jackson, David M. (Key3).

Key1	Key2	Key3
Jackson,	Andrew	
Jackson,	David	B.
Jackson,	David	M.

WordPerfect can sort in three different ways: by line, by merge file, and by paragraph. Each method has its own set of procedures.

Line Sort

Because Line Sort is the default, let's begin with that.

◾ Since you must have a file to sort, enter the following. Set left tabs at **3.2** and **4.3**, and decimal tabs at **6.0** and **7.1**. When you are finished, save the file as **LineSort.13**. You may, if you wish, retrieve the **LineSort.13** file from the Student Exercise Disk.

Jones, Mary Anne	Senior	628-43-5547	3.75	100.4
Johnson, William	Junior	546-90-7869	2.45	23.69
Jenkins, Samuel	Senior	554-87-8976	2.98	435.8
Johnson, Sandra	Soph.	453-97-6580	3.87	3.555
Jatte, Andrew S.	Fresh.	238-87-3241	2.93	97.2

To do a Line Sort, you must first define for WordPerfect what you want it to sort and where the information can be found. In other words, you must specify the type of information and its location as a field, line, and word. If there is more than one criterion to sort, you must also specify the order in which you want these items sorted.

The material you just entered and saved as **LineSort.13** consists of five columns (Name, Class, SS#, GPA, Amount). Each column is separated by a [Tab] command, and each line ends with a [HRt] command. These Tab and HRt commands are what WordPerfect will use to identify fields and count records.

Before moving ahead, there are some terms you should be familiar with:

Type

WordPerfect recognizes two types of information--alphanumeric and numeric. **Alphanumeric** items are composed of letters of the alphabet, or of numbers that are all the same length (such as the Social Security number). **Numeric** items consist of numbers that contain symbols, such as dollar signs, commas, or periods, and numbers that are unequal in length (such as those in field 5). Numeric items can be calculated.

Field

Each column or item that is set off by a Tab or Indent command is classified as a field. If you want WordPerfect to sort the last names in the list above, you tell it to sort on field 1. To sort GPAs, you would tell it to sort on field 4.

Word

Some fields contain more than one word separated by spaces (for instance, field 1 contains last and first names, and in some cases a middle name or initial). WordPerfect can sort on any of the three words, so you must tell it which one you want it to use. If you want it to sort on last names, you would specify word 1. First names would be word 2.

Jones, Mary Ann
Johnson, William

Negative Words

A problem sometimes arises when the same information occupies different positions in different records. This is the case in field 1, in which some of the records contain two words and some three. (WordPerfect defines as a word as all the characters from one blank space to the next.)

To handle situations like these, you can use negative numbers. Look at the following:

Salt Lake City, UT
Boise, ID
St. Paul, MN
Denver, CO

If you wished to sort the states, how would you tell WordPerfect which word to sort on? The position of the name of the state varies, since the number of words preceding it varies. However, it is the last word in every line. Therefore, you could specify first position going from right to left.

To tell WordPerfect to search backward, from right to left, use a minus sign before the number of the word (-1 in this case).

◾ Now, to see how this works, be sure that you have the **LineSort.13** file on the screen.

◾ Then enter **Merge/Sort (Ctrl-F9)** to call up the following prompt:

```
1 Merge; 2 Sort; 3 Sort Order: 0
```

◾ Since you want to sort, select **Sort (2)**. You will then be asked:

```
Input file to sort: (Screen)
```

WordPerfect wants to know the name of the file to sort--either one stored on your disk or the one displayed on the screen. To sort a file on your disk, type in its name. To sort a file on the screen, press **Enter**.

■ Since the file you wish to sort is on the screen, press **Enter**.

WordPerfect will then ask what you want to do with the file that results from the sorting operation.

```
Output file for sort: (Screen)
```

You can either send it directly to the disk or have it displayed on the screen. If it is to go to the disk, you must supply a file name. If it is to go to the screen, you need only press Enter. (It can then be saved to the disk in a second operation, using Save or Exit.)

■ Let's send the sorted file to the screen so you can see it. Press **Enter**. The Sorter menu will appear:

```
------------------------------- Sort by Line -------------------------------

Key Typ Field Word          Key Typ Field Word          Key Typ Field Word
 1   a     1     1            2                           3
 4                            5                           6
 7                            8                           9
Select


Action                      Order                       Type
Sort                        Ascending                   Line sort

1 Perform Action; 2 View; 3 Keys; 4 Select; 5 Action; 6 Order; 7 Type: 0
```

There are several things you must tell WordPerfect before it can do the sort. Before going any further, let's look over this menu and see what it requires.

Type of Sort

First you must select the type of sort you want to do—Line, Merge, or Paragraph. The menu above is set for a Line Sort. (Note the top line and the Type of Sort indicator.) If you wished to switch to one of the other types, you would select **Type (7)**. The following would appear on the bottom line:

```
Type: 1 Merge; 2 Line; 3 Paragraph: 0
```

Choosing **Merge (1)** or **Paragraph (3)** would change both indicators to the type of sort you selected. Try changing the type of sort a time or two to see what happens. Then return to Line Sort.

Key and Type of Data

You must also indicate the sequence (key) of the sort, so WordPerfect will know which field to sort on first, which second, and so on. **Keys (3)** will allow you to do this.

You will also use **Keys (3)** to specify the type of data (alphanumeric or numeric) to be sorted for each key, the field, and the word position in the field.

Select

If WordPerfect is to select data from a list, you must indicate that as well, using **Select (4)**. (More on this later.)

Action

Action (5) offers three commands: Sort, Select, and Select and Sort.

The Sort command will sort the entire list.

The Select command allows you to select specified items from the list.

The Select and Sort command sorts those items which have been selected into whatever order you identify.

TIP: The two choices involving selection (Select and Select and Sort) will only respond when a Select statement has already been entered.

Order

With **Order** (**6**), you can tell WordPerfect to sort in ascending order (going up from lowest to highest — 1 to 10 and A to Z) or descending order (coming down from highest to lowest— 10 to 1 and Z to A). Don't confuse this command with key order, which is specified under the Keys option.

View

The **View** (**2**) option will allow you to scroll through the file on the screen. This is very convenient if you forget the position of an item in the list or need to go back into your file temporarily to check something.

Perform Action

Finally, **Perform Action** (**1**) will activate the sorting/selecting process once you have specified all the other criteria.

To Review

Indicate what each of the following commands will do:

1 Perform Action ____

2 View ____

3 Keys ____

4 Select ____

5 Action ____

6 Order ____

7 Type ____

Now that you are acquainted with this menu, let's sort the list you entered alphabetically by last name.

◼ You should already have the file (**LineSort.13**) on the screen. You should also have pressed **Merge/Sort** (**Ctrl-F9**), chosen **Sort** (**2**), and indicated that the Input file is on the screen, the Output file should go to the screen, and the Sorter Menu should be displayed. If you haven't, do that now.

You must now give WordPerfect the rest of the information it needs to sort by last name. To do so, use the options shown across the bottom of the menu. The order in which you identify these criteria is not critical, but you must specify them all **before** selecting Perform Action (1).

TIP: Since you must enter several commands, and **Perform Action (1)** is the last command you will use, it may help to be sure you don't miss anything by doing the commands in reverse order, beginning with **Type (7)**.

◻ Now enter the following:

<table>
<tr><td>7 Type:</td><td>Line</td></tr>
<tr><td>6 Order:</td><td>Ascending</td></tr>
<tr><td>5 Action:</td><td>Sort</td></tr>
<tr><td>4 Select:</td><td>(Skip this for now—it applies only to the Select function)</td></tr>
<tr><td>3 Keys:</td><td>Since you are sorting on only one item, you will have only one key. Alphanumeric (a) is the default. Accept it by pressing the Enter key. (You could type n if you wished to change it.) Since the item you want to sort on is in the first field, enter 1 for field. And since it is also the first word in the field, enter 1 again. (You can use the Arrow keys and the Del or Backspace keys to edit and move the cursor as you wish.) When you are finished, the key information line should look like this:</td></tr>
</table>

Key Type Field Word

1   a   1   1

◻ Press **Exit (F7)** to return to the menu.

TIP: You may also use the **View (2)** option whenever you need to check your file.

◻ When you have entered all of the above information, select **Perform Action (1)** to Perform Action. Quick as a wink, the sort will be done.

Jatte, Andrew S.	Fresh.	238-87-3241	2.93	97.2
Jenkins, Samuel	Senior	554-87-8976	2.98	435.8
Johnson, Sandra	Soph.	453-97-6580	3.87	3.555
Johnson, William	Junior	546-90-7869	2.45	23.69
Jones, Mary Anne	Senior	628-43-5547	3.75	100.4

- Now do another sort, this time ranking GPA from lowest to highest. Enter the appropriate settings. When you are finished, save the sorted file as **GPASort.13** and print it.

- Finally, sort one more time, this time using two keys. Sort by both last (key1) and first (key2) name. Save this file as **NameSort.13** and print it.

- **Clear your screen** when you are finished.

If you are sorting a table that is within or part of another document, it is best to block the table, copy it, and transfer it to Doc 2. Sort it as Doc 2. Then block it again and return the sorted table to the original document in Doc 1. Sorting a table within a document can sometimes result in problems later with margins, tabs, etc., in the text that follows.

Merge Sorts

The list you will prepare to sort by Merge resembles the address list (secondary file) you created for the merge operation in Chapter 12. Like the Line Sort, it will have fields and records, and each field must be in the same place in each record. Like that file, you must use the ^R and ^E commands at the end of each field and record, and each item must be in the same place and on a separate line because WordPerfect will search for it by position. In fact, you could use the same file to both merge and sort if you wished.

Let's get started.

- First, enter the following list or retrieve **Merge.13** from the Student Exercise Disk. Do not leave any blank lines in the list. If you do not have any information for a field, maintain its position with an empty line and a ^R. Note that WordPerfect adds a hardpage [HPg] command at the end of each record when you enter ^E.

**Wilson, Bill J.^R
145 South 500 East^R
Provo, UT 84601^R
^E
Jensen, Mary Beth^R
2245 Eastridge Drive^R
Denver, CO 80201^R
^E
Scott, Thomas^R
1557 West Center^R
Fremont, CA 94537^R
^E**

> Anderson, Warren^R
> ^R
> Sandy, UT 84070^R
> ^E
> Collins, Sara^R
> 875 Marymount Road^R
> Wichita, KS 67213
> ^E

▣ If you enter the list, then save it as **Merge.13** using **Save** (**F10**) F10. Press **Merge/Sort** (**Ctrl-F9**) to bring up the Merge/Sort Menu.

```
1 Merge; 2 Sort; 3 Sort Order: 0
```

▣ Select **Sort** (**2**).

▣ Indicate that the Input file is on the screen by pressing **Enter**.

▣ Send the Output file to the screen by pressing **Enter**, and display the Sorter Menu.

▣ Then select **Type** (**7**), and indicate that the sort is a merge by selecting **Merge** (**1**).

You must now furnish the same kinds of information you did for the Line Sort. The main difference is in the way the fields and records are identified.

Line Sort uses Tab commands to tell where one field ends and another begins, but Merge Sort uses ^R commands. And, instead of using a [HRt] to count records, Merge Sort uses the ^E.

The following examples show how fields would be identified for Line Sort and Merge Sort:

Line Sort:

Smith, MaryBeth   Denver, CO 234-0986

Merge Sort:

Smith, Mary Beth^R
Denver, CO^R
234-0986^R
^E

Each record contains three fields. The first field consists of three words, the second field two. To sort by state, in both cases, you would enter the following for Key1: Type **alphanumeric**; Field **2**; Word **2** in both cases or:

Key
1   a   2   2

Occasionally, a Merge Sort record will contain a field with more than one line. In the example below, the street address and the city and state have all been included in one field. To designate the city for sorting, you would designate field 2, line 2, word 1.

Smith, Mary Beth^R
234 Stephens Avenue
Denver, CO^R
234-0986^R
^E

- For practice, Sort the merge list alphabetically by last name. Save the sort as **LastName.13**. You will see the following.

```
Anderson, Warren^R
^R
Sandy, UT 84070^R
^E
================================================
Collins, Sara^R
875 Marymount Road^R
Wichita, KS 67213
^E
================================================
Jensen, Mary Beth^R
2245 Eastridge Drive^R
Denver, CO 80201^R
^E
================================================
Scott, Thomas^R
1557 West Center^R
Fremont, CA 94537
^E
================================================
Wilson, Bill J.^R
145 South 500 East^R
Provo, UT 84601^R
^E
================================================
```

- Then sort by city within state. Save this sort as **CitySort.13**.

- Print both sorts and then clear your screen.

When these files are printed, the ^E and ^R commands will be printed as well. If you wanted to remove them, you could do a search for the ^E and ^R commands, just before printing, and eliminate them . You would need to do two searches--one for the ^E and one for the ^R. To do so, you would press Replace (Alt-F2). The choice to confirm would be optional. When asked what to search for, press MergeR (F9) for ^R or Merge Codes (Shift-F9) for ^E. Then press Esc. When the ^E and ^R commands disappear, resave your file and print. You can also search for [HPg] commands and replace them with [HRt][HRt] to separate each record and print them on the same page.

Paragraph Sorts

Now, let's try a Paragraph Sort.

- Type the following or retrieve **ParaSort.13** from the Student Exercise Disk. If you enter the following yourself, be sure to press the **Enter** key twice after each item. When you are finished, save it as **ParaSort.13**.

Key: The key identifies the sequence in which items are to be sorted. There can be up to nine keys.

Field: A field is a category within a record.

Type: The type of information can be either alphanumeric or numeric. Alphanumeric information can be a combination of letters and numbers, or all letters.

Order: Items may be sorted in either ascending or descending order.

WordPerfect defines as a paragraph any item that ends with two [HRt] commands. A paragraph can be as brief as one line or as long as a page. The paragraphs in a file do not all need to be the same size. WordPerfect will arrange them alphabetically or numerically by the first word in each para-graph. This type of sort lacks the flexibility of the other two, because it only sorts on one field. However, you do have more latitude about how the data is arranged within a given paragraph. For instance, you could set it up as a table or a list. The data does not need to be all alike, and you need not be constrained by position.

Now to do the sort itself:

- Press **Merge/Sort** (**Ctrl-F9**) and move to the Sort Menu.

- Change the type of sort to **Paragraph** (**3**).

- Specify the information for Key 1 to sort the first field alphabetically, and sort in ascending order.

- When you are finished, save the sorted list as **ParaSort.13** and print it. Then clear your screen.

To Review

Line sorts use ____________________, ______________ and ___________________ to signal the ends of words, fields and records.

Merge sorts use __________________ and ________________ to mark the end of fields and records.

Paragraph sorts use __________________ to indicate the ends of records.

Summary

In summary, to do a Sort:

    a. Enter the list and save it.

    b. Press Merge/Sort (Ctrl-F9).

    c. Choose Sort (2).

    d. Identify the Input and Output files.

    e. Specify sort criteria (type, order, keys) on the Sorter Menu.

    f. Perform action.

    g. Save and Print.

Selecting from a Database

The Select function will allow you to pull specified items from the input file and create a new file with them. This file can be arranged in either sorted or unsorted order. You will again use the Sort Menu, but now you will also use the select options that you have already seen.

For this exercise, you can reuse the files you already have named **Line-Sort.13** and **Merge.13**.

- For the first exercise, clear your screen and retrieve **LineSort.13**.

- Since you will use the sorter menu, press **Merge/Sort** (**Ctrl-F9**) to bring up the Merge/Sort Menu.

- Choose Sort (**2**).

- The Input file is on the screen. Press **Enter**.

- Identify the screen as the Output file too by pressing **Enter**.

- When the Sorter Menu appears, enter **Type** (**7**), and select **Line** (**1**), since that is the way your Input file is arranged.

Let's select students with GPAs over 3.0. To do so we'll need to use field 4.

- Identify Key1 as **numeric**, field **4**, word **1**, and press **Exit** (**F7**).

- Now enter Select (**4**) to bring up the following on the bottom line:

```
+(OR), *(AND), =, <>, >, <, >=, <=:   Press Exit when done
```

WordPerfect is asking what you want to select, and giving you some symbols to work with. If you have done any algebra or programming, many of them will look familiar.

As you can see, you have a number of options. You can select for:

One thing OR another (+)

One thing AND another (*)

Items equal to your specification (=)

Items not equal to your specification (<>)

Items greater than your specification (>)

Items less than your specification (<)

Items greater than or equal to your specification (>=)

Items less than or equal to your specification (<=)

Your choice will be placed under the Select heading in the menu and used to select from the Input file. Notice that WordPerfect can select and sort on both alphabetic and numeric criteria.

◻ Since we want to select students with GPAs greater than 3.0, type in the following:

Key1>3.0

NOTE:It is important to type Key1 as shown. Do not insert a space between the word Key and the number. The spacing of the rest of the statement is not critical. (The > and < symbols are located above the comma and period on the keyboard.)

◻ Press **Exit** (**F7**).

◻ Choose **Action** (**5**).

◻ You may choose either **Select & Sort** (**1**) or **Select Only** (**2**). (These commands will not respond if you haven't entered a Select statement.)

◻ Identify the order as **A**scending.

◻ Choose **Perfom Action** (**1**) to perform the select function.

In a couple of seconds, the output file will appear on your screen listing in ascending order those students whose GPAs are greater than 3.0.

◻ Save the file as **Select.13** and print it.

Now that you know how the select function works, you can use it to select (and sort) any number of things. You can get quite ingenious with the select statement if you wish, combining two or three criteria and using more than one key. For instance, the following select statement would specify seniors with GPAs over 3.0:

Key1>3.0*Key2=Senior.

For more details about Select functions, refer to your WordPerfect manual.

You can also use the file you created for Merge to select. You could even combine a select function with a merge operation to send letters to selected people on a list. The possibilities are tantalizing.

If you would like to experiment further with the sort and select commands, you can practice on the following information. It is named **Practlst.13** on the student exercise disk. Have fun!

Johnson, Robert	Automotive	3.85	226-6549
Jensen, Bradley	Automotive	3.45	225-5679
Jones, Roger	Diesel	3.57	226-6432
Jensen, Henry	Carpentry	2.97	375-9047
Johnson, Bill	Diesel	3.66	226-6579
Johnson, Amy	Marketing	2.45	374-5673
James, Alice	Accounting	3.92	373-4537
Jones, Chris	Accounting	2.24	226-6549
Jacobsen, Kevin	Data Proc.	2.89	226-6479
Jensen, William	Accounting	3.51	377-0986
Jespersen, Karl	Data Proc.	3.23	226-9843
Jesperson, Kelly	Data Proc.	3.86	373-5470
Jackson, Jerry	Management	2.97	374-5893
Jenson, Margaret	Management	2.72	374-9872
Johnston, Gerry	Data Proc.	1.98	226-6491
James, Alvin	General Ed.	2.86	374-9071
Jesperson, Steve	Data Proc	4.00	224-4014
Johnson, Reed	Accounting	3.74	226-6566
Jones, Sandra	Management	2.74	377-2362
Jason, Bruce	General Ed.	3.23	225-6539

To Review

What do each of the following symbols mean when used in a select statement?

= ____

* ____

> ____

< ___________________________________

\+ ___________________________________

<> ___________________________________

= ___________________________________

____

Summary

In summary, to Select:

a. Enter the list in line, merge, or paragraph format.

b. Press Merge/Sort (Ctrl-F9).

c. Select Sort (2).

d. Identify the Input and Output files.

e. Identify the Select/Sort criteria (keys, select statement).

f. Perform action.

g. Save and print.

Activities

You should have completed the following:

LineSort.13	*Information to Sort*
GPASort.13	*Line Sort by GPA*
NameSort.13	*Line Sort by last and first name*
Merge.13	*MergeList*
LastName.13	*Merge Sort alphabetically by last name*
CitySort.13	*Merge Sort by city within state*
ParaSort.13	*Paragraph Sort*
Select.13	*Select GPA>3.0 in ascending order*
Practlst.13	*Practice List*

Chapter Review

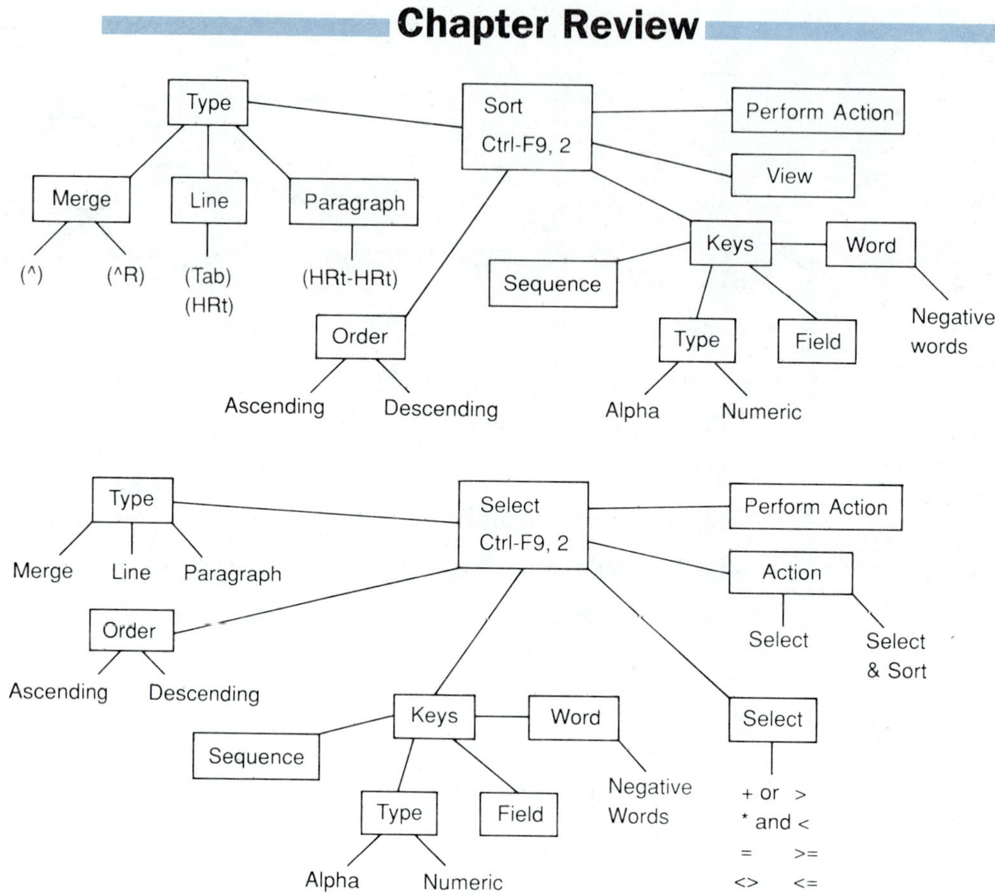

Self-Check Quiz 13

1. Describe the difference between a Line Sort and a Merge Sort in terms of how items are entered in the file.

2. What do the following signify to the sorter?

   ^R
   [HRt]
   ^E
   Space
   [TAB]
   [HRt][HRt]

3. What does the following command mean?

   Key
   3   n   2   1

4. What is an alphanumeric item?

5. What is a numeric item?

6. Define the following:

   Key
   Field
   Word

7. What would you select with each of the following criteria?

   Key2=Jones
   Key1<>100
   Key1>=6*Key2>10

8. How would A-Z and 1-10 be sorted by each of the following?
   Ascending
   Descending

9. What must be present for the Action command to work?

10. How many levels (or keys) will WordPerfect sort on?

Extra Practice

For extra practice on the material covered in this chapter, do the following:

a. Enter the following table and save it as **Pract13a**. Use whatever margins and tab settings you choose.

Chevrolet	1969	Camaro	V6	$2300
Pontiac	1982	Gran Prix	V6	$4200
Chevrolet	1984	Blazer	V8	$9200
Toyota	1985	Celica	V4	$6650
Ford	1979	LTD	V8	$2400
Chevrolet	1981	Blazer	V8	$5225

b. Sort the table by Year. Save as **Pract13b**.

c. Sort the table by Price, with the least expensive cars listed first. Save as **Pract13c**.

d. Sort the table by Make first, and then by Style. Save as **Pract13d**.

e. Select all V8 cars. Save as **Pract13e**.

f. Select all Chevrolets with V8 engines. Save as **Pract13f**.

g. Select all cars that cost less than $5000. Save as **Pract13g**.

h. Retrieve the list of names used for the merge exercise in Chapter 12 called **EpList.12**. Sort it alphabetically by last name. Then sort it again by city. Save your sorts as **Pract13h** and **Pract13i**.

i. Print the sorts. Use the Mark Files feature in List Files, using an * to indicate all the files to be sent to the printer in sequence.

j. Enter a list of names, ages, city, state, GPA, hobby, birthday, or any other pertinent information for your family, friends, a class, or any group. Sort the data in any way that will make it useful to you. Select some of the data from the database that is especially helpful.

14

Tabulation, Columns, and Math Functions

Up to now, you have been working with text material. But there will also be times when you want to create a table with headings centered over the columns or to present your material in more than one column like a newspaper. WordPerfect can help you do this. It can also help you do math functions by calculating some formulas and giving you subtotals, totals, and grand totals. When you have completed this chapter, you should be able to:

- Enter tables and other tabulated material, using correct format and placement.

- Center text from any point on the line.

- Format material in columns, using both newspaper and parallel style.

- Perform math functions with WordPerfect, including doing calculations and generating subtotals, totals, and grand totals.

Typing Tabulated Material

Take a close look at the following table. We will use it to explain how to type tabulated material. (The line numbers along the left side are for reference only.)

1.		INSTALLMENT CONTRACTS			
2.					
3.					
4.	<u>Customer</u>	<u>Item</u>	<u>Dept.</u>	<u>Down</u>	<u>Mo.</u>
5.					
6.	B. Jones	Towels	Bath	160.28	12
7.	R. Burningham	Suit	Menswear	98.50	10
8.	S. Stevens	Draperies	Domestics	48.40	8

You'll notice that the main heading is typed in all capital letters and centered. There are two blank lines between the main heading and the column headings. The column headings are typed in upper- and lower-case characters, underlined, and centered over the columns. There is one blank line between the column headings and the first item. This format is standard for all tables. The column items (lines 6, 7, and 8) may be either single- or double-spaced.

To Review

The main heading is _________________________ and _________________ on the line.

The column headings are typed in ___________ - and ____________ -case characters.

They should be _____________________________ and _____________________________ over the columns.

You should leave ________________ blank line(s) below the main heading and ________________ blank line(s) below the column headings.

What follows is a Preview of the steps you will be using to type tabulated material, and some guidelines for completing a tabulation problem. It is helpful to have an overview before you begin working with the individual parts. Therefore, before doing the problem, read through these instructions to familiarize yourself with the process. Pay particular attention to the procedure for identifying tab positions and centering the headings over the columns. Then complete the assignment according to the instructions given with it.

Set Margins (and Clear Screen If Necessary)

The first step when setting up a tabulation problem is to reset your margins to the edges of the page, usually 1 space in from each edge or 0.01 from both left and right. If you are working on a new problem, you should also clear the screen.

Type the Main Heading

Next, you will center and type the main heading in all capital letters. Then space down four lines.

Identify Tab Positions

To determine where to place the tabs, you will need to decide (a) how many spaces you want between the columns, and (b) which is the longest line in each column. The longest line can be either the column heading or a column item. If you are copying a draft or printed table, it is helpful to mark the longest line in each column in pencil to make it easy to find.

You should then press Center (Shift-F6) to activate the Center function. Type the longest line in the first column. Then space once for every space you want to leave between columns. Type the longest line in the second column, and insert spaces again. Continue until you have typed and centered a single line containing the longest item from each column, plus spaces between each of the columns. For instance, look at the example below. There are four columns in the table. The items shown are the longest from each of their respective columns, and there are five spaces between each column.

John Doesmith   Albany   235.58   September

TIP: The number of spaces between columns is often determined by appearance and the number of available spaces on a line. Usually a number between 3 and 8 will avoid either a spread out or crowded look in your table.

To determine the placement of the tabs, return the cursor to the left end of the line (the "J" in John) and begin moving the cursor along the line with the Right Arrow key. (Do **not** use the Space Bar.) As you do, look at the status line for the position (Pos) where each column begins, and write down the number to use as a tab setting. (Remember that columns that will be aligned at the decimal point should have the tab set at the decimal, not at the left of the column.) In the example above, you would note the positions of J, A, the decimal point, and S.

Then return the cursor to the left end of the line again (the "J" in John) and use Ctrl-End to delete the line you typed. Since it is probably composed of scrambled items from your table, you won't want to keep it any longer.

Set Tabs

Clear out any old tabs, and set new ones for each of the columns using the positions you identified in the previous step.

Type the Table

With the tabs set, to type the first line of the table. (You will type the column headings later.) Type the remainder of the table, using the Tab key to move from column to column.

Type the Column Headings

When you have finished typing the table, move the cursor up to the line you have chosen for the column headings (usually line 4 or near 1.66 inch).

Using the Space Bar, space over to the center of the first column. The cursor should be positioned above the center of the longest item in the column.

TIP: To do this you can (1) count the letters and spaces in the longest item and divide by two, (2) space over once for every two letters and spaces in the item, or (3) visually estimate the center of the column. (Methods 1 and 2 do not work well with proportionally spaced fonts.)

With the cursor at the center of the column, press Center (Shift-F6) to tell WordPerfect to center from the current cursor position. Then turn Underline (F8) on, type the column heading, and turn Underline (F8) off. WordPerfect will center the heading over the column.

Then press the Tab key, which both cancels the centering command and moves the cursor to the next tab. Space over to the center of the next column, press Center and Underline again, type the second column head, turn off Underline and press the Tab key. Repeat these steps for each remaining column heading.

TIP: When a tab has been set at the decimal point for a Tab Align column (usually a number), the cursor jumps to the decimal point when you press Tab. Since this may not be in the center of the column, the procedure outlined above must be modified to center the heading for this type of column. When you have finished the column heading in the column at the Left of the Tab Align column, press the Right Arrow key twice to end the centering command (instead of the Tab key). Then use your Space Bar to move the cursor to the center of the column and follow the procedure outlined above for centering the heading.

Center on the Page

After completing the table, center it on the page if you wish.

Save and Print

Save your table with an appropriate name and print it.

Now type the following table, according to the instructions below:

INSTALLMENT CONTRACTS

Customer	Item	Dept.	Down	Mo.
B. Jones	Towels	Bath	160.28	12
R. Burningham	Suit	Menswear	98.50	10
S. Stevens	Draperies	Domestics	48.40	8

- Begin with a clear screen. Set the margins at **0.01"** for both left and right sides (or as wide as possible).

- Press **Center (Shift-F6)** and type the main heading, **INSTALLMENT CON-TRACTS**. Press **Enter** three times to move the cursor to the fourth line down.

- For this table, insert 5 spaces between columns. You will see that the longest lines are **R. Burningham, Draperies, Domestics, $160.28** and **Mo.** Mark each of those lines.

- Press **Center (Shift-F6)** and type **R. Burningham**. Then press the **Space Bar** five times (to put five spaces between the columns). Type **Draperies**, and press the **Space Bar** five times. Type **Domestics** and press **Space Bar** five times. Type **$160.28** and press Space Bar five times. Type **Mo.** You have just centered and typed the longest line in each column and allowed for five spaces between columns.

◪ Move the cursor to the beginning of the line (**Home, Left Arrow**). Using the **Right Arrow** key, move the cursor along the line, noting the position where columns one, two, and three begin. These will be left tabs. Column four is a decimal tab so you should note the position of the decimal point. The last column, column five, can be right aligned, so note the last character in that one.

◪ Return the cursor to the left end of the line again (**Home, Left Arrow**). Be sure that you have written down your tab settings. Then delete the line you typed (R. Burningham, Draperies, etc.) using **Ctrl-End**.

◪ Press **Format (Shift-F8)** and choose Line (**1**) and Tab Set (**8**). When the tab display comes up, press **Home, Home, Left Arrow** to move to the far left of the line. Erase all existing tabs by pressing **Ctrl-End**. Then set new tabs at the positions you just determined. Remember to use a decimal tab in the fourth column and right align the fifth one.

◪ Press **Exit (F7)** twice when all the tabs are set to return to your document.

TIP: You may recall from Chapter 3 that you can set a tab by typing in the position number and pressing Enter. WordPerfect will jump to that position on the line and enter a left-justified (L) tab. If you wish, you can then change the type of tab by simply typing a different character (R, C, D, etc.) and pressing Enter. The new tab type will replace the previous one. When you have finished, press Exit (**F7**).

◪ Press **Enter** twice to space down two lines and type the three lines in the body of the table, using the **Tab** key to advance to the next column and the **Enter** key at the end of each line.

◪ Now, position the cursor at the left margin three lines below the main heading. You are ready to enter the column headings. **Tab** to the first column (Customer). Press the **space bar** once for every two letters or spaces in the column to find the middle of the column (use the longest line in the column, which in this case is **R. Burningham)**, and advance 6 spaces.

TIP: If you are using a proportional spacing font, you may need to make some adjustments in the headings to keep them centered over the columns.

◪ Press **Center (Shift-F6)** and **Underline (F8)**, type <u>Customer</u>, press **Underline (F8)**, and **Tab**. Repeat this procedure for each column heading. (Space to the center of the column, Center, Underline, type the column heading, end Underline, Tab to end the centering, and move to the next column.)

NOTE: Remember to use the Right Arrow key to deactivate the centering function in column 3 before moving to column 4 (the Tab Align column).

■ After typing all the column headings, move the cursor to the left margin on line 1 (**Home, Home, Up Arrow**). To center the page top-to-bottom, press **Format (Shift-F8)**, **Page (2)**, **Center Page (1)**, and **Exit (F7)**.

■ Save your table as **Contract.14** and print it.

■ For some practice on your own, type the table below using the format you have just learned. Save it as **SaleItem.14**, print it, and clear the screen.

SPRING SALE ITEMS

Amt.	Inventory Number	Item	List Price	%Disc
2	M23489	Dining Chair $	48.97	20.5
4	T24688	Sofa	985.90	25.0
10	M28901	Rugs	23.50	15.2
14	L89644	Lamps	89.00	30.0
7	J42891	Stereo	1,450.00	40.5

To Review

To set tabs for a table, you need to decide how much space to leave for

____

and ____.

To center column headings, you should press ___________________.

____

Summary

In summary, to type Tabulated Items:

a. Clear all tabs and set the widest possible margins.

b. Center and type the main heading.

c. Identify and set tabs.

d. Enter the table.

e. Insert and center the column headings.

f. Center the table on the page, if you wish.

g. Save and print.

Working with Text Columns

WordPerfect can print columns in both newspaper (shown top below) and parallel style (shown bottom below).

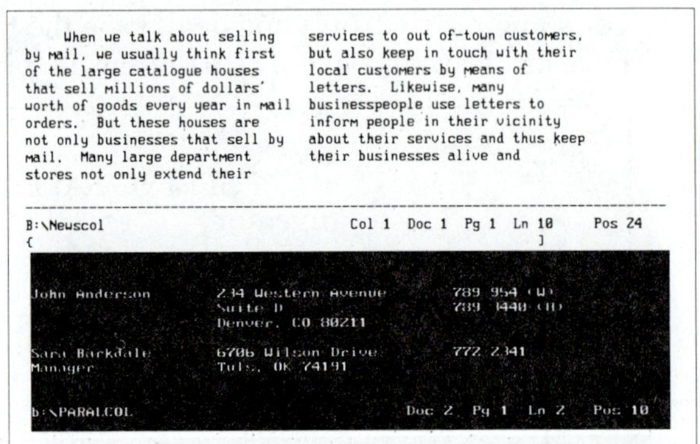

You will note that newspaper columns flow down the page and then back to the top as they move from column to column. Parallel columns flow across the page in groups.

TIP:

In addition, WordPerfect can print parallel columns with either block protect On or Off. When block protect is on, WordPerfect will keep each group of items together on the same page and will not allow the group to be split by a soft page return. If there is not enough room for the entire group on the first page, the entire group will be carried forward to the next. When block protect is off, parallel columns are allowed to spill over (or extend) from one page to the next. This feature is called extended parallel columns and is especially helpful for screenwriters and others requiring the ability to carry columns forward to the next page.

To print a document in columns, you begin by telling WordPerfect how many columns you want and how far apart they should be. Using the existing left and right margins, WordPerfect will automatically compute the margins for the columns. Then you type in the text of your document. When it is printed, it will appear as you have specified.

You can create both newspaper and parallel columns with the Math/Columns (Alt-F7) command by following the instructions below.

For this exercise, you will use the defaults for margins and tabs, and you won't need to change the settings. When you use the columns function on your own, however, it is best to have your margins and tab settings where you want them to be **before** you begin.

TIP:

Once a column definition code has been inserted into your document, you can turn columns on and off as often as you need. The same definition will be used again and again until another one is added.

Newspaper Style

First, let's work with newspaper-style columns--the type used in books and newspapers.

Define Columns

The first step is to tell WordPerfect how the columns should look.

◙ Start by pressing **Math Columns (Alt-F7)** to bring up the following prompt:

```
1 Math On; 2 Math Def; 3 Column On/Off; 4 Column Def: 0
```

◙ Choose Column **Def (4)** to begin column definition. The following menu will appear. Notice that two-column newspaper-type columns with 1/2 or (.5) inch between the columns is the default.

```
Text Column Definition

    1 - Type                                    Newspaper

    2 - Number of Columns                       2

    3 - Distance Between Columns

    4 - Margins

    Column    Left      Right    Column    Left      Right
      1:      1"        4"         13:
      2:      4.5"      7.5"       14:
      3:                           15:
      4:                           16:
      5:                           17:
      6:                           18:
      7:                           19:
      8:                           20:
      9:                           21:
     10:                           22:
     11:                           23:
     12:                           24:

Selection: 0
```

◙ To see the options available, press **Type (1)**. The following prompt will appear at the bottom of your screen.

> ```
> Column Type: 1 Newspaper; 2 Parallel; 3 Parallel with Block Protect: 0
> ```

- ◼ Select Newspaper (**1**) type. You will work with Parallel columns later.

- ◼ Since two columns is the default, you do not need to enter anything for that option. If you wanted another number, however, you could simply select Number of Columns (**2**) and type it in.

- ◼ Choose **D**istance between columns (**3**) and enter **.25** to indicate 1/4 inch between columns. WordPerfect will automatically compute the left and right margins for each of the two columns and display them in the menu.

TIP: WordPerfect assumes that you will want evenly spaced columns. If you do not, you can manually change any of the settings by selecting Margins (**4**) and then entering different margins beside any or all of those shown.

- ◼ If the margins are acceptable, press **Exit** (**F7**).

Turn Text Columns On

The Math/Columns menu will reappear.

- ◼ This time, type **3** to turn text columns On. Note that the status line now displays a Col indicator similar to that shown below. You can use this to tell when you have columns turned on.

> ```
> Col 1 Doc 1 Pg 1 Ln 0.66" Pos 0.01"
> ```

Enter the Text

You can either retrieve a file to be printed in column format or you can enter new text.

- ◼ For this exercise, type the following document or retrieve **NewsCol.14** from the Student Exercise Disk. If you don't want the first column to extend all the way to the bottom of the page before jumping back up to the top to begin the second column, you may press **Ctrl-Enter** (New Page) to tell WordPerfect where to begin the second column. Do not double-space between paragraphs.

When we talk about selling by mail, we usually think first of the large catalogue houses that sell millions of dollars' worth of goods every year in mail orders. But these houses are not the only businesses that sell by mail. Many large department stores not only extend their services to out-of-town customers, but also keep in touch with their local customers by means of letters. Likewise, many business people use letters to inform people in their vicinity about their services and thus keep their businesses alive and growing.

Sometimes the function of these letters is merely to introduce a new line of goods or a new model, or to lure the recipient into the store to see a product or a demonstration, or to meet the salesman. If customers are already acquainted with an item, the letter may be an effort to persuade them to place an order.

The writer of a sales letter must, first of all, have a thorough knowledge of the product, the jobs for which it may be used, its strength and dependability, and how it compares with competing articles on the market. It would be ideal to know equally as much about the recipient of the letter--his or her likes and dislikes, interests, and problems. Usually the writer does not know the customers individually, and thus addresses them as members of a group with certain characteristics, needs, and problems in common.

The writer tries to match the qualities of the product to the needs of the customer. It may be a matter of saving time or work or money; it may clear up a difficulty; or it may merely meet a desire or a need. Whichever seems the most compelling at the time becomes the chief selling point of the letter. If there are any secondary points, they are presented after the main point has been thoroughly explained. A good sales letter can be as thoughtful as a face-to-face sales presentation.

Moving Between Columns

If you need to move from column to column while typing, or after the text is entered, you may use the following commands. Remember that Go To is Ctrl-Home.

Go To, Left Arrow—Moves cursor to previous column.

Go To, Right Arrow—Moves cursor to next column.

Go To, Home, Left Arrow—Moves the cursor to the far left of the first column.

Go To, Home, Right Arrow—Moves the cursor to the last column.

TIP: The Home, Home, Up Arrow; Home, Home, Down Arrow; Home, Left Arrow; and Home Right Arrow commands can also be used within columns.

Turn Text Columns Off

When you have finished typing the material, you need to turn the Columns feature Off.

- Press **Math/Columns (Alt-F7)** and again choose **3** to turn text columns Off.

TIP: During editing of text printed in columns, it sometimes works more smoothly if each column is displayed separately on the screen. The Setup menu will allow you to do this. Press Setup (Shift-F1), choose Display (3), and select Side-by-side Column Display (8). Type **N**(o)and WordPerfect will then display each column individually. Be sure to return the setup menu to its original setting when you are finished.

Save and Print

The next step is to save your document with an appropriate name and print it.

- Save it as **NewsCol.14**, print it, and clear the screen.

TIP: You can use a variety of commands within the columns mode. For instance, pressing Delete to End of Page would erase the remainder of the contents of that column. If you wish to move part of a column, you should block the part you wish to move, and select cut or copy block. Do NOT use cut/copy column for this operation.

Summary

In summary, to type newspaper-style columns:

a. Press Math/Columns (Alt-F7).

b. Choose Column Definition (**4**).

c. Identify type, number of columns, and distance between columns. Also specify margins if different from those displayed.

d. Turn Text Columns On (3).

e. Enter (or retrieve) the text.

f. Press Math/Columns (Alt-F7) and 3 to turn Text Columns Off.

g. Save and print.

Parallel Columns (Extended and With Block Protect)

Parallel columns are different from newspaper columns in two major ways. First, the contents of several columns are related across the page, and second, the parts of each column are not of equal length. In addition, you can specify whether or not related columns are to be printed together on the same page by turning block protect on or off.

TIP: When you are using this method, the columns do not need to be of equal length. This allows you a great deal of flexibility in the kinds of information that you can enter as a unit.

- For practice, define columns for the following text using **Math/Columns** (**Alt-F7**), and Column **Def** (**4**). The text consists of three columns and two groups of information. Put 0.4" between the columns, and have the columns evenly spaced. Select parallel with block protect.

- Turn Text Columns On (**3**). Then enter the text. First, type **John Andrews**. Then press **Ctrl-Enter** to move to the second column and enter the complete address. (NOTE: WordPerfect wordwraps within a column; or you can press Enter to move to the next line in the column.) When you have entered Andrews's complete address, press **Ctrl-Enter** to move to the first line of the third column. When you have finished with the last column in the first group (Andrews's phone numbers), press **Ctrl-Enter** to begin the next group of items, which begins with Sara Barker's name.

John Andrews	234 Western Avenue Suite D Denver, CO 80211	789-9854 (W) 789-3440 (H)
Sara Barker Manager	6706 Wilson Drive Tulsa, OK 74106	772-2341
Jim Wilson Branch Mgr. Operations	2457 Georgetown Suite 43 2468 Roosevelt Denver, CO 80229	325-9807

- Turn Columns **Off** (**3**) when you are finished.

- Save your document as **ParalCol.14** and print it.

To Review

What information must you supply to define the columns?

What is the major difference between newspaper- and parallel-style columns? Between parallel with block protect and extended parallel?

Doing Math Functions with WordPerfect

WordPerfect can add subtotals, totals, and grand totals. It can subtract, and it can also use formulas. To see how this function works, let's create a table and do a little calculating.

Suppose that you work in a furniture store and have been asked to construct a table of the prices if several items were marked up 20 percent. You will need to generate some totals and a grand total and subtract out the amount for returns. WordPerfect can help you with these calculations.

First, glance at the table on the next page. Then let's review the steps to follow before you actually type it in.

1. **Type the main heading**: Center and type the main heading.

2. **Set margins and tabs**: Set your margins as wide as possible and clear all your tabs. Then set new tabs, using the procedure you learned previously.

   Since you want WordPerfect to perform a special function in this table, you must tell it what to expect and what to do before you type in the numbers. You will do this by performing the following steps, which will be explained in more detail later.

3. **Define the math columns**: This function tells WordPerfect what is in each of the columns (numbers, text, calculation, or total), and the formulas to use, if any.

4. **Set the math function On:** This command activates the math function so the calculations can take place.

5. **Enter the table**: You will use some special symbols as you key in the table to tell WordPerfect how to do its calculations.

   +   Generates a subtotal

= Generates a total (adds subtotals)

* Generates a grand total (adds totals)

N   Indicates a negative or subtraction

! Indicates a calculation. (This symbol need not be typed in. WordPerfect will enter it automatically when you press TAB if a calculation is specified for that column.)

6. **Calculate**: This command will cause WordPerfect to calculate the totals you have asked for. These totals will be automatically entered in the table where the special commands appear.

7. **Turn the math function Off**: When your table is complete you will deactivate the math function.

8. **Type the column headings**: Enter headings above the columns, following the procedure you learned earlier in this chapter.

9. **Insert underlines**: To insert the underlines necessary for the table, Block the spaces and numbers to be underlined and press Underline. The underline should be the same length as the longest number in the column (usually the total).

10. **Save and Print**: Save the document with an appropriate name and print it.

Now that you have an overview of how to use this function, let's try setting up the table. Follow the steps outlined below to enter the following:

```
                        FURNITURE SALES
        Item             Amount                    Markup

        Sofas            550.00  (TAB)             !(don't type !)
        Chairs           225.00                    !
        Love Seats       720.00                    !
          Subtotal          +        (press ENTER here to avoid !
                                      mark in third column)

        Tables           360.00                    !
        Stands            74.50                    !
          Subtotal          +
          Total             =
```

```
Dressers                820.00                              !
Beds                    640.00                              !
   Subtotal                +

Less Returns
Sofa                    320.00                              !
Stand                    28.00                              !
   Subtotal              N+
      Total               =

Grand Total               *

                      ========
```

■ Start with a clear screen. Set the margins at **.01** left and **.01** right (or as wide as they will go).

■ Center and type **FURNITURE SALES.**

■ Press **Enter** three times to move to the fourth line down. Set a left tab at **1.5** with a decimal tab at **4.0** and another at **5.0** for the three columns.

■ Press **Enter** twice more to leave room for the column headings. (You should now be on the sixth line down).

■ With the cursor at the point where you will start typing the table itself (sixth line, Pos 1.0"), press **Math/Columns (Alt-F7)**. This is the same key you used for the column function. This time, however, we will use the math commands.

■ You will see the following:

```
1 Math On; 2 Math Def; 3 Column On/Off; 4 Column Def: 0
```

As you did with the text columns, you must first define the math columns so WordPerfect will know which ones to calculate.

■ Press Math **Def (2)**. A menu resembling the following will appear:

```
Math Definition                 Use arrow keys to position cursor

Columns                         A B C D E F G H I J K L M N O P Q R S T U V W X

Type                            2 2 2 2 2 2 2 2 2 2 2 2 2 2 2 2 2 2 2 2 2 2 2 2

Negative Numbers                ( ( ( ( ( ( ( ( ( ( ( ( ( ( ( ( ( ( ( ( ( ( ( (

Number of Digits to             2 2 2 2 2 2 2 2 2 2 2 2 2 2 2 2 2 2 2 2 2 2 2 2
  the Right (0-4)

Calculation    1
   Formulas    2
               3
               4

Type of Column:
     0 = Calculation    1 = Text      2 = Numeric     3 = Total

Negative Numbers
     ( = Parentheses (50.00)           - = Minus Sign  -50.00



Press Exit when done
```

Looking it over, you can see that you can have up to 24 columns (A-X). (These may not all appear in your text because of printer limitations.)

Each column can be one of four types--Calculation, Text, Numeric, or Total. You can have the negative numbers displayed either in parentheses or with a minus sign, and you can specify the number of places to the right of the decimal point.

Your table should show what a 20 percent markup on several items would be. You'll use a formula and compute subtotals, a total, and a grand total.

There are three columns, which are designated A, B, and C. The A column is simply descriptive, so designate it as a text column. Column B, which lists the cost, is numeric. Column C shows the amount of markup and requires a formula to compute.

■ With the cursor under Column A, enter a **1** in the Type row to indicate that this will be a Text column.

■ The cursor will move automatically to Column B. Since it is already set for numeric, use the **Right Arrow** to accept the setting and move to Column C.

■ In Column C, type a **0** (zero) for Calculation. When you type the zero, the cursor will jump down beside the first calculation formula and show 1 C. WordPerfect wants you to tell it the formula to use.

- Since you are going to compute a 20 percent markup, type **B*.20** and press **Enter**. This tells WordPerfect to multiply the amount in the B column by .20 and to put the result in the C column.

  You won't have any negative numbers in this table, and two places after the decimal point is correct for dollar amounts. Therefore, you may now exit from the math-definition menu.

- Press **Exit** (**F7**) to return to the Math/Columns Menu.

  Since WordPerfect will not calculate unless it is in Math mode, you must now turn Math On to enter the table.

- Choose **Math** On (**1**). The word **Math** will appear in the lower left-hand corner of your screen. This lets you know that the math function is On.

- Begin to type in the table. Press **Tab,** type **Sofas**, press **Tab,** type **550.00**.

  When you tab to the second column, you will be in Tab Align mode. WordPerfect automatically activates the Tab Align command when you define a column as numeric.

- **Tab** to the Markup column.

  When you Tab to Column 3, which you defined as a calculation column, WordPerfect will automatically show an exclamation point. This symbol lets you know that it is ready to calculate. When you give it the command to do so, the amount will appear beside the exclamation point.

- Press **Enter**.

- Continue typing the table, using the **Tab** key to move from column to column. Press **Enter** at the end of each line.

- When you are ready to enter the subtotal line, press **Tab**, space twice to indent, type **Subtotal**, press **Tab**, type +, and press **Enter**.

TIP: Do not Tab to the C column and allow WordPerfect to insert the ! symbol if you do not want the markup to be calculated for the subtotal. Pressing Enter at the end of Column B will prevent the calculation symbol from being entered.

  When you want to calculate a subtotal, Tab to column B and type (+). This tells WordPerfect to add the numbers above the plus sign, and record the subtotal beside it, when you give it the command to calculate. (The + will not print on the printout.)

  An equal sign (=) is the command for a total. Wherever you type an equal sign, WordPerfect will add all the subtotals together and place the total beside it.

The asterisk (*) is the command for a grand total. WordPerfect will add the totals together and place that amount wherever you have typed an asterisk, when the command to calculate is given.

The letter N, in combination with one of the other calculation symbols, tells WordPerfect to add the column and then treat the total as a negative number, to be subtracted whenever it is used.

+　Subtotal
=　Total
*　Grand Total
N　Negative number

TIP: It is important to remember to Tab to the column where you intend to enter the special computation symbols (+, =, *, N). Tab codes must precede these symbols in order for WordPerfect to recognize them as calculation points.

When you have finished typing the table, you are ready to calculate the Markup column and the totals.

◾ Press **Math/Columns (Alt-F7)** again. The second option, Math Def, has now been changed to Calculate.

```
1 Math On; 2 Math Calculate; 3 Column On/Off; 4 Column Def: 0
```

◾ Select **Calculate (2)**. WordPerfect will do the rest.

All of a sudden, the totals will appear. As you will see, it has calculated across the rows (!) and totaled down the columns (+, =, *, N).

If you wish, you can calculate as you go along. It isn't necessary to wait until you've typed in the entire table. WordPerfect will do the math functions as soon as you have entered one of the operators (+, =, *, !, N). Simply press **Math/Columns (Alt-F7)**, and Calculate (2) to generate figures whenever you want.

TIP: If the table will not calculate, make sure that the cursor is between the Math On/Off codes (the Math prompt should appear in the lower left-hand corner) when you select Calculate. The math function must be On to calculate. If the cursor is outside the codes, or you have turned Math Off before calculating, the math function will not calculate. If your cursor is in the correct position but it still does not calculate, check to be sure you have entered the right symbols, and that they are entered between the alignment codes, like this [Align]+[c/a/Flrt].

- Now turn Math Off by pressing **Math/Columns** (**Alt-F7**) and choosing **1**.

- Go back and enter the column headings, centered, in the fourth line, following the procedure on page 361.

     The column headings can be keyed in before the table is typed and calculated, but waiting to do so eliminates several potential problems. If they are keyed in with the Math mode turned On, the automatic tab align, which the math definition command creates in numeric columns, makes centering difficult. If the column headings are keyed in before the Math mode is turned on and the columns are entered, it is hard to find the centers of the columns. Therefore, it is easiest to enter them after the table is calculated. Math is turned Off, and you can see where the column centers are.

- **Block** and **Underline** the numbers above the subtotals. Then, using the = sign, type a double underline under the grand total.

TIP: If you have difficulty entering the solid line separating amounts from totals, press Format (**Shift-F8**), Other (**4**), and select option **7** to underline spaces and tabs.

- Save your table under the name **MathTabl.14**, print it, and clear your screen.

To Review

List the steps to follow in using each of the following math functions:

Tabs ____

Define Columns ____

Turn Math On ____

Type Table ____

Calculate ____

Turn Math Off ____

Save and Print ____

What will happen when each of the following symbols is used with Math On?

+ ____

= ____

* ____

N ____

Summary

In summary, to use the Math Functions:

   a. Enter the main heading, and set margins and tabs.

   b. Define Math Columns (Alt-F7, 2).

   c. Press Math/Columns (Alt-F7) and turn Math On (1).

   d. Type the table, using special symbols where appropriate.

   e. Press Math/Columns (Alt-F7) and Calculate (2).

   f. Press Math/Columns (Alt-F7) and turn Math Off (1).

   g. Center and type column headings.

   h. Insert underlines where appropriate.

   i. Save and print.

Activities

You should have completed to following:

Contracts.14	*Installment Contracts table*
SaleItem.14	*Spring Sale Items table*
NewsCol.14	*Newspaper Text Columns*
ParalCol.14	*Parallel Text Columns*
MathTabl.14	*Math Table*

Chapter Review

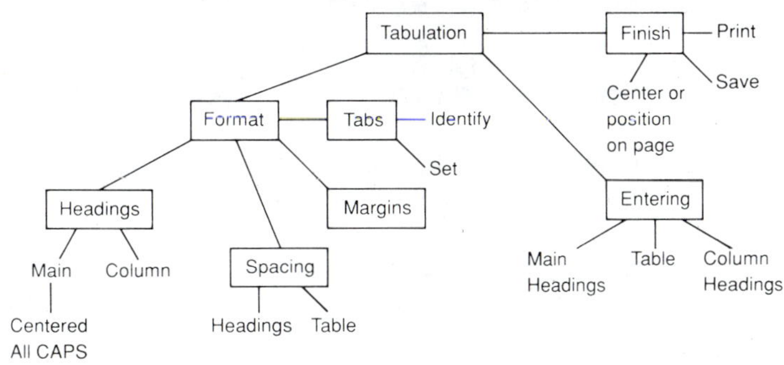

(continued)

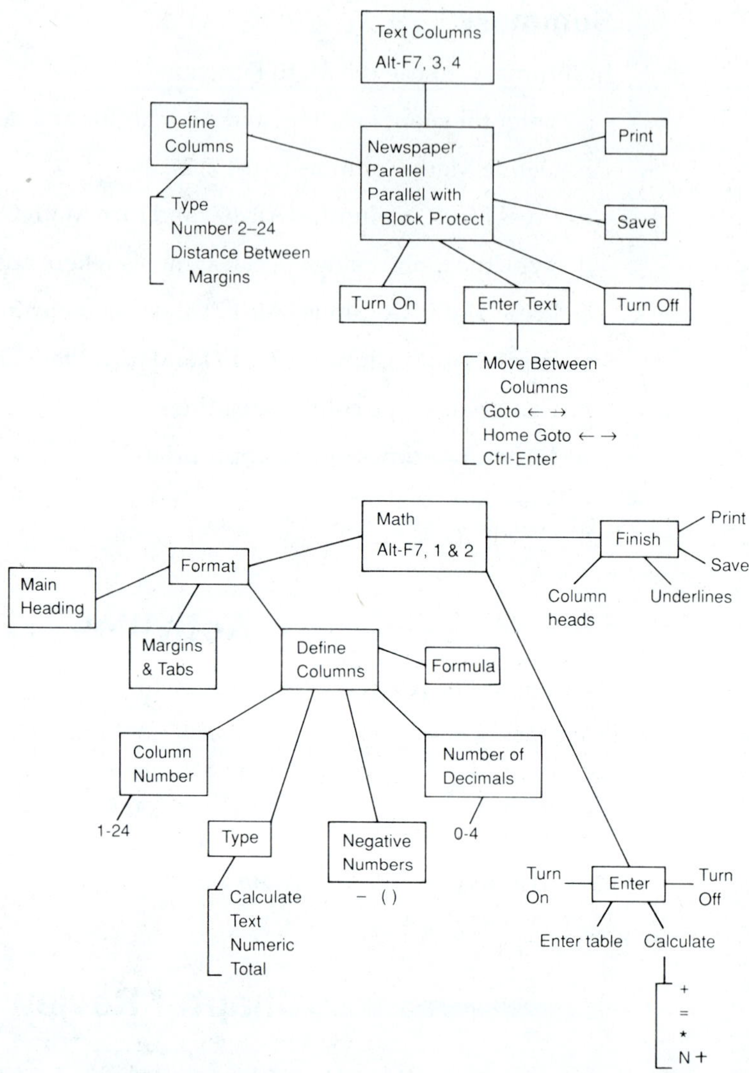

Self-Check Quiz 14

1. How should you space and type the title and column headings of a table?

2. What keystrokes erase all tabs at once?

3. Which keystrokes should you use to center column headings?

4. When must you set the margins and tabs for text to be printed in columns?

5. If you do not specify a break in newspaper-style columns, how will WordPerfect print them?

6. What information should you supply to define newspaper-style columns?

7. What information should you supply to define parallel-style columns with block protect? With extended parallel?

8. What information should you supply to define math columns?

9. How many text columns can be put on a standard-size page?

10. How can you determine margins for your columns?

11. Which keys do you press to turn the Columns function on and off?

12. What will each of the following commands generate?

    ! ____

    + ____

    N+ ____

    = ____

    * ____

    N= ____

13. What keystrokes should you use to tell WordPerfect to compute totals?

Extra Practice

For extra practice on the material covered in Chapter 14, do the following:

a. Set up and enter the following table:

INVENTORY ON HAND

(Current Date)

Part No.	Description	Qty	Location	Price
04311	Chair	4	E4-A	49.85
10988	Desk	2	B10-D	329.95
62319	Cabinet	2	B3-C	189.00
48222	Lamp	5	C14-A	74.25
10113	Stand	9	B3-C	29.95

b. Save it as **PRACT14a** and print.

c. Set up a two-column format for the material in Chapter 2 on TV viewers. When the setup is completed, retrieve **TV.2** and make two columns.

d. Save the two column document as **PRACT14b** and print it.

e. Enter the following table in three columns. Use block protect. Save it as **PRACT14c** and print it.

HOMES FOR SALE

June 1, 19--

Address	Features	Contact
236 Evergreen	3 bdrm	Landmark Realty
$130,500	2 bath	Sam Williams
	Full basement	229-0409
		Can be seen anytime
		after 4 p.m. daily.

66 South Market $198,200 Negotiable, Owner Anxious	4 bdrm large lot 2-car garage newly carpeted 4 years old	BJR Realty & Associates Betty Green 329-4116 Shows well. A very good value for the money.
1398 Southern $145,000	4 bdrm all brick prestige area vacant	Wilson Real Estate Marge Egan 229-6100 Available for immediate occupancy. Has been appraised at $160,000. FHA approved.

f. Assume you are contemplating a trip to a resort area. The costs vary by season, with a 20 percent discount for mid-season (March-June, September-October), and a 40 percent discount for low season (November-February). Enter the following table. Use appropriate math commands and formulas appropriate to compute the comparative costs by season, subtotals, totals, and grand total. When you are finished, save it as **PRACT14d** and print it.

ANALYSIS OF VACATION COSTS

High-Medium-Low Seasons

	High	Medium	Low
Transportation	340.00		
Lodging	550.00		
Subtotal			

<table>
<tr><td>Car Rental</td><td>150.00</td></tr>
<tr><td>Insurance</td><td>30.00</td></tr>
<tr><td>Subtotal</td><td></td></tr>
<tr><td>TOTAL</td><td></td></tr>
<tr><td>Food</td><td>200.00</td></tr>
<tr><td>Gratuities</td><td>40.00</td></tr>
<tr><td>Subtotal</td><td></td></tr>
<tr><td>Souvenirs</td><td>100.00</td></tr>
<tr><td>Miscellaneous Expense</td><td>75.00</td></tr>
<tr><td>Subtotal</td><td></td></tr>
<tr><td>TOTAL</td><td></td></tr>
<tr><td>GRAND TOTAL</td><td></td></tr>
</table>

g. Prepare a budget for your personal finances. Estimate your expenses for the coming month and enter them with the math function. Calculate your expected costs for food, lodging, transportation, clothing, and other expenses.

h. Set up a table to determine your automobile costs for the month. Include car payment, gasoline, insurance, repair, and any other expenses you may have on your car. Use the math features to calculate your costs.

15

Adding Graphics to Your Documents

One of the most exciting new features of Word-Perfect 5.0 is its ability to include graphics in your documents. These graphics include many shapes and designs and can consist of clip-art files, text, or files from a variety of other software programs. WordPerfect also has enhanced ability to create lines in any number of lengths, widths, and shades to add emphasis and variety to your document.

You'll work with all of these features in this chapter, and when you're finished you should be able to:

- create graphics boxes in a variety of formats.

- incorporate clip art, text, and other designs into your box.

- import graphics from other software programs into WordPerfect documents.

- use the appropriate editing commands to size and place graphics in the box as needed.

- modify graphics boxes using available options for borders, numbering, captions, and shading.

- add horizontal and vertical lines in a variety of ways.

There are two parts to adding graphics to a document. The first is creating a box or space for the graphic, and the second is inserting the graphic into the space. Both parts require several steps and have a variety of options. Since you cannot insert a graphic until the box is defined, let's work with the box first.

Creating a Graphics Box

Even though you will probably want to combine graphics and text in most of your documents later, for the time being let's experiment with the graphics box alone. We'll add the accompanying text later.

If the error message **"Insufficient file handles"** should appear, be sure that the statement "Files = 20" has been added to the CONFIG.SYS file on the DOS disk or root directory.

Now let's create a graphics box to see how it is done.

■ With a clear screen, press **Graphics (Alt-F9)**. The following menu will appear:

```
1 Figure; 2 Table; 3 Text Box; 4 User-defined Box; 5 Line: 0
```

WordPerfect allows four different kinds of graphics boxes. It also can create horizontal and vertical lines. Particularly notice the boxes. (We'll work with the lines later.) Even though they are identified separately, these boxes have many similarities and the process of defining each kind does not vary a great deal.

You can insert both text and graphics into any of the four kinds of boxes, and all can be used anywhere in the text. The major differences are in the defaults identified for each kind, and how they are displayed.

Another disparity, which is not as obvious, is that WordPerfect treats them differently when numbering, generating lists, and performing other functions. This allows you to distinguish among the different kinds of boxes even when they are combined in the same document.

The most noticeable difference is the style of border used for each kind of graphics box and the placement of the caption. Take a look at the following examples.

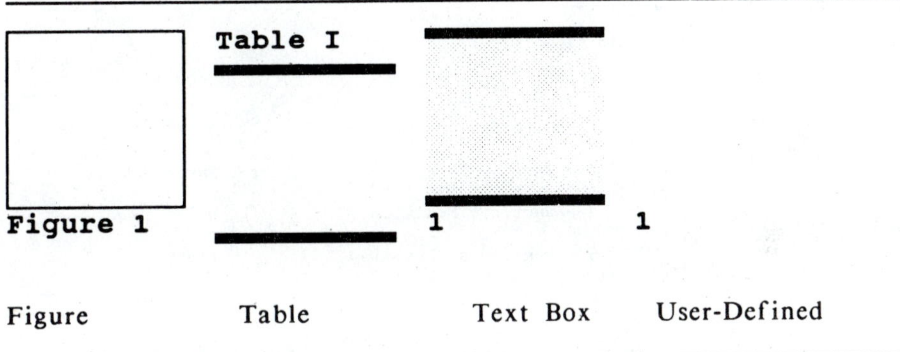

Figure   Table   Text Box   User-Defined

As you can see, a figure is enclosed in a box with single lines around it and the caption (Figure 1) is displayed below the box. A table has thick solid lines at the top and bottom with nothing on the side. The caption (Table I) is shown at the top in Roman numerals. A Text Box also has thick solid lines at the top and bottom with nothing on the side. It is shaded 10 percent and the caption simply shows a number (1) at the bottom. Finally, a User-Defined box has no lines around it, and the caption is shown at the bottom as a number (1). There are also other defaults that are not as noticeable, having to do with border space inside and outside the box.

Defaults on any of the four can be changed in a variety of ways, and you'll work with that later. Having some predefined boxes to use is very convenient however, and allows WordPerfect to distinguish among different kinds for lists and other uses. Generally, when you customize a box, you will probably use the User Defined kind. For the time being, let's see what happens when you select Figure.

■ Choose **Figure** (**1**). A new menu will appear.

```
Figure: 1 Create; 2 Edit; 3 New Number; 4 Options: 0
```

■ Select **Create (1)** to display the Figure Definition menu shown below.

```
Definition: Figure

    1 - Filename

    2 - Caption

    3 - Type                        Paragraph

    4 - Vertical Position           0"

    5 - Horizontal Position         Right

    6 - Size                        3.25" wide x 3.25" (high)

    7 - Wrap Text Around Box        Yes

    8 - Edit




Selection: 0
```

This menu allows you to specify a number of things about how the graphics box will be positioned on the page. It also allows you to identify the file (graphic) to be inserted into the box when it is printed.

Filename

After selecting this option, WordPerfect will ask for the filename of a graphic to be inserted into the box. We'll come back to this selection later once the position of the box has been defined.

Caption

The caption is the identifier (Figure 1, Table I) and any accompanying text that you wish to add to describe the contents of the graphics box. WordPerfect will automatically update the number of each new graphics box as it is created.

TIP: You cannot add captions to graphics boxes that are placed inside headers, footers, footnotes, and endnotes.

Type

There are three types of boxes: Paragraph (the default), Page, and Character. In most cases, the code for type of box is inserted at the cursor position. Therefore, it is important to place the cursor where you want the box to appear in the text before entering the commands to create it.

TIP: Note that **kind** of box refers to the appearance of the box, such as borders, shading, and caption. **Type** of box refers to how the box is placed within the surrounding text. Each kind of box (Figure, Table, Text Box, User Defined) can be any type (paragraph, page, character) meaning that you can place any kind of box in any of the three type positions.

A **Paragraph** type of box (any kind) is tied to the paragraph in which it appears and will stay with it as the text expands and shrinks with editing. Surrounding text in the paragraph will wrap around the box.

A **Page** type of box (any kind) is positioned at a specific or fixed place on the page and will not move, even if the paragraphs and text around it changes. Surrounding text on the page will adjust and wrap around the box.

A **Character** type of box (any kind) is treated as if it were a single character on the line. When WordPerfect encounters the code for this type of box, it simply prints the box as if it were the next character on the line, wherever that occurs. Text that precedes and follows the box is printed above and below it. Text on the same line can be aligned with the top, center, or bottom of the box. This is the only type of box that can be used inside footnotes and endnotes.

To Review:

List the differences between paragraph, page, and character types.

Vertical Position

This option determines where the box will be positioned vertically (up and down), either in the paragraph, or on the page (depending on what type it is).

If the box is a paragraph type, (any kind) the vertical position default is at the top of the paragraph (first line). The 0" you see on the screen means that the box will be positioned 0" from the top of the paragraph unless it is changed. If you want it positioned somewhere else in the paragraph, you must specify an offset, or distance from the top of the paragraph.

You can also place the cursor anywhere within the paragraph before creating the graphics box. The cursor position becomes the default location and WordPerfect will then insert the command and the box at the cursor position.

TIP: When printing, if the paragraph begins too close to the end of the page for the box to fit, the box is moved to the top of the next page.

If the box is a page type, (any kind) you may choose to have the box fill the full page (using margin boundaries), at the top margin, centered on the page, at the bottom margin, or you may specify an offset by setting a specific position. The current cursor position will be the default.

Character type boxes (any kind) will simply be placed where the line occurs in the text. Therefore you cannot specify a vertical position for these types.

Horizontal Position

This option specifies where the box will be placed horizontally (or from left to right) across the page.

If the box is a paragraph type, (any kind) it can be placed at the left margin, at the right margin, in the center of the page (or column), or spread between the left and right margins.

If the box is a page type, (any kind) you have several alternatives. You can place the box horizontally at the cursor based on the page margins (left, right, center, both left and right) or based on column margins (left, right, center, both left and right). You can also specify a fixed position (in inches, points, or centimeters) as an offset or distance from the left edge of the paper.

Because character type boxes (any kind) are placed with the line in which they occur, there is no optional setting for horizontal position.

Size

The size, or width and height, of the box can be determined in several ways.

WordPerfect can determine what is needed based on the default size of the graphic and offer it. You can press Enter to simply enter that size.

You can specify that the box must be a certain width and let WordPerfect determine the height needed, based on the graphic's requirements.

You can specify the height, and let WordPerfect determine the width needed based on the graphic's requirements.

Or you can specify a fixed distance for both the width and height and require WordPerfect to adjust (if possible) the size of the graphic to fit it.

In most cases, when you specify a width or height and let WordPerfect determine the other measurement, WordPerfect will adjust the size of the graphic proportionally. For instance, if you specify a small width, Word-Perfect will choose a correspondingly small height and reduce the graphic accordingly. The end result depends on the requirements of the particular graphic being inserted into the box. Some are square, some rectangular, and some are long and narrow. If exact measurement is an issue, use the fixed distance. If not, let WordPerfect make the final adjustments.

TIP: You must be careful when determining height and width that you do not cause the appearance or accuracy of the contents to be distorted.

Wrap Text Around Box

You may respond Yes or No to this item. If you say Yes, the text will be wrapped around the box. If you say No, the text will display across the full line and overwrite the box.

TIP: If you use the overwrite feature (no wrap) you can insert Hard Returns [HRt] to wrap text very close to the image. This would need to be done just before saving and printing. Remember that these hard returns will make your document harder to edit.

It is important to note that if the box is centered or positioned in the middle of the line, the text will wrap only on one side of the box. When the wrap text option is set to N(o), the outline will not display on the document editing screen. You must use View Document (Shift-F7, 6) to see it. Press Exit (**F7**) to leave View.

TIP: WordPerfect can wrap to a maximum of 20 boxes per page.

Edit

The edit option allows you to rotate, scale, and move the graphic image in the box. It also allows you to enter or edit text that is to be inserted into the box. You can rotate the text 90, 180, and 270 degrees on the page. However, your printer must be able to print it in rotated position if you wish a printout.

◼ Now let's create a graphics box using the defaults. As you can see, the box will be a paragraph type, meaning that it will stay with the paragraph the cursor is currently in. It will be placed beginning on the first line of the paragraph (0" offset). It will be aligned at the right margin, and the box itself will be 3.25" wide by 3.25" high. Finally, any text in the paragraph will wrap around the box. Since you are using the defaults, you do not need to make any selections at this point. The defaults will automatically be saved with the file when you exit.

If this box were printed as it now appears, you would see a single ruled 3.25 inch square box at the right margin (located at the current cursor position), without a caption.

◼ Let's add a caption to say "Figure 1 --It's Good News. Select **Caption** (**2**). Immediately you will be placed in an editing screen like that shown below.

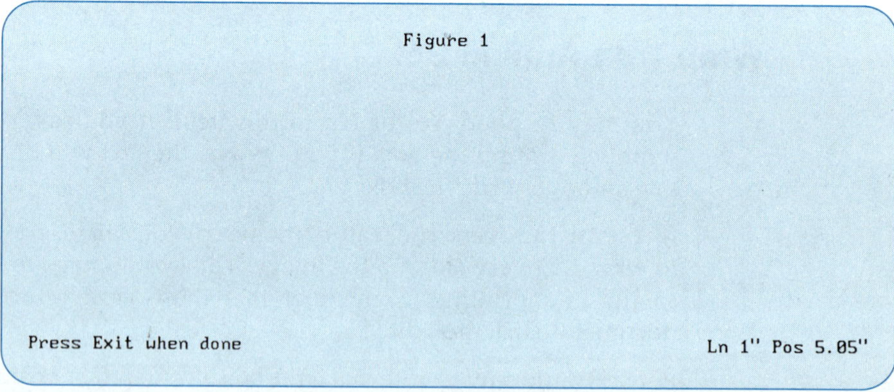

WordPerfect has supplied the indicator Figure 1. You may now type in the remainder of the caption and press Exit (**F7**).

◼ Type — **It's Good News** and press **Exit** (**F7**). You will be returned to the Figure Definition menu. Notice that the new caption has been inserted into the menu.

TIP: WordPerfect will keep track of the numbering of the figures (and tables and user defined boxes also) and automatically offer the next higher number when you select the caption.

☐ Press **Exit** (**F7**) to leave the menu and return to the main editing screen.

☐ Press **Enter**. At the top of the screen you will see the beginning of the first figure. Press **Enter** 20 or so times to bring the lines to the bottom of the box until it is completely displayed on the screen.

☐ To see how the box looks on the full page, press **Print** (**Shift-F7**) and View (**6**). When you are finished, press **Exit** (**F7**) to leave the view screen.

TIP: To view your graphic, you must have the printer defined correctly. If it is not, and nothing appears (or you get an error message), review the material in Chapter 1 and select the printer according to the instructions given there.

Now let's add some text to see how it is wrapped around the box. There are several ways to incorporate text at this point. You can type it in, retrieve another file, or the text could already be on the page and the box added to it.

☐ For this exercise, let's retrieve the file you created called **Boosters.5**. Position the cursor at the top left corner of the screen with **Home, Home, Up Arrow**, opposite the top of the box you just created.

TIP: Use **Reveal Codes** (**Alt-F3**) to be sure the cursor is positioned right of the code for Figure 1.

☐ Using **Retrieve** (**Shift-F10**) or **List Files** (**F5**), retrieve **Boosters.5** into this file. Then run the cursor through the text and reformat it to wrap around the box.

☐ Using **Save** (**F10**) save your file as **Graph.15**.

☐ Now, let's view the document again with the **View Document** (**6**) command. Pretty impressive.

Summary

In summary, to create a graphics box:

   a. Position the cursor where the box is to be placed.

   b. Press Graphics (Alt-F9).

   c. Select Figure (1), Table (2), Text Box (3), or User-Defined (4).

   d. Select Create (1).

   e. Supply information for type, vertical/horizontal position, size, and text wrap.

   f. Edit if necessary.

   g. Exit (F7).

Editing a Graphics Box

There are many ways to edit the position, size, and appearance of the graphics box. For some practice, let's move the box you just created to the left margin and make the size 2" square. Let's also have it begin one-fourth inch down in the paragraph rather than on the top line.

▣ Select **Graphics (Alt-F9)** and again choose Figure **(1)**.

▣ When the following menu appears, select Edit **(2)**.

```
Figure: 1 Create; 2 Edit; 3 New Number; 4 Options: 0
```

▣ When asked for the figure number to edit, enter **1** and press **Enter**. You will be returned to the Figure Definition screen.

▣ To drop the box down in the paragraph, select Vertical Position **(4)** and enter **.25** as the offset from the top of the paragraph. Then press **Enter**.

▣ To move the box to the left margin, select Horizontal Position **(5)** to bring up the following menu along the bottom of the screen.

```
Horizontal Position: 1 Left; 2 Right; 3 Center; 4 Both Left & Right: 0
```

▣ Choose Left **(1)**. Immediately the setting in the figure definition menu will change.

▣ To change the size, select Size **(6)** to display the following menu across the bottom of the screen.

```
1 Width (auto height); 2 Height (auto width); 3 Both Width and Height: 0
```

From this menu you can elect to set the width (1) or height (2) and allow WordPerfect to determine the remaining side. Or you can elect to set both width and height at fixed positions (3). Since the original graphics box is square, and you have not entered a graphic to influence the size, WordPerfect will maintain the square shape at this point.

If you selected either (1) or (2) and entered a 1" width/height, WordPerfect would automatically set a 1" height/width. Or if you selected (3) and entered a 1" height and width, you would still have a square box. The big difference between the auto (1 and 2) and fixed settings (3) would be more apparent when a graphic was added. If the graphic required something other than a square shape, the auto settings would adjust, but the fixed setting would not.

TIP: With a fixed size, instead of the shape of the box being changed, the graphic would be altered, possibly distorting it.

- For this exercise, select **Width (1)** and type **2** (meaning 2 inches). Then press **Enter**. Notice that WordPerfect automatically determines the height and enters both in the menu.

- Now press **Exit (F7)** to leave the menu and return to the document editing screen. Notice that the box has been moved from the right to the left side and that the size is smaller.

TIP: If the box does not move down 1/4 inch in the paragraph, use Reveal Codes (Alt-F3) to see if there are [HRt] codes between the figure code and the first line of text in the paragraph. If so, delete the [HRt] codes and the paragraph will move down.

- Again press **Print (Shift-F7)** and View Document (6) to see the changes. Press **Exit (F7)** to return to the document editing screen.

As you can see, it's very easy to position the graphics box where you want within the paragraph. You can use a variety of settings to change both the position and size of the box.

Some cautions include the following: Text will not wrap on both the right and left side of a box that is centered. If this creates a problem for the appearance of your document, you may want to avoid the centering option and use left or right only.

If the paragraph begins near the bottom of the page, and there is not enough room for the box on the page where it would normally be printed, the box will be moved upward in the paragraph (if possible). If it will not fit, the box will be moved to the top of the following page to be printed.

TIP: You can also change a Figure to a Table or a Text-Box. To do this, press Graphics (Alt-F9), Figure (1), and Edit (2) to bring up the figure definition menu. Then press Alt-F9. A menu will appear across the bottom of the screen listing the kinds of boxes. Select one of them and Exit (F7). WordPerfect will make the change immediately.

▣ Now save your document as **GraphBox.15** and print it.

To Review

What keystrokes must you use to change each of the following in a graphics box?

Position ____

Size ____

Type ____

____

Summary

In summary, to edit a graphics box?

     a. Select Graphics (Alt-F9) and the type of box you wish to edit.

     b. Choose Edit (2).

     c. Make appropriate changes in definition menu.

     d. Press Exit (F7) to save changes.

Options for Graphic Box Appearance and Display

There are a number of ways to change the way your graphics boxes appear. As you know, there are defaults for each kind (Figure, Table, Text-Box, User-Defined). However, the appearance of any of them can be altered using the options available. To see what they are, do the following:

▣ Clear your screen and select **Graphics (Alt-F9)**. Select **Figure (1)** and **Options (4)** from the menus as they appear. The Options menu looks like the following:

```
Options:     Figure

        1 - Border Style
                Left                           Single
                Right                          Single
                Top                            Single
                Bottom                         Single
        2 - Outside Border Space
                Left                           0.16"
                Right                          0.16"
                Top                            0.16"
                Bottom                         0.16"
        3 - Inside Border Space
                Left                           0"
                Right                          0"
                Top                            0"
                Bottom                         0"
        4 - First Level Numbering Method      Numbers
        5 - Second Level Numbering Method     Off
        6 - Caption Number Style              [BOLD]Figure 1[bold]
        7 - Position of Caption               Below box, Outside borders
        8 - Minimum Offset from Paragraph     0"
        9 - Gray Shading (% of black)         0%

Selection: 0
```

This menu allows you to change the appearance of lines used for the border. It also lets you alter the distance allowed between the border and the adjacent text (outside) as well as between the border and the graphic or text it contains (inside). You can also change the numbering method, the style and position of the caption, and the minimum offset from the paragraph that a graphics box may be placed. Finally, you can change the shading within the box from nothing (0) all the way to black (100).

TIP: The options define the setup and appearance of the Figure graphics boxes. *They must be entered before the graphics box is created.* The default options for a Table, Text-Box, and User-Defined box are different variations of this menu. If you change the defaults for one kind of box, such as a figure box, all subsequent graphics boxes of that same kind will be changed, but other kinds of graphics boxes will not.

Border Style

There are a number of Border Styles (1) that can be used. Any or all can be applied to the left, right, top, or bottom line.

■ Press **Border (1)** to bring up the following menu along the bottom of the screen:

```
1 None; 2 Single; 3 Double; 4 Dashed; 5 Dotted; 6 Thick; 7 Extra Thick: 0
```

■ Let's change the defaults to have a thick line on top and bottom of the box and dashed lines on the sides. To do this, enter Dashed (**4**) for the Left and Right border style and Thick (**6**) for Top and Bottom border style.

Inside and Outside Border Space

By default, WordPerfect will leave .16" between the border of the graphics box and text that is wrapped around it (option 2). It will not leave any extra space inside the box between the border and a graphic or text that it contains (option 3).

■ To change the border space to 1/4 inch both inside and outside the box, select Outside (**2**) and type **.25** for the left and right sides. Then select Inside (**3**) and type **.25** for the left and right sides. Leave the top and bottom at the default for both outside and inside.

Numbering Method

The default for first and second level numbering method (4, 5) also depends on the kind of box being created. First level figures are shown in Arabic numbers (1, 2, 3) preceded by the word Figure. Tables are shown with Roman numerals (I, II, III) preceded by the word Table. Text Boxes and User-Defined boxes have only Arabic numbers (1, 2, 3) with no accompanying word. The second level default for all kinds of boxes is Off.

You may choose a numbering method for both first and second level numbers. For instance: Figure 1-a or Figure 3-1. If you choose to change the default method, you have the following options:

```
1 Off; 2 Numbers; 3 Letters; 4 Roman Numerals: 0
```

Turning the numbers Off (**1**) will eliminate the numbering completely for all but the first level. You cannot turn numbering off for the first level.

TIP: There is a difference between having numbering turned off or absent (as above for the second level), and having it blank or not displayed, even though WordPerfect is still numbering the boxes internally. Numbering will be turned off (absent) with the option given above. Numbering will appear blank (not displayed) if you *do not* select the Caption option. If you *do* select Caption (2) from the figure definition screen (and numbering is not turned off), you can use backspace or Del to erase it, thus causing it to appear blank.

Selecting **Numbers (2)** or **Roman Numerals (4)** will change the default to that method.

Selecting **Letters (3)** will cause the numbering method to be shown as A, B, C, etc.

■ Turn the numbering method for the first level to Letters by pressing **First Level (4)** and **Letters (3)**. Turn the numbering method for the second level to Numbers by pressing **Second Level (5)** and **Numbers (2)**.

Captions

The Caption Number Style (6) determines the way the caption is displayed and printed. For instance, you may prefer Fig. 1 to Figure 1. Or you may want to call the illustrations something other than figures, tables, etc. If so, you can simply type the pattern in, and WordPerfect will use it to mark your graphics boxes.

TIP: If you enter "Fig. 1", WordPerfect will automatically increase the number to 2 for the next box.

The Position of the Caption (7) can be either below the box or above the box, based on selections available with this option. By default, the Table caption appears above the box. All other kinds of boxes show the caption below it.

TIP: The text of the caption will be automatically wrapped to match the size of the graphics box. It is possible to delete the figure number with backspace. It can be added by pressing Graphics (Alt-F9).

■ To see the difference, select **Caption Number Style (6)**, press **Bold (F6)** and type **Fig. A-1**. Press **Bold (F6)** again and then press **Enter**. View the box if you like.

TIP: You can also include font style commands in captions.

Minimum Offset from Paragraph

When WordPerfect cannot fit the graphics box on the page in its normal position in the paragraph, it will attempt to move the box upward in the paragraph to fit it in, assuming there has been some offset (or lowering) of the box to begin with. This option specifies the minimum amount that the box can be moved upward.

TIP: If you do not want the offset altered, set the minimum offset at some large number.

Gray Shading (% of black)

As you can see from the example of the Text Box given at the beginning of this chapter, shading can be added to graphics boxes. The Text Box you see there is shaded 10%. You can add shading from 0 to 100% (or none to total) to any of the graphics boxes.

- Select Gray Shading (**9**) and enter **15** to cause the box to be shaded 15% when it is created. Then **Exit** (**F7**) the menu.

TIP: Some printers support only a single shading level. In those cases, the shading should be set at 100%. Depending on the capability of your monitor and printer, you may not see a box or shading at this point. Do not be concerned, it is there and will print later.

- Now, with the options altered, create a Figure graphics box that will be printed in the center of the margins and is 1.5 inches wide.

- Then press **Print** (**Shift-F7**) and **View** (**6**) your document.

- Finally, save the graphics box as **GraphOpt.15** and print it.

Now that you are familiar with the commands used to position and display graphics boxes, create a Table and a Text Box. Then create a User-Defined box and modify it several ways until you feel comfortable with your ability to work with graphics boxes.

To Review:

List the options that can be changed when creating graphics boxes.

Adding Graphics to Boxes

Once the box is created, you will want to add some graphics. There are several ways to do this.

First, you can use any of the 30 clip art files from Publisher's Picture Paks for WordPerfect that are included with your WordPerfect program. There are arrows, clocks, computers, flags, and many other designs that you can simply insert. A complete listing is included in the Appendix.

Second, you can enter text using the edit mode. This can be a comment, a title, an excerpt, or a portion of the text you wish to highlight.

Third, you can import files into the graphics box. These can be other WordPerfect files, or they can be ASCII type files from programs such as Lotus 1-2-3 and other spreadsheets.

Fourth, you can use clip art type files from a variety of other paint and draw graphics programs such as PC Paintbrush, Freelance, Dr. Halo II, Windows, Paint, PC Paint Plus, GEM Paint, Auto CAD, Scan, and Publisher's Paintbrush.

To begin with, let's use one of the clip art files. These are stored on the Fonts/Graphics disk.

- ■ Retrieve the file you saved as **GraphBox.15** that contains an empty box and the Booster's file.

```
Definition: Figure

    1 - Filename

    2 - Caption                    Figure 1 It's Good News

    3 - Type                       Paragraph

    4 - Vertical Position          0.5"

    5 - Horizontal Position        Left

    6 - Size                       1" wide x 1" (high)

    7 - Wrap Text Around Box       Yes

    8 - Edit




Selection: 0
```

▣ Press **Graphics** (**Alt-F9**), select Figure (**1**), Edit (**2**), and specify Figure **1** to bring up the Figure definition menu for that box.

▣ Select Filename (**1**). The following menu will appear across the bottom of the screen.

At this point you can either type in the name of a file to be retrieved into the graphics box, or you can retrieve it from List Files (**F5**). Let's use the List Files (**F5**) first.

▣ Press **List Files** (**F5**). Remove your data disk from Drive B and insert the disk labelled Fonts/Graphics.

▣ When the prompt **Dir B:*.*** appears, press **Enter**.

▣ Press **Enter**. Immediately you will see a listing of all the files on the Fonts/Graphics disk.

TIP: If you are using a hard drive, the files should already be in the same directory as your WordPerfect program. If that is the case, you will not need to exchange disks, but simply press List Files (**F5**) and Enter to see the list of files.

▣ Look the files over carefully when they appear on the screen. Notice especially those that end with .WPG. These are the graphics files.

TIP: Since WordPerfect sometime rearranges files, the partial illustration shown below may not exactly match what you see. Your directory may also list files from the hard disk that are not found on the Fonts/Graphics disk.

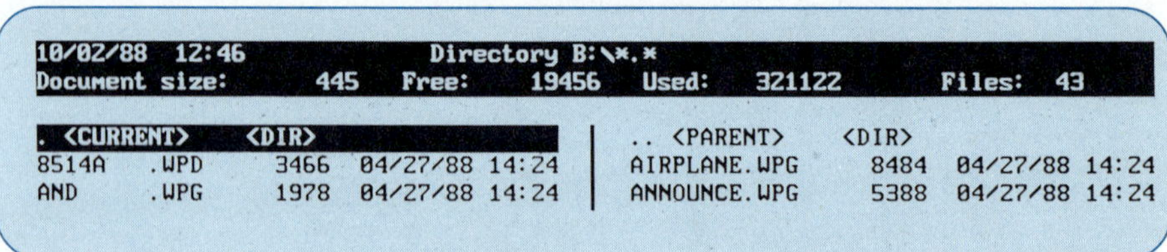

▣ Move the highlighter to the file titled **GOODNEWS.WPG** and select **Retrieve** (**1**). WordPerfect will make a copy of that graphics file from the Fonts/Graphics disk and insert it into the document in its memory. As it does this, it will display the message "Please wait -- Loading WP Graphics File."

 Rather than call the file from List Files (F5), you can simply type the filename (GOODNEWS.WPG) if you like. Note that you must always include the extension .WPG when entering graphics filenames this way. If you are using a hard disk, you must also include the path such as C:\WP50\GOOD-NEWS.WPG

The Figure definition menu will return, and you will see the name of the GOODNEWS.WPG file on the line beside the Filename item. It's as easy as that.

■ To see the graphic that has been inserted, select **Edit (8)** from the figure definition menu. In a few seconds the GOODNEWS graphic will appear on the screen as shown below.

 The clarity of what you see will depend on the graphics capability of your monitor.

■ When you have finished, **Exit (F7)** twice and save the file as **GoodNews.15**.

To Review:

List the different sources for adding graphics to a graphics box.

Summary

In summary, to add graphics to a graphics box:

a. Create the box.

b. Press Graphics (Alt-F9) and select the type of graphics box.

c. Select Edit (2).

d. Select Filename (1).

e. Enter the name of the graphics file.

f. Edit the graphic if desired.

g. Exit (F7).

h. View, save, and print.

Editing the Graphic

The Edit (8) menu allows you to move the graphic around in the box, make it larger or smaller, rotate it, and invert it and/or reverse it to a mirror image. The information at the top tells you which keys to press to alter the graphic as you wish, and the percentage shown in parentheses in the lower right corner indicates how much change will occur each time you press one of the directional keys.

Rotate, Move, and Scale

For instance, you can press the arrow keys to move the graphic up, down, left, and right in the box. Since 10% is displayed, each tap of a key will move the graphic 10% in the direction of the arrow. If you select Scale (2), you can use PgUp and PgDn to increase or decrease the scale and make the picture larger or smaller, again by 10% each time.

The + (Plus) key will rotate the graphic to the right (clockwise) and the – (Minus) key will rotate the graphic to the left (counterclockwise). Pressing the Ins (Insert) key will allow you to change the percentage shown in the lower right corner to 1, 5, 10, or 25 percent. If you wish to reset, or return to the original position, press Goto (Ctrl-Home).

TIP: Bitmapped graphics work a little differently than line draw graphics. Graphics with .WPG, HGPL, .PIC, CGM and .DXF extensions are line draw files. Graphics from all other WordPerfect supported files are considered bitmaps. The rotate and Screen Up/Down commands will not work with bitmapped files. The mirror image command does not work with line draw files.

- To see how the + (plus) and – (minus) keys work, use them to move the graphic around in the box. When you feel comfortable with what they will do, press **Goto** (**Ctrl-Home**) to return the graphic to its original position.

TIP: If you wanted to save the graphic in a modified position, you need only change it to the place and/or size you want and Exit (F7) the menu. WordPerfect will remember the changes and save and print the graphic that way.

Now let's use the options across the bottom of the menu. These allow you to type in the amount of change you want and make it in one jump.

- Select **M**ove (**1**). Immediately you will be asked the horizontal distance you wish to move.

TIP: Since the graphic is only 2 inches wide by 3.06 inches high, you cannot move a great distance without going completely out of the box.

- Type **.25** (1/4 inch) and press **Enter**. Immediately you will be asked for the vertical distance. This time type **.50** (1/2 inch) and press **Enter**. When the screen is redrawn, the graphic will be moved as you specified.
- Now select **S**cale (**2**). You will be asked for the distance to change on the X (horizontal) scale (100 is full size). Enter **30** to reduce the box from left to right. Leave the Y (vertical) scale at 100 and press **Enter**. Immediately the graphic will be redrawn, only this time it will appear tall and narrower than before.
- Select **S**cale (**2**) again and enter **125** for the X scale. Leave the Y scale at 100. When the box is redrawn it will be oversized horizontally.
- Press **Goto** (**Ctrl-Home**) to reset the graphic. Then select **R**otate (**3**). The prompt this time will ask for the number of degrees between 0 and 360 you would like to rotate the graphic. Type **45** and press Enter.
- You will then be asked if you want to switch the graphic to a mirror image. Responding **Y**(es) to this prompt will reverse the graphic if it is bitmapped. Since this is a line draw graphic, reversing this particular graphic will not make a noticeable difference. Enter **N**(o). When the graphic is redrawn, it will be rotated 45 degrees.
- Now to return the graphic to its original settings, again press **Goto** (**Ctrl-Home**).
- Then press **Exit** (**F7**) twice to leave the graphics menu and return to the document editing screen.

TIP: Notice that the graphic itself does not appear on the editing screen. You must use View Document (6) or the Edit (8) option on the Figure definition screen to see it.

◻ Using **Save** (**F10**), save your document as **Graphpix.15**.

◻ To take a look at the entire document including the graphic, press **Print** (**Shift-F7**) and View Document (6). When you are finished, press **Exit** (**F7**) to leave the View screen.

Immediately the page will appear on the screen, including the graphic. Isn't this amazing!

TIP: The clarity of what you see on the screen will depend on the graphics capability of your monitor.

◻ If you wish, view the screen at 100% (1) and 200% (2) as well. When you are finished, return it to **Full Page** (**3**) and **Exit** (**F7**) the menu.

◻ Resave your document as **Graphpix.15** and print it.

As you can see, adding clip-art files to a graphics box and then altering the position of the graphic is quite simple. If you wished to import files from another software program, you could save them in ASCII format and specify that filename in the definition menu. WordPerfect would find and insert the file. For instance, to import a Lotus 1-2-3 file, you need only save it as a .PIC file. Then indicate the name of the Lotus .PIC file at the filename prompt and it will be inserted into the graph box.

TIP: You can put only one graphic in a given box. However, you can create two or more boxes at the same location. When the graphics are printed, they will print over each other, making it appear that there are multiple graphics in the same box.

◻ For some additional practice, clear the screen and create several more graphics boxes. Retrieve a clip-art file into each of them. Save and print if you wish.

TIP: Here is a fast way to create more than one identical box. First, create the box using the regular steps. Then use Reveal Codes (Alt-F3) to find the embedded code. Position the cursor to the immediate right of the code and press backspace delete. Then press Cancel (F1) and Restore (1) to undelete and restore the figure. Now position the cursor where you wish the next box to appear and again press Cancel (F1) and Restore (1). Repeat this process as many times as you need. If you wish to change any or all of the boxes in a special way, such as to add different graphics to each, use the editing commands to do so.

To Review:

The direction of the X scale is: ____.

The direction of the Y scale is: ____.

The + (plus) key will rotate the graphic: _________________________________.

The - (minus) key will rotate the graphic: _______________________________.

Graphics files have a ___________ . _____________ extension.

Summary

To	Press
Rotate (3)	+ (plus) or - (minus)
Move (1)	Arrow keys
Scale (2)	PgUp and PgDn
Invert (4)	
Reset	Goto (Ctrl-Home)
Change %	Ins

Adding Text to a Graphics Box

Now let's add some text to a graphics box.

- Retrieve **Graphpix.15** and move the cursor to the first line of the last paragraph.

- Position the cursor at the beginning of the paragraph. Then create a Text Box graphics box for this exercise. Use the defaults to make it paragraph type and position it horizontally at the right margin. Do not change any of the other defaults.

- When the Text Box is created, select Edit (8) from the Text Box definition menu to bring up the editing screen.

- Enter the following sentence, in boldface: **Return the enclosed order form to receive six free issues of Business BOOSTERS.**

TIP: A short excerpt or quote from the text (often called a "pull quote") is frequently used this way to call attention to major points or highlight important information.

- Then press **Exit (F7)** to leave the screen. As you do, notice that WordPerfect has altered the size of the graphic shown on the definition menu. This often happens when WordPerfect must make changes to match the space available or the requirements of the graphic. Press **Exit (F7)** again to return to the document editing screen.

TIP: When you are working with text in the edit mode, you can use most of the editing commands that are available such as Reveal Codes, Block, Underline, Bold, etc. You can even block an item from one document (Doc 2) and move it into the editing screen of another (Doc 1), insert font changes, and retrieve other text files. Since the above sentence is stored within the graphics command, it will not display on the Reveal Codes screen.

- Use **Print (Shift-F7)** and View Document (**6**) to see what the text box looks like.

TIP: You can also put text into a box by using the Advance commands. To do this, you would type the text above or below the box, and then use the command to place it in the space where the box will appear.

- Save the file as **Graphtxt.15** and print it.

TIP: You can also include graphics boxes in styles, but the boxes must be empty or contain only text. Styles will not accept graphics boxes with clip-art and other graphics images.

Summary

In summary, to add text to a graphics box:

   a. Create the graphics box.

   b. Select Edit (2).

   c. Type the text.

   d. Press Exit (F7).

   e. View

   f. Save and print.

Creating Horizontal and Vertical Lines

WordPerfect can also add solid or shaded horizontal and vertical lines to your document.

Horizontal Lines

Horizontal lines can be positioned at or slightly to the left of the left margin, at or slightly to the right of the right margin, centered between the left and right margins, extending from the left to the right margin, between columns, or at some absolute horizontal position offset from the left margin on the line the cursor is on.

Vertical Lines

Vertical lines can be positioned at the top margin, at the bottom margin, centered between the top and bottom margins, or at an absolute position from the top of the page. They can also be placed between columns.

Length, Width, and Shading

For both horizontal and vertical lines, you must specify how long the line is to be, how wide the line is to be, and how much shading there should be. Note the sample lines on this page illustrating various shading, length, and line positions.

TIP: | The text of a document will not wrap around lines.

Creating Lines

For a little practice, let's add some lines to the **Graphtxt.15** document.

- With the **Graphtxt.15** file on your screen, press **Home, Home, Home, Up Arrow** to move to the very beginning of the document, to the left of all existing codes.

- Press **Enter** to move the text down three blank lines. Position the cursor on the top line above the three lines you just entered.

- Press **Graphics** (**Alt-F9**), select Line (**5**), and Horizontal Line (**1**) from the menus as they appear. The Graphics: Horizontal Line menu will then display as shown at the top of the next page.

```
Graphics: Horizontal Line

     1 - Horizontal Position              Left & Right

     2 - Length of Line

     3 - Width of Line                     0.01"

     4 - Gray Shading (% of black)         100%



Horizontal Pos: 1 Left 2 Right 3 Center 4 Both Left & Right 5 Set Position: 0
```

Horizontal Position

Horizontal, or side to side position, is the first option.

◻ Select **Horizontal Position** (**1**), which allows you to position the line as indicated in the following menu.

```
Horizontal Pos: 1 Left 2 Right 3 Center 4 Both Left & Right 5 Set Position: 0
```

The left and right settings, combined with the length measurement, determine how far the line extends from the left margin toward the middle of the page. The line can also be centered between the margins, or go all the way from the left to the right margin. The Set Position option allows you to enter a specific horizontal offset from the left edge of the page.

◻ Leave the default at **Both Left and Right** (**4**) so that the line will extend from the left margin to the right margin across the full page. With this selection, the length is calculated automatically.

◻ Leave the width at 0.01" and the shading at 100%. Press **Exit** (**F7**).

◻ Move the cursor down the page two lines and insert a second line like the one above.

TIP: Since this will be an identical line, use the delete/restore method to duplicate the command. Go back and delete the **HLine: Left & Right** code. Without moving the cursor, press Cancel (**F1**) and select Restore (**1**) to return the line to its original position. Then move the cursor down three lines and press Cancel (**F1**) again. Select **Restore** (**1**) to insert the second line. You will now have two lines across the page. Check View Document (**Shift-F7, 6**) to verify.

◼ Move the cursor between the two lines you just created and insert another horizontal line. Make this line .03 wide and shade it at 50 percent.

TIP: You cannot edit a line once it has been created. Therefore, if you wish to change the style, length, or shading you must delete the command and start over.

◼ Finally, add a similar line (.03 wide, 50% shading) at the bottom of the page.

◼ Then use **View Document** (**6**) to see the result.

◼ Save your document as **Graphlin.15** and print it.

TIP: If you wish, you can alter the spacing between the lines to obtain a different effect. Use Reveal Codes (Alt-F3) to position the cursor. Then press Enter or Del to add or remove [HRt] commands.

Lines have many possibilities for separating parts of your document, adding emphasis, and enhancing appearance. There are many ways they can be used to make your documents attractive and easy to read.

To Review:

List where each of the following can be placed on the page.

Horizontal lines ____

Vertical Lines ____

Summary

In summary, to add horizontal and vertical lines to your document:

a. Position the cursor.

b. Press Graphics (Alt-F9) and select Lines (5).

c. Indicate horizontal and vertical position.

d. Indicate length and width of line.

e. Indicate shading.

f. Exit (F7).

g. View, save, and print.

Experiment a little with both horizontal and vertical lines to become comfortable with this feature and what it will do. When you are finished, print your practice document. Then clear your screen and move ahead.

Combining Graphics Boxes, Lines and Columns

Quite often you will want to display the text you are working with in column format and then insert graphics and lines to improve its appearance. This is easy to do using the commands you have already learned. Try the following project for some practice and an opportunity to experiment with these commands.

◘ Retrieve the **JobsA.3** file and change the spacing to single spacing. Put the text into two columns.

◘ Add the title **FINDING A JOB** and center it over the column. Leave one blank line between the title and the first sentence of the paragraph.

◘ Since the table will not fit into the columns, delete it and display the items in single space, stacked form, like the following:

> Good References
> Degree
> Computer Background
> Experience
> Knowledge of Company
> Good Worker
> Gets Along With Others
> Dependable

◘ Create a new paragraph, beginning with the sentence "Next list the requirements..."

◘ Put a horizontal line across the second column at the end of the text. Use the defaults for length, width, and shading.

◘ Add a horizontal line at the top of the first column from left to right and shade it 70%.

◘ Add a vertical line down the left side of the page. Use the defaults for shading and width.

◘ Create a figure box to be placed at the left margin .20" down from the top of the second paragraph and insert the **NO1.WPG** clip-art graphic into it. Make the box no bigger than 1" wide. Wrap the text around the box.

◘ Create a text box in the next to the last paragraph. Enter the text **"Show how you will be able to serve the firm."** into the box. You determine placement and size.

■ Save your document as **GraphCol.15** and print it.

■ Then experiment with this project as you like. Change the lines, graphics, and other features to see what the result will be. Turn justification on and off. Try three columns. Spread the title across the columns. Put the title in a box and shade it. Move the graphics. Be creative. Print the results and share them with your instructor and classmates.

Activities

You should have completed the following:

Graph.15	*Figure 1*
GraphBox.15	*Figure 1 - Empty graphics box*
GoodNews.15	*Figure with GoodNews graphic*
GraphOpt.15	*Figure box with modified options*
GraphPix.15	*Figure with clip art*
GraphTxt.15	*Table with text*
GraphLin.15	*Document with horizontal lines*
GraphCol.15	*JobsA.3 in column format with graphics*

Chapter Review

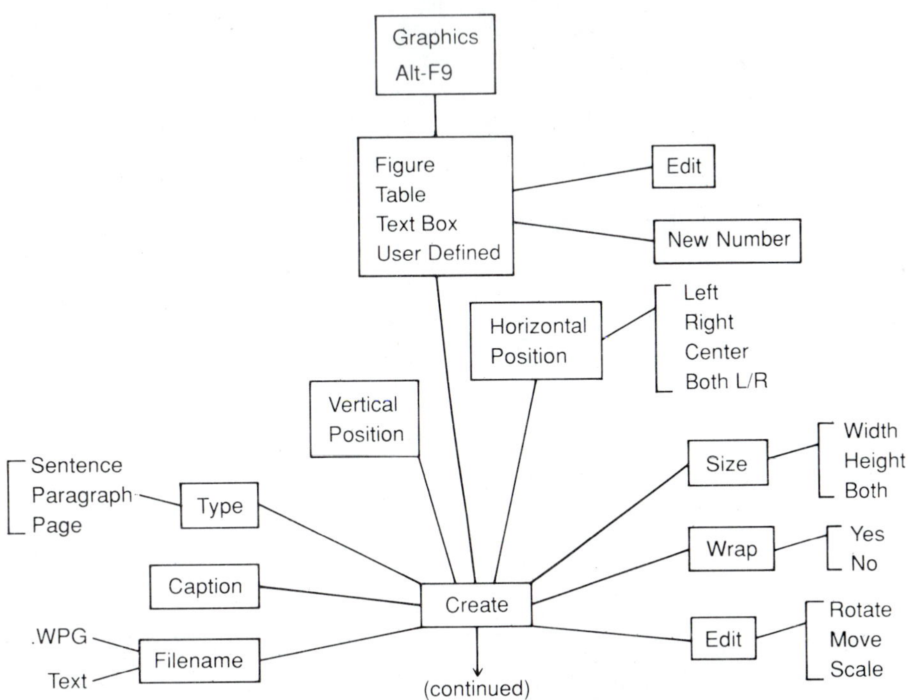

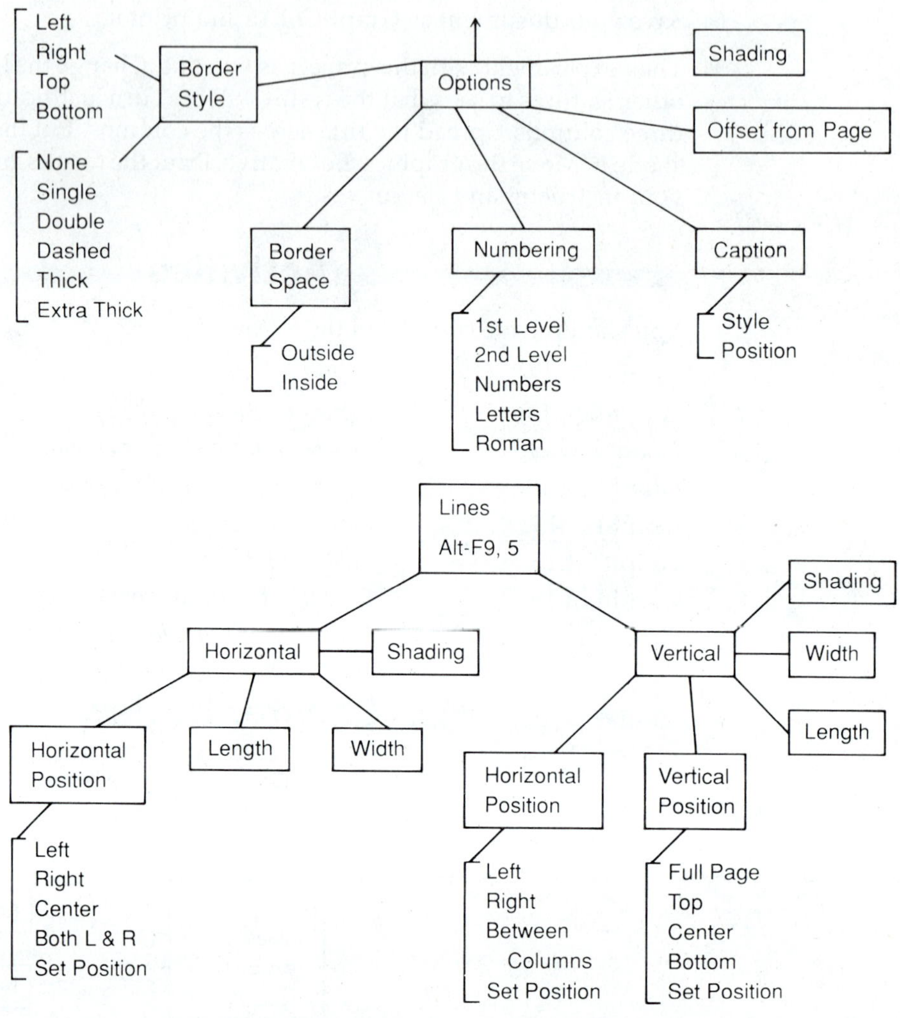

Self-Check Quiz 15

1. List the four types of graphics boxes.

2. Where are each of the following printed?

Paragraph ____

Page ____

Character ____

3. What information is found in the caption?

4. What is the default for vertical position on paragraph boxes?

5. Where can the text be printed with character-type boxes?

6. What does offset mean?

7. Why is it usually to your advantage to let WordPerfect determine the offset borders?

8. In Edit mode, which keys should you press to do the following:

   Rotate _______________

   Move _______________

   Scale _______________

   Return to defaults _______________

   Change the percentage _______________

9. What happens when the setting **Left & Right** is used to define a box?

10. What happens when the graphics box setting for Wrap around text is No?

11. List two or three advantages for having more than one kind of graphics box in your document.

12. Where is the border placed on each of the four kinds of graphics boxes?

13. What is inside and outside border space?

14. List at least four ways to add graphics or text to a graphics box.

15. What is a "Pull Quote?"

16. What keys should you press to make the graph larger? smaller? move it up? move it down? move it left? move it right?

17. What happens when the scale is entered as X = 40 and Y = 80?

18. What keystrokes allow you to see the graphic combined with the text of the document?

19. What information must you supply when creating lines?

20. How can you edit a line?

Extra Practice

For extra practice on the material covered in this chapter, do the following:

a. Retrieve the document you saved as **Pract4a** on Interviewing Tips. Add appropriate graphics (see list of available graphics in Appendix) and lines to enhance its appearance. Save it as **Pract15a** and print it.

b. Retrieve **Pract15a** and reformat the document with two columns. Change the position of the graphics and lines as necessary. Save it as **Pract15b** and print it.

c. Copy an article from the newspaper, your textbook, or another source. Add columns, graphics, and/or lines as appropriate. Save the completed document as **Pract15c** and print it.

d. Add appropriate graphics to one of your written school assignments and hand it in. Also include lines and columns if appropriate.

e. Create an advertisement, notice, invitation, or other bulletin for a group you belong to. Use graphics to make it more eye catching and attractive. Save your document as **Pract15d** and print it.

16

Working with Fonts, Special Printing Techniques, and Desktop Publishing

In addition to its graphics capability, WordPerfect 5.0 offers you access to many new fonts to lend emphasis and variety to your documents. With these fonts you can change the size and appearance of your text to make it larger, smaller, italicized, and bolded. You can even create outlines and shadows in your text. In addition, there are a number of special commands, such as kerning and word and letter spacing, that can be used to make your work look more professional when it is printed. With these new features, good layout and design are even more important as you work to make your documents look as appealing and attractive as possible.

When you are finished with this chapter, you will be able to:

- utilize a variety of font typefaces and sizes.
- change the initial and base font as needed.
- incorporate font size and appearance attributes.

- **use advanced printing techniques such as kerning, word and letter spacing, and line height, for special effects.**
- **list a number of recommendations for good page and document design using graphics and fonts.**

Initial and Base Fonts

Besides being able to insert boxes, lines, and graphics into your text, Word-Perfect will allow you to change the font size and style. Prior to version 5.0, WordPerfect was more limited in the number and type of fonts that were available, but now you have a wide range from which to choose. Which fonts are available in any particular situation will depend on the printer, but in most cases you will have a selection of several, including at least one to print larger and one to print smaller than normal type. In addition, you may have fonts that can print italics or that print in bold type.

There are several terms and definitions that will help you work with fonts. The following is a brief overview. Then we will do some exercises to see how they work.

Initial Font

You will recall that when the printer is defined with Print (Shift-F7), Select Printer (S), Edit (3), one of the things you are asked for on the menu shown on the next page is the Initial Font (6).

When Initial Font (6) is chosen, WordPerfect displays a list of fonts available for the printer you have selected.

TIP: If you have a laser printer or other type that accepts cartridges or downloadable soft fonts, be sure to specify them for WordPerfect using options 5 (Cartridges and Fonts) and 7 (Path for Downloadable Fonts and Printer Command Files) on the Printer: Edit menu (shown on the next page) before moving ahead.

```
Select Printer: Edit

        Filename                      IBPCGRPR.PRS

   1 - Name                           IBM PC Graphics Printer

   2 - Port                           LPT1:

   3 - Sheet Feeder                   None

   4 - Forms

   5 - Cartridges and Fonts

   6 - Initial Font                   Normal

   7 - Path for Downloadable
         Fonts and Printer
         Command Files




   Selection: 0
```

From the list of fonts, you must choose one font to be the Initial or default font; this will be used automatically when WordPerfect is started (or in the absence of other font changes). Because it is a default, the font setting does not appear when you press Reveal Codes (Alt-F3). If you want to change the font permanently, you should change the Initial Font (6).

TIP: It is possible to have access to more than one printer at a time. In that case, you may select a different initial font for each printer and have different fonts available for each printer.

☐ Before moving ahead, press **Print (Shift-F7)**, Select Printer (**S**), Edit (**3**), and note which font is set as the Initial Font for the printer you have selected. It will have an asterisk (*) beside it. Jot the name of the font down on the following line.

____

☐ Then select Initial Font (**6**) and note the fonts that are available on the printer you have selected. Write them down below. When you are finished, **Exit (F7)** to the document editing screen.

TIP: If a list of fonts does not display, or the message "Printer not selected" appears, remove your data disk from Drive B and insert the disk marked Printer 1 or the one labeled with the type of printer you have. Then press Print (Shift-F7), Select Printer (S), Additional Printers (2), Other Printers (2) and identify the B: drive as the drive where the printer files can be found. Press Enter and view the list of printers that appears. If your printer is not among them, remove the

TIP: Printer 1 disk, insert the Printer 2 or a second disk, and again select Other Printers (2). Continue searching (using Printer 3 and Printer 4 disks if necessary) until you find the name of your printer. Then Select (1) it and press Enter to update your file. As you do, note the helpful hints supplied for your printer. If you are using an EGA monitor or a Hercules Graphics card, you may need to use the Fonts/Graphics disk also. Follow the prompts as they appear. Then remove the printer disk and replace your data disk in Drive B. The list of fonts should then appear when you enter the appropriate commands.

The lines of code for fonts and graphics requires a great deal of computer memory. If you are using WordPerfect Library or other resident program, you may see a message indicating there is not enough memory left for the fonts. If so, exit the Library or other programs. This will free up additional memory for the fonts and allow you to access them.

Summary

In summary, to select an Initial Font:

a. Press Print (Shift-F7).

b. Choose Select Printer (S) and Edit (3).

c. Select Initial Font (6).

d. Highlight desired font.

e. Select (1) a font from the list.

f. Exit (F7) from menu.

Base Font

There are times when you will want to change the initial font temporarily, such as for a heading or to emphasize a word. In these instances, you should use another font command to change the setting. This command is found on the Font (Ctrl-F8) key. It is called the Base Font and will allow you to enter a command that will override the Initial Font setting. Because it is not a default, a font change code like the following can be seen when you press Reveal Codes (Alt-F3): [Font: Courier 10 pitch (PC-8)].

■ To see what the Font menu looks like, press **Font (Ctrl-F8)**.

```
1 Size; 2 Appearance; 3 Normal; 4 Base Font; 5 Print Color: 0
```

■ Select Base Font (**4**) to display a listing of fonts available for the printer you have selected. (This is the same list you saw when you selected the Initial Font.) The current font will have an asterisk (*) beside it.

What is listed will vary by printer. As an example, if you were using a Hewlett-Packard LaserJet Series II printer with a B cartridge, the following list of base fonts would be available.

Base Font

Courier 10 pitch (PC-8)
Courier 10 pitch (Roman-8)
Courier Bold 10 pitch (PC-8)
Courier Bold 10 pitch (Roman-8)
Helv 11pt (AE)
Helv 14.4pt Bold (B)
Letter Gothic 09.5pt 16.66 pitch
(Legal)(DA)
Line Printer 16.66 pitch (PC-8)

Line Printer 16.66 pitch
(Roman-8)
Solid Line Draw 10 pitch
Solid Line Draw 12 pitch
Tms Rmn 06pt (AC)
Tms Rmn 06pt Bold (AC)
Tms Rmn 08pt (AC)
Tms Rmn 08pt (B)
Tms Rmn 08pt Italic (AC)

Tms Rmn 10pt (AC)
*Tms Rmn 10pt (B)
Tms Rmn 10pt Bold (B)
Tms Rmn 10pt Italic (B)
Tms Rmn 12pt (AC)
Tms Rmn 14pt (AC)
Tms Rmn 18pt Bold (AC)
Tms Rmn 24pt Bold (AC)
Tms Rmn 30pt Bold (AC)

The list of base for an Okidata 192 is given below.

Condensed 17 Pitch Outline
Condensed Subscript 17 Pitch
Elite 12 Pitch DW Italics Utility
Elite 12 Pitch DW NLQ
Elite 12 Pitch Italics Utility

Pica 10 Pitch NLQ
Pica 10 Pitch DW Italics Utility
Pica 10 Pitch Italics Utility
Pica 10 Pitch NLQ

The list of fonts for your printer probably will be different, but the above list can be used to explain what appears.

First, notice that several font styles are shown. These include Courier, Helvetica, Letter Gothic, and Tms Rmn (Times Roman). In addition there are options for a line printer. Some of the fonts have variations, such as bold and italics. A sample of several of these font styles is shown below.

Courier 10 pitch
Helvetica 14.4pt Bold
Line Printer 16.66 pitch
Times Roman 10pt
Letter Gothic 9.5pt 16.66 pitch
Times Roman 10 point bold.
Times Roman 10 point Italic.

Second, there are a variety of sizes available. These are shown in both pitch (width of characters) and points (height of characters). It is important to note the difference so you will get the size you want.

Pitch refers to the number of characters that can be printed per inch. Therefore, the higher the pitch number, the more characters that will fit into an inch and the smaller the printed characters will be. As a result, 8 pitch will print larger letters than 14 pitch.

Point, on the other hand, is just the opposite. A point is 1/72 of an inch. Therefore, the more points a character has, the larger it is. As a result, a character that is 8 points will be smaller than one that is 14 points. *You must watch carefully to see whether the font is measured in pitch or point size.*

Courier 10 pitch.
Times Roman 8 point.
Times Roman 10 point.
Helvetica 14.4 point.
Line Printer 16.6 pitch

Third, the fonts have a notation in parentheses at the end of each one. This notation tells where the font is found. Some are internal fonts (PC-8 and Roman-8), some are soft fonts (AC and DA), and some are cartridge fonts (B). Not all fonts may be available. For instance, you may have a B cartridge but no soft fonts. Therefore, you could select from the internal fonts that come with the printer and those fonts marked B, but the fonts marked AC and DA would not work unless the software for the soft fonts was available. If your printer will not accept soft fonts, no notations will be found.

TIP: You may wonder why the fonts are listed when they cannot be used, and the reason is that the printer drivers must contain the code for them to be recognized when they are available. They are included in anticipation of the time when the software will be available to make them active.

Fourth, you may see some notations like NLQ (near letter quality), Pica (10 pitch), Elite (12 pitch), CPI (Characters per inch), DH (double high), DW (double wide), PS (proportional spacing), and others. If you cannot decipher what they mean, look in your printer manual or ask your instructor for a definition.

TIP: Remember that if you are using downloadable fonts, (or those on a disk) you must specify where they can be found by pressing Print (Shift-F7), Select Printer (S), Edit (3), Option 7 and entering a path.

To make selections from the Base Font menu, simply use the Up and Down Arrow Keys to move the highlighter to the font you want and press **Select (1)**.

◼ Press **Exit (F7)**, the **space bar**, or **Enter** to leave the menu and return to the editing screen.

To Review

What is the difference between each of the following:

Font Style ______________________________________

Font Size ____

Font Appearance _________________________________

Summary

In summary, to select a Base Font:

a. Press Font (Ctrl-F8).

b. Select Base Font (4).

c. Select (1) the desired font.

d. Exit (F7).

Font Attributes

In addition to choosing the font itself, there are a number of attributes (or characteristics) that you can also select. These generally relate to the size and appearance of the font being used.

◻ To see what the attributes are, press **Font (Ctrl-F8)** to reveal the following menu:

```
1 Size; 2 Appearance; 3 Normal; 4 Base Font; 5 Print Color: 0
```

Size

The first attribute category you can select is size. To see what sizes are available, do the following:

◻ Select Size (**1**) to display the menu shown on the next page:

> 1 Suprscpt; 2 Subscpt; 3 Fine; 4 Small; 5 Large; 6 Vry Large; 7 Ext Large: 0

Superscripts and subscripts are small characters that are printed above and below the line. You will work with them later.

The remaining options--Fine, Small, Large, Very Large, and Extra Large—-are variations of the current font. Look back at the Base font selection menu and notice that Tms Rmn shows several sizes: 6, 8, 10, 12, 14, 18, 24 and 30 point. Depending on what you have selected to be the Initial or Base Font (whichever is active), WordPerfect will use other available fonts to print as you specify.

Therefore, if you have selected Tms Rmn 10 point as the base font and then select Small (4) from the menu above, WordPerfect will print with a Tms Rmn font size that is smaller, perhaps 8 point. However, if you are using Tms Rmn 14 point as the base font and select small, WordPerfect may use 10 point as the small font. Finally, if you are using 6 point as the base font, WordPerfect will not have any fonts smaller to use for this option. As you can see, the size of print that ultimately results is relative to the current font size.

TIP: Any fonts used as either Initial, Base, or Attribute selections must be available on your computer. Therefore, even though the font may display in the list, it may not be available (such as the soft fonts in the illustration above). In that case, if WordPerfect cannot find a font that is "smaller" or otherwise matches the attribute you select, it will simply ignore the command and print in normal size.

Following is what each of the options looks like using Tms Rmn 10pt as the base font.

Superscript   Subscript   Fine   Small   **Large**
Very Large   **Extra Large**

TIP: Unless you have a special Ramfont card in your computer, the font changes will not display on your monitor. Color monitors can be set to display different characteristics in different colors, but no changes will be apparent on a monochrome monitor without the special graphics card. All changes will be apparent in the printout, however.

■ Press **Enter** to return to the document editing screen.

To end or turn appearance and size attributes off, you can do any of three things:

1. Press Right Arrow to move past the Attribute Off code that was inserted at the same time as the On code. (Use Reveal Codes (Alt-F3) to see it.)

2. Select Normal (3) from the menu, which will turn the attribute off.

3. Reselect the attribute which will turn it off.

Appearance

The second attribute category is appearance. To see the options available for this characteristic, do the following:

■ Press **Font (Ctrl-F8)** and select **Appearance (2)** to bring up the next menu.

```
1 Bold 2 Undrln 3 Dbl Und 4 Italc 5 Outln 6 Shadw 7 Sm Cap 8 Redln 9 Stkout: 0
```

The attributes shown can be applied to the current font, assuming the font will accept the command. (The functions of Redline (8) and Strikeout (9) are presented in another chapter.) Following is what each of the options looks like using Tms Rmn 10pt as the base font.

Bold   Underline   Double Underline

Italic   Outline   **Shadow**   SMALL CAPS

Redline   Strikeout

TIP:

Again, these attributes are applied to the current font. You may use more than one appearance attribute at a time if you wish. The Bold and Underline commands are identical to those found on the F6 and F8 keys. It is possible to indicate both a size and an appearance attribute at the same time. If the printer has the capability, the printed characters will display them both.

Normal and Print Color Attributes

The Normal (3) option will turn off all attributes and can be used to indicate the end of the text to be affected by the attribute(s) you have selected. The Print Color (5) option will allow you to select colors for various parts of your document if your printer will print in color.

Using Fonts

Now, let's add some different fonts to your text.

■ Retrieve the document you saved as **Graphlin.15**. Let's change the fonts on the title and some of the text.

■ Position the cursor at the left of the title **HOW MUCH MONEY WILL YOU MAKE THIS YEAR**. Press **Font (Ctrl-F8)** and select Base Font (**4**) from the menu at the bottom of the screen.

■ When the base font selections for your printer appears, select a font that is larger than the initial font you are currently using. (Remember that higher points and lower pitch are larger.)

■ Then move the cursor to the right of the title and again press **Font (Ctrl-F8)** and Base Font (**4**).

■ This time, select the font you want the text of the document printed in. This will likely be the same as the initial font selection in a 10 or 12 pitch or 9 to 11 point size.

■ To see the change, press **Print (Shift-F7)** and select View Document (**6**).

■ Now move to the heading **"Ideas to increase sales and profits"** and delete the underline. Change the heading to an italic type style. Do the same for the heading **"No office reading time"** by blocking the heading (**Alt-F4**) and pressing **Font (Ctrl-F8)**, Base Font (**4**), and making a selection.

■ Finally, move the cursor to the last sentence **"Mail in your order today!"** and **Block (Alt-F4)** it. Use **Switch (Shift-F3)** to change it to all upper case letters.

■ Then mark the sentence as a block again (**Alt-F4**) and press **Font (Ctrl-F8)**. Notice that an abbreviated menu appears indicating choices for Size (1) and Appearance (2). Select **A**ppearance (**2**).

TIP: Remember that you can remark a previous block by pressing Block (Alt-F4) and Ctrl-Home, Ctrl-Home.

■ From the Appearance menu, select **S**hadow (**6**). View the document if you wish. Then save it as **Graphatt.16** and print it.

Experiment with the attributes and fonts to become familiar with what they do and how they look.

The following is what resulted on my computer. Yours may differ because of different fonts, etc., but you can see what can be done.

HOW MUCH MONEY WILL YOU MAKE THIS YEAR?

This is a special invitation for you to join a group of businessmen who recently subscribed to the new business service called Business BOOSTERS...a monthly booklet containing ideas to increase sales and profits.

BOOSTERS is for businessmen who see business opportunities in the future and a chance to move ahead. BOOSTERS is for the smaller business firm that is determined to increase profits. Some of our subscribers are:

Reed Hansen	Hansen Auto Parts
J. L. Crandall	Downtown Office Supply
Shauri Wilson	Fashion Botique
Mark Thomas	Hidden Hollows Restaurant

Boosters is tied to your future . . .

Ideas to increase sales and profits. This service gives tips that have been tested, that work, that show a profit under today's conditions.

No office reading time. BOOSTERS is put up in the exact size of a railroad timetable to fit your busy schedule. It slips into your coat pocket. Ideas are pictured and illustrated with a brief description of how you can turn the ideas to profit.

Now you can quickly find out for yourself how much BOOSTERS can mean to you by accepting this invitation to join the 10,000 new readers. If you will

Mail the enclosed order form to receive six free issues of Business BOOSTERS.

mail the enclosed order form, we will send you immediately and free of charge six previous issues of BOOSTERS containing scores of profitable ideas you can use right now. That is a bonus just for trying BOOSTERS. Then, for only $3.68 we will extend to you the special Introductory Rate of 18 months of BOOSTERS.

MAIL IN YOUR ORDER TODAY!

Creating Styles for Font Changes

Combining styles and font changes is a natural with WordPerfect. You can create a style for any font (or other printer command) that you use frequently. To see how this works, do the following:

- Clear your screen then press **Style (Alt-F8)**, and select **Create (3)**.

- Select **Name (1)** and type **Lg font**.

- Use the defaults of **Type (2)** and **Paired (1)**.

- ▣ Select **Description (3)** and type the name of the font. For example **Courier 10 pitch**.

- ▣ Select **Codes (4)** and enter the beginning code by pressing **Font (Ctrl-F8)**, and **Base font (4)**, and selecting the appropriate large font.

- ▣ Move the cursor past the [**Comment**] marker and again select **Font (Ctrl-F8)** and **Base font (4)**. Then enter the font you wish to return to.

- ▣ Leave the Enter key setting at the default ([HRt]) and **Exit (F7)** the menu.

- ▣ Create a second style for a small font by following the same steps and substituting the appropriate name, description, and font code above the [Comment] for a smaller (or different) font. Enter the normal text font following the [Comment].

- ▣ Use **Save (6)** on the style menu to save these styles as **Fontsty1**.

    Now you can simply block the text you wish to change, select the appropriate style, and enter the codes quickly and easily. If you decide to change or edit a font contained in a style, the change will be made instantly throughout your document wherever the style is used. You can also **Retrieve (7)** the fonts file into other documents if you wish. For some practice, do the following:

- ▣ Retrieve **Vacation.6**.

- ▣ Use **Block (Alt-F4)** to block the main heading. Then press **Style (Alt-F8)** and select **Lg Font** by highlighting it and selecting **On (1)**.

- ▣ **Block (Alt-F4)** each of the side headings and turn the large font style on for each one.

- ▣ **Block (Alt-F4)** the table (Taxi, Train Fare, etc.) and turn the small font style on.

- ▣ Save the document as **Vacafont.16** and print it.

- ▣ Experiment with other fonts and styles. Also edit a style and change the font. Then reprint the document to see how the font has been automatically changed throughout the text.

Advanced Printing Techniques

Even though the graphics, line, and font options are amazing, that's still not all WordPerfect can do to help you with your desktop publishing. It can also help you improve the overall appearance of the text on the page with some special printer commands, such as kerning, word and letter spacing, and line height.

■ Press **Format** (**Shift-F8**), Other (**4**), and Printer Functions (**6**) to bring up the
following menu:

```
Format: Printer Functions

    1 - Kerning                                    No

    2 - Printer Command

    3 - Word Spacing                               Optimal
        Letter Spacing                             Optimal

    4 - Word Spacing Justification Limits
        Compressed to (0% - 100%)              60%
        Expanded to (100% - unlimited)         400%


Selection: 0
```

Kerning

Kerning is a technique used by printers to remove extra white space between
characters in words and make them easier to read. It is most often used with
proportioned type styles on specific letter pairs that fit together, such as WA,
VA, and others.

To use this command, position the cursor where you want kerning to start,
select Kerning (1), and Y(es). If your printer is capable of this command,
WordPerfect will make the necessary adjustments as the document is printed,
based on information contained in the .PRS (Printer Definition) file.

To turn kerning off, press Format (Shift-F8), Other (4), Printer Functions
(6) Kerning (1), and N(o).

Printer Command

The Printer Command (2) option on the menu shown at top of the page allows
you to enter special commands that take advantage of unique capabilities of
individual printers that are not found elsewhere in WordPerfect. Since most
printer options are already built into WordPerfect, you will probably not use
this option.

Word and Letter Spacing

Space between adjacent words and letters can be adjusted with this command.
There are four settings available. To see what they are, select **W**ord Spacing
(**3**) to bring up the following menu across the bottom of the screen:

```
Word Spacing: 1 Normal; 2 Optimal; 3 Percent of Optimal; 4 Set Pitch: 2
```

The Normal (1) setting is the spacing that looks best according to the printer manufacturer's opinion.

The Optimal (2) setting is the setting that looks best according to Word-Perfect Corporation's opinion. This may be same as the Normal setting, but there are some differences among printers.

The Percent of Optimal (3) setting allows you to set a width of your own as a percentage of the optimal setting. Percentages of less than 100% reduce the amount of space between words, and percentages greater than 100% increase it.

The Set Pitch (4) option allows you to enter an exact pitch setting. This setting will then be adjusted according to the specifications of the current font.

TIP: Remember that pitch identifies width, and point identifies height. The higher the pitch, the smaller the letters, and the higher the point, the larger the letters.

Some examples of the effect of word/letter spacing are as follows:

Optimal
Now is the time for all good men to come to the aid of their country.

Normal
Now is the time for all good men to come to the aid of their country.

80% of Optimal
Now is the time for all good men to come to the aid of their country.

120% of Optimal
Now is the time for all good men to come to the aid of their country.

70% of word spacing, optimal letter spacing
Now is the time for all good men to come to the aid of their country.

Optimal word spacing, 70% of letter spacing
Now is the time for all good men to come to the aid of their country.

8 pitch

Now is the time for all good men to
come to the aid of their country.

12 pitch
Now is the time for all good men to come to the aid of their country.

Word Spacing Justification Limits

This command specifies how much WordPerfect can expand or compress spacing between words when justifying lines. The defaults are 60% compression and 400% expansion, meaning that WordPerfect can compress up to about half and expand about four times the normal width of a space. When the limit is reached, WordPerfect adjusts the spacing between characters to justify the line. If excessive space is a problem on justified lines, you can change the defaults here (to something less than 400%) to help reduce it. Anything over 999% is considered unlimited.

TIP: You can also adjust the hyphenation commands to reduce excessive spacing.

To Review

Describe what happens when each of the following commands are used:

Kerning ____

Word/Letter Spacing _____________________________________

Line Height ____

Other Commands that Affect Appearance

Several of the other commands you have already learned can also be used to add graphics and/or other special effects to your documents.

Line Draw, Compose, and Others

Some of these other commands include Line Draw, Compose, Justification, and the Advance commands. You can also add columns to enhance readability and appearance. Incorporating these features with the graphics, line, and font commands gives you the ability to produce documents that are attractive, eye catching, and communicate your message in an emphatic way.

Line Height

Another command that can be used to alter the appearance of the page is Line Height. This is a measurement of the amount of space used by each line and is determined by measuring from the bottom of one line to the bottom of the next. Different fonts require different line heights. Bigger fonts require taller heights and hence can fit fewer lines into a given space, and smaller fonts require shorter heights and can fit more lines into a given space. WordPerfect makes the adjustments automatically to provide the space required. The default for 10 and 12 pitch fonts is six lines per inch or .16" per line.

TIP: You will not see the changes on the screen, but you can watch the status line to see the adjustments WordPerfect makes for different fonts.

If you should want to change the automatic line height setting to increase or reduce the normal amount, press Format (Shift-F8), Line (1), Line Height (4) to bring up the following menu:

```
1 Auto; 2 Fixed: 0
```

From this menu you could select Fixed (2). Then enter a line height measurement. WordPerfect will use the new setting from the cursor forward. If you wish to change back to an automatic line height measurement, you can follow the same sequence but select Auto (1) instead of Fixed from the menu.

TIP: Some printers can print only six lines per inch and this command will not function.

The line height command is often used to provide different line spacing between items on a page for variety and emphasis. An example of the effect of this command is shown in the following illustration, using a Tms Rmn 10pt font. Other sizes of font would produce similar results, but they would be adjusted to the size of font used.

Normal line height (.16 default for 10 point type)

Now is the time for all good men to come to the aid of their country.
Now is the time for all good men to come to the aid of their country.

Line height .25

Now is the time for all good men to come to the aid of their country.

Now is the time for all good men to come to the aid of their country.

Line height .10

Now is the time for all good men to come to the aid of their country.
Now is the time for all good men to come to the aid of their country.

Large font, no line height adjustment (.19 default for 14 point type)

Now is the time for all good men to come to the aid of their country. Now is the time for all good men to come to the aid of their country.

Large font, line height .30

Now is the time for all good men to come to the aid of their country. Now is the time for all good men to come to the aid of their country.

Graphics and Text Quality

Another command that can affect the appearance of your printed work is the setting for graphics and text quality on the Print (Shift-F7) menu.

■ Press **Print (Shift-F7)** to bring the menu to the screen. Then select Graphics Quality (**G**). The following menu will appear:

```
Graphics Quality: 1 Do Not Print; 2 Draft; 3 Medium; 4 High: 3
```

Some printers cannot print both graphics and text at the same time. As a result, printing must be done twice--once for graphics and once for text. When this is the case, the Do Not Print (1) option allows you to turn graphics printing off when the text is being printed and text printing off when the graphic is being printed.

Draft (2), Medium (3), and High (4) quality refer to the sharpness and intensity of printed graphs. The higher the quality, the longer the graph takes to print. You may want to use draft quality for preliminary copies and change the setting to Medium or High quality for final output.

◼ Press **Enter** to remove the Graphics Quality menu. Then select **Text Quality** (**T**) to bring up the quality menu again. The options on this menu are the same and affect text in a similar way. The setting you use can affect the sharpness and clarity of your printed documents.

Page Layout and Design Tips

You now have quite sophisticated tools to use as you work with desktop publishing. In addition to learning the new commands you can use, another major consideration is the design and arrangement of items on the page. You can do this effectively by following a few basic guidelines of page layout and design.

The Objective is to Communicate

Remember that you want to communicate with the reader. Anything that distracts from or interferes with that objective should be avoided. Information should be presented in an appealing and appropriate manner that makes understanding and comprehension easier. When graphics, fonts, and special printing techniques can be used to enhance the material and strengthen the communication value, they should be used. When they do not add to that value, they should be omitted, regardless of how clever or unique they are.

Preplan

It is always a good idea to preplan your document to determine design, placement, size, and arrangement of the material. As you arrange the elements on the page, keep in mind that the style and presentation should suit the information. Organize carefully to give important elements emphasis and to provide balance and variety.

The most noticeable point on a page is 2/5 down from the top on the right side. This space should contain your most important information. The least read area is the lower right corner; this should be reserved for less important items. You should avoid putting graphics and photos where the paper will be folded, and it is best to put photos near the top of the text they relate to. When doing newsletters and other similar items, apply the dollar bill test. Place a dollar bill vertically anywhere on the text. If the text under it is unbroken, revise your material to include some variety.

Once you have a sketch in hand (often called a thumbnail) you are ready to begin. You will find that preplanning will help you save time and avoid the need to make many corrections.

Design Considerations

You will also want to take into consideration the unique design requirements of different types of projects. Some authors break all common business documents into four major categories:

Reports, which include proposals, summaries, long memoranda, and other similar articles. These items are usually text based with standard margins, tabulation, and other format criteria. Graphs and tables are often included.

Directories, which include catalogs, price lists, and address and phone listings. These items usually employ tabulation and/or parallel columns. Headings, lines, fonts, and other methods of separating items are essential.

One-page items, including overhead transparencies, tables, charts, short listings, fliers, handbills, announcements and similar pieces. These items often include several fonts, tabulated or centered material, special spacing, and many graphics.

Newsletters, which include magazines, notices, advertisements, and bulletins. These often use newspaper columns, graphics, lines, and several fonts in their presentation.

Spacing, font style, appropriateness and use of graphics, type of material, user preference, company policy, and a host of other considerations must also be taken into account when designing the layout for your document.

Avoid a Cluttered Appearance

Unless it is an intentional part of your design, try to avoid a jumbled or gimmicky layout. It is best not to have more than two type families per page or more than five or six different sizes of type per page. In addition, you should be fairly consistent in the type style used for titles, headings, subheadings, the text of the body, captions, and credit lines. All items do not have to be the same style, but the styles used should enhance one other. In addition, like items should match, so the reader can follow from one to the next and recognize elements easily. If articles are continued on other pages, use jump lines to let readers know where to turn for the remainder of the article.

Font Selection

In general, fonts should be appropriate to the use and context of the material. Fancy fonts are best for text that is open and contains less information. Examples are fliers, announcements, and advertisements. When using such fonts, remember that a little goes a long way.

You should also select a font that is large enough to read easily. It is acceptable to mix font styles within a document, but they should compliment one another. As a rule of thumb, headlines for books, newsletters, newspaper articles, and other like items should be two to three-and-a-half times larger than the body text, and they should fit on one or two lines without hyphenation. If they do not, reduce the size of the font or shorten the headline. Characters in column heads and subheadings should be closer together and usually less than twice as large as the body text.

Helvetica and other sans-serif type fonts are popular choices for headlines and are used extensively in Europe for body text. Type styles such as Tms Rmn and Courier are widely used in America for body text. A popular combination is Helvetica for headlines and Times Roman for body text. Generally speaking, between 9 and 11 point type size is used for the text of a document, 14 point for subheadings, and up to 24 point size used for main headings.

It is a good idea to avoid the overuse of bold and underline and substitute an italics font instead. Use all capitals sparingly, and substitute small caps, which are easier to read, wherever possible.

Graphics

The impact of graphics can be summed up in the old saying that one picture is worth a thousand words. Graphics can include charts, drawings, symbols, photos, clip-art, text, and other items.

All graphics should be chosen carefully and should help convey the message of the text to the reader. It is generally more appealing if the graphics are not all the same size or design. They should also be positioned in various areas on the page rather than all in the same place. You may want to move, resize (enlarge or crop), rotate, or invert the graphic to provide a more specific illustration. Use bullets and enlarged, short quotes from the text to lend emphasis and draw attention to important items.

Other interesting visuals are lines, white space, shading, enlarging the first letter of a paragraph, and irregular shapes. Pull quotes, which are enlarged quotes or excerpts from the text, are often used to provide variety and highlight important points.

Headlines and Paragraphs

For interesting headlines, use active verbs, keywords, or catchy phrases. Headlines should not be longer than five to seven words. The current practice is to capitalize only proper nouns and the first letter of each word.

Paragraphs should not run more than about 10 lines and should include graphs, skipped lines, indentations, subheads, and other visual devices for variety.

Landscape and Portrait Orientation

Some printers will print in landscape orientation, which means that they will print on paper in sideways position. When this is the case, the long sides of the paper are considered to be the top and bottom. Portrait orientation means that the paper is in normal position with the short edges on top and bottom.

Portrait
Orientation

Landscape
Orientation

Columns, Lines, Justification, and Line Height

Many documents are printed in columnar format. Lines of no more than 45 characters are easier to read. Generally, two or three columns per page is preferred for ease of reading and flexibility of design. Some documents have part of the text in two column format and part in three, with a headline stretched over multiple columns. Paragraphs are generally not indented when columns are used.

Rules and lines can be used to separate items, enliven the pages, and add visual variety, especially when they are varied in length and weight. Many newsletters today use a ragged rather than a justified right margin. Ragged lines are often easier to read, and they help avoid wide spaces within words. This format also opens up the page and presents a friendlier appearance. Varied line height can also enhance the appearance and help to avoid a monotonous look.

Watch hyphenation carefully and avoid widow or orphan lines in the text.

Originality and Creativity

Finally, you should approach the design of your pages with a fresh eye and a search for new and innovative ways to present your data in a more meaningful and understandable way. Let your imagination go and have fun as you do.

Now let's use all these new commands.

■ Retrieve **GraphCol.15**, which is the article about finding a job with graphics and lines.

■ Use your creativity to change the appearance of this article. You could change the fonts for the headlines and italics. Add side headings if you wish and use a special font for them (depending on what your printer offers). Change the columns to three, and see what the article looks like with justification both on and off. Add a caption under the graphic. Change the word and letter spacing and reduce the line height to see what the difference will be. Change the position of the graphics boxes. Use the shadow, outline, redline, and small caps attributes where appropriate. Insert **"To be continued..."** at the end in a small font. Put the title into a box and shade it. Extend it over all columns like a banner.

■ When you are finished, save the article as **Fonts.16** and print it. Share the results with your instructor and classmates.

For additional practice, retrieve any of your previous documents. Add suitable graphics, change the fonts, and insert any printer commands that are appropriate. Have fun as you do. Save, print, and share your best efforts.

Activities

You should have completed the following:

Graphatt.16   *Font changes*
Fonts.16   *Graphlin.16 with changes*
VacaFont.16   *Vacation.6 with Style/Font changes*

Chapter Review

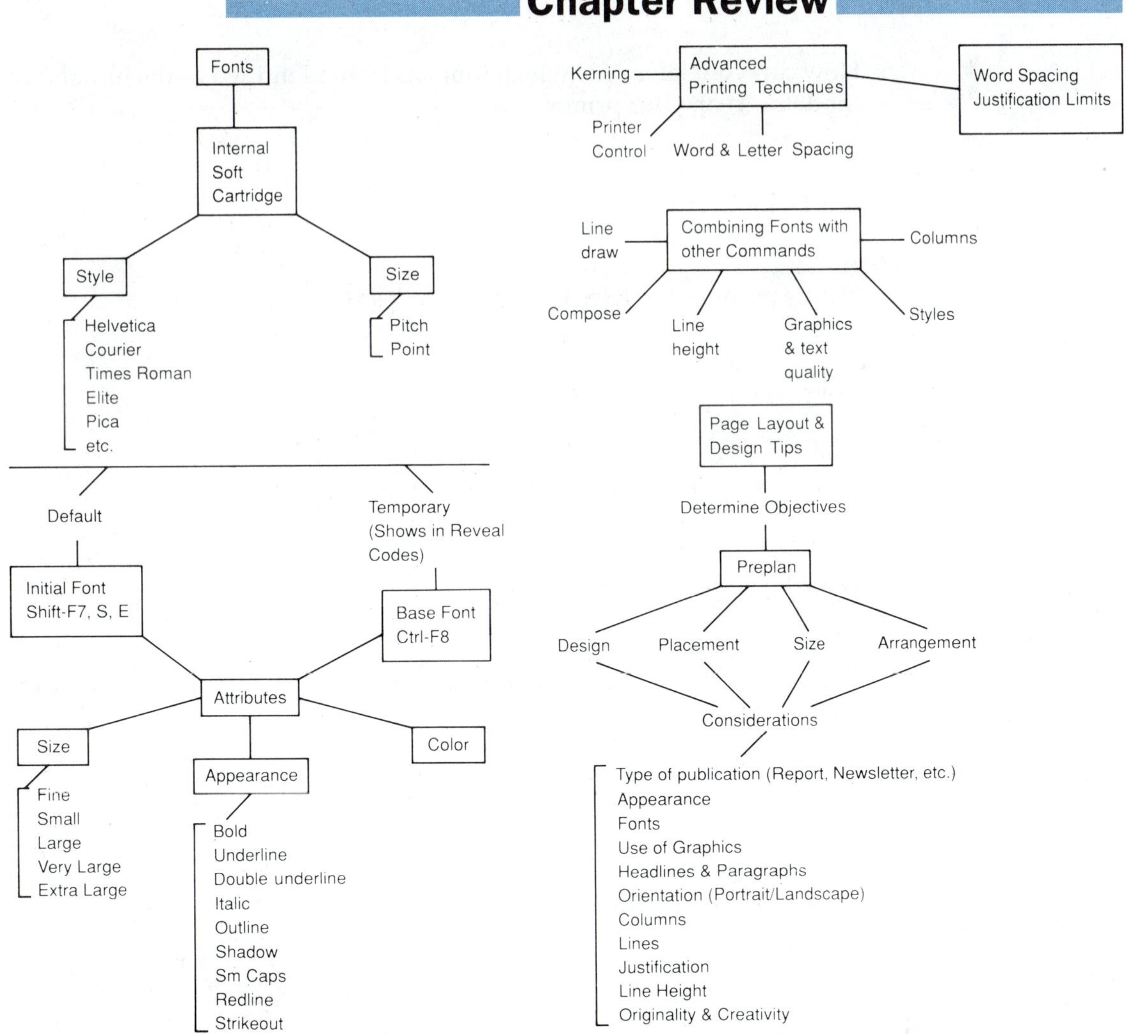

Self-Check Quiz 16

1. Describe the difference between the Initial font and a Base font.

2. What is an attribute?

3. List the attributes that are available for font size.

4. List the attributes that are available for font appearance.

5. How can you determine which font has been identified as the Initial font (or default) on your printer.

6. Define pitch as it relates to fonts.

7. Define point as it relates to fonts.

8. List several font styles or typefaces.

9. How can you tell where the code for fonts is located?

10. What keys should you press to select a different base font?

11. What happens if you select a font or font attribute that is not available on your printer?

12. What is Normal attribute on the Base Font menu used for?

13. What does kerning do?

14. What is the difference between optimal and normal word spacing?

15. What happens when the line height command is used?

16. Why might you use draft quality for printing text or graphs?

17. List several commands that can be combined with font and graphics to enhance the appearance of a document.

18. Why is communication a major consideration of page layout and design?

19. List several tips for good page layout.

20. Describe landscape and portrait orientation.

Extra Practice

Following are some projects to give you extra practice on the material covered in this chapter.

a. Design a business card for yourself. Include your name, address, phone number, and any special message you would like to have. Use lines, fonts, and incorporate a graphic if you wish. Most business cards are 3 1/2 inches wide by 2 inches high. Put multiple copies on a page, save the file as **Pract16a,** and print several. Give them to your friends.

b. Create a memo format (To, From, Date, Subject) using fonts, lines, and appropriate graphics if you wish to include them. Use line spacing, font attributes, word/letter spacing, pitch changes, or whatever other techniques you need to make it attractive and useful. Save the file as **Pract16b** and print it.

c. Design a newsletter header for an organization you belong to. Write two or three short articles of interest to other members and illustrate them with graphics, quotes, and tables. Save the file as **Pract16c** and print it.

d. Design a letterhead for your personal use. Put your name, address, and telephone number on it along with any other information you would like to include. Try not to use more than the top two inches or bottom one inch of the page. Be creative with lines, fonts, and spacing. Save the file as **Pract16d** and print it.

17

Helps for Manuscripts

WordPerfect can help you with many of the unique requirements of manuscripts, reports, and other documents. In addition, you can change the way text is printed and the way it appears on the page. When you have completed this chapter, you will be able to:

- change the top and/or bottom margins.

- specify whether page numbers will begin on odd or even pages.

- suppress printing of page numbers, headers, footers, footnotes, and endnotes.

- work with headers and footers.

- create and use footnotes and endnotes.

- use redline and strikeout commands to edit.

- add superscripts and subscripts to your text.

- use document compare to review changes made to a document.

Changing Top and Bottom Margins

As you know, WordPerfect automatically creates one-inch top and bottom margins on your printout. With most fonts, this is six lines. However, there will be times when you want to adjust either the top or bottom margin, or both--such as when you wish to bind your document across the top, or are using letterhead or special-sized paper such as mailing labels.

TIP: If the changes apply to only one page (such as the first page of a report), or occur infrequently, it is usually faster to use the Enter key to add lines [HRt] to the 1" top margin that the printer will automatically leave rather than changing the defaults. For instance, if you want a 1-1/2-inch top margin on the first page, it is easiest to use the Enter key to add three blank lines (1/2 inch) to the 1-inch top margin. However, if such changes are frequent, or affect several consecutive pages, it is easier to have WordPerfect do it since you need enter the command only once rather than on each page.

- For practice, retrieve **Acting.4**.

- Create a document summary, showing yourself as the author and typist. Provide appropriate comments.

  Let's assume that this document will be bound at the top, and you wish to leave a 1-1/2-inch top margin on all pages. To change the top margin, use the Page Format menu.

- Move the cursor to the extreme top left of the first page, with **Home, Home, Home, Up Arrow**. This is important because WordPerfect must get the margin change command at the very beginning of the document for it to affect the first page.

- Press **Format (Shift-F8)** to bring up the menu. Select **Page (2)** and bring up the menu shown on the next page.

- Select **Margins (5)** to set the top and bottom margins.

- When the cursor jumps to the setting for the Top Margin, type **1.5** and press **Enter**.

- Leave the 1" bottom margin as it is and **Exit (F7)** the menu.

```
Format: Page

    1 - Center Page (top to bottom)      No

    2 - Force Odd/Even Page

    3 - Headers

    4 - Footers

    5 - Margins - Top                     1"
                  Bottom                  1"

    6 - New Page Number                   1
          (example: 3 or iii)

    7 - Page Numbering                    No page numbering

    8 - Paper Size                        8.5" x 11"
                  Type                    Standard

    9 - Suppress (this page only)


Selection: 0
```

When the document is printed, WordPerfect will insert a 1-$1/2$-inch top margin on every page of your document. It will also alter the positions of page numbers and any headers or footers. The new top margin will remain in effect from this point on until you exit or it is changed again within the document.

TIP: If the top margin on the first page of your printout does not change, use Reveal Codes to check that the commands are located in the extreme upper left corner of your document. Unless these instructions are inserted at the very beginning of the page, WordPerfect will use the defaults. It is critical that they be the very first commands.

■ Now save your document as **Margins.17**. Then print it, to see if you have a 1-$1/2$ inch top margin and a 1-inch bottom margin.

TIP: If you hand feed forms into the printer, roll the paper up one inch past the printhead before entering a print command. From this point, WordPerfect will make appropriate adjustments for any changes in the top margin.

You can also change the bottom margins in the same way. Or if only one page is involved, you can cut the bottom margin off with a New Page command (Ctrl-Enter), forcing WordPerfect to begin a new page at that point. For more than one or two pages, however, or for material where the cut-off point may change because of editing, the adjustments outlined above work better.

How easy can it get?

To Review

The new top margin and page length you specify will remain in effect until: ____ .

Commands for changes in the top and bottom margin must be positioned

____ .

If you wish to change the top margin on only one page, you can use:

____ .

If you wish to change the bottom margin on only one page, you can use:

____ .

Summary

In summary, to change the Top and Bottom Margins:

a. Position the cursor at the very top of the page.

b. Press Format (Shift-F8).

c. Select Margins (5).

d. Indicate the desired width of the top and bottom margins in inches or other appropriate measurements.

e. Press Exit (F7).

Forcing Odd/Even Numbering

You already know how to enter the command to number pages. However, when working with a manuscript containing several parts, you may want to specify that certain pages must begin with an odd or an even number. For instance, you may want all chapters to begin on a right-hand page (odd numbers) or you may want a particular item to be printed on the left side of the publication (even pages).

If you do much editing to your document, it may be hard to guarantee where things will be printed since the page number can fluctuate as your document grows and shrinks with changes. To overcome this problem, you can enter a command that will tell WordPerfect to print a given page on either an odd or an even numbered page.

■ To see how this command works, again retrieve **Acting.4**.

■ Move the cursor to the top of your document with **Home, Home, Up Arrow**.

■ Then press **Format (Shift-F8)**, **Page (2)**, **Force Odd/Even (2)**. When the following prompt appears, select **Even (2)** and press **Exit (F7)**.

> 1 Odd; 2 Even: 0

WordPerfect will enter a code like the following: [Force:Even] at the cursor.

■ Press **Reveal Codes (Alt-F3)** to see the code in your text.

When this code is encountered by the printer, it will skip a page if necessary and put the text for that page on the next even numbered page. If the page already falls on an even number, the code is ignored. For example, if the page would originally have been numbered 3, WordPerfect will skip a page and print the contents on page 4. If the page would be printed on 6 anyway, it will remain on page 6.

TIP: If you watch the status line, you will note that the page change is reflected there.

■ Save the document as **ActingA1.17** and print it. Notice the blank first page, and that the document now begins on page 2.

Suppressing Page Numbers

Another command that affects the page numbering of your document is also found on the Page Format menu. This command allows you to suppress, or stop, the printing of page numbers, headers, and footers on specified pages.

As you know, the page number on the first page of a manuscript is often omitted or printed at the bottom of the page. Therefore, if you have already specified that page numbers are to be printed at the top center for the rest of your document, you will need to change the command for the first page.

■ To see how this is done, press Format (**Shift-F8**) and select **Page (2)**, and **Suppress** (This page only) (**9**). The following menu will appear:

```
Format: Suppress (this page only)

    1 - Suppress All Page Numbering, Headers and Footers

    2 - Suppress Headers and Footers

    3 - Print Page Number at Bottom Center   No

    4 - Suppress Page Numbering              No

    5 - Suppress Header A                    No

    6 - Suppress Header B                    No

    7 - Suppress Footer A                    No

    8 - Suppress Footer B                    No




Selection: 0
```

As you can see, you can suppress or omit headers, footers, and numbering on this page. You can also specify that the page number be printed at the bottom center on this page even if you have selected another style (such as top left) for the rest of your document. The other style will then be used for remaining pages.

To make choices from the menu, you need only enter your selections, respond to the prompts, and Exit.

Adding Headers and Footers

Long printed documents often have identifying information at the top and bottom of each page to orient the reader. For example, the header might be the chapter title; the footer might be the author's name. It would be time-consuming to retype the same material on each page. But there is a faster way. The Headers and Footers option on the Page Format menu will do it for you.

TIP: Do not confuse headers and footers with footnotes, which appear at the bottom of the page and indicate the original source of a quotation or idea. A header or footer can be any line of text you wish to have appear on each page. The commands for footnotes/endnotes and headers/footers are not interchangeable.

- ▣ Clear your screen and retrieve **Margins.17**.

- ▣ Again, move to the beginning of the document.

- ▣ Then press **Format (Shift-F8)** to bring up the menu.

- ▣ Since Headers and Footers appears under **Page** format, select **Page (2)**.

```
Format: Page

      1 - Center Page (top to bottom)     No

      2 - Force Odd/Even Page

      3 - Headers

      4 - Footers

      5 - Margins - Top                   1"
                    Bottom                1"

      6 - New Page Number                 1
            (example: 3 or iii)

      7 - Page Numbering                  No page numbering

      8 - Paper Size                      8.5" x 11"
                    Type                  Standard

      9 - Suppress (this page only)


Selection: 0
```

TIP: WordPerfect will allow you to have two headers and two footers, identified as A or B.

Entering Headers and Footers

Let's suppose that you want to enter a Header.

- ▣ Select **Headers (3)**. A prompt at the bottom left of your screen will ask if you want to enter Header A or Header B.

```
1 Header A; 2 Header B: 0
```

◼ Since this is the first header, type **1** for Header A.

◼ You will then see another prompt across the bottom of your screen like the following:

```
1 Discontinue; 2 Every Page; 3 Odd Pages; 4 Even Pages; 5 Edit: 0
```

WordPerfect is asking where you want this header printed. You can have it printed on every page or only on odd numbered or even numbered pages. This menu also allows you to discontinue a header from the point of the command forward or to edit an already existing header.

◼ Select Every **P**age (**2**) to have Header A printed on every page.

Immediately the screen will clear and you will see a prompt at the bottom similar to the following:

```
Press Exit when done                                    Ln 1" Pos 1"
```

You can now type whatever text you want to add as a header. As you can see, you can have several lines of text. Let's put the words PRELIMINARY COPY as header A at the top of every page.

◼ Type **PRELIMINARY COPY** and press **Exit (F7)**.

TIP: Pressing Exit (F7) saves the text of the header. Pressing Cancel (F1) would cancel the command and return to the Page Format menu without saving.

◼ Then press **Exit (F7)** once more to leave the Page Format menu and return to your document. Save it as **Header.17**.

That's all there is to it. You won't see the header on your screen, but when the document is printed, the words PRELIMINARY COPY will appear at the top of each page. Footers are created the same way. You can even have two of each if you want.

◼ If you want to see how the header looks on your document, use **Print (Shift-F7)**, and View (**6**) to see it, then print a copy.

TIP: Headers and footers are printed at the top margin and/or bottom margin of the page. They are *not* printed within the margins themselves. A space equivalent to approximately one blank line will be added between the header/footer and the document text. WordPerfect will automatically subtract the space needed to print headers/footers from that available between the top and bottom margins and make appropriate adjustments. Therefore, if you can usually print 54 lines of text on a page and you have a 3 line header, WordPerfect will subtract 4 lines (3 for the header and 1 for the blank space) from the 52 and print only 48 lines plus the header on a page.

Summary

In summary, to enter Headers and Footers:

a. Position the cursor at the beginning of the document or page.

b. Press Format (Shift-F8).

c. Select Page (2).

d. Select Headers (3) or Footers (4).

e. Indicate A or B header/footer.

f. Indicate the pattern of occurrence to print.

g. Enter the text of the header and/or footer, and its placement.

h. Press Exit (F7) to return to the document.

i. View if you wish.

- For practice with Headers and Footers, clear your screen if necessary and retrieve **Trips.6**.

- Add the header **TRAVEL BROCHURE COPY**, aligned at the right margin (Flush Right), and the footer **For publication in mid-May**, centered.

- Add a document comment at the beginning, indicating that this document is copy for a travel brochure to be published in mid-May.

- Resave the document with your changes as **HeadFoot.17**, and then print it.

Editing Headers and Footers

To change the footer to **For publication in mid-June**, do the following:

- Position the cursor after the footer you wish to edit. (Remember that WordPerfect works backward for the edit function.)

- Press **Format** (**Shift-F8**) to bring up the Format Menu.

- Select Page (**2**) and Headers (**3**).

- Choose Header **A** (**1**) and Edit (**5**).

- Make the change when the text is displayed, and press **Exit** (**F7**) to end Edit mode.

- Save this document as **EditHdFt.17** and print it.

To Review

Headers will be printed ____ .

Footers will be printed ____ .

To edit a Header/Footer, the cursor should be ____________________________ .

To see what a Header/Footer will look like when printed, you can press

____ .

Tips for Using Headers and Footers

When creating Headers and Footers, there are several things to keep in mind.

1. WordPerfect normally works forward. If you want the Header or Footer to be printed on the page you are working on, as well as subsequent pages, you must enter it at the very beginning of the page (Line 1 at the left margin). Otherwise it will be printed beginning on the next page. If you do not want the headers or footers to be printed on a particular page, use the Suppress command to stop it.

2. If the header or footer code is not at the beginning of your document, it may be moved from the top of the page when you add or remove text. You can keep this from happening in situations where headers and footers are added within the text by putting a hard page break in front of the code.

3. Remember that WordPerfect works from right to left in the edit mode. Therefore, you will want to position the cursor **after** or to the **right of** the code for the header or footer you wish to edit before choosing the edit option. When you have finished editing, press Exit to return to your document.

4. You can use many other functions in a Header/Footer if you wish. For instance, you can Center the Header/Footer, Underline it, Bold it, and so on.

5. Be careful that you don't put both an A and a B Header or Footer in the same place, or they will be printed one on top of the other. If you want to use two headers, for example, it would be best to position one at the left margin and the other flush right, or possibly centered.

6. WordPerfect will report any headers and/or footers that you have entered in the Page Format menu. A notation such as "HA Every Page" tells you that Header A will be printed on every page. Move the cursor past the header command, then press Format (Shift-F8), Page (2) if you wish to see this on your document.

7. If you wanted to include page numbering in the header or footer, you could do so by holding the **Ctrl** key down and typing **B**. This will insert a ^B command that will tell WordPerfect to number the pages consecutively from the command forward.

Using Headers and Footers

Headers and Footers have many uses. One of the most common is specialized numbering, or other identification formats that the page-numbering function of WordPerfect won't handle. For instance, you could use any of the following as a header or footer: 1-1, 1-2, 1-3, 10A, 6/10/89, Chapter 1, Set 2, etc.

Remember that the Extended Search feature (Home, F2) will search headers and footers as well as footnotes and endnotes. Spell checks of your documents will include the contents of headers and footers. However, if you wish to spell check only the header and/or footer, display it in an editing screen before activating the speller. That way, only the header/footer will be checked. See Chapter 5 for further instructions on using the speller function.

Entering Footnotes and Endnotes (Notes)

Footnotes and endnotes, (called notes) which can be quite a challenge on a typewriter, are even easier than headers and footers with WordPerfect. All you need to do is enter the text of the note (footnote or endnote); and WordPerfect will format it correctly, put it in the right spot, and even keep track of the numbers.

TIP: Footnotes are placed at the bottom of the page containing the reference. Endnotes are combined together either in a specified place within the document or at the end in summary fashion.

◼ To see how the footnote/endnote commands work, retrieve **VacaIndt.7**. Let's add a note or two.

Entering a Note

The process for entering either a footnote or an endnote is essentially the same. When you select the appropriate option from the menus as they are presented, WordPerfect puts the note in the correct format and proper place.

◼ For some practice, let's enter a footnote. Move the cursor to the end of the first paragraph, immediately following "memories linger long after the travel is ended."

◼ Press **Footnote (Ctrl-F7)**. The following prompt will appear at the bottom of your screen:

```
1 Footnote; 2 Endnote; 3 Endnote Placement: 0
```

From this point you have several options:

1. You can have the text you enter printed at the bottom of the page as a footnote.

2. You can have the text you enter printed at the end of your document as an endnote.

3. You can change the numbering of endnotes, or have them printed at the cursor rather than at the end of the document.

◼ To enter a footnote, select Footnote (**1**). The prompt will change to:

```
Footnote: 1 Create; 2 Edit; 3 New Number; 4 Options: 0
```

This same prompt would appear if you had chosen Endnotes (2), and as you can see, it allows you to create, edit, or change the numbering of notes. The Options choice allows you to specify the style and spacing of various parts of the footnote and/or endnote.

▣ Select **Footnote** (**1**) to create the footnote.

The screen will clear, and you will see a 1 (or whatever the number of the footnote) and something like the following prompt at the bottom of the screen:

> ` Press Exit when done `   ` Doc 1 Pg 1 Ln 1.5" Pos 1.56" `

At this point, all you need do is enter your footnote. WordPerfect will insert a superscript number in the text (if your printer is capable of printing them) and position the footnote at the bottom of the page when it is printed. It will also insert a two-inch dividing line between the text and the footnote(s) and single-space the footnote.

If you had selected Endnote, WordPerfect would again insert the superscript number in the text, store the endnote, and print it at the end of the document (assuming you have not specified another place for it to be printed).

TIP: You must remember to end notes with an Enter, so that if you have more than one note there will be a space between them. **Do not type the note number.** WordPerfect will insert it for you.

The note itself will not appear on the screen with the rest of your document. To see the note, you will need to press Reveal Codes (Alt-F3) or Print (Shift-F7) and View (6).

▣ For this footnote, type the following (you may underline the title instead of using italics):

> **Vincent Score,** *Travel Tips* **(Boston: Jetway Publishers, 1984), p. 10.**

▣ Now press **Enter** (to leave a blank line) and then Exit (**F7**). WordPerfect will take care of the rest. It will even adjust the amount of text on the page to allow room for the footnote at the bottom.

TIP: If the footnote is long, or the reference is near the bottom of the page and the entire footnote cannot be printed on the same page as its reference in the text, WordPerfect will put at least 1/2 inch (or 3 lines) of the footnote on the same page and carry the remainder over to the bottom of the next page.

If you wish to review the note, you can see the first 50 characters in Reveal Codes. You can also return to the footnote creation/editing screen (Ctrl-F7, 1, 1 or 2), or you can press Print (Shift-F7), View (6) to see it in its entirety.

◼ For more practice, move the cursor down to the heading **Sightseeing Tips**.

◼ Position the cursor at the end of the line. Press **Footnote** (**Ctrl-F7**), Footnote (**1**), **Create** (**1**). Then enter the following footnote:

> **L.H. Travels, *See Europe By Car* (London: Gatlin Press, 1983), p. 50.**

◼ Save your document as **Footnote.17** and print it.

Normally you won't use both footnotes and endnotes in the same document; you'll choose one or the other. But here, so you can easily compare how WordPerfect handles each kind, we'll use the same file.

◼ Retrieve **Footnote.17**, if necessary.

◼ Place the cursor immediately following the heading **Travel Plans And Cost**.

◼ Press **Footnote** (**Ctrl-F7**), choose Endnote (**2**) and Create (**1**) and type the following endnote. Remember that you do not need to type the number. WordPerfect will keep track of them for you. You should, however, allow two spaces between the number and the beginning of the endnote, so be sure to space twice before beginning to type.

> **George R. Wilson, *Touring the World* (San Francisco: Maxmillian Publishers, 1984), p. 125.**

◼ Now move to the heading **What to Take**, and add another endnote. (This will be number 2.)

Sandra Baxter, *Traveling Light* **(Denver: Travel Press: 1985), p. 21.**

▣ Oops, the page reference should be 201, not 21. Edit your endnote accordingly.

To put the endnotes on a separate page, with a title, do the following:

▣ Go to the end of your document and insert a hard page break. Type the word **ENDNOTES**, centered at the top of the new page you just created.

TIP: Be sure to leave two blank lines after the title if the document is single spaced and one blank line if it is double spaced.

▣ When you are finished, Save your work as **Endnote.17** and print it.

Endnote Placement

If you want the endnotes to be printed within the text of your document create them first. Then position the cursor where you want them placed and select option 3 from the Footnote (Ctrl-F7) menu.

You would be asked if you wanted to restart numbering, and if so, which number to start with. This means that WordPerfect can number the endnotes, position them, and then start numbering again.

Whether you renumber the endnotes or not, WordPerfect will insert a hard page command and display the following message on your screen:

```
Endnote Placement
It is not known how much space endnotes will occupy here.
Generate to determine.
```

To generate the endnotes to be entered at this command, press Mark Text (Alt-F5), Generate (6), and Generate Tables, Indexes, Automatic References, etc. (5). If you are asked if you want to replace existing tables, lists, indexes, then answer **Y**(es); WordPerfect will do the rest. The message on the screen will change to reflect the amount of space required for the endnotes and the change will also be reflected on the status line. When the document is printed, all endnotes generated to that point will be printed at the command.

TIP: You can place endnotes throughout your document if you wish. Simply enter an endnote placement command where you want them to be printed. WordPerfect will generate all endnotes between the previous command and this one and place them at the cursor.

Summary

In summary, to enter a Footnote or an Endnote:

a. Position the cursor immediately following the last word in the sentence or paragraph that the note refers to.

b. Press Footnote (**Ctrl-F7**).

c. Select option 1 or 2, to work with a footnote or an endnote.

d. Press 1 to create the note.

e. Enter the text of the note.

f. Press Exit (**F7**) and Enter to return to the document.

g. Create a header for the page on which the endnotes will be printed, if necessary, or specify other placement.

h. View if you wish.

i. Save and print

Now let's take a look at some of the other options on the footnote menu. Follow along to see how these commands work.

```
Footnote: 1 Create; 2 Edit; 3 New Number; 4 Options: 0
```

Editing a Note

For practice editing a note, let's change the author's name from *Travels* to *Tippets* in the second footnote.

◻ Call up the **Footnote** function (**Ctrl-F7**).

◻ Choose Footnote (**1**) and Edit (**2**).

◻ When you are asked for the number of the footnote you wish to edit, press **2** and Enter. WordPerfect will find and display footnote number 2.

■ Change the author's name from **Travels** to **Tippets**.

■ Press **Exit** (**F7**). The text will reappear with the changed footnote.

TIP: You can use many of the other WordPerfect features, such as Block, Move, and Spell, when editing a footnote or endnote.

Deleting a Note

To delete an entire note, you can use either Backspace or Del. Place the cursor under the note number and press either key. Confirm that you wish to delete with a Y. Subsequent notes will be automatically renumbered by WordPerfect.

New Number

Option 3 on the Footnote Menu allows you to specify how notes will be numbered. The default is to start with 1 and use the next highest number for each succeeding note throughout the document. However, you may wish to have the numbers keyed to the text, such as beginning with 10 for the first chapter, 20 for the second, etc. Or you may want them to begin again with 1 at the start of each new chapter. The New Number option allows you to do this.

Routine renumbering, such as when you change the order of notes, or delete or add notes in the middle of your text, will be done automatically by WordPerfect. Before printing, WordPerfect will renumber the notes consecutively.

Options

Option 4 lists the defaults used for footnotes and allows you to change them. The Options Menu looks like the one shown on the next page.

As you can see, there are a number of ways to alter how footnotes and endnotes are displayed. The column on the right side indicates the defaults; this is the format you will want to use most of the time. If you do not change them, notes will be single spaced with one line between them (0.16"). Footnotes will be separated from the text with a two-inch line, and printed at the bottom of each page.

```
Footnote Options

      1 - Spacing Within Footnotes            1
                Between Footnotes             0.16"

      2 - Amount of Note to Keep Together     0.5"

      3 - Style for Number in Text            [SUPRSCPT][Note Num][suprscpt]

      4 - Style for Number in Note                    [SUPRSCPT][Note Num][suprscp

      5 - Footnote Numbering Method           Numbers

      6 - Start Footnote Numbers each Page     No

      7 - Line Separating Text and Footnotes   2-inch Line

      8 - Print Continued Message              No

      9 - Footnotes at Bottom of Page          Yes



   Selection: 0
```

You can change the style of notes and enter up to 5 other letters or symbols. When five are used, WordPerfect will double them and start again. The continued message will cause the word "Continued" to be printed at the end of the footnote that is too long for the page and must be partially carried to the next.

TIP: Remember that to include the text of headers, footers, footnotes, and endnotes in a search, you must press Home before pressing the search keys. This is called an extended search.

To Review

To complete or exit from the Headers/Footers and Footnotes options, you should press ___________________.

To delete a note, press ___________________.

To see the text of a note, press ___________________.

When you have finished entering a note, you should press ___________________.

To insert a note number, you should press___________________.

Editing with Redline and Strikeout

WordPerfect provides several specialized ways to edit your material. The Redline and Strikeout features are two of them.

Redline allows you to mark a passage that you may have added and need approval for, or that you want to come back to later.

Strikeout allows you to mark text to be removed from your document.

The Redline command can insert a vertical bar in the left or alternating margins beside each line that is being added. Or it can be a shaded box around the text. These additions can also be printed in red, if you have a color printer. Not all printers can print all options, so you would have to test which ones are available on your printer.

The Strikeout command prints a row of dashes through a line of text. This material can be deleted from your text if you wish.

This text is marked with redline to be added.

This text ~~is marked~~ with strikeout to be deleted.

Redline and Strikeout allow you to mark where changes have been made in your document.

◼ Clear your screen, For a document to work with, retrieve **Nowis.2**.

Redline

To redline text in your document, you must first define how you want the redline markings to appear. This is accomplished on the Document Format, menu.

TIP: It is not necessary to define these markings each time. You can simply use the defaults if you wish.

◼ Press **Format (Shift-F8)** and select **Document (3)**. Again type **4** or **R** for Redline Method to display the following menu across the bottom of the screen.

```
Redline Method: 1 Printer Dependent; 2 Left; 3 Alternating: 1
```

TIP: If you have a color monitor or printer, you will also see an option for **Red (2)**. The numbers for **Left** and **Alternating** will be changed to 3 and 4 respectively.

If you select Printer Dependent (1), the printer will use its default.

If you select Red (2), the markings will be printed in red (assuming your printer has that capability). This option may not appear in the menu if you do not have a color monitor or printer.

If you select Left (2), the markings will be printed in the left margin. (This option will be 3 if Red was included.)

If you select Alternating (3), the markings will be printed in the left margin for even numbered pages and the right margin for odd numbered pages. (This option will be 4 if Red was included.)

◾ For now, select **Left** (**2 or 3**). You will then be asked to specify the character to be used to mark redlined text.

TIP: The default for this character is usually the upright bar, similar to the following |. However, you could use a slash (/), an equal (=), a pound sign (#), or whatever else you preferred. Laser and other printers often print shaded areas like the example shown on the previous page.

◾ Press the upright bar (|) and **Exit** (**F7**).

Now, let's mark some text. You can either turn the command on and enter the text, or you can mark a block of existing text and redline it.

◾ Press **Font** (**Ctrl-F8**), select **Appearance** (**2**), and **Redln** (**8**). Then type your name and the date as part of **Nowis.2** When you are finished, again choose **Font**, (**Ctrl-F8**), **Appearance** (**2**), and **Redln** (**8**) to turn the command off.

◾ Block a section of the text and mark it for redline.

◾ Save your document as **Redline.17** and print it. You will see a short vertical line in the left margin, indicating the text added and marked.

TIP: If you wish to redline material you have already typed, you can define a block of text using the Block feature, then press redline. The entire block will be marked when it is printed.

Summary

In summary, to mark text for Redline:

a. Press Font (Ctrl-F8), then choose Appearance (2), and Redln (8) to turn Redline On.

b. Enter the text you wish to have redlined.

c. Press Ctrl-F8, 2, 8, again to turn Redline Off.

d. Or mark a block of text and enter the Redline commands.

e. Save and print.

Strikeout

The strikeout feature is also activated from the Font (**Ctrl-F8**) command. Text marked for strikeout can be deleted from your document.

▣ To mark text for Strikeout, use the Block key to highlight the text you want to remove. For this exercise, block the words **good men** in the first sentence.

▣ Then press **Font** (**Ctrl-F8**) to call up the following prompt:

```
Attribute: 1 Size; 2 Appearance: 0
```

▣ Choose **Appearance** (**2**) and Stkout (**9**).

▣ Save your document as **Stkout.17** and print it. The blocked text will have a row of hyphens running through it, like the example shown above.

Summary

In summary, to mark text for Strikeout:

a. Block the text you wish to have marked for Strikeout.

b. Press Font (Ctrl-F8) and choose option 2 for Appearance.

c. Choose 9 for Strikeout.

d. Save and print.

Removing Redline Markings and Text Marked for Strikeout

If you wish, you can delete Redline markings and material marked for Strikeout before you print. This is fairly simple.

▣ Just press **Mark Text** (**Alt-F5**) and choose **Generate** (**6**).

▣ Select option **1** to Remove Redline Markings and Strikeout text from the Document. When you are asked if you want to delete the marked text, answer **Y**(es).

WordPerfect will search your document and delete any Redline markings leaving the text in. It will also delete all text that is marked for Strikeout.

To Review

Text that is Redlined will be marked with a vertical line in the

_______________________ .

Text that is marked for Strikeout will have _________________________________ .

Marking Text with Super/Subscripts

You have already seen how the text references to footnotes and endnotes are inserted. WordPerfect simply prints them for you, 1/2 line above the text. There may be times when you will want to print characters other than footnote and endnote references slightly above or below the line. Examples are mathematical formulas and explanatory comments.

NOTE: Not all printers will print super/subscripts. If your printout does not position them above or below the line, check with your instructor or the printer manual to learn if the printer has this capability.

To print characters other than footnote and endnote references slightly above (Superscript) or below (Subscript) the line, you can use the Super/Subscript command.

◼ Press **Font (Ctrl-F8)** and select **Size (1)** to bring up the following menu:

```
1 Suprscpt; 2 Subscpt; 3 Fine; 4 Small; 5 Large; 6 Ury Large; 7 Ext Large: 0
```

TIP: Superscript characters are printed above the lines of text; subscript characters fall below it. Because the character on the screen does not appear as a superscript or subscript, you may want to check Reveal Codes to make sure that WordPerfect has inserted a command to print it in the appropriate way.

To streamline this process, WordPerfect will allow you to enter the text, mark it as a block and then press Super/Subscript. Try the following exercise to see what these characters look like.

◼ Type the following:

> This is a superscript.
>
> This is a subscript.

Mark the word **superscript** as a block.

- Press **Font (Ctrl-F8)** and select Size **(1)**. Then select Superscript **(1)**.

- Mark the word **subscript** as a block.

- Press **Font (Ctrl-F8)**, Size **(1)**, and Subscript **(2)**.

- Save the document as **Supersub.17** and print it. If your printer has the capability of printing superscripts and subscripts, you will see the words printed above and below the line, like the following:

This is a ^{superscript}.

This is a $_{subscript}$.

Summary

In summary, to print Super/Subscripts:

a. Mark the text you wish to have Super/Subscripted as a block.

b. Press Font (Ctrl-F8) and Size (1).

c. Choose option 1 or 2 for Super/Subscript.

Correlating Text with Document Compare

One of the exciting new features of WordPerfect 5.0 is the ability to compare a document on the screen with one on the disk. All changes made in a phrase are marked. A phrase is defined as text between punctuation marks, such as a period, question mark, comma, or exclamation point; or text between a punctuation mark and a hard return.

When the document is printed, you will see that:

1. Text in the on-screen document that does not exist in the file on disk is redlined.

2. Text found in the file on disk but not in the document on-screen is copied to the on-screen document and marked with strikeout codes.

TIP: As a result, some words that were not changed may be marked along with actual changes in a given phrase. However, the Document Compare feature will help identify places where changes were made and point them out.

To see how it works, let's edit the **Acting.4** file and then use it for document comparison.

- Retrieve **Acting.4** and make the following changes.

- Delete the sentence: **"Where movement alone is involved, the case is somewhat different."**

- Change the word **"klieg"** to **"theater."**

- Delete the listing in the table for the Ritz theater and add the following in its place: **Academy 520.**

- To the end of the first sentence, add the words **"by participating in community or civic productions."**

- Move the entire section titled **"Voice"** above the section titled **"Movement."**

  NOTE: **Do not** save the revised file under the same name as the file on the disk. Doing so will make the file on-screen the same as the one on disk, and the document compare feature will not work.

- Save the file as **ActingB.17** using **Save** (**F10**). Do not clear the screen and memory.

- With the edited document on the screen, press **Mark Text** (**Alt-F5**), and **Generate** (**6**) to display the following menu:

```
Mark Text: Generate

    1 - Remove Redline Markings and Strikeout Text from Document

    2 - Compare Screen and Disk Documents and Add Redline and Strikeout

    3 - Expand Master Document

    4 - Condense Master Document

    5 - Generate Tables, Indexes, Automatic References, etc.


Selection: 0
```

- Type **2** or **C** to compare the screen and disk documents.

- Enter the name of the unchanged file on disk to compare with. In this case, the name is **Acting.4**.

- WordPerfect will immediately begin comparing the two documents, indicating differences by inserting redline and strikeout markings in the on-screen document.

- When it is finished, save the changed document as **ActingC.17** and print it. On the printout, you will see the redline and strikeout markings showing places where the two files differ.

Removing Redline and Strikeout Markings after Document Compare

You can now review the document on the screen and make whatever additional changes you wish. If you decide to delete any redline and/or strikeout markings so the original editing is reversed, you may do so now. When the document is edited to your satisfaction, you can command WordPerfect to remove all remaining redline markings and leave the inserted text in the document. It will also delete all text marked for strikeout.

- To do this, again press **Mark Text (Alt-F5)** and **Generate (6)**. At the Mark Text-Generate menu, select **Remove Redline Markings (1)** and delete text marked with Strikeout from the document.

  Quick as a wink, WordPerfect will obey your command, and the resulting document will contain the new text (redlined) and omit that which was deleted (strikeout).

- Again save the file. Use the name **ActingD.17** and print it.

Summary

To compare documents:

a. Enter the original document and save it on the disk.

b. Make editing changes in the on-screen document.

c. Press Mark Text (Alt-F5), and Generate (6), to compare the on-screen document with the file on disk.

d. Supply the name of the file on disk to compare to.

e. Make any additional editing changes.

f. Press Mark Text (Alt-F5), Generate (6), 1 to remove the redline and strikeout markings, thus entering and deleting text as appropriate.

g. Save and print.

Actitivies

You should have completed the following:

Margins.17	*Changed top margin to 1-1/2 inches.*
ActingA.17	*Force even page*
Header.17	*Headers*
Headfoot.17	*Header and footer*
EditHdFt.17	*Edited header*
Footnote.17	*VacaIndt.7 with footnote*
Endnote.17	*VacaIndt.7 with endnote*
Redline.17	*Text marked with redline*
Stkout.17	*Text marked with strikeout*
Supersub.17	*Superscripts and subscripts*
ActingB.17	*Edited document*
ActingC.17	*Document showing redline and Strikeout markings*
ActingD.17	*Completed document with redline and strikeout removed*

Chapter Review

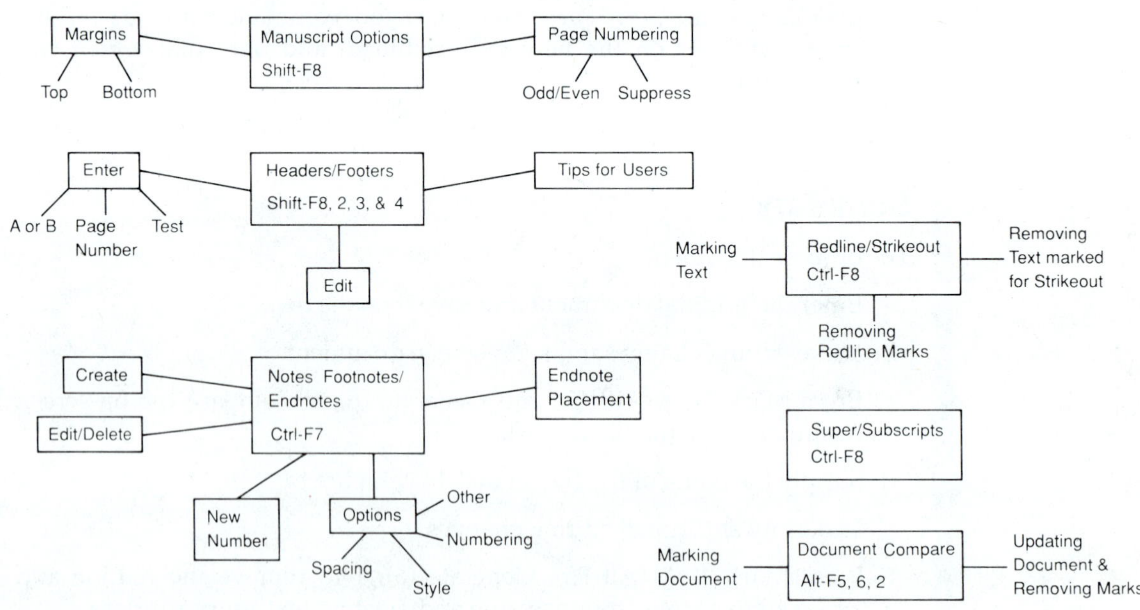

Self-Check Quiz 17

1. Which keystrokes should you use to edit the headers/footers and footnotes commands?

2. How will your text appear when you use the Redline command?

3. How will your text appear when you use the Strikeout command?

4. What number would you enter to change the top margin to two inches?

5. What keys should you press to be sure that WordPerfect will include footnotes, endnotes, headers, and footers in a search?

6. If you wanted to leave a 2- inch top margin on only one page, what could you do?

7. What is the default for top and bottom margins?

8. What will happen when the command [Force:Odd] is encountered by the printer?

9. What does it mean to suppress printing?

10. How do headers and footers differ?

11. What will the command ^B do?

12. What does "HA Every Page" mean?

13. What is the difference between a footnote and an endnote?

14. What is the difference between redline and strikeout?

15. How does Document Compare work?

16. What must be done to remove strikeout marks?

Extra Practice

For extra practice on the material covered in this chapter, do the following:

a. Retrieve **Pract6c** (use the revised document on Employment Opportunities if you do not have **Pract6c** on your disk).

b. Resave it as **Pract17a**. Then use **Pract17a** for the following:

c. Turn Right Justification off.

d. Change the top margin to allow a 1- $1/2$-inch top margin on all pages.

e. Adjust the bottom margin so there will be a 1-inch bottom margin when the document is printed.

f. Assume this paper is part of an assignment for one of your classes. To help you remember, add two headers. Put one at the left margin and one at the right. Use a different font if you wish. The headers should say:

ENGL103	**JOB APPLICATION PAPER**

g. At the end of the sentence in the first paragraph that ends "...and ask you to come in for an interview." add the following endnote: (Underline the title if you do not have an italics font.)

> Lou Larsen, *Getting That New Job*. (San Francisco: Hart Publishing Co, 1986), p. 52.

h. Add a second endnote at the end of the paragraph that begins "Apply for a Specific Job." Position the cursor following the sentence "...and how you will be able to serve the firm." (Underline the title if you do not have an italics font.)

> **Don Barlow, "Writing Good Business Letters,"** *Computing Magazine* **(July, 1987), p. 17-22.**

i. Move to the end of your document, press Ctrl-End to start a new page, and center the title ENDNOTES.

j. Mark for strikeout the fourth sentence in the first paragraph, which begins, "Some of the ads require you to write to a box number..."

k. Redline and add the words "with vague references" to the sentence that begins "Beating around the bush (with vague references) about what..." Don't include the parentheses.

l. Resave the document with changes as **Pract17b.**

m. Print the document.

n. Use List Files (F5) to retrieve **Pract5a.** (You may use **JobsA.3** if you do not have **Pract5a.**)

o. Add the following paragraph at the end of the document. Use the hard hyphen command to be sure the dash does not get separated in printing and the words "self-conscious" remain together.

> **Once you have obtained an appointment for an interview, you should prepare to make the best possible impression. Some things to consider are:**
>
> **1.** *Your appearance.* **You should be neat, clean, and well groomed. Your clothing should be appropriate for the job you are applying for--neither too elaborate nor too casual.**
>
> **2.** *Manners and speech.* **Try not to appear too self-conscious or nervous. Smile and be pleasant and friendly. Speak clearly and use good grammar.**

p. Proofread and check your document carefully. Use Conditional End of Page commands, if necessary, to control where the pages end. Then save your document as **Pract17c** and print it.

q. Use Document Compare to compare **Pract17b** with **Pract17c**. Save the result as **Pract17d** and print it.

r. Use WordPerfect to write a term paper or report for one of your classes or work responsibilities. Use footnotes/endnotes and headers/footers as appropriate. Use the redline and strikeout commands to help you edit it. Turn justification off if you wish. Use the line draw feature and font and pitch changes to highlight parts of the title page or cover and center it on the page. Include graphics if they are appropriate. When you are finished, save and print it.

The following exercises will provide extra practice as well:

s. Retrieve **JobsA.3** on Job Opportunities and resave it using the name **Pract17e**.

t. Then using **Pract17e** change the margins to 1-1/2" left and right and change the spacing to double.

u. Center and bold the following title at the beginning of the document: **TIPS FOR JOB APPLICATION**.

v. Insert the following paragraphs a double space below the title:

Finding a job is often a challenging task. There are, however, a number of things you can do to assist you in this search. Following are several helpful pointers that should improve your chances for success.

Do a Self-Evaluation

The first thing you must do is consider what you have to offer a prospective employer and what your job requirements are. Prepare a resume showing your training, skills, and experience. BE sure it is neat and well done. Ask yourself questions about what you need in a job. Is location important to you? What hours can you work? Do you have transportation? How much salary must you earn? What do you have to offer an employer? What skills do you lack for the kind of work you want?

> **Write down and take with you important information that your employer will need to know such as:**
>
> **Your Social Security Number**
> **Your home telephone number**
> **Dates and places of previous employment**
> **Addresses and names of previous employers**
> **Names, addresses, occupations, and phone numbers of your references.**
> **A transcript from your school**

w. Move to the beginning of your document and turn Widow/Orphan protection ON.

x. Resave your document under the name **Pract17e** and clear your screen.

y. Use List Files (**F5**) to retrieve **Pract17e**.

z. Number the pages at the top right. Put the page number for the first page at the bottom center.

aa. Add the following side headings at the beginning of each of the paragraphs after the material you just inserted. Bold and underline all headings. You may use an italic font on these and the previous headings instead of bold and underline.

> **Use the Newspaper**
> **Make a Check List**
> **Apply for a Specific Job**
> **Ask for an Interview**

bb. Check your document to be sure all pages end correctly. Use Conditional End of Page to avoid having headings separated from the first two lines of text in a paragraph. Also use Conditional End of Page to make sure the list of items to write down and take to an interview are kept together on the same page.

cc. At the very end of the document create a new page using Ctrl-End to insert a hard page break. Prepare a cover sheet for your document with the title, your name, and today's date arranged attractively on the page. Turn page numbering off for the cover page.

dd. Save again using Exit (F7) under the name **Pract17f** and print one copy of your revised document.

18

Beginnings, Endings, Reference Sections, and Working with Large Documents

When you produce a document for other people to read, you'll often want to include a Table of Contents and/or an Index. You may want to develop an outline for your own use while writing. And if your document gets large, you may want to break it into several smaller files that can be recombined later. Finally, as you edit and change your document, you may find that the location of footnotes, figures, and other items within it also changes creating a need to update tables, indexes, and other references. Word-Perfect can help you do all these things quite easily. When you have completed this chapter, you will be able to:

- create a Table of Contents and a list of items.

- develop outlines using WordPerfect.

- generate an Index and a concordance File.

- create a master document with subdocuments.

- condense and expand a master document.

- use the automatic reference feature to create and update references.

Creating a Table of Contents and Various Lists

The steps for creating a Table of Contents and a list of items are essentially the same. You simply indicate that you want to define one or the other from the Mark Text (Alt-F5) menu, and then do the following:

1. Tell WordPerfect how to display and print the page numbers by defining the style and number position from a menu.

2. Mark or block each heading that is to be included in the Table of Contents and specify the level or list number where it is to appear.

3. Generate the Table of Contents or list.

For some practice, let's create a Table of Contents by following the three steps outlined above.

◩ For something to work with, clear your screen and type the following text or retrieve the **Reading.18** file from the Student Exercise Disk.

   a. Use default settings for the margins and paragraph tabs.

   b. Double-space the text. Remove any extra lines if necessary.

READING FOR RELAXATION

<u>Introduction</u>

Recently there has been a noticeable increase in the popularity of reading as a pastime. It seems that more and more people are reacting to the pressures and complexity of our society by relaxing with a good book.

A visit to the local library or bookstore can present the casual reader with a wide variety of books on every imaginable topic.

<u>Choosing Books</u>

Not every book will provide the diversion or information one seeks. Several considerations, such as the writing style and the reading level, should be kept in mind when choosing a book. Another factor is the type of book one likes or wants at the moment. Some books deal with actual situations, while others deal with situations created by the author.

Real-Life Situations

Books in this category report actual happenings or events, usually supported by documentation of some kind. In a narrative or storylike way, they describe the circumstances and people involved.

1. <u>Historical accounts</u>: Historical accounts usually portray some major event, such as the Second World War or the westward movement. These accounts often provide informative insights into why things happened as they did.

2. <u>Biographies</u>: A biography is a type of historical account that deals with the events in one person's life. Some biographies focus on a certain aspect or period of the subject's life, while others tell the complete life story. For example, a biography of a U. S. president could recount his life from birth to death or focus on the years he was in office.

Author-Created Situations

Books of this type may seem very true-to-life and may draw on reality, but they are essentially products of the author's imagination.

1. <u>Fiction</u>: A book of fiction is a story about some fictitious people, circumstances, or events. It can be, for instance, a mystery, an adventure, a western tale, a romance, or a combination of types. Many people enjoy the distraction and change of scene that fiction offers.

2. <u>Fantasy</u>: A fantasy is sheer make-believe, usually about something extraordinary, like outer space or talking animals. Many fantasies take place in the future. These stories are pure diversion, but they often spark curiosity and creativity.

<u>Conclusion</u>

There are many other types of books as well. By browsing through the shelves of a library or a bookstore, you will come across many intriguing publications to provide relaxation and diversion.

◼ Save the document as **Reading.18** and print it.

Defining the Table of Contents

Now you are ready for the first step, which is to define the Table of Contents.

◼ Position the cursor at the beginning of your document and press **Ctrl-Enter** to create a new first page. Put the cursor at the top of the new page.

◼ Center and type the main title, **TABLE OF CONTENTS**. Press **Enter** at least twice to move the cursor down the page two lines, or wherever you want the Table of Contents to begin.

◼ Press **Mark Text (Alt-F5)**. The following menu will appear:

```
1 Auto Ref; 2 Subdoc; 3 Index; 4 ToA Short Form; 5 Define; 6 Generate: 0
```

◼ Select **D**efine **(5)** to bring up the following menu:

```
Mark Text: Define

    1 - Define Table of Contents

    2 - Define List

    3 - Define Index

    4 - Define Table of Authorities

    5 - Edit Table of Authorities Full Form


Selection: 0
```

◼ Select Table of **C**ontents **(1)**. The next menu will be:

```
Table of Contents Definition

    1 - Number of Levels                         1

    2 - Display Last Level in                    No
        Wrapped Format

    3 - Page Numbering - Level 1        Flush right with leader
                         Level 2
                         Level 3
                         Level 4
                         Level 5


Selection: 0
```

As you can see, you can select up to five levels, each indented under or
subordinate to the one above it. Each level represents a heading and could be
illustrated like the following:

    I.   Level 1
       A.   Level 2
          1.   Level 3
             (a)   Level 4
             (1)   Level 5

The headings in a report could be shown as follows:

      Level 1 —Side Heading
      Level 1 —Side Heading
         Level 2 — Paragraph Heading
            Level 3 — Numbered Paragraph Heading
            Level 3 — Numbered Paragraph Heading
         Level 2 — Paragraph Heading
            Level 3 — Numbered Paragraph Heading
      Level 1 — Side Heading

Additional levels (4 and 5) would be indented further under Level 3. You
can decide how many levels to specify by looking over the text of your
document and determining how much detail is needed in the Table of Contents. However, in long documents it is customary to list, at most, only two
levels of heads in the Table of Contents.

■ Since there are three levels in your report, (1. Side, 2. Paragraph, and 3.
Numbered paragraph heading), press **1** to select number of levels and enter **3**
levels.

Immediately the default page number position will display as flush right with leaders beside each of the three levels.

▣ Select **P**age Numbering (**3**) to display the following menu indicating that other options are also available.

> ```
> 1 None; 2 Pg # Follows; 3 (Pg #) Follows; 4 Flush Rt; 5 Flush Rt with Leader
> ```

If you select **None** (**1**), no page numbers will be printed in the Table of Contents.

If you select **Pg#** Follows (**2**), the page number will be printed immediately following the heading title.

If you select (**Pg#**) Follows (**3**), the page number will be printed enclosed in parentheses immediately following the heading title.

If you select **Flush Rt** (**4**), the page number will be printed at the right margin.

If you select Flush Rt with Leader (**5**), the page number will be printed at the right margin with leaders (periods--. . .) between it and the end of the heading title.

For example, if all five levels were on page 10, the five styles for displaying page numbers would appear as follows:

Style for Level 1
    Style for Level 2   10
        Style for Level 3   (10)
           Style for Level 4   **10**
               Style for Level 5 10

TIP: You may use as few or as many levels as you need, and you can use any page numbering style with any level.

Wrapped items are separated by semicolons and listed one after the other, with the page numbers displayed inside parentheses. Nonwrapped items are stacked one below the other. Both styles are shown as follows:

Wrapped
Title (34); Next Title (42); Next Title (55).

Nonwrapped

Title	34
Next Title	42
Next Title	55

■ For this exercise, indicate page numbering style **5** for level 1 headings (flush right with leaders) and style **4** (flush right no leaders) for levels 2 and 3. Do not wrap the titles.

■ Press **Exit** (**F7**) twice to clear the menu. You have now defined the Table of Contents. In other words, you have identified how it is to be printed and where it is to appear when it is generated.

TIP: | It is a good idea to check Reveal Codes (**Alt-F3**) frequently to see what codes have been inserted and whether they are in the right place so your table of contents will appear as you expect it to.

Marking the Text

Step two is to mark all of the side and paragraph headings in **Reading for Relaxation** for the Table of Contents. To mark the text, do the following:

■ Move the cursor to the first side heading, **Introduction**, and block it, using **Block** (**Alt-F4**).

■ Then press **Mark Text** (**Alt-F5**) to bring up the following menu:

```
Mark for: 1 ToC; 2 List; 3 Index; 4 ToA: 0
```

This menu enables you to mark the block you just highlighted for a Table of Contents (**1**), a List (**2**), an Index (**3**), or a Table of Authorities (**4**).

■ Since you are working on a Table of Contents, press **1** or **T**.

The following prompt will appear:

```
ToC Level:
```

WordPerfect is asking you on which level this heading should be displayed. You have already specified that there are three levels for this Table of Contents and indicated how the page numbers should be shown. Now WordPerfect needs to know which of the three levels this particular heading is so it will know how to print it.

■ Press **1** to indicate that this is a first-level heading.

■ Now work through the rest of your document, marking each heading and specifying its level as 1, 2, or 3.

TIP: Since all of the headings are underlined, you could use the Search command to find the rest of them quickly.

■ Press **Search** (**F2**) to bring up the forward search prompt.

■ Then press **Underline** (**F8**) to indicate a search for the Underline command.

■ Finally, press **Esc** or **F2** to start the search.

The cursor will jump to the next underlined item, the side heading **Choosing Books** <D>.

■ Mark it as a block, press **Mark Text** (**Alt-F5**), choose **ToC** (**1**) and again indicate the level as **1**.

■ Continue using the Search, Block, and Mark Text commands to find and mark the rest of the underlined headings for the Table of Contents.

■ When you get to the paragraph headings, **Real-Life Situations** and **Author-Created Situations**, indicate that they are Level 2.

■ The headings **Historical Accounts**, **Biographies**, **Fiction**, and **Fantasy** are all Level 3 headings.

■ The last heading, **Conclusion**, is a Level 1 heading.

Generating the Table of Contents

When you have marked all the headings, you are ready for step three, which is to generate the Table of Contents.

It does not matter where the cursor is positioned when you generate the Table of Contents. Everything will appear at the point where the Table of Contents definition commands were entered in step one.

■ Again press **Mark Text** (**Alt-F5**) and choose Generate (**6**).

■ When the Mark Text: Generate menu appears, choose **5** to generate the tables.

```
Mark Text: Generate

       1 - Remove Redline Markings and Strikeout Text from Document

       2 - Compare Screen and Disk Documents and Add Redline and Strikeout

       3 - Expand Master Document

       4 - Condense Master Document

       5 - Generate Tables, Indexes, Automatic References, etc.


Selection: 0
```

The following prompt will appear across the bottom of your screen:

```
Existing tables, lists, and indexes will be replaced.  Continue? (Y/N) Yes
```

◼ Enter **Y(es)** to continue. You will then see the prompt **Generation in Progress. Pass: #, Page #** indicating that the Table of Contents is being generated from the text you marked.

As soon as the Table of Contents has been generated, it will display on the screen on the page where you defined it.

TIP: You may need to clean up the format of the items in the Table of Contents. WordPerfect sometimes carries over other commands used in the text, such as Underline, Tab, and Bold, when the items are marked. These extra commands may need to be deleted and/or revised in the Table of Contents.

You may also need to insert a page-numbering command at the beginning of the text to prevent the Table of Contents from being numbered page 1, and the first page of your document page 2. If you wish to do this, position the cursor at the top of the first page of text, press Format (Shift-F8), Page (2), and select New Page Number (6). Start your document with page 1 and press Exit (F7). You could also insert a similar command at the top of the Table of Contents and show the page number as **ii** in Roman numerals. You will probably need to regenerate both the document and the Table of Contents to make the page numbers in both correct.

◼ Save your document as **TofC.18** and print it.

Generating a list of items, such as illustrations, tables, charts, or diagrams, is essentially the same as doing a Table of Contents. You define the numbering style, block the item you wish to include in the list, mark the level, and then generate the list.

To Review

Indicate what you should do in each of the following steps to create a Table of Contents or list:

Define

Mark the items and their level

Generate the table

Summary

In summary, to create a Table of Contents:

a. Enter and save the text.

b. Position the cursor at the top of the document and press Ctrl/Enter to create a new page.

c. Move the cursor to the top of the new page and center the title Table of Contents. Enter any other text you want to include on the page.

d. Press Enter twice to move the cursor down the page. Then press Mark Text (Alt-F5), 5, 1 to define the Table of Contents.

e. Indicate the levels and page number positions for each level.

f. Block each heading or text excerpt to be included in the Table of Contents.

g. Press Mark Text (Alt-F5), 1, and indicate the level of each item.

h. Press Mark Text (Alt-F5), 6, 5, Y(es) to generate the Table of Contents.

i. Do any necessary reformatting.

j. Save and print.

Making an Outline

An outline is similar in format to a Table of Contents because it lists the main topics or ideas in order. However, the outline is developed **before** you write, for your own use to organize your thoughts, sequence your material, and make sure your data is complete. It is therefore more detailed. A Table of Contents is generated **after** you have written and is for the benefit of your readers, to help them find sections or items within the text.

They are alike in several respects, however, including the fact that main topics are shown with indented subtopics underneath. Following are examples of an outline and a Table of Contents developed from the same material:

<u>Outline:</u>

WRITING A PAPER

  I. Format
     A. Margins
     B. Spacing
     C. Appearance
 II. Content
     A. Choice of topic
        1. Should be of importance
        2. Reference material must be available
     B. Organization
        1. Should have a beginning, middle, and end
        2. Ideas should flow logically

<u>Table of Contents:</u>

WRITING A PAPER

  I. Format 2
       Margins
       Spacing
       Appearance

 II. Content 6
       Topic
           Importance
           Reference Materials

       Organization
           Structure
           Logic

Clearly, an outline and a Table of Contents are quite similar in form and content. Since you have already learned how to generate a Table of Contents, let's try an outline. You must write the content, but WordPerfect will make it easy for you to get it on paper in the proper form by automatically adding the letters and/or numbers as you type.

■ For practice, enter the outline previously shown. First, clear your screen. Use the defaults for tabs, margins, and spacing. Center and type the heading **WRITING A PAPER,** and then space down two lines.

■ Press **Date/Outline (Shift-F5)** to bring up the following menu:

```
1 Date Text; 2 Date Code; 3 Date Format; 4 Outline; 5 Para Num; 6 Define: 0
```

■ Select Outline (**4**). The word **Outline** will appear in the lower left-hand corner of your screen.

■ Press **Enter**. The Roman numeral **I.** will appear on your screen.

■ Now press the **Left Indent (F4)** key and type the word **Format**.

■ Then press **Enter** again. Immediately a **II.** will appear on your screen.

■ Press **Tab**, and the **II.** will change to **A**.

■ Press **Left Indent (F4)** and enter **Margins**. Then press **Enter**.

■ When the **II.** reappears, again press **Tab** to bring up the **B**. Then press **Left Indent (F4)** and enter **Spacing**.

■ Continue on until the entire outline is entered. Use the **Tab** and **Left Indent (F4)** keys to control the numbering sequence and format of the text.

■ When you are finished, press **Date/Outline (Shift-F5)** and **4** to turn Outline Off.

■ Save your document as **Outline.18** and print it.

One of the nice features of this command is that it will automatically update itself if you revise the outline. To see how this works, let's add some items to the outline.

■ Position the cursor at the right of the word **Spacing** that appears as item B under **Format**.

◾ Press **Enter** and then **Tab** to place the cursor immediately under the **B**. The letter **C** will appear.

◾ Type **Use of Graphics** beside the new **C**.

◾ **Then** move the cursor down the page a line or two. **Do not press Enter**. Immediately the former **C** will change to a **D**.

◾ Position the cursor at the end of the line that says **Should be of importance.** and press **Enter**.

◾ **Tab** to place the cursor under the **1**. A new **2** will appear. Type **Should relate to assignment**. and move the cursor down the page with the Arrow keys. Again, WordPerfect will automatically update the numbers. Can you see the possibilities of this command?

◾ Save the revised outline as **OutlineA.18** and print it.

As you have just seen, when **Outline** appears in the lower left-hand corner of your screen, WordPerfect automatically supplies outline numbers for you, in I., A., 1., a., etc., sequence. If you wanted to use another format, you could press Date/Outline (Shift-F5), Define (6), and redefine how they are displayed.

◾ To see what is available, press **Date/Outline (Shift-F5)**, Define (6), and take a look.

```
Paragraph Number Definition

    1 - Starting Paragraph Number            1
        (in legal style)

                                        Levels
                            1    2    3    4    5    6    7    8
    2 - Paragraph           1.   a.   i.   (1)  (a)  (i)  1)   a)
    3 - Outline             I.   A.   1.   a.   (1)  (a)  i)   a)
    4 - Legal (1.1.1)       1    .1   .1   .1   .1   .1   .1   .1
    5 - Bullets             •    o    -    ■    *    +    •    x
    6 - User-defined

    Current Definition      I.   A.   1.   a.   (1)  (a)  i)   a)

        Number Style               Punctuation
        1 - Digits                 #    - No punctuation
        A - Upper case letters     #.   - Trailing period
        a - Lower case letters     #)   - Trailing parenthesis
        I - Upper case roman       (#)  - Enclosing parentheses
        i - Lower case roman       .#   - All levels separated by period
        Other character - Bullet        (e.g.  2.1.3.4)


    Selection: 0
```

◾ As you can see, there are a variety of other options available. Experiment with any of them you wish to see how they work. When you are finished, press **Cancel (F1)** twice to return to your document.

To Review

List at least three different numbering styles that WordPerfect will use for Outlines.

Summary

In summary, to create an Outline:

a. Position the cursor where the outline is to begin.

b. Press Date/Outline (Shift-F5),Define (6) to identify a numbering style (if necessary).

c. Press Date/Outline (Shift-F5), Outline (4) to turn Outline On.

d. Enter the text of the outline. Press Tab to change the number or letter. Press Left Indent (F4) to indent.

e. Press Date/Outline (Shift-F5), Outline (4) to turn Outline Off.

f. Save and print.

Developing Indexes

An index lists all the pages on which a certain topic is treated. It can be a very helpful feature in a long document. Take a look at the index at the back of this book. Then let's use the document you named **TofC.18** to see how an index is generated.

◾ Clear your screen and retrieve **TofC.18**.

To create an index, you will use the Define-Mark-Generate sequence again. First, however, you will need to prepare a place for the index to appear.

◾ Move your cursor to the end of your document (**Home, Home, Down Arrow**) and press **Ctrl-Enter** to begin a new page.

◾ With the cursor on the first line of the new page, center and type the title **INDEX**.

- Then press **Enter** three times to insert blank lines between the heading and where the index items are to begin.

TIP: If your document is double-spaced, you will also need to change the spacing to single for the index.

Defining the Index

The first step is to define the index, so do the following:

- Press **Mark Text (Alt-F5)** again, and choose **Define (5)**.

- Choose option **3** to define an index.

- You will be asked if a concordance file is being used. For the time being, press **Enter** to say No.

- When the Index Definition menu shown below appears, type **5** or **L** to have the page numbers of index entries displayed at the right margin with leaders. Your index is now defined.

```
Index Definition

    1 - No Page Numbers

    2 - Page Numbers Follow Entries

    3 - (Page Numbers) Follow Entries

    4 - Flush Right Page Numbers

    5 - Flush Right Page Numbers with Leaders


Selection: 0
```

Marking the Text

Now you are ready to mark the text. Several different types of books are mentioned in **TofC.18**; let's list all the types in the index.

TIP: Use the Search function to find all occurrences of the words you want to mark for the index. (Do not include references to the Table of Contents in your index.) If you wish, you can create a macro to do the searches and mark the text. See your WordPerfect manual for additional instructions on how to do this.)

- ■ Move to the beginning of your document (**Home, Home, Up Arrow**).

- ■ Search for the word **Historical** and highlight it as a **Block (Alt-F4)**.

- ■ Then press **Mark Text (Alt-F5)** and select Index (3) when the following menu appears.

```
Mark for: 1 ToC; 2 List; 3 Index; 4 ToA: 0
```

- ■ When you are asked for a heading, key in **Types** and press **Enter**.

TIP: WordPerfect will print each word you enter just as you typed it. Be sure to capitalize each word as you want it to appear in the index.

- ■ Type **Historical** as the subheading or press **Enter** to accept it, if it is offered.

TIP: WordPerfect will offer the marked word(s) as a possible heading. If you wish to use them, all you need do is press Enter.

- ■ Mark each occurrence of the word **Historical** in the document as a subheading for **Types**.

- ■ Move to the word **Biographies** and block it.

- ■ Again press **Mark Text (Alt-F5)** and choose Index (3).

- ■ Enter **Types** as the heading and **Biographies** as the subheading.

- ■ Repeat the above process with **Fiction** and **Fantasy**. Enter **Types** as the heading each time, and the word you have blocked as the subheading.

- ■ There are also brief references to **mystery**, **adventure**, **western tale**, and **romance**. Move to each of those words and repeat the above procedure (listing **Types** as the main heading and the blocked word as the subheading).

TIP: Remember that you may need to watch how WordPerfect deals with capital letters at the beginning of words when it searches.

- ■ Now block and mark **Choosing Books**. This time, however, you will not have a subheading. Simply press **Enter** when asked for one.

- ■ Also mark the words **Real-Life Situations** and **Author-Created Situations** as headings for the index. Again you will have no subheading.

TIP: To add words to the index that are not in the text, simply enter them as headings or subheadings when requested.

Generating the Index

To generate the index, do the following:

- Press **Mark Text** (**Alt-F5**), Generate (**6**), Generate Tables, etc., (**5**) and **Y(es)**.

    Wait a minute, then bingo! There it is. Amazing.

- Save the file as **Index.18** and print it. It should have both a Table of Contents and an index.

TIP: When the index is generated, WordPerfect inserts a [Def Mark] code at the beginning of the index and an [End Def] code at the end. If you should add text between these codes and then regenerate the index, the additional text will be deleted.

To Review

Give an example of how each of the five index numbering styles would be displayed.

Summary

In summary, to create an index:

a. Make a place for the index by creating a new page at the end of your document and entering the title.

b. Define the index by pressing Mark Text (Alt-F5), 5, 3, concordance file (Y/N), and indicate how the page numbers are to be displayed.

c. Find and block the entries you wish to include in the index.

d. Identify an entry by pressing Mark Text (Alt-F5) and choosing option 3.

e. Enter the main heading.

f. Enter the subheading, if any.

g. Generate the index by pressing **Mark Text** (Alt-F5), 6, 5, Y(es).

h. Save and print.

Using a Concordance File to Create an Index

As easy as it is to create an index with the commands you have just learned, it can be even easier with a concordance file. A concordance file is a separate file that you create, containing all the words you want listed in the index. WordPerfect will then mesh your text file and the concordance file as it generates the index. The page numbers for each entry you have listed in either the concordance file or the text will be listed in the index when it is finished. This saves you having to mark each entry individually within the text of the document. Sound interesting? To see how a concordance file works, let's create another index for **TofC.18**.

Creating the Concordance File

You must make a separate file for the concordance file, clear your screen and do the following:

TIP: If you like, you can switch to Doc 2 to create the concordance file.

◾ Let's assume you will use the same entries in this index as before. Beginning at the left margin at the top of your screen, type each word shown below on a separate line, followed by an Enter command. You may, if you wish, retrieve the **Confile.18** file from the Student Exercise Disk. When you are finished, your screen should look like the following:

```
Types
Historical
Biographies
Fiction
Fantasy
Mystery
Adventure
Western Tale
Romance
Choosing Books
Real-Life Situations
Author-Created Situations



                                          Doc 1 Pg 1 Ln 3" Pos 3.5"
```

TIP: The Enter, or Hard Return, command at the end of each entry in a concordance file is very important and **must** be included. Without it, WordPerfect will not be able to create the index accurately.

◼ Save this new document with the name **ConfileA.18** and clear your screen.

TIP: An index will be generated more quickly if this list is first arranged in alphabetical order. You could use the Sort command to alphabetize the list before saving it if you wished.

Generating an Index with a Concordance File

Even though it doesn't have any subheadings yet, let's generate an index to see how this command works.

◼ Retrieve **TofC.18**.

TIP: Do not be concerned that you may already have an index at the end of this document. It will be erased when the new index is generated.

◼ Move the cursor to the end of the document. Begin a new page, set the spacing to 1 for single-space, and enter the heading **INDEX**.

◼ Press **Enter** two or three times to move the cursor to where you want the index to begin.

◼ Press **Mark Text (Alt-F5)**, **Define (5)**, and **Define Index (3)**. When you are asked for the name of the concordance file, enter **ConfileA.18**.

◼ Choose whatever treatment of page numbers you prefer when the Index Definition menu appears.

◼ Then press **Mark Text (Alt-F5)**, Generate (6) again, and type **5** or **G** to generate an index. Say **Y(es)** to replace existing tables.

In a few seconds the index entries will appear in alphabetical order, with appropriate page numbers. WordPerfect will use each of the items you listed in the concordance file as a heading, and will supply the appropriate format.

◼ Save the document as **TextConA.18** and print it.

TIP: If you should change the numbering style and then regenerate an index, you must be sure to delete the previous [Def Mark] code. Otherwise the index will be generated twice.

Using Subheadings

However, doing it this way, you don't yet have any subheadings. To generate subheadings using a concordance file, you must mark them in the concordance file first. Let's do that now.

◼ **Clear your screen** and retrieve **ConfileA.18**.

TIP: If you prefer, switch to Doc 2 to retrieve **ConfileA.18**.

- Place the cursor on the word **Types**.

- Press **Mark Text (Alt-F5)** and select Index (**3**).

- Enter **Types** as the Index heading.

TIP: When the cursor is on a word, WordPerfect will offer it as the heading. If you wish, you may simply press Enter to accept the word as the heading. This is an easy way to re-enter the same word multiple times without having to retype it each time it is used.

When you are asked for the Subheading, enter **Historical**.

- Repeat this process for the words **Biographies, Fiction, Fantasy, Mystery, Adventure, Western Tale,** and **Romance**, showing **Types** as the heading each time and the different words as the individual subheadings.

Since WordPerfect will use each item in the concordance file as a heading, if a word does not have a subheading, you do not need to mark it further. (This is the case for **Choosing Books, Real-Life Situations** and **Author-Created Situations**.)

TIP: If you want to use a particular entry *only* as a subheading, but do not want it to appear as a side heading, do not enter it as a heading in the concordance file. Simply show it as a subheading when asked.

Therefore, if you wanted Types to appear as a side heading with Historical, Biographies, Fiction, Fantasy, Mystery, Adventure, Western Tale, and Romance as subheadings only, you would omit all the subheading words from the list and enter them when asked.

Since we have included Historical, Biographies, Fiction, Fantasy, Mystery, Adventure, Western Tale, and Romance in our concordance file list and marked them as subheadings also, they will appear as both side headings and subheadings in the index.

- Now that you have marked the words in the concordance file to include subheadings, Save the file as **ConfileB.18** and clear your screen with **Exit (F7)**.

- Again Retrieve **TofC.18**. Move the cursor to the end of the document (**Home, Home, Down Arrow**).

- Press **Ctrl/Enter** to begin a new page. Center the title **INDEX** at the top. Change the spacing to single spacing for the index.

- Press **Enter** three times to move the cursor down the page a little. Then press **Mark Text (Alt-F5)**, and Define (**5**), and Define Index (**3**). Enter **ConfileB.18** as the name of the concordance file, and choose a page number position.

■ Now you are ready to generate the index. Press **Mark Text (Alt-F5)**, **Generate (6)**, **Generate Tables, etc. (5)**, and **Y**(es).

When the index appears, both headings and subheadings will be shown. If you change your document by adding, moving, or deleting text so that the page numbers shown are no longer accurate, simply re-generate the index and the page numbers will be changed. What could be easier?

■ Save this file as **TextConB.18** and print it.

To Review

Indicate what is contained in each of the following:

Table of Contents ____

Index ____

Concordance File ____

Summary

In summary, to create an index using a concordance file:

a. Create and save a separate concordance file listing items to be indexed as headings and subheadings as appropriate.

b. With the main document on the screen prepare a page for the index, with a title.

c. Define the index using Mark Text (Alt-F5), Define (5), 3. Enter the name of the concordance file, and select a page-number position.

d. Generate the index using Mark Text (Alt-F5), Generate (6), 5, Y(es).

e. Save and print the index.

Working with Master Documents

A new feature of WordPerfect 5.0 is the ability to link several documents together with a Master Document and then to expand and condense that document. This capability would be very useful if you were preparing a lengthy report with several parts, writing a book, or working with some other large project. In that case, individual parts or chapters could be created and saved separately, making it easier and faster to work with smaller files. Then the master document would allow you to link them all together so that when you were ready to number the pages, prepare the table of contents, indexes, lists, or do other functions that required access to all files simultaneously, it would appear to WordPerfect as if they were all combined into one large file. Obviously, this command is most useful for longer projects. However, rather than take the time to key in many pages and create several files to use to practice with, let's do a little improvising and use the **Reading.18** file to see how this command works.

▣ Retrieve **Reading.18** to the screen.

▣ Create several small files that can be combined later using the master document. To do this, **Block (Alt-F4)** the first three paragraphs and Save them (F10) using the name **Intro.18**. Then **Block (Alt-F4)** the section headed **Real-Life Situations** including the items numbered 1 and 2. Save the block as **Pt1Real.18**. Now **Block (Alt-F4)** the section headed **Author-Created Situations**, again including items 1 and 2. Save it as **Pt2Auth.18**. Finally, **Block (Alt-F4)** the **Conclusion** and save it as **Concl.18**.

When you are finished, you should have four files named **Intro.18**, **Pt1Real.18**, **Pt2Auth.18**, and **Concl.18**. Even though these files are small, the command would work the same if they were many pages long.

Creating a Master Document

Now let's create a master document and use it to generate a table of contents.

▣ Clear the screen with **Exit (F7)**.

It is important to note that this master document will be a separate file that can contain, among other things, text not found in any of the other files (such as a title or other information), commands that will affect all subdocuments (such as those for a table of contents or index), and commands to integrate other files (so WordPerfect will know where you want imported files put).

▣ Press **Mark Text (Alt-F5)** to bring up the following menu:

```
1 Auto Ref; 2 Subdoc; 3 Index; 4 ToA Short Form; 5 Define; 6 Generate: 0
```

◼ Each of the individual files you created for the parts of the **Reading.18** file (**Intro.18**, **Pt1Real.18**, **Pt2Auth.18**, **Concl.18**) will be considered to be subdocuments in the Master document, so type **2** or **S**.

◼ When you are asked for the Subdoc Filename, type **Intro.18**. WordPerfect will insert a command similar to the following:

```
Subdoc: INTRO.18
```

◼ Move the cursor down two lines, and again press **Mark Text** (**Alt-F5**). Select **Subdoc** (**2**).

◼ When you are asked for the Subdoc Filename, type **Pt1Real.18**. Immediately Subdoc: **Pt1Real.18** will appear on the screen.

◼ Again move the cursor down a couple of lines and indicate **Pt2Auth.18** for the subdocument. Do the same for **Concl.18**. Your screen will look like the following:

```
Subdoc: INTRO.18



Subdoc: PTREAL.18



Subdoc: PTZAUTH.18



Subdoc: CONCL.18


                                      Doc 1 Pg 1 Ln 2" Pos 1"
```

Expanding the Master Document

Now let's expand this document to see what happens.

▣ Press **Mark Text (Alt-F5)** and select **Generate (6)**. The following menu will appear:

```
Mark Text: Generate

    1 - Remove Redline Markings and Strikeout Text from Document

    2 - Compare Screen and Disk Documents and Add Redline and Strikeout

    3 - Expand Master Document

    4 - Condense Master Document

    5 - Generate Tables, Indexes, Automatic References, etc.


Selection: 0
```

▣ Select **E**xpand Master Document (**3**). Immediately a message will appear at the bottom of the screen telling you that WordPerfect is expanding the master document and indicating which file is being retrieved at the moment.

As soon as the expansion is finished, the screen will clear and the combined document will appear. Notice that each subdocument appears at the point where the command was positioned in the master document. As you can see, it is important to consider spacing between parts when entering the commands since the files will be shown where you indicate.

TIP: You will also notice boxes showing where each subdocument starts and ends. These boxes are for information only and will not print.

From this point you can do a number of things and, in general, the file can be used as if it had been created as a single document. Among other things, you could save the expanded document under another name. You could add to or edit it. You could print it, or you could even use it as a subdocument in another master document.

TIP: It is important to note that before printing, the master document must be fully expanded. You cannot print a condensed document.

▣ Right now, let's add a title. Watch the status line to be sure you are on the first line. Then center, bold, and type the following: **MASTER DOCUMENT EXPANSION**. Be sure to leave two blank lines between the title and the Introduction.

◉ Next move the cursor to the fifth paragraph titled **Historical accounts**. Add the words **and frequently contain pictures** at the end of the second sentence.

◉ Number the pages at the bottom in the center.

◉ Finally, move to the beginning of the document, and add a table of contents. You determine settings and style.

◉ When you are finished, print the complete document. Make any needed adjustments and reprint if necessary. Save it as **MastDoc.18**.

Condensing a Master Document

When you have finished working with the entire document, you will probably want to return to the condensed version to save disk space.

◉ To do this, press **Mark Text (Alt-F5)** select **Generate (6)** and **Condense Master Document (4)**.

You will be asked if you want to save the subdocuments with the following prompt:

```
Save Subdocs? (Y/N) Yes
```

Your response at this point will depend on whether you have made changes to the subdocuments while they were expanded in the master document. If so, you will need to save in order to retain the changes.

◉ Since you added text to the end of one of the paragraphs, you should respond with **Y(es)** at this point or the changes will be lost.

◉ WordPerfect will then ask if it should replace the file with the following:

```
Replace INTRO.18? 1 Yes; 2 No; 3 Replace all Remaining: 0
```

■ At this point you could respond with Yes or **Replace all Remaining**. If you respond Yes, WordPerfect will ask you if it should replace each individual file as it comes to it. If you answer **Replace all Remaining**, it will automatically replace all files on the disk with what is on the screen as it saves. Choose either.

■ When the document is condensed, save it as **Mastcond.18**. Notice that it contains the codes for page numbering and the Table of Contents as well as all commands for retrieving other files should you need to do so again.

To Review

List several situations in which a Master Document would be useful.

Summary

In summary, to create, expand, and condense a master document:

1. Create and save individual files.

2. Clear the screen and press Mark Text (ALT-F5). Select Subdoc (2).

3. Identify the name of the files, one by one, to be used as subdocuments.

4. Expand the document by pressing Mark Text (ALT-F5), Generate (6), Expand Master Document (3).

5. Make any necessary editing changes and enter desired commands.

6. Print and/or save if desired.

7. Condense the document by pressing Mark Text (ALT-F5), Generate (6), Condense Master Document (4).

8. Save if desired.

Using Automatic Referencing for Multiple References

Another command new with WordPerfect 5.0 is automatic referencing. Using this command, you can tie or link a title, heading, footnote, etc., (target) to a page number, a paragraph/outline number, a footnote or endnote number, or a graphics box number (reference).

Then if in the process of editing and revising, you move items that have been identified as targets around, the place where they can be found (reference) is easily updated. As a result, when a footnote that was originally on page 10 is moved to page 21, the reference will be automatically changed to show the new location.

To make this work, WordPerfect asks you to identify three things:

1. The *target* or information you are referring to, which could be something like a table, a section of a book, or a quotation.

2. The *reference* which is composed of two parts including (a) where the reference notation is at present and (b) whether the reference should be shown by page number, paragraph number, footnote/endnote number, or graphics box number.

3. The *name* to be used for both the target and the reference. WordPerfect will use this name to match the target and reference notations together as it searches through your document.

TIP: Using this technique, you could mark several targets with the same name. This would then enable you to show more than one item in the reference. For example: (See illustrations on pages 23, 35, 44.) WordPerfect will add the necessary space and comma between items. You can also have more than one reference type in any given reference.

For example, look at the following example of a target and reference.

[Target] Page 5
According to the latest information available from the National Weather Service: "Current weather patterns appear to be changing with slightly warmer temperatures being recorded worldwide over the past several years."

[Reference] Page 9
Statements by weather service personnel (See page 5) indicate a warming trend in the world's atmosphere.

TIP: It may help to remember which is a reference and which is the target if you think of a reference as something referring to or pointing at a target. The target can be identified by the number of the page it is on, the number of the paragraph it is in, its number if it is a footnote or endnote, or by its box number if it is displayed in graphic form.

▣ For some practice with this command, retrieve the **Reading.18** file again. The spacing should be double.

▣ Add the following paragraph to the end.

> Whether your preference is for books based in reality or for creations of the author's mind, you're sure to find many titles that can offer an interesting respite from the pressures of the day.

◻ Save the document as **AutoRef.18.**

Marking the Reference

Now let's add some references to see how this is done.

◻ Move the cursor to the right of the word **reality** in the paragraph you just added. Type the following: **(See Real-Life page)**

◻ Put the cursor in the blank space following the word "page." Now let's mark the reference.

◻ Press **Mark Text (Alt-F5)** and select Auto Ref **(1)**. The following menu will appear:

```
Mark Text: Automatic Reference

    1 - Mark Reference

    2 - Mark Target

    3 - Mark Both Reference and Target




Selection: 0
```

As you can see, it is possible to mark the reference or the target separately or you can mark them both at the same time.

TIP: There are times when you may type information that you know will be used later in a reference. But you have not yet gotten to the point where it should be entered. In that case, you can mark the target as you go along. If so, you need only supply the target name. Then when you get to the place to put the reference, enter it as well. WordPerfect will then match things up and complete the process. If you enter the reference before a target is identified, WordPerfect will place a question mark (?) for the page number and then replace it with the appropriate number when the target is specified.

■ For now, let's mark them both to see how things work, so select **Both (3)** to indicate both. A new menu will appear.

TIP: When using this option, it is best to have the cursor positioned at the reference point before beginning the command.

```
Tie Reference to:

    1 - Page Number

    2 - Paragraph/Outline Number

    3 - Footnote Number

    4 - Endnote Number

    5 - Graphics Box Number

After selecting a reference type, go to the location of the item you want to
reference in your document and press Enter to mark it as the "target".




    Selection: 0
```

Marking the Target

This menu is asking you to identify what the reference should be linked or tied to. As you can see, you have several options.

■ Select **Page Number (1)**.

Immediately a prompt at the bottom of the screen will tell you to:

```
Press Enter to select page.                              Doc 1 Pg 1 Ln 1" Pos 1"
```

■ WordPerfect is asking you to tell it where the target is. Move the cursor to the right of the heading **Real-Life Situations** and press **Enter**.

The next prompt will be:

```
Target Name:
```

A name may already appear. If you wish to use it, simply press Enter. If not, you must supply a name that can be used to mark both the target and the reference. WordPerfect will then keep track of the location of the target names and insert those page numbers at the point of the reference.

■ Type **Real** and press **Enter**. Quick as a wink, WordPerfect will enter the page number of the target marked Real next to the reference. If you look in Reveal Codes, you will see the following codes next to the target and reference: [Target(Real)]. [Ref(Real): Pg 1]. Pretty impressive.

Updating the References

Now, if you should edit or change your document so that the target information (with the code) was no longer on page 1, you could regenerate the references and WordPerfect would simply change the page numbers shown to match the new location. To do this, you could press Mark Text (Alt-F5), Generate (6), Generate Tables, Indexes, Automatic References, etc. (5) and Y(es) to bring everything up to date again.

Using Automatic References in Master Documents

You can also use the automatic reference feature with master documents. In this case, it is possible to have targets in one document and the reference in another. Then you can simply expand the document and regenerate the references to update them.

TIP: If you should enter the target and reference separately, it is important to use the same target name for each command. If you should have several targets to be listed in one reference, each target should also be marked with the common name.

- For additional practice, add the following item at the right of the word **mind** in the last paragraph. **(See Author-Created page.)**

- Then create an automatic reference to tie this reference to the title **Author-Created Situations** as the target.

- When you are finished, resave the document as **AutoRef.18** and print it.

To Review

List the five things that automatic references can be tied to:

Summary

In summary, to create an Automatic Reference:

1. Enter the text to be marked as a target for reference. (This can be marked either now or later.)

2. Enter the text of the notation indicating a reference. (This can be marked either singly or together with the target.)

3. Position the cursor in a blank space following the notation.

4. Press Mark Text (Alt-F5) and select Auto-Ref with 1 or R.

5. Specify the target, reference, or both to be marked.

6. Indicate what the reference is to be tied to.

7. Move the cursor to the target location and press Enter.

8. Supply a target name and press Enter.

Activities

You should have completed the following:

Reading.18   *Reading for Relaxation.18*
TofC.18   *Table of Contents*

Outline.18	*Outline*
OutlineA.18	*Revised Outline*
Index.18	*Index*
ConfileA.18	*Concordance file*
TextConA.18	*Index using Concordance file 1*
ConfileB.18	*Concordance file with subheads*
TextConB.18	*Index using Concordance file 2*
Intro.18	
Pt1Real.18	
Pt1Auth.18	
Concl.18	
MastDoc.18	*Expanded document*
MastCond.18	*Condensed document*
AutoRef.18	*Reading.18 with Automatic References*

Chapter Review

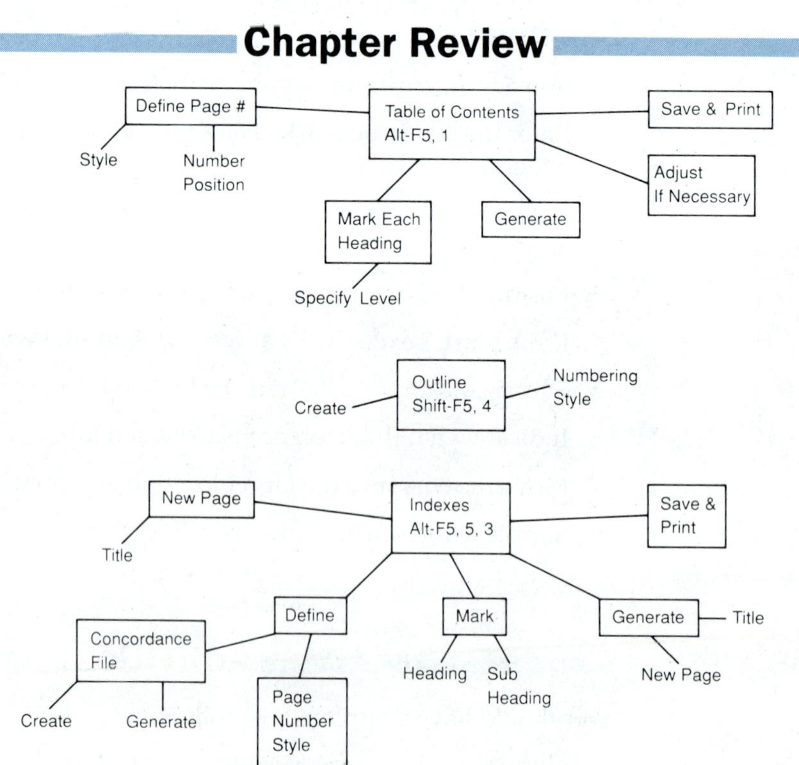

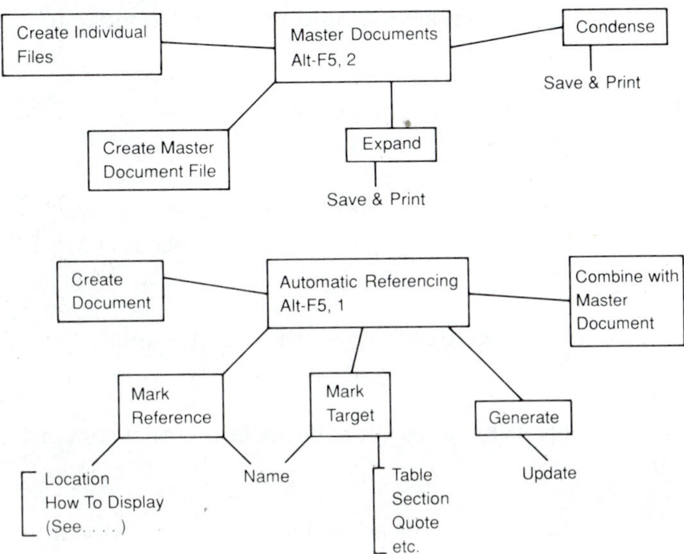

Self-Check Quiz 18

1. When preparing a table of contents, index, etc., what keystrokes must you enter for each of the following?

   Definition: ____

   Marking Text: ____

   Generation: ____

2. Which keys do you press to bring up the menu that allows you to define a table of contents, list or index?

3. How many levels can you include in a table of contents?

4. What is the difference between the way wrapped and nonwrapped lines are displayed in a table of contents?

5. Why must you block text before marking it?

6. Why should you prepare an outline before you write?

7. Which keys should you press to move to the next number in an outline?

8. What is a concordance file used for?

9. What is the difference between the way WordPerfect uses a heading and a subheading with concordance files?

10. What does a concordance file contain?

11. What does WordPerfect do with a concordance file?

12. What is the advantage of a master document?

13. What is a subdocument and how is it used?

14. What happens when you expand the master document?

15. What happens when you condense the master document?

16. What information must you supply when doing automatic referencing?

17. What is contained in the target?

18. What is contained in the reference?

19. What is the target name used for?

20. What must you do to update a document with automatic referencing?

Extra Practice

For extra practice on the material covered in this chapter, do the following:

a. Create a table of contents for the revised material on Trips in **Pract6c**. Use flush right with leaders for the numbering style. Indicate that there are two levels. Have the second level appear in nonwrapped format. When you are finished, save as **Pract18a** and print.

b. Create an index for the same document. Identify words and topics you think would help readers trying to locate specific items in the text and include them in your index. When you are finished, resave as **Pract18b** and print.

c. Create an index using a concordance file with the following entries: Fabrics, Care, Shoes. When you are finished, save as **Pract18c** and print it.

d. Create an outline for **JobsA.3**. When you are finished, save it as **Pract18d** and print it.

e. Using one of your textbooks or other material, create an appropriate table of contents and index. Use a concordance file. Save them as **Pract18e** and print.

f. Create an outline for **Pract18e** and save it as **Pract18f**. When you are finished, print it.

g. Create a master document and identify the files Charlie.1, Acting.4, and Reading.18 as subdocuments. Add the title **WORD PROCESSING EX-ERCISES**. Expand the master document and create a table of contents. Print the document. Then condense and save the document as **Pract18g**.

19

Using WordPerfect for Legal Applications

It's easy to see that word processing can be used for many different tasks. Because legal offices have a number of unique needs, WordPerfect has some distinctive commands designed especially for them. In this chapter you'll learn some specialized techniques for working with legal applications. When you have completed it, you should be able to:

- use the line numbering command to number the lines of a document in a variety of ways.

- define, mark, and generate a Table of Authorities for legal papers, using both long and short form entries.

Numbering Lines

When a document is to be discussed in detail, in a meeting or in correspondence, it is often helpful to number the lines on each page. Then reference can be made to "the information on Line 23," etc., during the discussion or in the letter. Doing so makes it easier for others to find and follow references to a particular point in the document without becoming confused. Line numbering is common for legal documents, so that the judge, attorneys, and others can quickly and easily find their way in a document. Line numbers also allow for precision about exactly what is being referred to, making misunderstandings or mistakes less likely. A document can be printed with line numbers in the left margin for reference, as shown on page 514.

- For practice with this command, retrieve **CharlieA.19**.

- Position the cursor at the beginning of the document (or wherever you want numbering to begin).

- Press **Format (Shift-F8)** to bring up the Format Menu.

- Select **Line (1)** to bring up the Line Format menu:

```
Format: Line

    1 - Hyphenation                         Off

    2 - Hyphenation Zone - Left             10%
                           Right            4%

    3 - Justification                       Yes

    4 - Line Height                         Auto

    5 - Line Numbering                      No

    6 - Line Spacing                        1

    7 - Margins - Left                      1"
                  Right                     1"

    8 - Tab Set                             0", every 0.5"

    9 - Widow/Orphan Protection             No

Selection: 0
```

▣ Select Line **Numbering (5)** and enter **Y**(es) to turn numbering on and bring up the Line Numbering menu shown below:

```
Format: Line Numbering

    1 - Count Blank Lines                      Yes

    2 - Number Every n Lines, where n is       1

    3 - Position of Number from Left Edge      0.6"

    4 - Starting Number                        1

    5 - Restart Numbering on Each Page         Yes


Selection: 0
```

If you accept the defaults, blank lines will not be counted, each line will be numbered without skipping, the numbers will be printed in the left margin slightly more than $1/2$ inch from the edge of the page, and each new page will begin with 1. Any or all of these settings may be changed, depending on your preference and the needs of your document. For now, let's use the default settings.

▣ Press **Exit (F7)** to accept the defaults and return to your document.

▣ If you were creating a new document, you would simply enter the text at this point. Since the text of **CharlieA.19** is already on your screen, simply move to the point where you want the line numbering to end--in this case, the end of the document, using **Home, Home, Down Arrow**. You must now turn line numbering off.

▣ Again, bring up the **Format** Menu by pressing **Shift-F8**.

▣ Select **Line Format (1)** and **Line Numbering (5)**.

▣ Enter **N**(o) to turn line numbering off.

▣ Again, press **Exit (F7)** to return to your document.

TIP: Since the line numbers are printed in the left margin, you will not see them displayed on your screen. If you wish to view them, press Print (**Shift-F7**) and View Document (**6**), to see your document. Press Exit (**F7**) to return to the regular screen when you are finished.

▣ Save this document as **LineNum.19** and print it. Line numbers should appear down the left side of the page like those in the following example.

```
 1        Charlie is the name of my miniature Doberman pinscher who
 2   is just eight months old. Dobermans come of German stock and are
 3   well known as watchdogs and seeing-eye dogs for the blind. Charlie
 4   is a proud specimen of the breed. His chest and forelegs are
 5   powerful, and he has slim, tapering hindquarters. Some Dobermans
 6   are copper-colored, but Charlie is black and tan. He has a short,
 7   smooth coat and generally looks like a terrier.
 8
 9        Charlie is practically full-grown, even though he is less than
10   a year old. He stands about eleven inches high and weighs less than
11   six pounds. He has an independent nature, an iron will, and is very
12   venturesome. When we are outside he is kept on a leash because he
13   has a strong desire to chase anything that moves including flies,
14   birds, kites, cats, and even shadows. On the other hand, he is the
15   kind of dog that becomes attached to just one person; and he gives
16   all his devotion and obedience to me.
17
18        Charlie had a pretty rough start in life. When he was just a
19   few months old, he was taken away from his mother and given to
20   me. That changed his young life completely.




C:\WP50\CHARLIE                                    Doc 1 Pg 1 Ln 1" Pos 5.03"
```

You may go back and change some of the defaults to have WordPerfect skip lines as it numbers them, or change the location where the numbers are printed. Remember to delete the previous line number code first (use Reveal Codes), so that the new codes will work. You can turn Line Numbering On and Off as often as you wish throughout your document.

TIP: This command will number the lines of footnotes and endnotes, but not those in headers and footers.

To Review

The line numbering command is found on the _________________________ menu.

Two options you can specify for format are: _________________________.

Summary

In summary, to Number Lines:

a. Move the cursor to the point where you want Line Numbering to begin.

b. Press Format (Shift-F8) and select Line format (1).

c. Press 5 to select Line Numbering and Y(es) to turn it on.

d. Make any changes in the defaults you wish.

e. Enter the text of your document (or move to the point you want line numbering to end).

f. Again press Format (Shift-F8), Line (1), and Line Numbering (5).

g. Enter N(o) to turn Line Numbering off.

h. Exit, save, and print.

Creating a Table of Authorities

A Table of Authorities is like a legal bibliography, which lists all the legal and other sources used to support an argument in a legal brief and shows every page on which those materials are cited. A list of authorities is useful because it informs a judge or attorney which cases, statutes, or other sources were examined in the preparation of the brief. It also provides a quick reference for complete citations to any materials used in the brief (document).

A Table of Authorities can be divided into as many as 16 sections or categories, and each section can be assigned a different format. The authorities in each section are sorted alphanumerically by WordPerfect. Examples of categories often used are Cases, Constitutional Provisions, Statues, Regulations, Legislative material, and Treaties.

For practice in creating a Table of Authorities, let's first create the document on which it will be based.

Type the following excerpt from a legal brief or retrieve **TablAuth.19** from the Student Exercise Disk.

a. Use the default settings for margins and paragraph tabs.

b. Space the text as illustrated.

c. Underline sections as indicated.

d. Use hard hyphens and spaces between numbers to keep them together.

<u>Post Code Case Law Supports the Application of U.C.C. Section 1-207 (1978) to Conditional Full Payment Check Situations.</u>

1. New York case law strongly supports the application of Section 1-207 to conditional full payment check situations.

> The first state to adopt a position with respect to the application of Section 1-207 to conditional check situations was the state of New York. A long line of cases concluding that Section 1-207 applies in conditional check situations has been decided in New York since the adoption of the U.C.C. <u>See, e.g. Continental Information Systems Corp. v. Mutual Ins. Co.</u>, 77 A.D.2d 316, 452 N.Y.S.2d 952 (1980); <u>Schenectady Steel Co. v. Bruno Trimpoli General Construction Co.</u>, 43 A.D.2d 234, 350 N.Y.S.2d 920 (1974); <u>Aguire v. Harper & Row Publishers</u>, 114 Misc. 2d 828, 452 N.Y.S.2d 852 (1980); <u>Lange-Finn Construction Co. v. Albany Steel and Iron Supply Co.</u>, 94 Misc. 2d 15, 403 N.Y.S.2d 1012 (Sup. Ct. 1978); <u>Hanna v. Perkins</u>, 2 U.C.C. Rep Serv. (Callaghan) 1044 (N.Y. County Ct. 1965). Each of these decisions is at least partially based upon the New York annotations to the Code, discussed earlier.
>
> White and Summers expressed approval of the New York position when they said, "We believe, and virtually all post-Code courts agree, that 1-207 authorizes the payee to endorse under protest and accept the amount of the check without forsaking his claim to any additional sum allegedly due him." J. White & R. Summers, <u>Handbook of the Law Under the Uniform Commercial Code</u> 544 (2d ed. 1980).
>
> 2. Other States Support the New York Position.
>
> The first court of last resort to rule upon the interpretation to be given to Section 1-207 was the Supreme Court of South Dakota. In <u>Scholl v. Tallman</u>, 247 N.W.2d 490 (S.D. 1976), the court concluded that the law in South Dakota supported the application of 1-207 to conditional check situations.

- Save your document as **TablAuth.19**.

A Table of Authorities is created in much the same way as is a Table of Contents, list, or index. That is, you must define it, mark the text to be included, and generate it.

A Table of Authorities is, however, a little more complex than an index or list because it often contains several sections. You must also specify both long and short forms of the reference as well as the format in which they are to be printed. However, WordPerfect can handle the task easily.

Now that you have created a document, you need to (1) insert a new page number code at the top of the first page of your document so that the Table of Authorities will not be counted with the pages of your document, and (2) prepare a page where the Table of Authorities should appear.

◼ Move to the top of the first page of your document and press **Format (Shift-F8)**, Page (**2**), New Page Number (**6**), and type **1** to begin numbering the pages of the document with 1. Otherwise, the Table of Authorities will be shown as page 1 and the references in your table will not be accurate.

◼ Press **Home, Home, Home, Up Arrow** to position the cursor to the left of the new page code you just inserted and press **Ctrl-Enter** to begin a new page.

◼ Enter the title **TABLE OF AUTHORITIES**, centered on the first line of the new page. Press **Enter** three times to add spacing after the title.

Defining a Table of Authorities

There are several items to consider when defining the Table of Authorities.

1. You should decide which type of authority each section of your table will contain. Commonly used categories are Cases, Constitutional Provisions, Statutes, and Miscellaneous.

2. Then you will need to type the headings of the sections you choose to include, in order. After each heading, press the Enter key twice to add spacing.

3. After typing each section heading, you must specify the format of that section, including whether you want dot leaders from the title to the page number, underlining commands to be carried over from the original, and blank lines between the references.

Looking over the report you have just entered, it appears that three sections could be included in the Table of Authorities--Cases, Statutes, and Miscellaneous.

◼ For the first section, type **CASES:** at the left margin (where the cursor is on the fourth line down, about 1.46"). Press **Flush Right (Alt-F6)**, type **Page No.**, and press **Enter**.

◼ To define how you want the items in this section to appear, select **Mark Text (Alt-F5)**, Define (**5**), and Define Table of Authorities (**4**).

You will be asked which section number you wish to define.

◼ Enter **1** for the first section and press **Enter**. When the Table of Authorities Definition menu appears, press **Exit (F7)** to accept and save the defaults for dot leaders, underlining, and space between references, and leave the menu.

```
Definition for Table of Authorities 1

    1 - Dot Leaders                          Yes

    2 - Underlining Allowed                  No

    3 - Blank Line Between Authorities       Yes




Selection: 0
```

◼ Now enter the title for the second section. Using the **Enter** key, move the cursor down three more lines (to the seventh line about 1.92"). Type **STATUTES:** at the left margin and press **Enter**.

◼ Press **Mark Text** (**Alt-F5**), Define (**5**), Define Table of Authorities (**4**), section **2**, and **Enter**. If the menu shows the correct responses next to your preferences for leaders, underlining, and blank lines, press **Exit** (**F7**) to save them and leave the menu. Otherwise change them before exiting.

◼ Space down to the tenth line (about 2.38"). Type **MISCELLANEOUS:** at the left margin and press **Enter**.

◼ Press **Mark Text** (**Alt-F5**), **Define** (**5**), and Define Table of Authorities (**4**), section **3**. Again select the format and press **Exit**.

Marking the Text for a Table of Authorities

When you have finished defining the sections, you can move on to marking the text. There are some things that are different about marking for a Table of Authorities, however.

The first time an authority is cited, it is entered in its entirety. This is called the *long* or *full form* and can be up to 30 lines long. When marking subsequent references to that same authority in the text, you may use a shortened version of the title, or *short form*. The short form is typically a shorthand version or nickname for the long form. For example, a case called *American Food Purveyors v. Lindsay Meats,* 153 G App. 383, 265 S.E.2d 325 (1979) the first time it is marked for inclusion in the Table of Authorities might be shortened to *Lindsay* the next time. Each authority cited must have a unique short-form title.

When you mark an item for inclusion in the Table of Authorities the **first** time, WordPerfect will ask you to supply:

1. A section number from 1 to 16.

2. The format of the long-form text, including spacing, indentation, and the like.

3. The name for the short form.

After marking the reference with the full form the first time, you may then use the short form for each subsequent citation. WordPerfect will match the full- and short-form references for you when the table is generated.

TIP: To edit the long form of a reference you have listed, place the cursor after the [Full Form] command in Reveal Codes. Then leave Reveal Codes and press Mark Text (**Alt-F5**), Define (**5**), and Edit Table of Authorities Full Form (**5**). The reference will be redisplayed on the screen. When you have made the corrections, press Exit (**F7**) to save the change and return to your document.

■ At the beginning of your document, Block **U.C.C. Sec. 1-207 (1978)**. Press **Mark Text** (**Alt-F5**), and type **4** or **A** to mark it for a Table of Authorities. Since this is a Statute, enter **2** for the section number and press **Enter**.

You will see the full-form reference displayed on your screen. You can use most of the editing and formatting features of WordPerfect to edit the text as you want it to appear in the Table of Authorities. You can shorten the lines with the Enter key, indent the beginnings of all lines after the first line, and make any other changes you wish. You can also use underlining and other features.

```
U.C.C. Sec. 1-207 (1978).



Press Exit when done                                    Ln 1" Pos 1"
```

■ Since the full form of this reference is only one line, you can press **Exit** (**F7**) to accept having it listed on one line in the Table of Authorities.

You will now be asked for the short form of this citation. WordPerfect displays the first part of the full-form text as a suggestion for the short form. You can press the Enter key to accept the suggestion, edit the displayed text, or type a different short form of your own. The short form must be unique, since it is used to identify other occurrences of the same authority in the text.

◾ Type **207** as the short form of this reference, and press **Exit (F7)**.

```
Short Form: 207
```

◾ Press **Search (F2)** to search for the next occurrence of this citation. Type **207** as the item to search. Then press **Search (F2)** to start.

TIP: If there are footnotes, headers, footers, and the like, in your document, you will want to use the extended search, with Home, Search (F2).

◾ When 207 is found, press **Mark Text (Alt-F5), 4**. The short-form name you have entered will be displayed. Press **Enter** to mark the text.

```
1 Auto Ref; 2 Subdoc; 3 Index; 4 ToA Short Form; 5 Define; 6 Generate: 0
```

◾ Continue searching and marking until all occurrences of **207** are marked.

◾ Continue to mark the authorities listed in the document. Next, **Block (Alt-F4)** the full reference for **Continental Information Systems Corp. v. Mutual Life Ins. Co.**, including the numbers that follow it. Press **Mark Text (Alt-F5), 4**. Type **1** for the section number and press **Enter**.

On the screen, the reference will look like the following:

```
Continental Information Systems Corp., v. Mutual Life Ins. Co.,77
A.D.2d 316, 452 N.Y.S. 2d 952 (1980)
```

TIP: A common format for a Table of Authorities is to list the case name on the first line, and the rest of the citation on the second and succeeding lines, with all but the first line indented from the left margin. However, if the case name is very short (less than half a line), more of the citation can be on the first line. If the case name is very long, part of the name may be carried to the next line. Generally, the first line of a citation in a Table of Authorities is about $1/2$ to $2/3$ of the line.

■ Edit this citation reference to look like the following:

Continental Information Systems Corp., v. Mutual Life Ins. Co.,
77 A.D.2d 316, 452 N.Y.S.2d 952 (1980)

■ Supply an appropriate short-form name for this reference.

■ Continue marking references in the document. The Schenectady, Aguire, Lange-Finn, Hanna, and Scholl citations are all cases and will be in section **1**. The White & Summers reference should be marked for section **3**. Be sure to **Block (Alt-F4)** the complete citation reference for the full form, and then do a **Search (F2)** for any other occurrences of the citation.

TIP: Be sure to consistently underline all items you wish to find with Search (F2) so that no occurrences will be overlooked.

Generating the Table of Authorities

When all the items to be included are marked, you are ready to generate the table. Though the cursor may be anywhere in the document, the Table will appear where the Table of Authorities definition commands [DefMark:ToA,#] are placed.

■ Press **Mark Text (Alt-F5)**, Generate (**6**), **Generate Tables, Indexes, Automatic** References, etc. (**5**), and **Y**(es) to generate the Table.

■ Then display the Table of Authorities on the screen and check it to be sure everything is correct and complete. If a reference needs to be edited, follow the procedure described in the TIP for editing the full form. If necessary, regenerate the table after the changes have been made.

■ Save the document as **TablAuth.A** and print it.

To Review

What information are you asked to supply when you define and mark the text for a Table of Authorities?

Summary

In summary, to create a Table of Authorities:

a. Put a new page number command at the top of your document.

b. Prepare a page with the title *Table of Authorities*.

c. Move the cursor to the place where you want each section in the Table of Authorities to appear. Type the section heading, press Enter, and then press Mark Text (**Alt-F5**), Define (**5**), **4**.

d. Indicate how each section is to be formatted.

e. Mark the citations to be listed, specifying both the long-form and short-form titles.

f. Press Mark Text (**Alt-F5**), Generate (**6**), **5**, **Y**(es) to generate the Table.

g. Save and print.

Activities

You should have completed the following:

LineNum.19	*CharlieA.1 with lines numbered*
TablAuth.19	*Table of Authorities*

Chapter Review

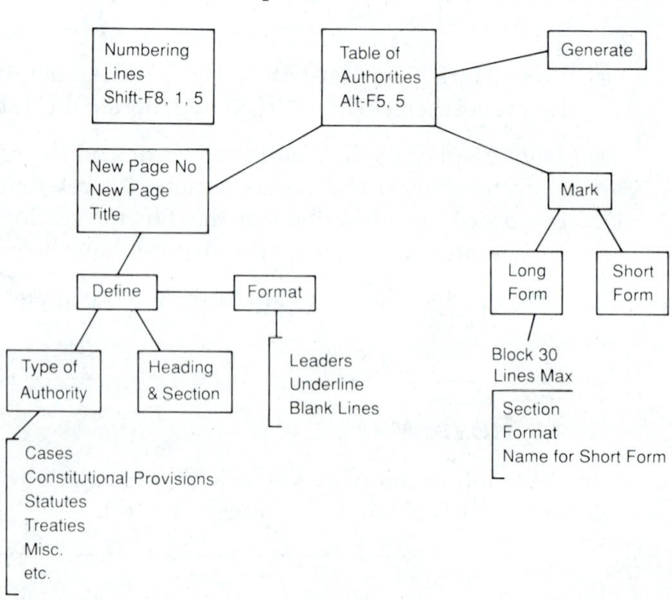

Self-Check Quiz 19

1. When numbering lines, what will happen if you tell WordPerfect to count all blank lines?

2. What command can you use to see the line numbers displayed on the screen?

3. Where are line numbers printed?

4. Place a check beside each of the following that WordPerfect will include when numbering lines:

   Headers _______

   Footers _______

   Endnotes _______

   Footnotes _______

5. What is contained in a Table of Authorities?

6. How many different sections or categories can be included in a Table of Authorities?

7. How does WordPerfect sort the entries in each section of a Table of Authorities?

8. List several categories often used in a Table of Authorities.

9. Why should you create a new page for the Table of Authorities?

10. When preparing a Table of Authorities, what keystrokes are required for each of the following?

    Definition: _______________________________

    Marking Text: _______________________________

    Generation: _______________________________

11. What is the maximum length for a long form entry in a Table of Authorities?

12. What information must you supply for a full-form reference in the Table of Authorities the first time it is entered?

13. Why must you change the page number command at the top of your document when creating a Table of Authorities?

14. What is a short-form reference for a Table of Authorities?

Extra Practice

For extra practice on the material covered in this chapter, do the following:

a. Turn line numbering On. Do not count the blank lines. Then type the first paragraph of **NewsCol.14** in Chapter 14 about selling by mail. When you are finished, save your document as **Pract19a** and print it.

b. Enter the following legal document. Double space the body of the text. When you are finished, add line numbering beginning with "Undisputed Facts" and create a Table of Authorities.

R. ARTHUR JONES, #3257
ATTORNEY FOR PLAINTIFF
678 MAIN STREET
SAN MATEO, CALIFORNIA 94033
TELEPHONE: 662-1449

IN THE THIRD JUDICIAL CIRCUIT COURT OF SAN MATEO,

SAN MATEO DEPARTMENT, STATE OF CALIFORNIA

<table>
<tr><td>JERRY WILSON

Plaintiff,

v

WALTER JONES,

Defendant.</td><td>)
)
)
)
)
)
)
)
)
)
)
)</td><td>MEMORANDUM IN SUPPORT
OF PLAINTIFF'S MOTION FOR
SUMMARY JUDGMENT

Civil No. 23-5-7690 CV.</td></tr>
</table>

UNDISPUTED FACTS

1. On or about January 23, 1987 Defendant, Walter Jones, properly executed and delivered an Installment Promissory Note (the "Note") a copy of which is attached as Exhibit A and is incorporated by reference, having a face amount of $6,532 plus 12% interest payable to the order of Plaintiff, Jerry Wilson.

2. Defendant promised to make payments of $123.72 on the 15th day of each month to Plaintiff at his home beginning February 15, 1987 and terminating upon full payment of the entire amount of the Note together with 12% interest.

3. The Note provided that if Defendant defaulted in the payment of any installment thereon, that the holder could elect to accelerate the Note.

4. Defendant has made no payments on the Note.

5. Plaintiff gave Defendant notice by certified mail of Plaintiff's election to accelerate the entire balance of the Note. A copy of this notice is attached as Exhibit B and is incorporated by reference.

6. Plaintiff was required to obtain counsel to appear on his behalf to assert his claim and has obligated himself to pay a reasonable attorney's fee for such services.

7. Under the terms of the Note Defendant is obligated to Plaintiff for attorney's fees and costs incurred in enforcing the Note.

8. Defendant is indebted to Plaintiff for Defendant's breach of his obligations under the Note in the principal amount of $6,788.00 together with 12% interest from February 24, 1987 until paid, for $55.00 Court costs, and reasonable attorney fees.

ARGUMENT

Defendant alleges facts in his answer which are irrelevant to the outcome of this case. The bare assertion by Defendant that he signed the Note under duress cannot obstruct summary judgment. Defendant's unsubstantiated claim is without merit, therefore Plaintiff must be permitted to recover from Defendant for the amount of the Note, interest, attorney's fees and costs.

DURESS HAS NOT BEEN DEMONSTRATED

Shaw Ranch, Inc. v. Stiller, 619 P.2d 1390, 1391 (California 1980) is dispositive in determining whether a claim for duress may preclude summary judgment.   In affirming a motion for summary judgment on a Promissory Note, the Court noted that to invalidate a contract, the objecting party must "show (1) that the other contracting party committed a wrongful act (2) which put the initial party in fear such as to compel him to act against his will." Id. at 1391. The Court held the defendants did not raise a factual issue by alleging a defense of duress when they failed to demonstrate plaintiff had acted wrongfully. The mere fact that conditions were imposed by a contracting party to insure against his financial loss did not prevent summary judgment. Id. at 1391.

The well accepted rationale of the Court was to avoid labeling all incentives or conditions as duress. If the Court permitted the defense of duress to succeed when one party insisted upon a writing or condition, the validity of most contracts could be easily challenged. Id. at 1392. This was substantiated by Jensen and Warren in their interpretation of the Uniform Commercial Code Section 2-352 (1981) A.D.3rd 643, 321.

In <u>Morgan v. Industrial Design Assoc.</u>, 657 P.2d 751, 753 (1982), the Supreme Court of California recognized the Plaintiff's allegations of duress as an attempt to fabricate a factual dispute. The Court affirmed the Third District Court's grant of summary judgment. Further, the Court held that whether undisputed facts are sufficient to constitute duress is a question of law. <u>Id</u>. at 753.

This Court should rule on the identical question of law and accordingly grant summary judgment in favor of Plaintiff.

<u>AWARDING ATTORNEY FEES IS APPROPRIATE</u>

Courts routinely award attorney's fees and costs when granting motions for summary judgment to enforce promissory notes which provide for the payment of attorney's fees and costs. <u>See Shaw Ranch, Inc. v. Stiller</u>, 619 P.2d 1390 (1980), <u>Landward Real Estate, Inc. v. Peck</u>, 672 P.2d 746, 752 (1983). Defendant agreed to pay reasonable attorney fees, legal expenses and lawful collection costs in addition to principal and interest in the event of default under the Note. In light of the parties' agreed allocation of these expenses and California Supreme Court decisions, Plaintiff is entitled to an award of attorney fees and costs.

<u>SUMMARY JUDGMENT SHOULD BE GRANTED</u>

Summary judgment is the appropriate remedy at any time it becomes apparent "there no genuine issue as to any material fact and that the moving party is entitled to judgment as a matter of law." Rule 56 (c), California Rules of Civil Procedure.

It is undisputed that Defendant executed a Note in favor of Plaintiff and then breached his obligations thereunder by failing to make payments. In view of the decisive facts, summary judgment is the appropriate remedy. Accordingly, Plaintiff respectfully requests judgment.

DATED this ________ day of ______________ 1987.

____
R. ARTHUR JONES
Attorney for Plaintiff

<u>MAILING CERTIFICATE</u>

I, the undersigned, hereby certify that I mailed true and accurate copies of the foregoing Motion for Summary Judgment together with supporting affidavits, postage prepaid, this _________ day of ____________ 1987, addressed as follows:

JERRY WILSON
233 Edwards Drive
San Mateo, California 94522

Supplementary Exercises

Congratulations! You have just been hired as Business Manager and Administrative Assistant to Mr. James Brown, Vice President of Leisure Services Incorporated. Leisure Services owns and operates Hideaway Lodge resort hotels located at some of the most popular western vacation areas: Jackson Hole, Wyoming; Yellowstone National Park, Montana; Grand Canyon, Arizona; Yosemite National Park, California; and Lake Powell, Utah. Your responsibilities are to supervise the main-office personnel and functions, including accounting, personnel, coordinating and scheduling events for the resorts, and maintaining communication among the various different resorts.

Use the WordPerfect skills you have learned to complete the following documents, which are designed to give you additional practice with word-processing operations. Be sure to proofread carefully and correct any errors. Follow the format instructions that accompany each assignment. If certain aspects of the format are not specified, use your best judgment. After completing the exercises, submit them to your instructor.

NOTE: These exercises are keyed to the Chapters in the text and may be completed as soon as you have finished the corresponding material in the book. For instance, you should be able to do Supplementary Exercise 7 as soon as you have completed the exercises in Chapter 7.

Supplementary Exercise 1

Type the following document—the first page of an employee handbook—following the format instructions given.

Format

Use default settings for margins, tabs, and spacing.
Proofread carefully and correct any errors you find.
Save as **SE1** and print.

Welcome to Leisure Services Incorporated! We are glad to have you as a member of the staff.

Leisure Services is a resort-hotel management company. It owns and operates Hideaway Lodge resort hotels at some of the most beautiful and popular western vacation sites. Each hotel is uniquely designed to accentuate the natural beauty of the area.

As an employee in the main office of LSI, you will be assisting us in our efforts to provide quality service at all of our resorts. The work you do will help assure that all hotel visitors and employees will be served in an efficient and timely manner.

Our facilities are known for their family-oriented atmosphere. The staff at each of the hotels is trained to extend warm, friendly, and courteous service to all of the guests we serve.

The visitors at our resort hotels spend their days relaxing, swimming, golfing, playing tennis, exercising, and exploring the fascinating shops and points of interest around the hotel. Some of our resorts offer special attractions such as boating, horseback riding, and fishing. Each hotel has two restaurants—one for family-style, casual meals and one for more formal dining. There is also nightly entertainment offered for the guests' enjoyment.

All employees of LSI are expected to conduct themselves in a professional manner at all times. You are expected to be punctual, abide by the rules and regulations of the company, and do your best in your assigned duties. Each employee, no matter what level your position, is a key member of the team we are building to provide the best service possible. We count on you to perform your duties to the best of your ability and to respect your supervisor and your coworkers at all times.

Detailed procedures for handling work assignments are essential for the successful operation of a service-oriented business such as LSI. The procedures that have been developed to facilitate accurate and thorough completion of each type of work assignment are detailed in the following pages of this handbook. As you are called upon to assist the executive staff in various assignments, read the related procedure carefully and study the examples. Refer to the procedures frequently as you perform the work assigned to you. This will help you handle your work with a minimum of supervision. When you need additional information about the assignment, ask your supervisor for clarification.

We feel that employee suggestions for improvement are always important. Any ideas you have that might improve the service we offer to our guests, reduce costs, or improve our operations will be given careful consideration for implementation. Just put them in the suggestion box located by the time clock.

We are glad to have you as part of the Leisure Services staff and hope you will enjoy working as part of the team.

Supplementary Exercise 2

Type the following revision of the Parking Regulations.

Format

Use the default settings for margins, tabs, and spacing.

Use quick cursor movement and delete commands as you work with the document.

Save as **SE2** and print two copies.

PARKING REGULATIONS
LEISURE SERVICES INCORPORATED

Parking areas at Hideaway Lodge resort hotels are designated as employee, guest, or handicapped.

Parking in employee lots is allowed only with the appropriate sticker displayed in the rear window of the vehicle. Employees are not allowed to park in the guest parking areas; violators are subject to immediate dismissal.

Employee parking stickers are available at the Director's office in each of the Hideaway Lodge resorts.

A sticker is valid for the duration of the staff member's employment, and should be placed in the lower left-hand corner of the rear window of the vehicle. Apply the sticker according to the instructions printed on the back. Stickers for motorcycles and scooters should be placed on the back bumper.

Employees who change vehicles during the year should remove the old sticker and return the remnants of it before a new sticker will be issued. The sticker must also be returned at the termination of employment with LSI.

Guests of the hotel are given a guest parking permit when they register. The dates of their stay are listed on the permit and the permit is valid only during the days listed. Unauthorized vehicles parked in the guest parking areas will be towed away at the owner's expense.

Areas marked for handicapped parking are reserved for those who have a special handicapped parking permit visible in the front window of the vehicle. These permits are available at the hotel check-in desk when a guest registers.

Supplementary Exercise 3a

Type the following revision of the Employee Fair Treatment Policy for the employee handbook.

Format

Set both left and right margins at 1½ inches.

Set eight-space paragraph indentations (convert to inches).

Double-space the document.

Triple-space after heading and before body of document.

Turn the Justification off.

Save as **SE3a** and print.

EMPLOYEE FAIR TREATMENT POLICY
LEISURE SERVICES INCORPORATED

Leisure Services Incorporated believes that every employee, regardless of position, should be treated in a fair and just manner, and with respect.

Employees will be considered for training and promotions strictly on the basis of their qualifications.

In spite of our best efforts, mistakes may be made. It is our desire to correct such mistakes as soon as they happen. NO MEMBER OF MANAGEMENT IS TOO BUSY TO HEAR AND RESPOND TO YOUR COMPLAINTS OR PROBLEMS.

If you have a complaint or a problem, you should follow the steps below:

First, tell your immediate supervisor. Most problems can be solved at this level if you are willing to accurately outline the problem to your supervisor. Your supervisor wants to resolve the problem as much as you do. Feel free to express ALL your concerns so that a meaningful solution to the problem can be found.

Second, if your problem has not been resolved to your satisfaction, contact your manager. He or she will then endeavor to evaluate all the facts and settle the problem in a fair way.

Third, if you still feel that the problem is not resolved, your manager will make an appointment for you to see the Personnel Director.

For problems that you want to discuss only with the Personnel Director, feel free to contact him or her directly.

It is our desire that all employee suggestions and complaints be given full and fair consideration. Be assured that there will be no recrimination or discrimination against an employee who registers a suggestion or complaint.

Supplementary Exercise 3b

Type the following list of Leisure Services Incorporated Executive Staff.

Format

Set both left and right margins at 1½ inches.
Set a left-justified tab at 5.0", with leaders between the two columns.
Double-space between entries.
Triple-space between the heading and the body of document.
Save as **SE3b** and print.

LEISURE SERVICES INCORPORATED
EXECUTIVE OFFICERS
JULY 1, 19__

President	Stephen L. Parley
Vice President	James Brown
Executive Assistant	Janelle Swenson
Controller	Dave Stilinger
Sales Director	Carter W. Ellison
Advertising Director	Susan P. Collings
Marketing Director	Lawrence J. Thomas
Hotel Services Director	Lisa Pickford

Personnel Director	James P. Stevenson
Convention Director	Harvey M. Anderson
Business Manager	(your name)

Supplementary Exercise 4a

Type the following letter.

Format

Set left and right margins at 1.8 inches.

Use full block style with mixed punctuation.

Indent paragraphs ½ inch.

Put your initials as typist.

Begin 2 inches down the page or center it on the page by positioning the cursor in upper left corner and pressing Shift-F8, Page(2), Center(1), Yes.

Save as **SE4a** and print.

Today's date

Mr. John Michaelson
Myers and Bowling, CPA's
638 Boulder Avenue
Boise, ID 83709

Dear Mr. Michaelson:

Thank you for your inquiry about the facilities and services of Hideaway Lodge in Jackson Hole, Wyoming.

We are enclosing a brochure describing all the services that are available for your executive retreat. We take great pride in providing a warm, friendly atmosphere along with facilities that will enhance any business meeting.

As you will see, we can offer you a choice of five different meeting rooms, use of either a banquet room or a private dining room for your meals, and the option of Continental breakfasts and/or refreshment breaks.

Recreational activities available for your group would include swimming, golf, horseback riding, fishing, and tennis. You may also take advantage of a sightseeing trip through the beautiful Teton Mountains. If you have any questions or would like additional information, please call our toll-free number, 1-800-555-1234. We will be happy to help you plan the details for your retreat.

Sincerely,

Harvey M. Anderson
Convention Director

(your initials)
Enclosure

Supplementary Exercise 4b

Type the following letter.

Format

Set both left and right margins at 1½ inches.
Use modified block style with mixed punctuation.
Put your initials as typist.
Begin three inches down or use center Page command.
Save as **SE4b** and print.

Today's Date

Mr. John Michaelson
Myers and Bowling, CPAs
638 Boulder Avenue
Boise, ID 83709

Dear Mr. Michaelson:

Thank you for choosing the Hideaway Lodge in Jackson Hole, Wyoming for your recent executive retreat. We hope your stay at the Hideaway was pleasant and that you enjoyed the services as much as we enjoyed having you stay with us.

We hope that you and your executives will stay with us again and that you will recommend the Hideaway Lodge to your family and friends.

If we can be of further assistance in planning future business or personal visits to any of the Hideaway Lodges, please contact us at our toll-free number, 1-800-555-1234.

Sincerely,

Harvey M. Anderson
Convention Director

Supplementary Exercise 4c

Type the following menu.

Format

Center each line.
Bold the first line of each menu item.

Triple-space between the date and the menu items.
Triple-space between menu items.
Save as **SE4c** and print.

HIDEAWAY LODGE
Dinner Menu
August 13, 19__

BROILED HALIBUT
with lemon and herb butter
Rice pilaf
$8.75

PRIME RIB (8 oz.)
served au jus
Baked potato
$11.95

CHICKEN CACCIATORE
onions, peppers, and mushrooms
in an herb tomato sauce
Buttered noodles
$9.75

ROULADES OF BEEF
stuffed with mushrooms and mushroom sauce
Duchess potatoes
$10.95

All menus include:
  your choice of soup du jour,
    garden salad, or fruit cup
  vegetable of the day
  hot dinner roll
  coffee, tea, or milk

DESSERTS

Ice cream or sherbet	$1.25
Fruit or cream pie	$1.95
Walnut layer cake	$2.25
Carrot cake	$2.25
Chocolate parfait	$2.50
Black Forest cake	$3.00

Supplementary Exercise 4d

Type the following policy on employee personal appearance.

Format

Set both left and right margins at 1½ inches.
Indent paragraphs at ½ inch.
Use double-spacing throughout.
Use auto hyphenation.
Use correct format.
Bold and underline all side headings.
Save as **SE4d** and print.

POLICY ON EMPLOYEE PERSONAL APPEARANCE
LEISURE SERVICES INCORPORATED

General:

All employees of Leisure Services Incorporated, regardless of position, are expected to be neat and clean in clothing and personal appearance. Generally accepted standards of personal hygiene are used as a guideline. If you are in doubt, consult your supervisor.

Office Staff:

Members of the general office staff should dress in clothing that is compatible with a businesslike environment. Dresses and skirts should be no shorter than one inch above the top of the knee. Pants and blouses should represent the image of a business office, not a casual gathering. Jeans, painters' overalls, tank tops, etc. are not permitted.

Resort Staff:

So that our guests, management, and other staff members can identify you as an employee of the resort, a uniform and name tag are provided for you. They should be worn at all times while you are on duty at the resort. Uniforms must be kept clean, and must not be shorter than one inch above the knee. Uniformed employees must be in complete uniform whenever they are in guest areas of the resort.

Supplementary Exercise 4e

Type the following memo.

Format

Set both left and right margins at 2 inches.
Set up the heading as shown.
Change the tab-alignment character to : (colon), and use tab alignment to line up the heading as shown.
Triple-space between the heading and the body of the memo.
Single-space paragraphs with a double space between paragraphs.
Save as **SE4e** and print.

      TO: All LSI Office-Support Personnel

  FROM: Janelle Swenson

  DATE: August 4, 19__

SUBJECT: Microcomputer Training

On August 13, Mr. Paul Samson of Computers Unlimited will offer training on the microcomputers that have recently been installed in our office. There will be two separate training sessions, one from 9 to 11 a.m. and another from 1 to 3 p.m. <u>All office support personnel must attend one of these training sessions.</u>

Supervisors and managers should arrange schedules so that all offices are covered during these times and all the employees attend one of the sessions.

Please indicate on the enclosed scheduling form the names of the employees who will attend the morning session and the names of those who will attend the afternoon session. Return the completed form to my office by 5 p.m. on August 7.

(your initials)
Enclosure

Supplementary Exercise 5

Retrieve **SE3a** and make the following changes.

> Use the speller option, and check the spelling for the entire document.
>
> Use the Thesaurus and find an alternate word for the word "fair".
>
> Use search and replace to change all appropriate occurrences of "fair" with the new word you have selected.
>
> Save the revised document as **SE5** and print.

Supplementary Exercise 6

Retrieve **SE1** and make the following changes:

Search and Replace the initials LSI with Leisure Services Incorporated for the entire text.

Move the paragraph that begins with the sentence "As an employee..." to follow the paragraph that ends with the sentence "There is also nightly entertainment...."

Save the document as **SE6** and print.

Supplementary Exercise 7a

Type the following document.

Format

Set left and right margins at 1½ inches.

Put the entire announcement on one page.

Triple-space after the heading.

Single-space the text with a double space between paragraphs.

Use tab-alignment and left-indent features for the indented information section.

Use hard hyphens for the word "corn-on-the-cob."

Save as **SE7a** and print.

LEISURE SERVICES INCORPORATED
ANNUAL SUMMER PICNIC

MARK YOUR CALENDARS! It's time for our Annual Summer Picnic again! The picnic is scheduled for September 4, and everyone is invited to come and have a good time.

Stacy Kimball and Inez Lopez are in charge of the activities this year. They tell us that it will be an event you will not want to miss.

Here are the details, so you will know the who, what, when, where, and cost:

WHO:	All employees of LSI and their families or a guest.
WHAT:	<u>Food</u>—barbecued chicken, a variety of salads, baked beans, corn-on-the-cob, chips, drinks, and watermelon.
	<u>Activities</u>—softball, volleyball, relay races, and contests.
WHEN:	September 4, 19__; from 11 a.m. to 5 p.m.
WHERE:	Little Creek Park
COST:	Free!

Whether you plan to attend or not, please return the form at the bottom of this announcement to Ms. Swenson by Wednesday, September 1. Please indicate how many of your family will be attending with you. That will allow us to have an accurate count when we make the final arrangements for the food and activities.

I (will, will not) be attending the picnic on September 4, 19____.

Name ______________________________________ Number __________

Supplementary Exercise 7b

Type the following information sheet on Safety Rules.

Format

Use default settings for the margins and tabs.
Double-space the text.
Single-space the numbered items, and indent them ½ inch from the left and right margins.
Double-space between numbered items.
Save as **SE7b** and print.

LEISURE SERVICES INCORPORATED
SAFETY RULES

Safe work habits are a necessary part of any job to prevent serious injury. You need to learn the possible hazards of your job and use the safety devices that are provided. Company safety regulations have been established to help you avoid injury. ALL EMPLOYEES ARE EXPECTED TO PRACTICE THE FOLLOWING SAFETY RULES:

1. Report <u>every</u> accident or injury to your supervisor immediately, no matter how slight.

2. Ask for instructions before using any equipment with which you are not familiar.

3. When lifting, bend your knees and keep your back as straight as possible while crouching down. Avoid jerking or twisting as you lift, and lift slowly. If the item is too heavy, get someone to help you.

4. Walk up and down stairs one at a time, using a free hand to hold onto the handrail.

5. Running and horseplay are strictly forbidden in company buildings and on the grounds.

6. Keep your area clear and free of debris. This will promote safety and efficiency.

7. Obey "No Smoking" rules to avoid a fire that could endanger your life and the lives of others.

8. If you become aware of any unsafe conditions or practices, report them to your supervisor.

9. Use the safety devices provided by your supervisor.

10. Follow any additional safety rules outlined by your supervisor.

First-aid kits are located at the check-in desk, by the swimming pool, and in the restaurant kitchens. Locate the one nearest your working station and become familiar with its contents. If you use the kit to take care of an injury, please fill out the first-aid log that accompanies the kit.

Supplementary Exercise 8

Type the following letter.

Format

Use full-block style with mixed punctuation.
Set the margins at 1½ inches.
Use correct letter format and center on the page.
The writer of the letter is J. P. Stephenson, Personnel Director.
Save as a locked document using the name **SE8** and any password you choose.
Print.

(Today's date)

Simplex Business Systems, Inc.
ATTENTION: Personnel Manager
3567 Washington Avenue
Salt Lake City, UT 84003

Gentlemen:

This letter is in reply to your request of July 6, 19__, in which you ask for a brief summary of Susan Collings' work record with our firm.

Susan was employed by LSI as a clerk in the business office from December 3, 1985 until March 3, 1987. She has a pleasant disposition and was friendly and neat. However, her work record with our company indicates that she was far from reliable. She frequently arrived late for work, took extended coffee and lunch breaks, and her work was completed carelessly and often had to be redone.

We dislike having to give a negative report on a former employee, but under the circumstances feel obligated to relate the record as it exists.

Sincerely,

Supplementary Exercise 9

Do the following:

Format

Create a style for the letter in **SE4a**. Include margins, tabulations, and
other appropriate commands.

Add a document summary and comment to **SE2** indicating Ms.
Janelle Swenson as the author, and your name as typist. The comment should say that this revison is effective on July 2, 1989.

Save as **SE9** and print.

Supplementary Exercise 11

Create the following macros:

1. Format for a document that has 1½ inch margins, ½ inch paragraph
    indentation, widow/orphan on, and justification off. Save it as **FORMAT**.

2. A memo-heading form using tab align feature to align the colons in the
    format shown below. Save it as **MEMO**.


```
                    LEISURE SERVICES INCORPORATED


           TO:
         FROM:
      SUBJECT:
         DATE:       (Insert date with Shift-F5)
```

Supplementary Exercise 12

Complete the following merge exercise.

Create a secondary merge file from the following list.

Create a primary file from the letter below showing the correct field codes.

Merge the primary and secondary files. Save the merged letters as SE12.

Secondary File Format

Field 1 is the person's full name.
Field 2 is the business name.
Field 3 is the street address.
Field 4 is the city, state, and zip code.
Field 5 is the name for the salutation.
Save as SEC12a.

Mr. Leonard Rushton
ACME Business Services
6312 West 13 Street
Denver, CO 70202
Mr. Rushton

Mr. Anthony Johnston
Johnston & Johnston
1011 Pacfic Avenue
San Diego, CA 90873
Mr. Johnston

Mr. Milton Beatty

529 Roosevelt Avenue
Seattle, WA 90821
Mr. Beatty

Mr. Paul Ryan
Ryan Office Systems
22 Busson Road
Portland, OR 94501
Mr. Ryan

Miss Ann Jeffreys

7423 Kings Place
Phoenix, AZ 70342
Miss Jeffreys

Mrs. Joan Stadler
Computer Training Int'l
734 Creek Road
Salt Lake City, UT 80611
Mrs. Stadler

Ms. Barbara Lawson
Lake Business College

Silver Lake, ID 80761
Ms. Lawson

Mrs. Laura Zimmerman
Modern Hotel Design
6721 Greenwood Drive
Boise, ID 89431
Mrs. Zimmerman

Mr. Larry Stevens
Brown and Stevens, CPA's
Third and Vine Streets
Sacramento, CA 90706
Mr. Stevens

Mr. Frank Thompson
Superior Restaurant Supplies, Inc.
284 Spring Street
Pleasant Hill, CA 93420
Mr. Thompson

Primary File Format

Center the letter on the page.
Set left and right margins of 1½ inches.
Use modified block style.
Use mixed punctuation.
Follow standard letter format.
Save as **PRIM12a**.

(Today's Date)

(Field 1)
(Field 2)
(Field 3)
(Field 4)

Dear (Field 5):

Thank you for your interest in Hideaway Lodge.

Enclosed is a brochure that describes the meeting facilities and catering services available at any of the Hideaway Lodge resort hotels. Our warm, friendly atmosphere, beautifully decorated rooms, and excellent food will enhance any meeting or conference you may be planning.

We strive to meet any special needs your group may have. For example, several of our meeting rooms have recently been equipped with new electrical systems that will accommodate the use of computers and other new, technology-related equipment.

Our varied recreational offerings provide opportunities to enjoy favorite activities and acquire new skills.

We hope you will find the brochure helpful and informative. Please don't hesitate to call us, (Field 5), at 1-800-555-1234 if you need any additional information or service.

Cordially,

Carter W. Ellison
Sales Director

(your initials)
Enclosure

Supplementary Exercise 13a

Enter the following database and then apply the directions given after the database.

Format

Set tabs at 2.5, 3.5, 5.0, and 6.0 inches.
Treat the column headings as shown.
Center on the page.
Save as **SE13a** and print.

Hideaway Lodge Contracts
May, 1989

Contract	Date	Contact	Room	Charge
587-001	7, 8	C. Brooks	C	$1,932
587-008	23	Z. Williams	D	1,057
587-003	10	B. Jackson	A	6,409
587-006	10	D. Franklin	B	1,474
587-002	9	L. Jones	C	1,049
587-005	6	A. Thompson	D	2,700
587-004	5	H. Miller	B	767
587-007	14	D. Maxwell	A	6,468
587-009	27	K. Anderson	B	665

Perform the following sorts. Save and print each sort.

1. Sort the entries into numerical order by the contract number. Save as **Sort1**.

2. Sort with Date as key 1 and Room as key 2. Save as **Sort2**.

3. Sort according to charge, with the highest charge first and the lowest charge last. Save as **Sort3**.

Supplementary Exercise 13b

Do the following merge sorts with the secondary file saved as **SEC9b**. Save and print each sort.

1.   Sort alphabetically by last name. Save as **Sort4**.

2.   Sort by state (Key1) and then by city within the state (Key2). Save as **Sort5**.

Supplementary Exercise 13c

Enter the following table. Then do a paragraph sort alphabetically according to the first column.

Format

Set tab at 4.0 inches.
Center on the page.
Save the table as **SE13c** and print.
Save the sort as **Sort6**.

HIDEAWAY LODGE
Refreshment Breaks

Tea Time	Three blends of tea, coffee, assorted open-face sandwiches, chocolate mints ($4.25/person)
Ice Cream Coolers	Ice-cream sundaes, homemade ice cream, ice-cream floats ($3.00/person)
Summer Refreshers	Fresh lemonade, popsicles, flavored slushes, ice-cream bars ($2.50/person)
Winter Warmups	Coffee, tea, hot chocolate, assorted cookies, doughnuts, cheese and crackers ($4.50/person)

| Ballgame Antics | Hot dogs, soft pretzels, chips, beer, soft drinks ($3.75/person) |
| Healthy Happenings | Fresh fruits, granola bars, yogurt, mineral water ($3.50/person) |

Supplementary Exercise 14a

Type the following table.

Format

You determine tab settings for the columns.
Center the table on the page.
Center each line of the column heading over the column.
Double-space the body of the table.
Save as **SE14a** and print.

HIDEAWAY LODGE
Meeting Room Capacities and Charges

Room	Theater Style	Schoolroom Style	Banquet Style	Reception Style	Charge Per Hour
A	225	125	180	250	$35
B	150	90	125	150	$25
C	100	60	90	130	$20
D	50	30	40	50	$15
A/B	400	225	330	400	$55

Supplementay Exercise 14b

Type the following text for a company newsletter.

Format

Set left and right margins at 1½ inches.

Center the main heading before setting up the columns.

Use 2 evenly spaced, newspaper style columns.

Leave 10 blank lines at the end of the first article to allow a picture to be placed between the articles.

Insert your name where indicated in the text.

Save as **SE14b** and print.

LSI NEWSLETTER

LSI MANAGMENT WORKSHOP SERIES

Ms. Janelle Swenson, Executive Assistant, has announced a series of workshops to be given during the coming year for all supervisory and management personnel in the main office of Leisure Services Incorporated.

The workshops are designed to inform all levels of management about the implications and applications of the computer and related technology for the services offered by LSI.

Each workshop will run for four weeks, with a two-hour session once a week. Management personnel should make arrangements to attend the workshops on the dates listed on the registration form.

These workshops have been offered in other travel-service related organizations, and have proven very effective at helping all levels of management understand the uses and benefits of computers.

CHANGES ANNOUNCED

Mr. Stephen L. Parley, President of LSI, recently announced the promotion of Janelle Swenson from Business Manager to the newly created position of Executive Assistant. Ms. Swenson has been with LSI since September 1980 and worked in the Personnel, Marketing,

Sales, and Hotel Services departments before being named Business Manager in June 1986. Her wide variety of assignments at LSI along with her previous work experience in other organizations give Janelle the background to handle this new, demanding, and challenging position.

Replacing Ms. Swenson as Business Manager will be (your name). As a recent graduate of the Business Management program at State University, (your name) was named outstanding Business graduate and has had previous experience in travel-service organizations. We welcome (your name) as a new member of the LSI team.

Supplementary Exercise 12c

Type the following table using the parallel columns feature.

Format

Choose whatever margin and column settings you wish.
Center the table on the page.
Save as **SE14c** and print.

LSI MANAGEMENT LECTURE SERIES

Dates	Topic	Speaker
Sept. 7, 14, 21, 28	The Personal Computer and Its Impact on Management	Ryan Collings, President The Management Group Phoenix, Arizona

Oct. 5, 12, 19, 26	Data Security—An Information-Age Concern	Susan Lindsey, Consultant Data Security Systems, Inc. San Francisco, California
Nov. 2, 9, 16, 23	An Experimental Approach to Electronic Mail	Pauline Hayward, Professor UCLA Los Angeles, California
Dec. 7, 14, 21, 28	Networking Computers in the Office	Sam Porter, Vice President Standard Systems Denver, Colorado

Supplementary Exercise 14d

Type the following financial statement.

Format

You determine column settings.

Center the table on the page.

Using the math function, enter the correct formula and calculate the percent column to three decimals.

TIP: Current assets is 24.7% and long-term investments is 9.8%. Remember that to compute percentages you should divide the amount by the total. Try the formula B/913628.

Underline items as shown in the statement.

Save as **SE14d** and print.

LEISURE SERVICES INCORPORATED
Balance Sheet Analysis
December 31, 19__

Assets	**Amount**	**Percent**
Current assets	$225,786	
Long-term investments	89,700	
Inventory	275,726	
Buildings	322,416	
Total assets	$913,628	
Liabilities		
Current liabilities	$188,400	
Long-term debt	238,420	
Total liabilities	$426,820	
Capital		
Common stock	$387,500	
Retained earnings	99,308	
Total capital	$486,808	
Total liabilities and capital	$913,628	

Supplementary Exercise 15

Retrieve **SE7a** and do the following:

Format

Add graphics, horizontal and vertical lines to the picnic flier to
make it eye catching and appealing.

Save the revised document as **SE15** and print it.

Supplementary Exercise 16a

Retrieve **SE4c** and do the following:

Format

Select large and small fonts for the menu items to differentiate
categories and items.

Select line height and other commands to make the menu look attractive and professionally done.

You may wish to add lines and graphics.

Save as **SE16a** and print.

Supplementary Exercise 16b

Do the following:

Format

Create a new letterhead design for Leisure Services Incorporated. Use
graphics, horizontal and vertical lines and any other desktop
publishing feature you need. The return address to include is P. O.
Box 2240, Jackson, WY 83001. The phone number is (307) 733-3210.

Save as **SE16b** and print.

Use the letterhead for **SE4a** and **SE4b**.

Save as **SE16c** and print.

Supplementary Exercise 17

Type the following manuscript.

Format

Set margins at 1½ inches.
Use a 1½ inch top margin on the first page only.
The text of the footnotes is given in parentheses at the location in the text for the footnote.
Single-space and indent quotations 5 spaces from each margin.
Double-space the text.
Turn the Justification off.
You may choose different fonts for main and side heads.
Add page numbers at the bottom center of each page.
Save as **SE17** and print.

LEISURE SERVICES INCORPORATED
Management Philosophy

Leisure Services Incorporated believes in a management philosophy that encompasses combining people and resources to achieve long- and short-term company goals. Instead of producing a product, those in LSI management positions find themselves directing the energies and talents of their employees toward accomplishment of established company goals.

LSI Management Levels

Because of the diversity of tasks in the LSI organization, management has been organized into three general levels. Each level has its own particular function and reporting line.

Supervisors   The base level of LSI management is the supervisory level. Supervisors assign workers to specific job tasks and evaluate their performance. They have the responsibility of putting into action directives from the Manager level of management. They report directly to the Manager in charge of their sphere of responsiblities.

Managers The middle management level of LSI are the managers. This level is composed of executives who direct the specific functions at each Leisure Services resort location. Managers are responsible for making decisions about the operation of each resort, and for developing procedures to implement plans that originate with the company executives. The reporting line for Managers is to the specific Director who oversees the function in question.

Executives The top management level at LSI is made up of the president and other key company executives. The main functions of this level are developing long-range plans, coordinating the various resort locations, and overseeing expansion projects. Directors in the LSI organization report directly to the president.

Management Functions

To effectively pursue company goals, the members of all three levels of management at LSI have adopted the management steps outlined by Dressler:

> Managers are thus the ones who "make things happen" in the organization, by doing the planning, organizing, staffing, leading, and controlling that are required for the enterprise to function. (Footnote 1: Gary Dressler, Management Fundamentals, 3rd ed. (Reston, VA: Reston Publishing Company, Inc., 1982), p. 7.)

Plan The planning function of management is to foresee future trends and plan a course of action responsive to those forecasts that will achieve the company's goals. Such factors as company size, resources needed, and growth potential must be considered.

Organize After a plan has been made, workers and resources must be organized to accomplish it. Since most plans require the cooperation of many people, large tasks are usually broken down into specific smaller tasks that can be performed by a single worker skilled at that particular assignment.

> The use of specialization...makes the best use of workers' abilities, makes worker training simpler, and increases the skill of workers....It is simpler to check the work done by each worker. (Footnote 2: Arthur R. Olsen and John W. Kennedy, Economics—Principles and Applications, 9th ed. (Cincinnati: South-Western Publishing Co., 1978), p. 48.)

While the Directors usually formulate the broad, general structure, Managers and Supervisors are often given the responsibility to make specific assignments.

<u>Direct</u> When specialization is employed to accomplish a task, Managers and Supervisors must oversee the efforts of each worker and coordinate the overall operation to avoid a situation that could delay the completion of the plan. Motivating the workers to perform their jobs becomes a major supervisory responsibility.

<u>Control</u> Management at all levels is constantly evaluating the performance of the organization to determine whether its goals are being met. After evaluating the progress, steps are taken to correct any areas where there could be improvement.

Supplementary Exercise 18

Retrieve **SE17** and create a Table of Contents and Index as instructed.

Table of Contents Format

Include two levels of entries in the Table of Contents: side headings and paragraph headings.

You determine how pages will be displayed, etc.

Index Format

Enter LSI Management Levels as a main heading, and supervisors, managers, and executives as subheadings.

Enter Management Functions as a main heading, and Plan, Organize, Direct and Control as subheadings.

Decide a format for displaying numbers.

Decide whether or not to use a concordance file.

After completing the table of contents and the index, save the entire document at **SE18** and print.

Supplementary Exercise 19

Retrieve **SE4d** and do the following:

Format

Number the lines beginning with the main heading.
Save your document as **SE19** and print.

Appendix A
Diskette Care and
Handling Guideline

To protect against failure of the diskette, equipment malfunction, and/or loss of data, it is important to handle diskettes with care and good judgment. The following tips will help you avoid some of the more common problems.

Do not touch any exposed surface of the diskette. Oil, dust, or other particles on your hands and clothing can easily scratch, contaminate, or otherwise damage the surface, causing errors.

Do not bend or fold the diskette. Creases or irregularities on the diskette or jacket can cause alignment problems in the drive, interfering with the proper operation of the disk and drive mechanism.

Do not use paper clips, elastic bands, or tape on the diskette. Any indentation or mark on the surface of the protective jacket can interrupt the smooth spinning of the disk within the machine and cause read/write errors.

Do not eat, drink, or smoke while handling the diskette. Spills and/or residue can damage the diskette surface and destroy data.

Do not place heavy objects on top of the diskette. Books, briefcases, and binders have sharp corners and can leave marks, creases, and tears on the diskette and jacket.

Do not write on the diskette label with a ballpoint pen or pencil. Use a felt-tip pen, particularly to write on a label that is already attached to the diskette. If possible, write identifying information on the label **before** it is applied to the diskette.

Do not expose the diskette to excessive heat or sunlight. Never leave a diskette in a window, in a car, or any other place where high temperatures could cause the diskette to melt or warp.

Do not use magnets or magnetized objects near diskettes. Data can be erased or scrambled by a nearby magnetic field.

Do not expose the diskette to extreme cold. If a diskette becomes very cold, allow it to return to room temperature before using it.

Do not attempt to clean the diskette with alcohol or other solvents. Use a cleaning procedure specially designed for disks, or replace the diskette with a new one.

Always keep the diskette in its protective envelope when it is not in use. Doing so allows you to handle the disk freely, and helps keep it clean.

Always store diskettes in an upright, vertical position. To avoid damage or warping, keep them in their protective sleeves and in a covered container when they are not in use.

Never force the diskette when you are inserting it into or removing it from the machine. Make certain there is not already a disk in the drive, that you are inserting it correctly, and that nothing is in the way.

Never open the drive door or attempt to insert or remove a diskette when the red light is on. Doing so can cause major—and possibly permanent—damage to the internal mechanism and/or the diskette.

Always handle the diskette by the label end. Insert it into the machine label up/label last. Doing so will help to avoid damage caused by mishandling and improper alignment in the machine. Remember that diskettes are like fine phonograph records. They should be treated with care and respect if you wish to get maximum trouble-free service from them.

Finally, **save your files often** and make a back-up copy of any data you wish to protect from loss. Then, should an accident occur or the machine malfunction, you can easily retrieve your data without having to re-enter it.

Appendix B
Letter and Punctuation Styles and Format

Letter Styles

The two most common letter styles are the full block and the modified block. They are similar in many respects, but you should be able to tell them apart and use them accurately. Study the two illustrations shown on pages 566 and 567. Notice that both letters are centered vertically and horizontally on the page. Both have a date line, inside address, salutation, complimentary closing, signature line(s), and reference initials and/or enclosure notations.

Both also have four lines between the date and the inside address, and between the complimentary close and the signature lines. There are double spaces between the inside address and the salutation, between the salutation and the body of the letter, between paragraphs, and between the letter and the complimentary close.

If you type a letter for someone else to sign, put your initials a double space below the signature lines, flush left. If the letter includes enclosures, they should be noted a double space below the reference initials.

June 21, 19—

Mr. James Doe
Andrews Metalworks
2357 Industrial Way
Reston, VA 23476

Dear Mr. Doe

Thank you for your recent order. The merchandise you requested has been shipped today.

We appreciate the opportunity of serving you over the past ten years and want you to know that you are a valued customer. We want to provide you with the finest, most economical service possible. In our book, you're #1.

Sincerely

William Armbruster
Manager

ri

Full-Block Style   Open Punctuation

Full Block. In the full-block letter style, every line begins at the left margin — the date, the salutation, the closing lines, everything. Do not indent paragraphs.

June 21, 19__

Mrs. Sara Anne Wilson
President
Industro Electronics
Wichita, KS 66215

Dear Mrs. Wilson:

Enclosed with this letter is a copy of our latest brochure showing the new ITTR printer. You will notice that it is fully compatible with all of the major machines and that it supports a variety of peripherals.

To introduce this printer, we are offering a 20-percent discount on all orders placed before September 1. You may call our toll-free number to place your order. Your printer will be on its way to you within the week.

Sincerely,

H. R. Jackson
Sales Department

ri
Enclosure

Modified-Block Style   Mixed Punctuation

Modified Block. In the modified-block letter style, the date line and the closing lines (complimentary close and signature lines) begin at the center point. Paragraphs may or may not be indented. In all other respects the letters are the same.

PUNCTUATION STYLES

The two punctuation styles you should be familiar with are called *open* and *mixed*. They affect only the punctuation that appears after the salutation and the complimentary close. No other punctuation is affected.

Open Punctuation

When open punctuation is used, there is **no** punctuation after **either** the salutation or the complimentary close.

Mixed Punctuation

With mixed punctuation, there is a colon after the salutation and a comma after the complimentary close. **Both** marks of punctuation should be used.

Note that the choice of punctuation style is an all-or-nothing situation. Either use both marks or don't use either one. Using only one is incorrect.

Generally speaking, open punctuation is used with full-block style letters. The mixed punctuation is more commonly used with modified-block style letters.

If you have questions, be sure to ask your instructor for assistance. Don't guess, and don't think that "anything goes." This is **not** the case. Learn the correct way to set up letters, so that your work will represent you as a knowledgeable and careful correspondent.

Appendix C
WordPerfect 5.0
Command Locator

Advance Line	Shift-F8, 4,1
Advance Up/Dn	Shift-F8, 4, 1, 1-6
Aided Hyphenation	Shift-F8, 1, 1
Alignment Character Set	Shift-F8, 4, 3
Auto Hyphenation	Shift-F8, 1, 2
Auto Referencing	Alt-F5, 1
Auto Rewrite	Shift-F1, 3, 1
Auxilliary Files	Shift-F1, 7
Backup	Shift-F1, 1
Backward Search	Shift-F2
Base Font	Ctrl-F8, 4
Binding Width	Shift-F7, B
Block On/Off	Alt-F4
Block Protect	Alt-F4, Shift-F8
Bold	F6
Bottom Margin	Shift-F8, 2, 5
Cancel	F1
Cancel Print Job	Shift-F7, 4, C
Cancel Printer	Shift-F7, 4, 1
Capitalization Lock	Caps Lock
Center	Shift-F6
Center on Column	Shift-F6

Center Page (Top to Bottom)	Shift-F8, 2, 1
Change Default Directory	F5, =
Clear Screen	F7, Y/N, N
Columns Definition	Alt-F7, 4
Columns On/Off	Alt-F7, 3
Compose	Ctrl-2
Concordance File	Alt-F5, 5,
Conditional End of Page	Shift-F8, 4, 2
Copy Block	Ctrl-F4
Copy File	F5, Enter, 8
Current Document Size	F5, Enter
Cursor Movement	Scrn UP/DN, ESC, GoTo
. . . .	Arrow Keys, PGUP/DN
Cursor Speed	Shift-F1, 2
Cut Block	Ctrl-F4
Date	Shift-F5, 1-3
Date Code	Shift-F5, 2
Date Format	Shift-F5, 3
Date Text	Shift-F5, 1
Define Macro	Ctrl-F10
Delete Block	Alt-F4, Mark, DEL,
Delete EOL	Ctrl-END
Delete File	F5, Enter, 2
Delete Left	Backspace
Delete Right	DEL
Delete to End of Page	Ctrl-PGDN
Delete Word	Ctrl-Backspace
Directory	F5, Enter
Display Disk Space	F5, Enter

GoTo	Ctrl-7 (with Numlock on)
GoTo	Ctrl-Home
Graphics	Alt-F9
H-Zone	Shift-F8, 4, 1
Hard Hyphen	Home-Hyphen
Hard Page	Ctrl-Enter
Hard Return	Enter
Hard Space	Home, Space
Headers	Shift-F8, 2, 3
Help	F3
Home	7
Index	Alt-F5, 5
Initial Settings	Shift-F1, 5
Insert/Typeover	Ins
Invoke Macro	Alt-F10
Justification On/Off	Shift-F8, 1, 3
Kerning	Shift-F8, 4, 6, 1
Keyboard Layout	Shift-F1, 6
Leading	Shift-F8, 1, 4, 2
Left Indent	F4
Left Margin Release	Shift-Tab
Left/Right Indent	Shift-F4
Left/Right Temporary Margin	Shift-F4
Left Temporary Margin	F4
Letter Styles	Appendix
Line Draw	Ctrl-F3, 2
Line Format	Shift-F8, 1
Line Numbering	Shift-F8, 1, 5
Line Spacing	Shift-F8, 1, 6

Lines per Inch	Shift-F8, 1, 4
List	Alt-F5, 5, 2
List Files	F5, Enter
Locking Files	Ctrl-F5, 4-5
Look	F5, Enter, 6
Macro	Alt-F10
Macro Define	Ctrl-F10
Macro Edit	Ctrl-F10
Margins	Shift-F8, 1, 7
Mark Text	Alt-F5
Master Document	Alt-F5, 6
Math Columns	Alt-F7
Math Definitions	Alt-F7, 2
Math Off/On	Alt-F7, 1
Merge	Ctrl-F9, 1
Merge Codes	Shift/F9
Merge Commands	Alt-F9
Merge End of Record	Shift-F9
Merge Return	F9
Move	Ctrl-F4, 1-4
New Current Page Number	Shift-F8, 2, 6
New Page	Ctrl-Enter
Number of Copies	Shift-F7, N
Odd/Even Page	Shift-F8, 2, 7
Orphan/Widow	Shift-F8, 1, 9
Outline	Alt-F5, 1
Overstrike	Shift-F8, 4, 5
Page Break	Ctrl-Enter
Page Down	PGDN

Retrieve Document	Shift-F10
Retrieve Text (Block)	Ctrl-F4, 4
Return	Enter
Reveal Codes	Alt-F3
Reverse Search	Shift-F2
Rewrite Screen	Ctrl-F3, 0
Ruler Line	Ctrl-F3, 1, 23
Save in WP 4.2 format	Ctrl-F5, 4
Save Text	F10 or Exit
Screen	Ctrl-F3
Screen	Ctrl-F3, 0
Screen Down	Plus (+)
Screen Up	Minus (-)
Search & Replace w/Confirm	Alt-F2, Y
Search & Replace	Alt-F2, N
Search Forward	F2
Search Reverse	Shift-F2
Select	Ctrl-F9, 2
Send Printer a "Go"	Shift-F7, 4, G
Setup	Shift-F1
Shell	Ctrl-F1
Soft Hyphen	Ctrl-(hyphen)
Sort	Ctrl-F9, 2
Spacing	Shift-F8, 1, 6
Speller	Ctrl-F2
Split Screen	Ctrl-F3, 1
Stop Printer	Shift-F7, 4, S
Strikeout	Ctrl-F8, 2, 9
Styles	Alt-F8

Appendix D
Codes Used in
Reveal Codes

The following is a listing of codes, together with their meaning, used in
Reveal Codes.

[ ]	Hard Space
[-]	Hyphen
-	Soft Hyphen
/	Cancel Hyphenation
[Adv]	Advance
[Align]	Tab Align
[Block]	Beginning of Block
[Block Pro]	Block Protection
[Bold]	Bold
[Box Num]	Graphics Box Caption
[C/A/FlRt]	End of Center Tab Align or Flush Right
[Center Pg]	Center Page Top to Bottom
[Cntr]	Center
[Cndl EOP]	Conditional End of Page
[Col Def]	Column Definition
[Col Off]	End of Text Columns
[Col On]	Beginning of Text Columns
[Comment]	Document Comment
[Color]	Print Color
[Date]	Date/Time Function

[Dbl Und]	Double Underline
[Decml Char]	Decimal Character/Thousands Separator
[Def Mark:Index]	Index Definition
[Def Mark:Listn]	List Definition
[Def Mark:ToC]	Table of Contents Definition
[End Def]	End of Index, List, or Table of Contents
[End Opt]	Endnote Options
[Endnote]	Endnote
[Endnote Placement]	Endnote Placement
[Ext Large]	Extra Large Print
[Figure]	Figure Box
[Fig Opt]	Figure Box Options
[Fine]	Fine Print
[Flsh Rt]	Flush Right
[Footnote]	Footnote
[Font]	Base Font
[Footer]	Footer
[Force]	Force Odd/Even Page
[Form]	Form (Printer Selection)
[FtnOpt]	Footnote/Endnote Options
[Full Form]	Table of Authorities, Full Form
[HLine]	Horizontal Line
[Header]	Header
[HPg]	Hard Page
[HRt]	Hard Return
[Hyph]	Hyphenation
[HZone]	Hyphenation Zone
[->Indent]	Indent
[->Indent<-]	Left/Right Indent

[Index]	Index
[ISRt]	Invisible Soft Return
[Italc]	Italics
[Just]	Right Justification
[Just Lim]	Word/Letter Spacing Justification Limits
[Kern]	Kerning
[L/R Mar]	Left and Right Margins
[Lang]	Language
[Large]	Large Print
[Line Height]	Line Height
[Ln Num]	Line Numbering
[<-Mar Rel]	Left Margin Release
[Mark:List]	List Entry
[Mark:ToC[	Table of Contents Entry
[Math Def]	Definition of Math Columns
[Math Off]	End of Math
[Math On]	Beginning of Math
!	Formula Calculation
t	Subtotal Entry
+	Calculate Subtotal
T	Total Entry
=	Calculate Total
*	Calculate Grand Total
[Note Num]	Footnote/Endnote Reference
[Outln]	Outline (attribute)
[Ovrstk]	Overstrike
[Paper Sz/Typ]	Paper Size and Type
[Par Num]	Paragraph Number
[Par Num Def]	Paragraph Numbering Definition

[Pg Num]	New Page Number
[Pg Num Pos]	Page Number Position
[Ptr Cmnd]	Printer Command
[RedLn]	Redline
[Ref]	Reference (Automatic)
[Set End Num]	Set New Endnote Number
[Set Fig Num]	Set New Figure Box Number
[Set Ftn Number]	Set New Footnote Number
[Set Tab Num]	Set New Table Box Number
[Set Text Num]	Set New User-Defined Box Number
[Shadwn]	Shadow
[Sm Cap]	Small Caps
[Small]	Small Print
[SPg]	Soft New Page
[SRt]	Soft Return
[StkOut]	Strikeout
[Style]	Styles
[Subdoc]	Subdocument (Master Documents)
[SubScrpt]	Subscript
[SuprScrpt]	Superscript
[Suppress]	Suppress Page Format
[T/B Mar]	Top and Bottom Margins
[Tab]	Tab
[TabOpt]	Table Box Options
[Tab Set]	Tab Set
[Table]	Table Box
[Target]	Target (Auto Reference)
[Text Box]	Text Box
[Txt Opt]	Text Box Options

[Und]	Underlining
[Undrin]	Underline Spaces/Tabs
[Usr Box]	User-Defined Box
[Usr Opt]	User Defined Box options
[VLine]	Vertical Line
[Vry Large]	Very Large Print
[W/O]	Widow/Orphan
[Wrd/LtrSpacing]	Word and Letter Spacing

Appendix E
Character Sets

Shown below are eleven of the thirteen character sets that can be accessed by WordPerfect using the Compose (Ctrl-2) command. Character set twelve is user defined using the Printer Definition Program. Not all printers have fonts to print all characters; therefore, you will need to test your printer's ability before using many of the characters listed.

Character Set 0 (ASCII)

```
        0 1 2 3 4 5 6 7 8 9 0 1 2 3 4 5 6 7 8 9 0 1 2 3 4 5 6 7 8 9
  0
 30       !  "  ?  $  %  &  '  (  )  *  +  ,  -  .  /  0  1  2  3  4  5  6  7  8  9  :  ;
 60   <  =  >  ?  @  A  B  C  D  E  F  G  H  I  J  K  L  M  N  O  P  Q  R  S  T  U  V  W  X  Y
 90   Z  [  \  ]  ^  _  `  a  b  c  d  e  f  g  h  i  j  k  l  m  n  o  p  q  r  s  t  u  v  w
120   x  y  z  {  ¦  }  ~
```

Character Set 1 (Multinational 1)

```
        0 1 2 3 4 5 6 7 8 9 0 1 2 3 4 5 6 7 8 9 0 1 2 3 4 5 6 7 8 9
  0   `  ·  ~  ^     _  /  ´  ¨  ¯  ˗  ¸  ‚  ‚  °  ·  ˝        ˘  ´  —  ˘  ß  ı  ȷ  Á  á  Â  â
 30   Ä  ä  À  à  Å  å  Æ  æ  Ç  ç  É  é  Ê  ê  Ë  ë  È  è  Í  í  Î  î  Ï  ï  Ì  ì  Ñ  ñ  Ó  ó
 60   Ô  ô  Ö  ö  Ò  ò  Ú  ú  Û  û  Ü  ü  Ù  ù  Ÿ  ÿ  Ã  ã  Đ  đ  Ø  ø  Õ  õ  Ý  ý  Đ  ð  Þ  þ
 90   Ă  ă  Ā  ā  Ą  ą  Ć  ć  Č  č  Ĉ  ĉ  Ċ  ċ  Ď  ď  Ě  ě  Ė  ė  Ē  ē  Ę  ę  Ǵ  ǵ  Ğ  ğ  Ǧ  ǧ
120   Ģ  ģ  Ĝ  ĝ  Ġ  ġ  Ĥ  ĥ  Ħ  ħ  İ  i  Ī  ī  Į  į  Ĩ  ĩ  Ĳ  ĳ  Ĵ  ĵ  Ķ  ķ  Ĺ  ĺ  Ľ  ľ  Ļ  ļ
150   Ŀ  ŀ  Ł  ł  Ń  ń  Ṅ  ṅ  Ň  ň  Ņ  ņ  Ő  ő  Ō  ō  Œ  œ  Ŕ  ŕ  Ř  ř  Ŗ  ŗ  Ś  ś  Š  š  Ş  ş
180   Ŝ  ŝ  Ť  ť  Ţ  ţ  Ŧ  ŧ  Ŭ  ŭ  Ű  ű  Ū  ū  Ų  ų  Ů  ů  Ũ  ũ  Ŵ  ŵ  Ŷ  ŷ  Ź  ź  Ž  ž  Ż  ż
210   Ŋ  ŋ  D̄  đ  L̄  Ī  Ñ  ñ  Ŗ  ŗ  Š  š  Ŧ  ŧ  Ŷ  ŷ  Ỳ  ỳ  D'  ď  O'  ơ  U'  ư
```

Character Set 2 (Multinational 2)

```
        0 1 2 3 4 5 6 7 8 9 0 1 2 3 4 5 6 7 8 9 0 1 2 3 4 5 6 7 8 9
  0   .  ..  °  ∘  ,  ^  =  —  K  ˇ  ʔ  '        ,  ʻ  ¬  ∟  ⌐  |  ∪  ˘  '  "
```

Character Set 3 (Box Drawing)

Character Set 4 (Typographic Symbols)

Character Set 5 (Iconic Symbols)

Character Set 6 (Math/Scientific)

Character Set 7 (Math/Scientific Extension)

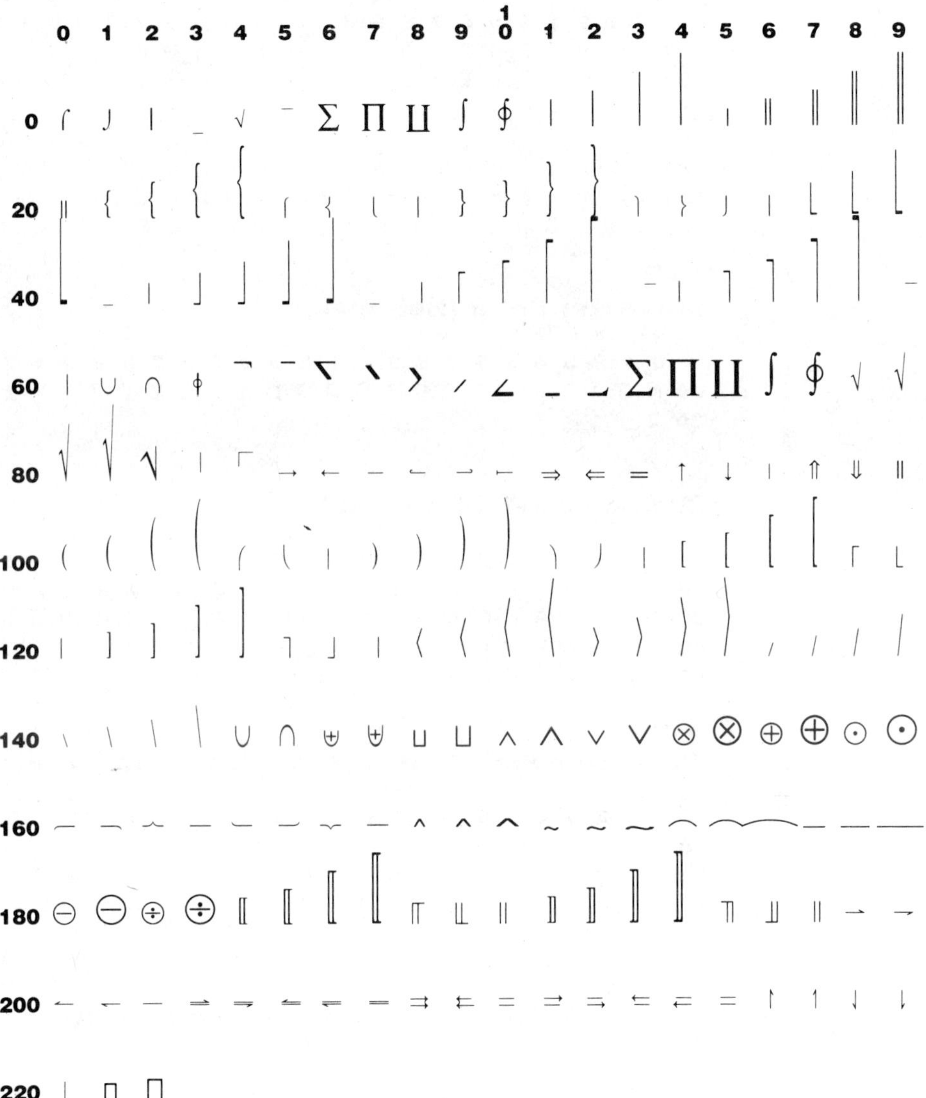

Character Set 8 (Greek)

```
              1                   2
  0 1 2 3 4 5 6 7 8 9 0 1 2 3 4 5 6 7 8 9 0 1 2 3 4 5 6 7 8 9
  0 Α α Β β B в Γ γ Δ δ Ε ε Ζ ζ Η η Θ θ Ι ι Κ κ Λ λ Μ μ Ν ξ Ξ
 30 Ο ο Π π Ρ ρ Σ σ Σ ς Τ τ Υ υ Φ φ Χ χ Ψ ψ Ω ω ά ΄ ή ί ϊ ö ύ ü
 60 ϋ ε ϑ ϰ ϖ ρ Υ φ ω · ; ΄ ΄ ΄ ΄ ΄ ΄ ΄ ΄ ΄
 90 ΄ ΄ ΄ ΄ ΄ ΄ ΄ à â ą ą́ à ă ă ā â ā ą ą̄ ā ā ā ā ą ą̄ ą̄ Ä Ē É É Ě
120 Ė Ē Ē ή ή̄ ή ή̄ ή ή̄ ή ή̄ ή ή̄ ή ή̄ ή ή̄ ή ή̄ ή ή̄ ή ή̄ ή ή̄ ή ή̄ ί ῑ ί ῑ ί ῑ ϊ ῑ
150 ῑ ί ϊ ϊ ϊ ό ό ό̄ ό ό̄ ό ό̄ ό ό̄ ύ ῡ ύ ῡ ύ ῡ ύ ῡ ύ ῡ ϋ ῡ ϋ ϋ ῶ φ φ φ̄ φ̄
180 ώ ώ́ ώ ώ̄ φ φ φ̄ φ̄ ώ ώ ώ̄ ώ̄ φ̄ φ̄ φ̄ ΄ , ϛ F ϙ ϡ
```

Character Set 9 (Hebrew)

```
              1                   2
  0 1 2 3 4 5 6 7 8 9 0 1 2 3 4 5 6 7 8 9 0 1 2 3 4 5 6 7 8 9
  0 א ב ב ג ד ה ו ז ח ט י כ ך ל מ ם נ ן ס ע פ ף צ ץ ק ר ש ש ת
 30 פּ ִ ֵ ֶ ַ ָ ְ ֹ ֻ ׳
```

Character Set 10 (Cyrillic)

```
              1                   2
  0 1 2 3 4 5 6 7 8 9 0 1 2 3 4 5 6 7 8 9 0 1 2 3 4 5 6 7 8 9
  0 А а Б б В в Г г Д д Е е Ё ё Ж ж З з И и Й й К к Л л М м Н н
 30 О о П п Р р С с Т т У у Ф ф Х х Ц ц Ч ч Ш ш Щ щ Ъ ъ Ы ы Ь ь
 60 Э э Ю ю Я я Ґ ґ Ђ ђ Ѓ ѓ Є є Ѕ ѕ І і Ї ї Ј ј Љ љ Њ њ Ћ ћ Ќ ќ
 90 Ў ў Џ џ Ѣ ѣ Ѳ ѳ Ѵ ѵ Ѫ ѫ
```

Character Set 11 (Hiragana—Japanese Kana)

```
              1                   2
  0 1 2 3 4 5 6 7 8 9 0 1 2 3 4 5 6 7 8 9 0 1 2 3 4 5 6 7 8 9
  0 ぁ ぃ ぅ ぇ ぉ っ ゃ ゅ ょ    ゎ ゖ あ い う え お か き く け こ が ぎ ぐ げ ご さ し す
 30 せ そ ざ じ ず ぜ ぞ た ち つ て と だ ぢ づ で ど な に ぬ ね の は ひ ふ へ ほ ば び ぶ
 60 べ ぼ ぱ ぴ ぷ ぺ ぽ ま み む め も や ゆ よ ら り る れ ろ わ を ん 【 】 〖 〗 「 」 『
 90 』 ． 。 、 ゝ ゞ 〃 ー ゚ ゙
```

Character Set 11 (Katakana—Japanese Kana)

```
              1                   2
  0 1 2 3 4 5 6 7 8 9 0 1 2 3 4 5 6 7 8 9 0 1 2 3 4 5 6 7 8 9
  0 ァ ィ ゥ ェ ォ ッ ャ ュ ョ ヴ ヵ ヶ ア イ ウ エ オ カ キ ク ケ コ ガ ギ グ ゲ ゴ サ シ ス
 30 セ ソ ザ ジ ズ ゼ ゾ タ チ ツ テ ト ダ ヂ ヅ デ ド ナ ニ ヌ ネ ノ ハ ヒ フ ヘ ホ バ ビ ブ
 60 ベ ボ パ ピ プ ペ ポ マ ミ ム メ モ ヤ ユ ヨ ラ リ ル レ ロ ワ ヲ ン 【 】 〖 〗 「 」 『
 90 』 ． 。 、 ヽ ヾ 〃 ー ゚ ゙
```

Character Set 12 (User)

Character Set 12 is a user-defined character set.

Appendix F
Graphics Images* for
WordPerfect® 5.0

AIRPLANE

AND

ANNOUNCE

APPLAUSE

ARROW1

ARROW2

CONFIDEN

AWARD

BADNEWS

BOOK

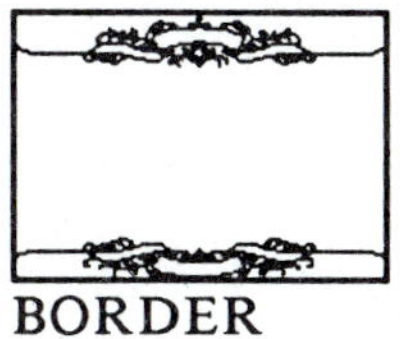
BORDER

CHECK

CLOCK

---

*from Publisher's PicturePaks for WordPerfect

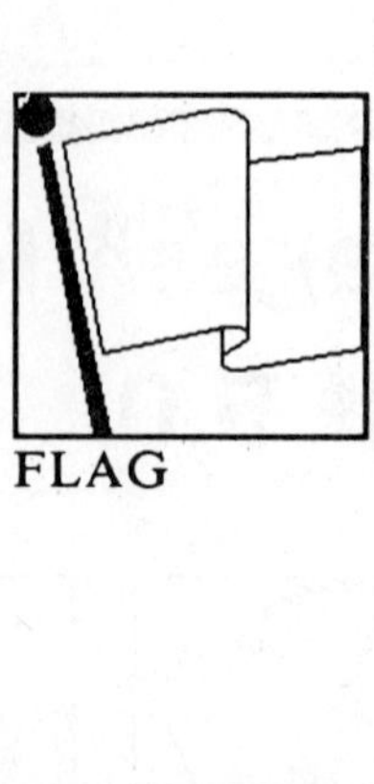

FLAG

GAVEL

GOODNEWS

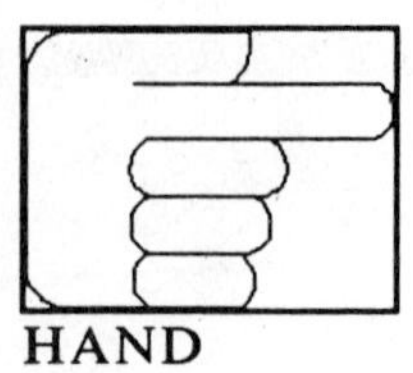

HAND

HOURGLAS

KEY

MAPSYMBL

NEWSPAPR

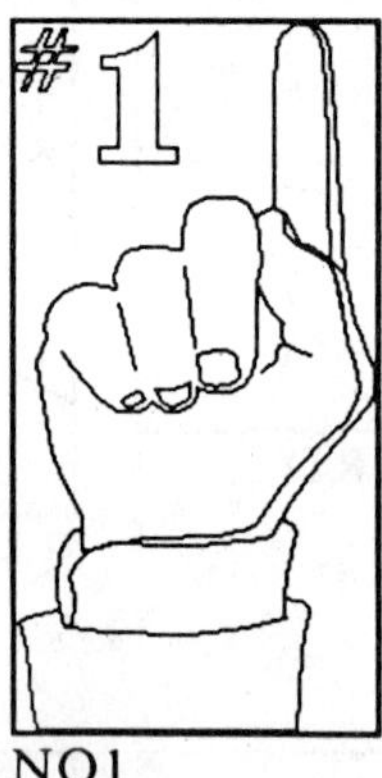

NO1

PC

PENCIL

PHONE

PRESENT

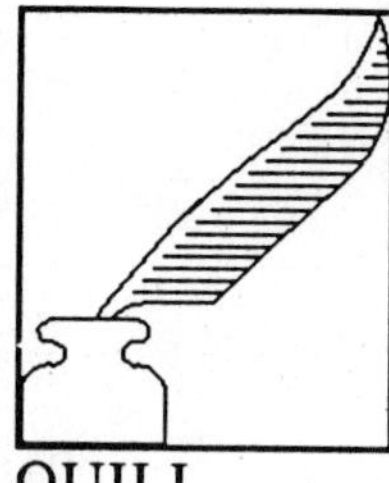
QUILL

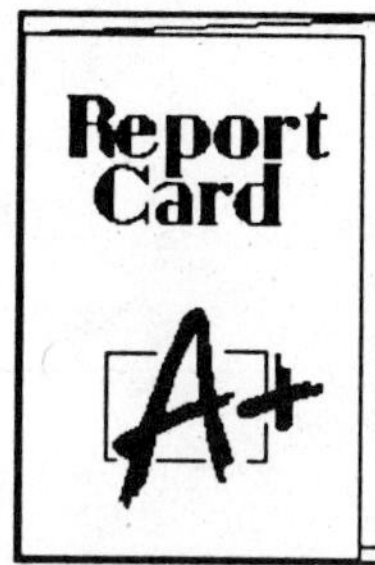
Report
Card
A+
RPTCARD

THINKER

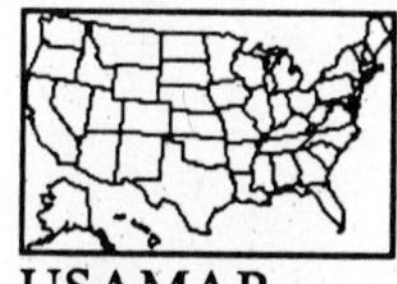
USAMAP

Answer Key for
Self-Check Quizzes

Self-Check Quiz 1 Answers

1. a. Backspace/Delete
      *Erases text above
      and to left of cursor*
   b. ENTER, *moves cursor to
      beginning of next line*
   c. TAB, *moves cursor
      to next tab stop*
   d. ↑ *Moves cursor up one line*

2. Red = Control
   Blue = Alt
   Black = none
   Green = shift

3. a. Enter
   b. Edit
   c. Format
   d. Save
   e. Print
   f. Retrieve

4. Postion of cursor is on first document, page 3, 2" from top of page, 1.9" from left margin. Document CHARLIE is on B drive.

5. Label up, label last

6. Save (F10) allows the document to stay on screen for editing. Save (F7) clears memory and the screen.

7. a. DEL
      Deletes above & to right
   b. INS (Typeover)
      *Old character deleted
      New character inserted*
   c. TAB
      *Cursor moves to next
      TAB stop*
   d. ENTER
      Cursor moves to new line
   e. BACKSPACE
      Deletes character to left of cursor
   f. UP ARROW
      Cursor moves up a line

8. Del deletes above and to the right of the cursor, while Backspace Delete deletes the character to the left of the cursor.

9. Save — F10
   Exit — F7 and (Y)es when asked regarding save

10. You do not need to memorize all the settings for the fonts available. WordPerfect has a built-in conversion table that makes the changes automatically.

11. That the disk is being read or written to.

12. Retrieve (Shift-F10), type name of document to be retrieved

13. Print (Shift-F7) option 1 or 2

14. Different printers read codes differently; therefore, the printer to be used must be defined.

15. COM1   Serial port

    LPT1   Parallel port

16. Neither can be interchanged. They do not represent the same command to WordPerfect.

Self-Check Quiz 2 Answers

1. a. Home, Up Arrow   *Goes to top of screen*

   b. Home, Right Arrow   *Goes to right end of line*

   c. Home, Left Arrow   *Goes to left end of line*

   d. Home, Down Arrow   *Goes to bottom of screen*

   e. Ctrl-Left Arrow   *Moves one word to left*

   f. Ctrl-Right Arrow   *Moves one word to right*

   g. Home, Home, Up Arrow   *Goes to beginning of document*

   h. Home, Home, Down Arrow   *Goes to end of document*

   i. PageUp   *Moves cursor up one page*

   j. PageDn   *Moves cursor down one page*

   k. Screen Up   *Moves cursor up one screenful*

   l. Screen Down   *Moves cursor down one screenful*

2. a. Backspace (held down)   *Continuous delete to left*

   b. DEL (held down)   *Continuous delete above, right*

   c. Ctrl-Backspace   *Deletes word at cursor*

   d. Ctrl-End   *Deletes from cursor to end of line*

   e. Ctrl-PgDn   *Deletes from cursor to end of page*

   f. Home, Backspace   *Deletes from cursor to next blank space on left*

   g. Home, Del   *Deletes from cursor to next blank space on right*

   h. Home, Del (typeover on)   *Deletes from cursor to next word on right*

3. Cancel

4. Because the documents will be combined otherwise

5. Exit (F7), Save Y/N

6. Cancel (F1)

7. Ctrl-7

8. *When typeover is On,* TAB will move the cursor through the text without inserting spaces or TAB commands. *When typeover is Off,* spaces and/or TAB commands are inserted when the TAB key or space bar is pressed.

9. Moves the cursor a specified number of lines, spaces, characters, etc., in the direction of the arrow used. It can also insert a specified number of duplicate characters at the cursor or repeat a command.

10. Three

11. Press Print (Shift F7), Number of copies (N), and type in the number of copies desired

12. Press Print (Shift-F7), Page (2), and the page the cursor is on will be printed.

    Press Print (Shift-F7), Document on Disk (3), type the name of document you want printed, then type in the number of the page you want printed as prompted

13. Print from the screen (Shift-F7), choose 1 or 2

    Print from the disk (Shift-F7), choose 3, then type name of document you want printed.

    List Files (F5), highlight file, press Print (4).

14. Print jobs in process or in line for printing will be canceled. The reset command or Go must be given for the printer to begin printing again

15. Print (Shift-7), Control printer (4), Cancel (1), Type asterisk (*), Cancel ALL print jobs, type (Y)es

16. Retrieve Printer Control menu, press Stop (5), then press Go (4), to start the same job from the beginning

17. The restart command = Go

18. Check the printer selection to be sure it is correct

    Check to be sure the printer is turned on and has paper

    Check the status of the Printer Control menu—see if the printer is waiting for a Go

19. Gives information about the print jobs, problems that may be occurring, instructions that you should do, etc.

20. Pages 1 to 4, page 9, pages 12 to 21, and pages 40 to the end of the document

21. 3-8,11,14,33-

22. From the Control Printer menu—current page will be listed

23. Job status—whether the job is printing or not

    Paper—size of paper being used

    Location—where WordPerfect expects to find the paper

    Page number—which page numbers are printing

    Current copy—which copy is currently printing when multiple copies have been specified

24. Close Up ↻

    Move Right ⌐

    Delete ℓ

    Move Left ⊏

    Ignore Correction STET

    Underline _____ underline

    Add a Space ∧#

    Delete and Close Up ℯ

Transpose

Bold

New Paragraph

Comma

Insert

Period

25. You will see your document displayed as it will be printed on the page—reduced in size to display the entire page.

26. WordPerfect will shift the text ½ inch to the right on odd-numbered pages and ½ inch to the left on even-numbered pages

27. Cancel (Control Printer menu, choose 1, number of job to be canceled)

    Stop printing (Control Printer Menu, Choose 5, Stop)

    Ctrl-NumLock

28. Ctrl-NumLock

Self-Check Quiz 3 Answers

1. Format (Shift-F8), Line (1), Margins (7), type new margins

2. Format (Shift-F8), Line (1), Line Spacing (6), Type 2

3. Format (Shift-F8), Line (1), Tab Set (8), change tabs as needed

4. Format (Shift-F8), Line (1), Tab Set (8), clear tabs if necessary, type 0.5,0.5

5. Screen Up/Down or Cursor Up/Down

6. Page Up/Down or Home, Home, Up Arrow/Down Arrow

7. Help (F3)

8. All function keys

9. 0.7" left and 0.25" right;
   determines point for line to end and cursor to wrap around.

10. Reveal Codes (Alt-F3)

11. Save (F10)

12. Left Justified *Words flow from left to right*

    Right Justified *Words flow from right to left*

    Centered *Centers from tab setting*

    Decimal *Aligns at decimal*

    Leaders *Will insert leaders between end of previous entry and beginning of current one*

13. Auto = *WordPerfect will insert hyphens if necessary*

    Manual = *WordPerfect will ask for assistance with division of words and placement of hyphens*

14. Ctrl-Hyphen

15. 2.0,0.7

Self-Check Quiz 4 Answers

1.

	To Turn On:	To Turn Off:
Center	Shift-F6	Enter
Underline	F8	F8
Bold	F6	F6
Flush Right	Alt-F6	Enter

2. If your margins are 1.0" and .50", what point will WordPerfect enter from? 4.5

3. What do the following lines signify?
   ——————————————————————— Soft Page—WordPerfect generated
   = ================Hard Page—User generated

4. $15,400.03   5.3%

   TXT.FIL   28.999301

5. (Center)   (Underline)   (Bold)
   (Tab Align)   Page Break   (Flush Right)

6. A row of double dashes will appear across the page.

   It means a Hard Page command has been entered.

7. Block protect—block the 15 lines (Alt-F4), Press Shift-F8, Type (Y)es

8. Check Reveal Codes (Alt-F3) or observe status line

9. *Hard Page* is user generated and shows as a double dashed line on screen, whereas a *Soft Page* is WordPerfect generated and shows a single dashed line on screen

10. Exit (F7), No

11. Keeps one-liners of paragraphs from occurring on the bottom or top of a page

12. Format (Shift-F8), Page (2), Page numbers (7), Top center (2)

Self-Check Quiz 5 Answers

1. Numbers, abbreviations, misused words, homonyms

2. There is no match for the word in the speller dictionary

3. Select Look up (5) from the speller

4. It matches words with those listed in the speller dictionary

5. The speller will indicate the word count when it has finished spell-checking the document

6. *Synonyms* are words that mean the same but have different spellings

   Homonyms are words that sound alike but are spelled differently

   The *speller* does not check the accuracy of use of either

7. A headword is a word that has other synonyms identified for it.

   Words that are headwords have dots (.) in front of them when they are listed by the thesaurus

8. Choose Look up Word (3) from the Thesaurus menu and then enter the word when asked by the prompt. The Thesaurus will immediately jump to the new word and display the synonyms listed in its dictionary.

9. Select Replace Word (1) and the letter corresponding to your choice of word from the Thesaurus menu

10. (a) stands for adjective

11. A word that means the opposite of another word

Self-Check Quiz 6 Answers

1. It doesn't matter where the cursor is positioned; Arrow must agree with direction of the search

2. Up/Down arrow keys will change directions

3. ESC and F2

4. a. Move   *Removes text from original place and moves it to another place*

   b. Copy   *Leaves the original text in the same place but makes a copy of it in another place*

   c. Delete   *Deletes block*

   d. Retrieve Text   *Recalls block from temporary memory and inserts it at the cursor*

5. a. Sentence   *Everything from the cursor to the next period*

   b. Paragraph   *Everything from the cursor to the next Hard Return (HRt) command*

   c. Page   *Everything from the cursor to the next Page Break (H/SPg)*

6. Screen (Ctrl-F3), Window (1), enter 23

7. Bold, underline, caps, copy, move, print, save, delete, append, etc.

8. If no block is marked, will move to Doc 2. If a block is marked, will allow change from upper- to lowercase characters or vice versa

9. GoTo (Ctrl-7) twice, then Alt-F4

10. Using Search *with Confirmation,* WordPerfect will stop at each occurrence to let you confirm.

    Search *without Confirmation* will automatically change each occurrence of the word.

11. Use the extended search when your document has footnotes, endnotes, headers or footers.

12. The block can be added to the end of another file on disk, or added as a separate file on the disk.

13. Columns must be separated by Tabs, Tab Align, Indent, or Hard Return codes. Rectangle will move from upper left to lower right of blocked area.

14. Switch (Shift-F3)

15. Single: 24

    Double: 23

Self-Check Quiz 7 Answers

1. Tab = *Indents specified number of spaces at one place and returns to original left margin*

   Left indent = *Indents specified number of spaces at left margin and continues to use that point as a new (temporary) left margin until* ENTER *key is pressed*

   Left/Right indent = *Indents specified number of spaces equally from both left and right margins and continues to use that point as new (temporary) margins until* ENTER *key is pressed*

2. The ENTER key

3. The left margin will indent to the next tab settings. The right margin will indent an equal amount.

4. *Date* text will enter the current date and it will remain that date when the document is retrieved at a later date.

   The Date Code enters a code that will cause the current or updated date from DOS to display whenever the document is retrieved.

5. The percent (%) will cause the month or day to be abbreviated to three letters

6. Date Code option

7. WordPerfect will put the two characters in the same space

8. They are alike in that both will put two characters in the same space; however, the *overstrike* command is limited to the characters on the keyboard whereas *Compose* can use various character sets as well.

9. A listing of the special ASCII characters available

10. 6,43: *First number* represents the character set, *the second,* the particular symbol within the character set

11. Advance Up/Down and Left/Right commands move relative to the cursor position when they are entered

12. Enter another command to move to a different position or return to the original line by entering another command in the opposite direction.

13. The top of the page.

14. WordPerfect will automatically insert a corner when the direction of the arrow is changed.

15. Cancel (F1), or Exit (F7)

16. Ctrl-Hyphen (-)

17. Hard hyphen (home hyphen) = *WordPerfect will treat the words joined by hard hyphens as one unit*

    Hard space (home space bar) = *Word Perfect will retain the space as it was typed and not treat the words on either side of the hard space as a single unit*

    Hard page = *The position of a hard page command will not change if text changes*

    Soft hyphen (Ctrl/Hyphen) = *Lets you control an end-of-line hyphen if the word falls at the end of a line. The hyphen is ignored if the word does not fall at the end of the line; the hyphen will not appear in the text.*

    Soft space = *Soft spaces tell WordPerfect the end and beginning of words and the words can fall on different lines between soft spaces.*

    Soft page = *Position of the soft page break can vary depending on text above it.*

18. Home hyphen, home hyphen (—) A dash should not have a space either before or after it when it is used in a sentence.

19. The Tab spaces are underlined

Self-Check Quiz 8 Answers

1. List Files (F7); ENTER; will show free disk space

2. Check List Files

3. Retrieve, Copy, Print, Delete, Rename, Look, Word Search, Name Search, Text In, Other Directory

4. American Standard Code for Information Interchange

5. It will search for a name pattern and find all the files with that name pattern in it

6. Mark all highlighted files at once with Alt-F5 or Home*. Unmark all files with the same command

7. List Files (F5); ENTER

8. Rename = List Files (F5), ENTER, Highlight filename; Rename (3); enter new name; ENTER

   Delete = List Files (F5); ENTER; Highlight filename; Delete (2); Confirm deletion (Y/N)

9. Exit temporarily to operating system

10. You must supply the correct password when prompted using any of the printing methods

11. To guard against typing errors

12. Use an asterisk (*)

13. They are lost

14. a. All the files relating to the Harris contract:
       List files (F5), Name Search, type Harris

    b. All files created during the last month:
       List files (F5), check dates of each file

    c. All files mentioning the name of William B. Jenks:
       List files (F5), Word Search (9), Entire Doc (3), Type William B. Jenks

> d. All files referring to either the downtown or mall stores:
> List files (F5), Word Search (9), Entire Doc (3), type Downtown
> (,) Mall

15. What appears on the screen will be printed

16. Use the Remove command

    Retrieve the locked file into an unlocked file. When the combined file is saved, it will not be locked

17. 25 characters

18. Type the word EXIT (do not press Exit [F7]), press ENTER

Self-Check Quiz 9 Answers

1. Making format changes, changing margins, setting tabs, inserting font and printer commands, entering functions such as bold, underline, etc.

2. *Paired styles* begin and end with codes at both points. You must block the material you want the style to affect or turn Style on and off.

   Open styles affect the document from its location forward. It has no end of its own.

3. To use them again in other documents

4. A Style Library is set up to store created styles for use over and over again. It is more efficient and easier to find the style you desire if it is stored in a library. To retrieve a style into a document go to the style menu and select Retrieve (7), enter the path of the directory and the filename.

5. *The codes above the box* are the codes to turn on the commands you desire.

   The codes after the box are the codes to end the current commands and to affect the text after the style.

6. With the down arrow

7. Each occurrence of that style will automatically change to include the new format.

8. Author's name, who typed the document, when it was last updated, comments, etc.

9. Up to 780 characters

10. AFTER the comment

11. Anywhere in the document

Self-Check Quiz 10 Answers

1. An extra copy of your document to protect against the possibility of data loss due to a power failure or equipment malfunction

2. Automatically backs up the current document at specified intervals

3. It creates an Original document backup that is useful in cases where you make changes, save them, then decide you want to return to the original version of the document

4. These changes become defaults and are retained by WordPerfect

5. Move the cursor completely through the text (Home Home Down Arrow) to cause the formatting codes to be entered and enable you to print

6. 31,4 = Month Day, Year

7. Inches = "

8. Because of the different fonts now available, the current vertical measurement (Ln) will change according to the line height and the current measurement (Pos) will change according to the pitch required for any given font.

9. Inches, centimeters, points, and lines/columns

10. Horizontal measure will change according to the pitch and width of a given character. All characters are not equal when using a proportional font.

11. *First,* create a forms definition containing the size, location, orientation, and other information about each form you plan to use and store it with the printer definitions.

    Second, each time you enter a print job, you must let WordPerfect know how to find the correct forms definition for that particular item.

12. Print (Shift-F7), Select Printers (S), Edit (3), Forms (4), Choose a predefined form and answer whether it is portrait or landscape orientation and where the form is initially present

13. With the form defined, select one for use. Press Print (Shift-F8), Page (2), Paper size/type, (8), Choose size of paper

14. WordPerfect will automatically match the Paper size/type code you have just entered to a form definition and use the form from that point on.

15. When the options on 1 - 7 do not meet your needs, choose ALL OTHERS

16. It means you will use continuous feed paper on print jobs on your forms.

17. *Portrait orientation* has the short sides at the top and bottom.

    Landscape orientation has the long sides at the top and bottom.

18. Use Page Offset to identify variations you need to compensate for in printing, such as an extra wide margin, tractor feed holes, binding at the top, etc.

Self-Check Quiz 11 Answers

1. A group of words, lines, sentences, functions, or a combination of all that can be saved and recalled and used over and over without reentering.

2. Press Macro Def (Ctrl-F10) to begin defining the macro
   Name the macro, type in the macro description
   Enter the macro itself
   Press Ctrl/F10 to turn Macro off

3. Position the cursor where you wish the macro to appear
   Press Alt/F10 (Macro)
   Enter macro name when prompted
   Press ENTER and macro will be retrieved

4. 2-8 characters
   Alt and one letter
   ENTER

5. Bold, Center, Page length, Margins, Tab settings, Print commands, Center page command, Headers, Footers, Page number position

6. ESC (type the number that you want to macro to repeat), Press Alt/F10 (Macro), Type in the name of your macro

7. Press Ctrl-F10 and Type the name of the macro you want to edit, Edit (2)

8. Create a macro. Create another macro and recall the first macro (Alt-F10) in the place you want it to appear in the second macro.

9. To allow you to assign new keys for functions already used by Word-Perfect

10. The keyboard definition allows you to change the location of commands on the keyboard layout

11. You must supply the new assigned key for the function you wish, and you must supply the name of the function to be assigned to the new key(s).

12. Press Setup (Shift-F1), Keyboard Layout (6), Name of macro, and Keyboard Layout (6), Choose Macro Retrieve (6), type the keys you wish to assign the macro to, Press those keys and Enter. Type in the Macro name when you are asked.

Self-Check Quiz 12 Answers

1. No colon after the salutation (Dear —), no comma after the complimentary close (Sincerely)

2. Category within a record from ^R to ^R

3. All data on one item — from ^E to ^E

4. Leave a blank line with a ^R

5. The text of the information to be sent to all and the merge field (^F) codes

6. The variable information such as names and address with ^E and ^R codes

7. ^R means End of Field

    ^E means End of Record

8. WordPerfect will insert the system date at that point

9. ^O — ^O

10. ^C

11. Merge R (F9)

12. It indicates to WordPerfect not to leave a blank line if there is no information in that field

13. The date will always be current

14. ^T

15. ^N^P^P tells WordPerfect to ignore the hard page command and to step the merge to the next record until the end of the file is reached.

Self-Check Quiz 13 Answers

1. Line sort items are separated by Tab commands and appear across the page

    Merge sort items are separated by ^R and ^E command and appear stacked

2. ^R   *End of a field* (merge sort)

    [HRt]   *End of a record* (line sort)

    ^E   *End of a record* (merge sort)

    Space   *Separates words in a field* (all sorts)

    [TAB]   *End of a field* (line sort)

    [HRt][HRt]   *End of a record* (paragraph sort)

3. Sort on the third key in priority, it is numeric, use the second field and the first word of that field

4. An item that has alphabetic and/or numeric characters that are to be treated as alphabetic characters

5. An item that is all numbers that can be calculated

6. Key   *Indicates the sequence or order of priority for sort or selection operation. Can be from 1 to 9*

   Field   *Each column or item separated by a Tab or ^R command in a record*

   Word   *Each item in a field separated by a space*

7. Key2=Jones   *All records having Jones in Key2 priority*

   Key1<>100   *All items not equal to 100*

   Key1>=6*Key2>10   *All items greater than or equal to 6 in key 1 and from those all items greater than 10 in key 2.*

8. Ascending A-Z, 1-10

   Descending Z-A, 10-1

9. A select statement or argument must have been previously entered

10. Up to 9

Self-Check Quiz 14 Answers

1. *Main* = Centered and ALL CAPITAL letters

   Column = Centered over columns in upper- and lowercase and *underlined*

2. Ctrl/4 (EOL/End)

3. Space to midpoint of column and press Center (Shift-F6)

4. Before entering column mode

5. In one long column to line 54 and then wrap to column 2

6. Press Math/Columns (Alt-F7), Col. Def (4), specify type, number of columns, distance between margins

7. Spacing, even or uneven
   Number of spaces between columns
   Type of columns
   Number of columns
   Select Block Protect
   Margins and tabs

8. Type of Column
   How to handle negative numbers
   Number of digits to right of decimal
   Formulas (if any)

9. Two to five

10. Set the left and right margins before defining columns and WordPerfect will calculate internal margins automatically if you elect evenly spaced columns

    Set the left and right column margins you prefer when prompted if columns are to be unevenly spaced

11. Math/Columns (Alt-F7) Col On/off (3)

12. !   *Calculation*

    +   *Subtotal*

    N+   *Subtraction*

    =   *Total*

    *   *Grand total*

    N=   *Negative total*

13. Math/Columns (Alt-F7), Calculate (2)

Self-Check Quiz 15 Answers

1. Figure, Table, Text box, and User defined

2. Paragraph   *Printed within the paragraph it is tied to*

   Page   *Printed at a specific or fixed place on the page*

   Character   *Printed as the next character on the line of text*

3. The caption is an identifier such as "Figure 1" and any additional information to describe the contents

4. At the top of the paragraph

5. At the top, center, or bottom of the box

6. *Offset* means the number of inches from the top of the paragraph in which the box will be printed

7. WordPerfect will select an offset border to go with the graphic you choose. In this way the graphic will not be distorted.

8. *Rotate*   Plus (+) or Minus (-)

   Move   Arrow Keys (1)

   Scale   PgUp and PgDn (2)

   Return to defaults   GoTo (Ctrl-Home)

   Change the percentage   Ins (Typeover)

9. The box is printed on the right or left of the page

10. The text will display across the full line and overwrite the box

11. Improves appearance and gives variety to the document, you can also generate lists of figures, tables, etc.

12. Figure = *Single line around it*

    Table = *thick solid lines on top and bottom with nothing on the sides*

    Text box = *Thick solid lines on top and bottom with 10% shading*

    User defined = *Has no lines around it*

13. *Inside border space* is the space between the border and graphic or text within the box

    Outside border space is how close the text on the outside will come to the box

14. Use clip-art files included in WordPerfect
    Enter text
    Import files into the box
    Use clip-art files from a variety of graphics programs

15. A quote pulled from the text and put into a box for emphasis

16. *Larger* = PgUp
    Smaller = PgDn
    Up = Up arrow
    Down = Down arrow
    Move left = Left arrow
    Move right = Right arrow

17. The graphic will be oversized vertically

18. View Document

19. Graphics (Alt-F9, Line (5), Vertical or Horizontal (1 or 2), Choose length of line, Width of line, and % shading

20. Lines cannot be edited. If you wish it changed, delete and start again.

Self-Check Quiz 16 Answers

1. The *initial font* is defined with the Print Key (Shift- F7) and is a default. The *Base font* (Ctrl-F8,4) lets you change the initial font temporarily.

2. An attribute is the characteristic you can select for the font such as size or appearance.

3. Superscipt, subscript, fine, small, large, very large, extra large

4. Bold, italic, underline, double underlines, redline, shadow, strikeout

5. From the Print menu (Shift-F7), Select (5), Edit (3), Initial font (6)

6. The *higher the pitch* number the *smaller the font* is.

7. The *higher the point* number the *larger the font* is.

8. Courier, Script, Gothic, Italics, Roman

9. If the font is a *base font* it shows in Reveal Codes.
   Initial fonts are shown in the Print (Shift-F7) menu.

10. Press Font (Ctrl-F8), select Base Font (4), Select (1), Choose the desired font, Exit (F7)

11. The command is ignored, or may be printed differently.

12. To turn off attributes or to indicate the end of the text to be affected by the attributes.

13. *Kerning* is a technique used by printers to remove extra white spaces between characters in words and make them easier to read.

14. *Optimal word spacing* is a setting of space between letters and words that looks best according to WordPerfect Corp's opinion. *Normal word spacing* is the spacing that looks best according to the printer manufacturer's opinion.

15. The amount of vertical space allocated to each line is altered

16. Draft quality doesn't take as long to print graphics as does Medium and High

17. Line Height
    Kerning
    Justification
    Word/Letter Spacing

18. Because the objective of a document is to communicate to the reader

19. Preplan
    Avoid a cluttered appearance
    Don't use too many fonts, select appropriate fonts
    Keep headlines short

20. *Landscape orientation* has the long sides at the top and bottom

    Portrait orientation has the short sides at the top and bottom

Self-Check Quiz 17 Answers

1. Place cursor at end of document. Press format (Shift F8), Page (2), Header or Footer (3 or 4), Edit (5), make changes, then Exit (F7).

2. Words have a shaded box around them or | is printed in the margin beside lines marked for redline

3. Strikeout has dashed lines running through the marked text.

4. 2"

5. Use the Extended Search (Home F2).

6. Use the ENTER key and return six times before typing document.

7. 1" top and bottom

8. WordPerfect will skip a page if necessary to put text on the next odd page.

9. If a page number, header, or footer has been *suppressed* on a certain page, it will *not print*.

10. *Headers* are printed at the TOP of each page of the document, whereas *footers* are printed at the BOTTOM.

11. It will include a page number in the header or footer at the ^B and automatically increase it one number for each page.

12. It means that Header A will be printed on every page.

13. *Footnotes* are placed at the bottom of the page containing the reference. *Endnotes* are combined together either within a specified place within the document or at the end in summary form.

14. *Redline* allows you to mark a passage that you may have added and need approval for or that you want to come back to later. *Strikeout* marks text to be deleted.

15. It will compare a document on the screen with one on the disk. All changes in a phrase are marked. Text in the on-screen document that does not exist in the file on disk is redlined. Text found in the file on disk but not the on-screen file is marked with strikeout codes.

16. Mark Text (Alt F5), Generate (6), Remove markings (1).

Self-Check Quiz 18 Answers

1. *Definition:*   Specifying number of levels, page number position, how the text is to be printed, etc.

   Marking Text: Indicating what is to be included, the level, whether it is a heading or subheading, etc.

   Generation: Giving command to WordPerfect to generate index, table of contents, etc.

2. Mark Text (Alt-F5), Generate (6)

3. Five

4. *Wrapped lines* have titles with page numbers in parentheses listed on one line.

   Nonwrapped lines put each title with its corresponding page number on a separate line.

5. So WordPerfect will know what is to be included and where it begins and ends

6. To assist you in collecting your thoughts, organizing your material, sequencing ideas, etc.

7. ENTER and Tab

8. It is a separate file you create containing all the words you want listed in the index.

9. Different commands. They are positioned differently on the page. A subheading is indented under and relates to a heading.

10. The words to be included in the index

11. It uses it to find matching words in the text for inclusion in the index.

12. You can prepare small files or parts of a document. Through the Master Document you can link them all together, and it would appear to WordPerfect as a single document. Functions that require all files simultaneously could be used by WordPerfect.

13. A smaller document that is part of a master document

14. Each of the subdocuments is combined into the one master document

15. You return the expanded master document to its condensed version or parts to save space on the disk

16. The Target, the Reference, and the Name

17. The information to which you are referring

18. Two parts: (1) the Reference notation where it is at present (2) whether the reference should be shown by page number, paragraph number, footnote/endnote number, or graphics box number.

19. It is used by WordPerfect to match the target and reference notation together.

20. Press Mark Text (Alt-F5), Generate (6), Generate Tables (5), (Y)es to bring everything up to date again.

Self-Check Quiz 19 Answers

1. All lines (both with text and without text) will be numbered.

2. The View Command

3. In the left margin slightly less than ½ inch from the edge of the page

4. Headers
   Footers
   Endnotes ✔
   Footnotes ✔

5. A list of all legal and other sources used to support an argument in a legal brief that shows every page on which those materials are cited.

6. Up to 16

7. WordPerfect sorts each section alphanumerically.

8. Case, constitutional provisions, regulations, legislative material, treaties, statutes, and miscellaneous

9. So it will not be counted with the pages of your document

10. *Definition:*   Mark text (Alt-F5), Define (5), Table of Authorities

    Marking Text: Block the text (Alt-F4), Mark text (Alt-F5), Type 4, Enter section number and press Enter

    Generation: Mark text (Alt-F5), Generate (6), Generate tables, etc. (5)

11. Up to 30 lines long

12. A section number from 1 to 16
    The format of the long-form text, including spacing, indention, etc.
    The name for the short form

13. So the Table of Authorities will not be numbered and the references in it are different than the table

14. It is typically a shorthand version or nickname for the long form.

<h1 style="text-align:center">Index</h1>

School Software Direct Order Form

☐ Ship to student   ☐ Ship to reseller (replacement stock)

Qualifying teachers, as well as college, university, and other post-secondary students, can now purchase WordPerfect Corporation (WPCORP) software directly from WPCORP at a reduced price. To qualify, a participant must be a full-time teacher/administrator or currently enrolled as a full-time post-secondary student, and must agree in writing not to resell or transfer any package purchased under this program.

If you satisfy these qualifying conditions and would like to purchase software directly from WPCORP under the School Software Program, complete the following six steps and sign at the bottom of the form.

Step 1. From the list below, select the appropriate software and disk size for your computer (please note that you are limited to *one* package of each program) and mark an "x" in the corresponding box(es).

Product	Price*	Disk Size
☐ WordPerfect 5.0—IBM Personal Computers	$135.00	☐ 3½" ☐ 5¼"
☐ WordPerfect 4.2—IBM PC & Compatibles	$125.00	☐ 3½" ☐ 5¼"
☐ WordPerfect—Apple IIe/IIc	59.00	☐ 3½" & 5¼"
☐ WordPerfect—Apple IIGS	59.00	☐ 3½"
☐ WordPerfect—Amiga	99.00	☐ 3½"
☐ WordPerfect—Atari ST	99.00	☐ 3½"
☐ WordPerfect—Macintosh	99.00	☐ 3½"
☐ PlanPerfect—IBM PC & Compatibles	99.00	☐ 3½" ☐ 5¼"
☐ DataPerfect—IBM PC & Compatibles	150.00	☐ 3½" & 5¼"
☐ WordPerfect Library—IBM PC & Compatibles	59.00	☐ 3½" & 5¼"
☐ WordPerfect Library—Amiga	59.00	☐ 3½"
☐ WordPerfect Executive—IBM PC & Compatibles	79.00	☐ 3½" & 5¼"
☐ Junior WordPerfect—IBM PC & Compatibles	35.00	☐ 5¼"
☐ WordPerfect, Foreign Versions—IBM PC & Compatibles	175.00	☐ 3½" ☐ 5¼"
Language _____________		
☐ WordPerfect Speller, Foreign Versions—IBM PC & Compatibles	40.00	☐ 3½" ☐ 5¼"
Language _____________		

No changes or additions can be made to this list.

Step 2. Make a photocopy of your current Student ID or Faculty card *and* a photocopy of some well known form of identification displaying your social security number, such as your Driver License or Social Security Card. (WPCORP will hold this information strictly confidential and use it only to guard against duplicate purchases.) Your school ID must show current enrollment. (If it does not show a date, you must send verification of current enrollment.) If you have serious reservations about providing a social security number, call the Education Division at (801) 227-7131 to establish clearance to purchase any of the above software products at these special prices.

Step 3. Enter your social security number: __ __ __ – __ __ – __ __ __ __ .

Step 4. Enclose payment for the total cost of the package(s) ordered with personal check, money order, Visa, or MasterCard.

Account # ____________________   Expiration Date __________   ☐ VISA   ☐ MasterCard

(Make check or money order payable to WordPerfect Corporation.)

Step 5. List your shipping address and the address of your local computer store (dealer) in the space provided:

Ship To ____________________   Designated Dealer Houghton Mifflin Company

Phone ____________________   Phone ____________________

Step 6. Enclose this signed and completed form, the photocopies of your identification cards, and your signed check or money order (or Visa or MasterCard account number and expiration date) in an envelope and mail to School Software Program, WordPerfect Corporation, 1555 N. Technology Way, Orem, UT 84057.

The information provided herein is correct and accurate, and I will abide by the restricting conditions outlined by WPCORP in this document. I understand that at its sole discretion, WPCORP may refuse any order for any reason.

Signature ____________________   Date ____________________

Utah residents add 6.25% sales tax. Prices are quoted in U.S. dollars and apply to U.S. delivery for U.S. customers only.

WordPerfect Corporation • 1555 N. Technology Way • Orem, Utah 84057 • (801) 225-5000